011993693

Cambridge Studies in Medieval Life and Thought

RICHARD III

Cambridge studies in medieval life and thought
Fourth series

General Editor:

J. C. HOLT
Professor of Medieval History and
Master of Fitzwilliam College, University of Cambridge

Advisory Editors:

C. N. L. BROOKE
Dixie Professor of Ecclesiastical History and
Fellow of Gonville and Caius College,
University of Cambridge

D. E. LUSCOMBE
Professor of Medieval History, University of Sheffield

The series Cambridge Studies in Medieval Life and Thought was inaugurated by G. G. Coulton in 1920. Professor J. C. Holt now acts as General Editor of a Fourth Series, with Professor C. N. L. Brooke and Professor D. E. Luscombe as Advisory Editors. The series aims to bring together outstanding work by medieval scholars over a wide range of human endeavour extending from political economy to the history of ideas.

Titles in the series

RICHARD III

A Study of Service

ROSEMARY HORROX

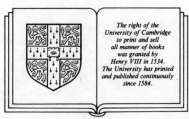

The right of the
University of Cambridge
to print and sell
all manner of books
was granted by
Henry VIII in 1534.
The University has printed
and published continuously
since 1584.

CAMBRIDGE UNIVERSITY PRESS

CAMBRIDGE

NEW YORK   NEW ROCHELLE   MELBOURNE   SYDNEY

Published by the Press Syndicate of the University of Cambridge
The Pitt Building, Trumpington Street, Cambridge CB2 IRP
32 East 57th Street, New York, NY 10022, USA
10 Stamford Road, Oakleigh, Melbourne 3166, Australia

First published 1989

Printed in Great Britain by the University Press, Cambridge

British Library cataloguing in publication data

Horrox, Rosemary
Richard III: a study of service. –
(Cambridge studies in medieval life and
thought. Fourth series; v. 11).
1. England. Richard III – King of England
I. Title
942.04′6′0924

Library of Congress cataloguing in publication data

Horrox, Rosemary.
Richard III, a study of service/Rosemary Horrox.
p.   cm. – (Cambridge studies in medieval life and thought;
4th ser., 11)
Bibliography.
Includes index.
ISBN 0 521 33428 4
1. Richard III, King of England, 1452–1485.   2. Great Britain –
Kings and rulers – Biography.   3. Great Britain – History – Richard
III, 1483–1485. I. Title. II. Series.
DA620.H65 1989
942.04′6′0924–dc19
[B]   88–22899 CIP

ISBN 0 521 33428 4

For Martin

CONTENTS

ACKNOWLEDGEMENTS

This book has its roots in my Ph.D. thesis for the University of Cambridge on 'The Extent and Use of Crown Patronage under Richard III', a topic which was suggested and supervised by Gerald Harriss. His help with the thesis, and his friendly and supportive interest in its subsequent slow progress towards print have been greatly valued. David Morgan generously read the introduction and chapter 5 in draft. They are much improved for his suggestions but he should not be held responsible for any remaining errors and misapprehensions. Further debts are acknowledged in the footnotes, but among those who have supplied me with references or ideas I should thank in particular Christine Carpenter, Margaret Condon, Michael Hicks, Michael K. Jones, Tony Pollard and Roger Virgoe. Bill Hampton has been an unfailing resource in genealogical matters.

Richard III is still capable of arousing strong feelings, as anyone rash enough to give public lectures on him soon discovers. I am the more grateful to my students, both undergraduate and extramural, who have submitted with good grace to having my ideas tried out on them and whose dissent has always been constructive and good-natured.

The British Academy awarded me a research grant which allowed me to work on material in London at a time when I was based in the north. I have met with great courtesy and help from all the archivists and librarians with whom I have had dealings. As the book approached completion it has benefited from the editorial care of Professor J. C. Holt and Professor Christopher Brooke.

My greatest debt is to my husband, without whose moral and material support the book would not have been written at all. The book is for him.

ABBREVIATIONS

Full details of the books listed below are supplied in the
bibliography.

Archaeol. I	'An extract relating to the burial of K. Edward IV', *Archaeologia* I (1770)
BB	*The Household of Edward IV, the Black Book and the Ordinance of 1478,* ed. Myers
BIHR	*Bulletin of the Institute of Historical Research*
BL	British Library
Cat. Anc. Deeds	*A Descriptive Catalogue of Ancient Deeds in the Public Record Office* (6 vols.)
CCR	*Calendar of Close Rolls*
CFR	*Calendar of Fine Rolls*
CP	*Complete Peerage,* Cokayne, revised Gibbs et al. (13 vols.)
CPR	*Calendar of Patent Rolls*
Crowland	*The Crowland Chronicle Continuations* ed. Pronay and Cox
EETS	Early English Text Society
EHR	*English Historical Review*
Harl. 433	*B.L.Harleian MS 433* ed. Horrox and Hammond
HMC	*Historical Manuscripts Commission*
Inqs p.m.	*Calendar of Inquisitions post mortem, Henry VII* (3 vols.)
Mancini	Dominic Mancini, *Usurpation of Richard III* ed. Armstrong (2nd edn, 1969)
PL	*Paston Letters and Papers of the Fifteenth Century* ed. Davis (2 vols.)
PRO	Public Record Office
RO	Record Office
Rot. Parl.	*Rotuli Parliamentorum*

Test. Ebor.	*Testamenta Eboracensia*, Surtees Society
TRHS	*Transactions of the Royal Historical Society*
VCH	*Victoria County History*
Vergil	Polydore Vergil, *Angliae Historiae libri viginti-septem* (Basel, 1555)
WAM	Westminster Abbey Muniments

Secondary material is cited by author/date; printed primary sources by title or author/title as appropriate.

Manuscripts are cited by call number only; full details of classes are supplied in the bibliography.

INTRODUCTION
THE ROOTS OF SERVICE

Studies of the reign of Richard III have multiplied in recent years, but most of them have remained focussed on the traditional subjects: the character and motivation of the king himself and the fate of his nephews. Attempts to discuss the reign in terms of late medieval government, particularly in its own right rather than as an adjunct to Edward IV's reign, have been far less frequent. No doubt this is largely because of the reign's brevity, but it is perhaps also due to a sense that the tensions of the reign make it untypical. However, at least one aspect of royal government is illuminated by the very fact that the king's authority was under pressure, and that is the role of the king's servants. Medieval kings relied heavily on the co-operation of their subjects in putting their wishes into practice. Although the king had a central bureaucracy, there remained large areas of activity where he was dependent on less formal help. It was to local men that he turned for the administration of his estates, the maintenance of order, the raising of troops and innumerable other tasks. Effective royal authority thus required that men of local standing should be willing to put their knowledge and influence at the king's disposal; that they should become the king's servants as well as his subjects. Their service is the central theme of this book, and the dramatic upheavals of Richard's reign provide a particularly good chance of exploring what it meant in practice, both to the men who performed it and the crown which needed it.

Service of this kind was not only the concern of kings, and much of what can be said about royal service is also true of the relationship between other lords and their men. Perhaps the most important characteristic of the relationship was its mutuality: service was performed in the expectation that it would bring some return. This could be a straightforward grant – of an annual fee, office or even, in rare cases, land. But the return was often less tangible, and hence less visible, than this. It was expected that a lord would put his influence behind his servant if required. This was the 'good lordship' to which fifteenth-century correspondents incessantly appeal, and the ways in which it could be manifest are endless. In asking for lordship, contemporaries rarely felt it necessary to define what they wanted: it was essentially an open-ended relationship, as a letter of c.1464 makes plain. The writer, John Neville, then earl of Northumberland, was enlisting the help of his kinsman lord Fitzhugh for his retainer John Aglionby, who had just been elected mayor of Carlisle. Neville was both offering and requesting lordship (a reminder of the complexities of obligation) but in neither case is it defined: '...and therefore, brother, I would desire and heartily pray you during the time of his said mayoralty you would stand his good lord, so that I might understand you his more tender lord at the instance of this my writing.'[1]

Here, Northumberland was taking direct action on his servant's behalf, but lordship could also have an effect independent of the lord himself. Contemporaries were alert to connections between an individual and a lord, as can be seen in an Essex example of the mid 1470s: 'John Herde said that Thomas Adam is not for us, for he saith that Avery and his fellowship draw much to his house and that he is my lord of Gloucester's farmer, whereof I was not aware. And so I have sent Thomas Adam his way home.'[2] As a result, the mere fact of lordship could have a bearing on an individual's standing in local affairs. In 1483 Thomas Wrangwish was recognized as a strong candidate for the mayoralty of York, because 'he is the man that my lord of Gloucester will do for'.[3] Such connections were accordingly worth publicizing. In a Wiltshire dispute of 1460 a Welshman who claimed to be a servant of the earl of March was able to persuade the sheriff to ignore a writ, presumably just by name-dropping, since March disowned him when the matter was brought to his attention. Royal service offered similar possibilities, as Gruffydd Vaughan ap Einion discovered when he tried (and failed) to find a lawyer prepared to take his part against Sir Richard Croft, treasurer of the household of Edward IV's son.[4] The acknowledged servant also stood to

[1] Cumbria RO, D/AY1/146, 149 (revised numbering). In this and all subsequent quotations, spelling and punctuation have been modernized.
[2] Essex RO, D/DCe/L54.
[3] Raine, *York Records* I p. 68.
[4] *Tropenell Cart.* II p. 64; Lowe 1977, p. 296.

benefit from the gifts of those seeking access to the lord. These were often very modest, such as the $2\frac{1}{2}d$ which Thomas Playter spent on drink for a servant of the chief baron of the exchequer, but more substantial gains were possible. The city of Hull paid five marks to an esquire of the earl of Suffolk when it was trying to enlist the earl's help over a new charter.[5]

Lordship and its benefits were attractive. Some idea of *how* attractive can be gained from the perennial interest in charms to capture the favour of the great. One fifteenth-century source recommended vervain (*verbena officinalis*): 'Whoso beareth it upon him, he shall have love of great masters, and they shall not refuse his askings but grant him with good will that that he will.' The longing for favour is perhaps even more explicit in the wistful enquiry of Sir William Neville in the next century, whether it were possible 'to have a ring made that should bring a man in favour with his prince'.[6] It was the possibility of favour which provided the main inducement to service: thus patronage was the lord's contribution to the relationship of lord and man, just as service was the man's. But the relationship between patronage and service was less straightforward than this might imply. Lords did not usually buy service in the crude sense of using patronage to secure a particular return. On the contrary, patronage was usually the reward for past service and petitioners were careful to specify their claims on a lord's favour. Men without a tradition of service felt themselves to be at a disadvantage, which they sometimes sought to remedy by citing the service of a close kinsman. When William Curwen petitioned the king for an office he did so on the strength of his father's 'faithful and diligent attendance and labour', although the petition seems to have failed.[7] A petitioner without even a vicarious claim to favour could only promise future service and hope that the lord was convinced.[8] But if service was usually assumed to precede patronage, it was of course the *possibility* of patronage which motivated service, and to that extent patronage can be said to generate service. It was also recognized that once a man had benefited from patronage his obligations towards the lord were strengthened, and petitioners usually coupled their reference to past service with a promise of

---

[5] Richmond 1981b, p. 47; Boyle, *Hull Charters* p. 47.
[6] Stephens, 'Extracts' pp. 395–6; Kittredge 1929, p. 110.
[7] Cumbria RO, D/Cu/1/1, undated but probably c.1471.
[8] McFarlane 1973, p. 109.

more to come. It was common form to begin a petition to the king with some variant of the appeal: 'Please it your highness in consideration of the true and faithful service which N has done and during his life intends to do unto your most noble grace...' This was not just an empty form of words and lords did on occasion threaten their servants with a cancellation of patronage.[9]

There was no precise equation between the level of patronage and the amount of service which it recompensed or demanded, although there was a general sense of what was fair. In the 1470s an unknown servant of the duchess of York wrote to John Prince, one of his colleagues:

my brother Sandes and I were never so sorry for man as we have been for you since your departing. Considering that so many men be slain daily and also your great cost and charge for to ride with 2 men and 3 horses by so long time...being at so great cost outward and at home and here in the law, it is great heaviness to us that love you as often as we think upon it. For I have spoken with Coton, with my master Verney's son and other that belong to my lady and they say you need not to have been at this cost, no more than they or other of my lady's feed men that have £40 by year, some £20 by year and yet go not passing 4 or 5 mile with her. Wherewith her good grace is as well pleased as though they had ridden an 100 mile. For when the journey and cost is done, the labour and cost is forgotten.[10]

In practice, as this implies, the relationship between levels of service and patronage was a loose one. It is also one which cannot be reckoned in narrowly financial terms. The duchess' backing won Prince a major dispute over his land, against powerful opponents, and he probably regarded this an adequate return for his 'cost and charge'.[11]

This lack of a precise correlation between service and patronage has a bearing on any attempt to define good and bad patronage. No doubt a servant needed to feel that he was on balance benefiting from the relationship, or at least not losing. But it was probably more important for him to feel that if ever he needed his lord's support it would be forthcoming, and to that extent lordship could be said to operate on something of a credit basis.

[9] *Harl. 433* I p. 44; Goodman 1981, pp. 133–7.
[10] Essex RO, D/DCe/L57.
[11] *Ibid.* D/DQ/14/124, particularly 3/40, 41, 43; D/DCe/L63–4. Some of the material is printed by Waller 1895a, 1895b, 1898. I hope to re-edit the whole collection.

'Bad' patronage was not a matter of a lord getting his sums wrong in individual cases, for that could be rectified. It was, rather, a situation in which the servant could not feel confident of future benefit. Undue favouritism on the lord's part might have this effect. So might political ineptitude. Or it might be the result of a psychological failing such as miserliness: a mean good lord was a contradiction in terms. The motto which Henry III had written over the gable of the Painted Chamber at Westminster puts the matter in a nutshell: He who does not give what he holds does not receive what he wishes.[12]

So far service has been discussed largely in terms of self-interest, but it was also conditioned by the duty of obedience which men owed to their rulers. This was not only impressed on them as a social and religious requirement but also had an obvious political dimension. If the ultimate secular authority were flouted a collapse of order might follow, from which the political classes stood to lose more than they might gain. The main beneficiary of this perception was inevitably the crown, although it is possible that other major lords reaped some benefit, particularly if they were in a position to dominate a specific region. The duke of Gloucester's control of the north in the 1470s, for instance, may have owed something to a recognition that his hegemony provided stability in a recently unsettled area. As far as the crown itself was concerned, this contributed to the king's ability to call on the support of men other than his acknowledged servants.

That support could not be taken entirely for granted: there was an element of reciprocity involved. The king could call on the help of all his subjects because his power was expected to be at the service of the whole community, not just his immediate circle of servants; and the obedience of his subjects rested in part on their assumption that he would employ that power in a proper fashion. To this extent the relationship of king and subject mirrors the more formal relationship of lord and man. The parallel is not exact. Subjects approaching the king for help appealed not to his lordship, which would imply a relationship and hence some obligation on the king's part, but to his grace, which was by definition unconstrained.[13] Only the great men of the realm, or acknowledged royal servants, could legitimately request the king's

---

[12] 'Ke ne dune ke ne tine ne prent ke desire', Tristram 1950, I p. 92; see also, Murray 1978, p. 354.

[13] As, for instance, in the petition of John Paston II to Edward IV: *PL* I pp. 487–9.

good lordship, and the familiar definition of the king as the 'good lord of all good lords', although correct as far as it goes, only expresses one side of the king's role.[14] The king's relations with his subjects, however, like those of lord and man, called for mutual trust and hence, inevitably, had a personal dimension. The character and ability of the king had to inspire confidence in his subjects. Exactly why an individual king succeeded or failed in this can be obscure, although the brute fact of success or failure is usually obvious enough. It is one of the ironies of Richard III's own reign that, having succeeded triumphantly in winning the confidence of the north as duke of Gloucester, he failed to repeat the process on a larger scale as king.

Lordship was thus a more complex matter than a mere distribution of grants among the deserving. Equally complex was the service it was intended to secure. Like lordship, service conferred intangible as well as tangible benefits upon its recipients. For a lord, as for his men, service was intimately related to status. A lord who could call on the support of many servants was not only likely to be more effective in practical terms, their backing also contributed to his 'worship': the respect in which he was held. This was of ever-present concern to fifteenth-century lords, as their surviving letters make clear, and although the service they commanded was not the only factor it was an important one. Lords were interested both in the quantity of service and in its quality, since their own standing was manifest in the influence and social status of their servants. This equation of worship and service is made most explicit in the desire of lords to muster a good turn-out of their supporters on special occasions. When the duke of Norfolk came of age in 1465 he ordered all his servants to attend on him in London when he received his lands from the king. Their presence was specifically for the duke's worship, and to underline the point they were told to come wearing the duke's livery, the visible expression of service.[15] Under such conditions an inability to command an adequate following would entail a serious loss of face and on one occasion the duke of Suffolk reputedly refused to come to London because many of his servants had gone home for Christmas and he was not properly attended.[16] Medieval kings

[14] McFarlane 1973, p. 119. For an explicit equation of Edward IV with a good lord: Loades 1986, pp. 2–3.
[15] *PL* II p. 430.
[16] McFarlane 1973, p. 106.

showed the same concern. It was rare for them to be inadequately attended, although for that very reason when it did happen the political impact was severe. A merely adequate attendance was not, however, enough, and kings usually showed themselves alert to the importance of putting on a good show.[17]

However, few lords would have considered display alone an adequate return on their lordship. Their servants were expected to perform a remarkably wide range of other duties. Every aspect of a lord's life, whether public or private, involved his servants in some activity. There was, moreover, very little attempt to compartmentalize this activity. Service was not seen as a matter of performing defined duties attached to a specific office. It was essentially a personal relationship between two men, in which the servant could be called upon to do whatever the lord needed done. This would not normally be something inappropriate to the servant's station: a knight would not be expected to scour dishes or a yeoman to lead an army. In practice, however, this was not much of a restriction: some menial service was considered honourable if performed for a lord of sufficiently high rank. Knights, for instance, would be willing to wait on the king at table or supervise his dressing. Conversely, the status of a lord had a bearing on the perceived status of his servants. An esquire in the king's service outranked most other esquires and could, by implication, be given greater responsibilities.[18] Service was thus almost completely open-ended, and just as petitioners asked for lordship without specifying its form, so lords demanded service. Surviving indentures are rarely more detailed than this, except in the case of military service, where the costs involved meant that obligations and rewards needed to be carefully specified, something which has often led to undue weight being put on the military aspects of late medieval service. In reality, it was the unstated multiplicity of peacetime service which was valued most highly by the majority of lords.[19]

What this multiplicity could mean in practice is illustrated most easily by royal servants, whose careers are more fully documented than those of their counterparts in aristocratic service. It is clear that they could be called upon to do almost anything, although it is also true that a lord would seek where possible to utilize the

---

[17] *BB* pp. 4–5.
[18] Furnivall, *Babees Book* p. 191; Pegge 1791, pp. 30–1.
[19] Harriss 1981, pp. x–xi.

particular connections and abilities of his servants. It made no sense for a lord to demand service which could not be performed. This usually meant that men would be employed within areas where they already had influence and where their local knowledge was at the lord's disposal. When Richard III ordered the Norfolk tenants of Mountgrace priory (Yorks.) to wear no livery but that of the prior, he put responsibility for the matter into the hands of Sir Hugh Hastings, who had connections with both Norfolk and Yorkshire.[20]

Geographical specialization of this sort could still subsume a wide range of activity. The service performed by Thomas Fowler, a Yorkist esquire of the body, was centred on Buckinghamshire. Here he served on royal commissions, including that of the peace, acted as escheator, and in 1478 and 1483 was pricked as sheriff for Buckinghamshire and the associated county of Bedfordshire. He was also active in the administration of the royal estates in the two counties. Edward IV made him feodary of the duchy of Lancaster lands there and his responsibilities grew under Richard III. After the rebellion of 1483, Fowler was put in sole charge of seizing the lands and goods of traitors in the two counties and shortly afterwards was made steward of the forfeited Stafford estates in the region, including Buckingham itself.[21] As usual, the *minutiae* of these responsibilites are barely visible, but in August 1483 Fowler appears selling wood to fund repairs to the manor of Creslow (Bucks.) and he was involved in further wood sales later in the reign. He also took on *ad hoc* tasks in the region, including raising loans for the crown and searching for treasure reputedly buried in or near Sudbuy in Eaton Socon (Beds.).[22]

Lords were also willing to exploit mercantile connections. Christopher Coleyns, a citizen and draper of London, was employed by both Yorkist kings on business with a maritime flavour, such as attacking pirates and victualling the king's ships.[23] In some cases it was personal expertise which was recognized and used. Avery Cornburgh had a long and varied career in royal service but seems to have specialized increasingly in financial

[20] *Harl. 433* II p. 159; Hastings was of Fenwick (Yorks.) and Elsing (Norf.).
[21] *CFR* 1471–85 nos. 168, 455, 797; *CPR* 1476–85 p. 411; *Harl. 433* II pp. 32–3; Somerville 1953, I p. 592.
[22] *Harl. 433* II pp. 9, 158, 183–4, 203, III pp. 128, 132.
[23] PRO, E 404/78/2/44, 404/78/3/49.

matters.[24] All of this could impose a certain coherence on the service performed by an individual, as too could the tendency in matters of service for one thing to lead to another. Thus the Yorkist controller of the works at Windsor, the Kentish man Thomas Cancellor, was employed on other royal business in the Thames valley. Under Richard III he was one of a group of commissioners appointed to investigate a dispute between the abbot of Abingdon and his tenants. He was also much involved with wood sales in the region, sometimes, but not always, with the intention of putting the revenues towards building costs at Windsor.[25] But this coherence should not be exaggerated. There might be no connection between the tasks performed by one man beyond the need to have them carried out reliably. Even servants with some specialized duties were likely to take on additional, unrelated tasks. Coleyns, for instance, was also constable of Queenborough castle (Kent).[26] Such diversity was taken for granted by both sides and no one would have found it odd that Thomas Elrington, after spending months purveying workmen and supplies for Dunbar and seeing to their transport, should be sent to seize forfeited land in the Home Counties.[27]

The demands of service, both in time and effort, must have been considerable. In c.1470 Sir Richard Harcourt, finding himself under pressure, wrote to Thomas Stonor: 'And as for the day of marriage I would right fain be there, in good faith, if I might have leisure, for you know well the business that I have about the king's matters at this time.'[28] Much of this activity was in response to *ad hoc* commands which have left no trace in royal sources. When Edward IV intervened in a disputed mayoral election in York in 1482 he told the city:

that you conform you to that that may best serve for the weal and quiet of our said city, according to such advertisements and instructions as we have given to our trusty and welbeloved Sir Edmund Hastings knight and Miles Metcalfe, bearers hereof, to whom we will you give faith and

[24] Chrimes 1972, p. 121. He was also responsible for the finances of the Scottish expedition of 1481, and perhaps that to France in 1475: Collier, *Household Books* p. 4; Southampton City RO, SC 5/1/15 fo. 15v.

[25] *Harl. 433* I pp. 204–5, 232, II pp. 183–4, 211; *CPR 1476–85* p. 552.

[26] *Harl. 433* I p. 207, II pp. 203, 213.

[27] *Ibid.* II pp. 101–2, 149–50, 184.

[28] *Stonor Letters* I p. 113.

credence as to ourself in all that on our behalf they shall show unto you touching the premises.[29]

Behind the letter lies not only a command to the bearers but some briefing on the problem and the king's wishes, but the process is now completely invisible. If it was written down, a central copy either was not taken or has not survived. It is, however, just as likely that it was all done orally; instructions by word of mouth seem to have been acceptable to all concerned.[30]

As a result, historians have perhaps tended to underestimate the amount of time that local men spent on other people's business. A royal commission to look into flooding of the marshland between Tenterden and Lydd had five of the leading men of Kent riding to and fro to consult with each other and with affected parties.[31] The formal grant of office, likewise, almost always entailed real work for somebody. Sometimes, no doubt, the nominal holder appointed a deputy, arranged some payment for him, and left him to get on with it. But one should not assume that this was always the case. In the 1470s, when he was one of the most eminent royal servants in Kent, Sir John Fogge was willing to involve himself in the details of estate management on behalf of the prior of Christchurch:

Please it you to wit that I have been at Westwell and taken a view of your deer... Sir, I have taken such direction there as I trust to God shall please you. William your parker abideth still, but I have set a controller upon him by his own agreement, at his cost and charge, and I doubt not there shall neither great game nor small game be taken away without I shall have knowledge of the same... Furthermore I have had Clement Woodward and Culling together and their books varieth not but 2s and odd money... Sir, also that you will remember to send for your hogs which be in your park, for in good faith if they go there still till All Hallowtide all your fawns will die, for they have rooted the whole wood over and over.[32]

This expenditure of time and effort was worthwhile. Service was one half of a mutual relationship, and had the possibilities of patronage to be set against it. But even this was not the whole story. Service could be its own reward. Many of the forms of

---

[29] Raine, *York Records* I p. 49.
[30] *Harl. 433* I pp. xxvii–xxviii.
[31] *Christ Church Letters* pp. 27–8, 95.
[32] *Ibid.* pp. 26–7, 95.

service discussed so far have one thing in common: they allowed the men concerned to exercise authority. Whether it was Thomas Fowler deciding what wood to sell to whom, or Edmund Hastings setting out the king's wishes, service had brought influence and thus an enhancement of their standing. There is no doubt that this was valued. When a correspondent of William Stonor urged him to try for the shrievalty and concluded, 'for it will get you acquaintance and it is better to govern than to be governed', he was enunciating a general principle.[33] Men wanted a share in the responsibilities on offer and their selection was welcomed as testimony to their standing. This is most obvious in the case of high-status jobs such as the commission of the peace or the shrievalty, but it applies also to *ad hoc* responsibilities. Although selection itself was valued, however, this did not mean that the attendant duties could then be hastily handed on to a subordinate while the nominal holder enjoyed the title. Influence and authority resided in taking action and if all the work was delegated, then much of the influence would go with it. This has an obvious bearing on contemporary attitudes to grants of office, which were not just seen as an excuse for a fee but as an opportunity to exercise practical authority. The willingness to take on responsibilities for the sake of the standing which they brought was also an element in the situation discussed earlier, in which lords, and especially the king, could call on the support of men who stood in no particular relationship to them. Alongside a sense that such obedience was necessary was no doubt also an awareness that it was personally advantageous.

The view that service could be inherently worthwhile was not, of course, universal. Some men may either not have welcomed authority or have considered the cost in time and effort too heavy.[34] More general, perhaps, was a feeling that local influence was valuable but that more distant involvement was not, unless it entailed *major* new responsibilities. It is unlikely that Fogge would have interviewed woodwards and assessed pig damage had Westwell not been within a few miles of his home. This was not just a matter of convenience; he would also have felt that Westwell and its problems fell within his proper sphere of influence. The same assumption can be seen in a letter of c.1502, written by Sir

---

[33] *Stonor Letters* II pp. 134–5.
[34] John Hopton may have been such a one: Richmond 1981a.

Thomas Darcy in pursuit of two offices in the honour of Pontefract, where his own land lay: 'Sir, it is the first that ever I laboured for within mine own country, and of my faith I had liefer have it than 10 times so great an office in far parts, and I trust there be few that better should see to the woods and game there.'[35] Darcy was unsuccessful, but his argument was valid. In calling upon local service, lords were benefiting from existing influence; in providing it, men were enhancing that influence in the place where it mattered most, their own country. Except in special cases, neither side was as interested in service in areas outside the servant's own knowledge. But, even admitting this limitation, it is clear that the idea of service as inherently rewarding needs to be built into any picture of the relationship between service and patronage. Patronage was not simply the incentive to service; the provision of an opportunity to serve might itself be a form of patronage.

What seemed at first a straightforward relationship between service and lordship has thus proved considerably more complex. Not only do both elements take a wide variety of forms, but there was no exact correlation between service, status and reward. Consequently, a retinue was not one hierarchy but several, which never quite matched. This is most obvious in the case of the royal household, where there was a formal hierarchy of office. That hierarchy was primarily social and ceremonial: it did not, in individual cases, correspond to the hierarchies of reward or political importance which could also be constructed. In the case of aristocratic retinues, which lacked a formal structure, modern attempts to impose one run into difficulties for the same reason. They involve an uneasy compromise between different criteria: social status, position within the lord's administration or the permanence of any legal bond between lord and man.[36] These apparent confusions are the concomitant of medieval perceptions of service. It was open-ended, so that the possession of a particular post was not a definition of the service required. It was also, above all, a personal relationship, and personal factors might therefore outweigh more formal considerations.

---

[35] WAM 16063, dated by the death of Sir John Neville, which caused the vacancy. The offices went to Sir Thomas Wortley, another local man: Somerville 1953, p. 518.
[36] Harriss 1981, p. xi

Introduction

In practice, of course, broad correlations did exist. The system could not have functioned otherwise. Thus it is possible to distinguish different levels of service, characterized by their role and level of reward, but the categories need to be kept very wide to be workable. As soon as one looks for greater precision the picture begins to fragment. In the case of the royal connection the most satisfactory division is threefold. At one extreme were the men who were not formally royal servants at all, but who might still be called upon for help by the crown. In theory this group was limitless, but in practice it was restricted to men of some influence who were known to the king, in other words men of some standing, however slight, at a local level. The acknowledged royal servants are potentially far harder to subdivide, but the Yorkist kings made their own division. Both used office in the royal household as a way of giving formal expression to their relationship with their closest supporters – although 'closest' is only a relative term with a household of several hundred. Thus the household represents the top level of royal service, with the non-household servants occupying the middle ground. Basic as this division may seem, it is far from cut and dried. It can be surprisingly difficult to be sure who was in the household, and the line between acknowledged and unacknowledged servants is blurred. The three groups also subsume a wide range of service. The problem is particularly acute with the household, which includes the humblest of menial servants as well as the men of independent influence discussed hitherto. But, for all its problems, this threefold division is the most workable and corresponds most closely to contemporary usage, which usually distinguished between subjects, servants and the holders of specific household office.

The first category, the subjects, can be dealt with briefly. They stood to gain little from their service beyond any influence deriving from its performance, but the demands upon them seem to have been correspondingly limited. They were rarely, if ever, expected to act outside their own sphere of influence – indeed it was that personal knowledge and influence which the king wanted to tap. Although generalizations are dangerous when so much service is invisible, the subjects seem to have been called on mainly to provide information or to investigate and settle local problems. They are not usually found running errands for the king or administering the royal demesne. Their role, in short, was

13

not so much to act for the king as to supply 'self-government at the king's command'.[37]

The second group, the non-household servants, may be characterized as having a larger role, which entailed their acting more specifically on the king's behalf. Apart from this, the underlying assumptions were very similar, with the king seeking to exploit the personal influence of the men concerned. This meant that, again, they were largely to be found acting within their own areas of interest. It also meant that their exact role would depend on their own standing, and here the range was very wide. It can be illustrated by two of the northern servants of Richard III. One, Duncan Huetson, was a butcher of Wentbridge (Yorks.) and his service probably consisted largely of organizing supplies for the household in the north, for which he was rewarded with an annuity of 4 marks.[38] At the other extreme was John Crakenthorpe, head of the Newbiggin (Westm.) family since his father's death in 1466. He sat as commissioner of the peace in both Cumberland and Westmorland and under Richard III was receiver of the royal land in Cumberland and was also one of those chosen to treat with the Scots.[39] Both men are described simply as king's servant, although their standing is clearly very different. Both also demonstrate a further difference between the acknowledged servants and the subjects, which is that the former had some chance (although by no means a certainty) of receiving a tangible reward for their efforts.

The household (excluding the menial servants) was the group from which the heaviest commitment was expected. They had a domestic role about the king's person and were also used extensively on other royal business. At a local level they normally provided the upper levels of the king's estate management and took on a wide range of other *ad hoc* duties, with particular responsibility for matters which touched the king most closely, such as arresting rebels or seizing forfeited land. They were also the men most likely to be called on to perform service outside their own areas, since their household status gave them influence independent of their local standing. Sir Gilbert Debenham, a knight of the body of Wenham (Suff.), was used by Richard III to seize the property of Sir William Brandon in Southwark (Sur-

---

[37] A phrase coined by A. B. White in the book of the same name: White, 1933.

[38] PRO, DL 42/20 fo. 20A; York, Prob. Reg. 5 fo. 302–v; *Harl. 433* II pp. 173–4.

[39] PRO, C 81/1530/5; *Harl. 433* II p. 28; *Inqs p.m.* II no. 820.

rey), for example, and Henry VII used the Cornishman Richard Nanfan to carry a message to Nottingham.[40] As this implies, it was the household which ran most of the king's errands. For lesser figures, such as the yeomen of the crown, this was often a matter of straightforward fetching and carrying. David ap Jenkins, for instance, had the job on one occasion of carrying valuable plate from Richard III's household in the north down to the king at Westminster.[41] More eminent figures might be used to represent the king or disseminate his wishes. In 1479 two of Edward IV's household men were sent to meet the Burgundian ambassadors and conduct them to London, and it was a household man, Edward Gower, whom Richard III used to convey his views on a truce to the king of Scots.[42] But if the household were kept busy, they were encouraged by the prospect of major gains. They had all the indirect advantages of service with a great lord. They had also, by this date, acquired a virtual monopoly of the most valuable forms of tangible royal patronage. No household man could rely on receiving a royal grant, but his expectations were better than those of anyone outside the household, and enough men benefited substantially to provide a potent encouragement for the rest.

The reward open to the household was the justification for their heavy workload. It also bought their reliability. Gains from royal service could be substantial; many Yorkist servants could have echoed the Hertfordshire esquire John Sturgeon who willed prayers, 'specially for the soul of the noble and victorious prince king Edward IV, by whose service I have had my poor substance which God hath lent me.'[43] The possibility of such gain would be threatened by disobedience, or even perhaps by seeming unenthusiastic. Clement Paston, commenting on the poor showing of his nephew John II at court, thought at first that John should come home: 'But then I considered that if he should now come home, the king would think that when he should do him any service somewhere, that then he would have him home, the which should cause him not to be had in favour.'[44]

It was this reliability which made household men the obvious

---

[40] PRO, KB 9/369/5; *Harl. 433* II p. 175; *Records of Nottingham* III p. 262.
[41] *Harl. 433* II pp. 212–3.
[42] Canterbury RO, FA 6 fo. 6v; *Harl. 433* III pp. 105–6.
[43] PRO, Prob 11/9 fo. 143v.
[44] *PL* I p. 200.

choice for particularly sensitive tasks, but it was also valued within the regular framework of royal authority at a local level. Here all kings relied extensively on the influence and connections of the local gentry, whose support was generally forthcoming even when they had no formal association with the crown. Having a household element among the gentry gave added assurance that the king's wishes would be met. It could never be more than an element. Cost precluded the taking of all the gentry into the king's service; and in any case royal service would presumably have lost much of its attraction had it been open to all comers. That being so, no king could afford to rely entirely on his own household men for action, since this would have entailed turning his back on other useful influence. But there does seem to have been a degree of royal discrimination in favour of household men. Yorkist sheriffs, for instance, include a higher number of household men than their numbers would warrant. In 1482 about a fifth of the candidates for sheriff are known to have held household office, but among those actually chosen the proportion rises to a third.[45] For the king this meant more accountability from his officials. For the household men such discrimination was a valued manifestation of royal favour and as such a further inducement to service.

Under the Yorkists the household, and to a lesser extent other royal servants, were thus a crucial element in the king's authority at a local level. But it is important not to exaggerate their role. It is true that household men were, in some respects, expected to remain permanently alert to the king's interests. Estate officials were expected to take steps to ensure the effective exploitation of land in their care. All royal servants performed the general function of acting as a line of communication between the king and the country at large, and one aspect of this was that they were expected to keep the king informed of what was going on. The *Black Book* of Edward IV's household recommended that the king's esquires be chosen from a spread of counties, 'by whom it may be known the disposition of the countries'.[46] This was exactly the role envisaged for Thomas Stafford when Richard III gave him office in Wiltshire in the aftermath of the 1483 rebellion. Stafford's subordinates were warned to 'be unto him and none other from henceforth attending, helping, answering and assisting

---

[45] PRO, C 81/1391/19.
[46] *BB* p. 127.

16

as the case shall require; so that by his report we may fully understand what towardness and loving dispositions ye bear towards us, which accordingly we will remember'.[47] Henry VII's household performed the same role. In 1489 the king assured the city of Coventry: 'We perceive that reports have been made unto you that Richard Reynold and Joan his wife, at their being in our household, should noise and slander that our city, saying that there should not be three true men unto us that wear scarlet... We let you wit that we bear no such miscontent nor opinion against you.'[48] This was an important contribution to effective royal government. The Yorkist kings seem on the whole to have been well informed about personalities and events at a local level. To take only a single example, when Richard III set about raising a loan he was able to issue the commissioners not only with a list of men to be approached, but with a note of how much each should be asked to lend.[49]

In most other respects, however, the household was not expected to devote itself single-mindedly to the king's interests. Royal service would hardly have been a tempting prospect otherwise. All but the most humble of royal servants had their own concerns. They did not expect to shelve these on entering the king's service; on the contrary, part of the attraction of royal service was the chance it gave for private interests to be pursued with more muscle. John Paston III, contemplating entry into the king's service, was frank about his motives. He had a dispute on his hands and wanted 'the king to take my service and my quarrel together'.[50] Everyone accepted that royal servants would use their position for their own ends; it was part of the price the king paid for their obedience when he needed it. As a result, the royal servants in a given region did not necessarily form a cohesive group. Their private interests could clash dramatically, as in the notorious Stanley/Harrington dispute in the north west in Edward IV's reign.[51] This is an extreme example, but it is a reminder that kings, like other lords, could not regard their following as a unity. Even the household has to be seen as a collection of disparate individuals. It became a unity only when

[47] *Harl. 433* II p. 37.
[48] *Coventry Leet Book*, pp. 535–6. Reynold was punished for tale-bearing.
[49] *Crowland* pp. 152–3; *Harl. 433* III pp. 128–33.
[50] *PL* I p. 617.
[51] The dispute is surveyed by M. K. Jones 1986a.

mobilized in pursuit of a specific purpose and, once that was accomplished, it fragmented again: Service, in other words, did not displace personal interests; it coexisted with them, and it was able to do so because service largely entailed obedience to *specific* commands.

This perception of service has wider implications. It has often been pointed out that late-medieval loyalty does not seem to have been exclusive. Men acted for more than one lord and, where evidence survives, can be shown to have received fees from more than one as well. John Howard was able to draw up an impressive list of fees and offices.[52] Lesser figures, too, might have links with more than one master. The Eyres of Padley (Derbs.) had connections with the earls of Shrewsbury and the Lovells, and perhaps with other landowners as well.[53] Traditionally, such multiple obligations have been seen as a black mark against bastard feudalism, with exclusive loyalty tacitly regarded as the ideal, but this is to misunderstand the nature of contemporary service. Because it dealt so largely in specifics, service did not have to be undivided to be effective. This is most obvious in the case of lawyers, who regularly served several masters simultaneously.[54] They were providing a particular expertise which they could sell to several buyers. Other forms of service were not far removed from this. A lord was looking for connections and influence, and a man who had them could legitimately put them at the disposal of more than one master. This would not normally cause problems, because he would usually be called upon to apply his influence to specific ends, just as a lawyer would be called upon to advise on a particular problem. The Eyres demonstrate this at a local level. They were active in the estate administration of their several lords, where their local knowledge and contacts could be exploited. Similar considerations prevailed at a national level: a well-connected figure such as William Catesby under Richard III was granted fees by a variety of men against the day when they might need to call upon his influence.[55]

Where the interests of two lords clashed profoundly, the performance of even specific services for both of them might, of

---

[52] Turner, *Manners and Expenses* pp. 456–7.
[53] Meredith 1964, pp. 1–3.
[54] McFarlane 1981, pp. 251–2. See also the examples in Horrox 1981, pp. 151–2; Ramsey 1985, pp. 104–6.
[55] Roskell 1959b, pp. 161–4.

course, become impossible, and a choice would need to be made between them.[56] Even under normal circumstances it is likely that one relationship took precedence over the others, if only because some forms of service (notably personal attendance or fighting) could by their very nature only be performed for one lord at a time. However, this still left room for a whole range of other connections, all involving an element of service. This variety of connections had obvious advantages for the servants concerned, but it should not be assumed that all the benefits were on their side and that lords acquiesced grudgingly. Some would-be retainers, it is true, held out their lack of other ties as an inducement, implying that exclusivity was valued. Gerard Salvin of Croxdale (Durham) assured the duke of Gloucester that he was 'a poor gentleman at my liberty, studying to take a master where I will and please'.[57] But in practice lords do not seem to have worried about their servants' other commitments as long as their own commands were obeyed. Even this may be too negative a view of their attitude. Servants were primarily a way of getting things done, and the men who could do that most effectively were men within the local power structure, men, that is, with their own connections and obligations. A man who stood aside from all this was more likely to be a liability than an asset (there is, for instance, no evidence that Salvin got his fee); indeed, since service often entailed the exercise of authority, a much-employed man might well be regarded as a more attractive servant than one with no commitments.

These assumptions about service are common to both royal and aristocratic retinues. In theory, service to the king took precedence over all other ties, even among men who had no formal connections with him. Salvin, immediately after the passage quoted above, went on, 'and I love none so well as you under God and the king'. It was a commonplace for indentures of retainer to except the obedience owed to the king, but this might well be ignored in a direct conflict of interest between the immediate lord and the king. Among the king's own servants his precedence was rather more secure – but one is still talking only of precedence, not exclusivity. Even within the household, royal service coexisted with other relationships. Two of Edward IV's grooms wrote to Sir William Plumpton as 'our right good master'

[56] Pollard 1968, pp. 245–6.
[57] Surtees 1816–40, IV p. 115.

and offered him 'our daily service at all times' in return for a favour to a Knaresborough acquaintance.[58] At the upper levels of the household, too, servants took on other responsibilities. Many acted as estate officials for other lords. In 1477 the esquire of the body John Sapcote was acting as receiver for Katherine, dowager duchess of Norfolk, while the knight of the body Thomas Burgh was steward of her lordship of Epworth.[59]

Such appointments have usually been regarded as sinecures – *douceurs* to have the good will of the recipients.[60] But the example of Sir John Fogge, quoted earlier, suggests that this was not necessarily the case. Fogge was giving real service to the prior. In appointing Fogge the prior no doubt had one eye on his useful court connections, but his specialized local knowledge was probably at least as important. Burgh lived only a few miles from Epworth at Gainsborough (Lincs.). John Howard's collection of stewardships fell within his geographical area of influence. Sometimes the official may have done nothing, but this cannot be assumed, even in the case of busy royal servants.

It is clear that the Yorkist kings did not frown on these other commitments. This is spelt out by the willingness of both Edward IV and Richard III to take the servants of other lords into their household with no expectation that the earlier connection would be broken off. Under Edward IV there was a significant overlap between the royal household and the affinities of Hastings and Gloucester. Richard III took several retainers of the earl of Northumberland into his household who then maintained links with the earl. Typical of these is Sir William Gascoigne, the earl's brother-in-law and his deputy steward at Knaresborough. He had entered Richard's household by September 1483 and was later given an annuity of £20, but he continued to receive his fee from the earl, with whom he clearly maintained close links.[61] In cases like this it is generally impossible to be sure which loyalty was paramount – unless there were a direct conflict. The king's claims might then prevail, as in the case of the former Neville servants who backed Edward IV in 1471, but equally they might not, and household men drawn from the Stanley connection fought against Richard III at Bosworth. Examples such as these emphasize the

[58] *Plumpton Corresp.* pp. 24–5.
[59] Lancashire RO, DDK/1746/15 m. 2 dorse.
[60] McFarlane 1981, pp. 252–3.
[61] PRO, DL 5/1 fo. 33v; DL 42/20 fos. 32v, 54–v; Cumbria RO, D/Lec/29/8.

extent to which both relationships remained a reality. Of course, conflicts were not anticipated. Shared allegiances developed only when the nobles concerned were thought to be loyal to the crown and when their men could thus be regarded as the king's men at one remove. Even so, it is a striking comment on royal attitudes to service that such dual loyalties could seem acceptable. These attitudes are explicable when one remembers the household's role. It is only if the king's servants are regarded as some sort of royalist party that undivided commitment to the king's concerns might seem desirable. Medieval kings were more realistic. Service for them was a way of wielding effective power, and the test of good service lay in what it achieved. When lord Strange wrote to William Stonor, 'If ye cherish my tenants, I will cherish you', he was being unduly brusque, but had put his finger on the crucial spot.[62] Service was to be judged by practical results.

This picture of royal service as one strand, albeit an important one, in the activity of men who had other interests and responsibilities has another major consequence. It is accepted that medieval kings needed the support of their leading subjects if they were to translate their wishes into effective action. Normally, discussion of this aspect of royal authority distinguishes between the king's relationship with his nobles and with lesser figures. It used to be argued that the nobility's interests were basically opposed to those of the crown, while those of the smaller landowners and the like were not, so that the crown would make common ground with its lesser subjects against the separatist tendencies of the magnates. Now, however, the emphasis is on the fact that nobility and king normally co-operated, that such co-operation was in both their interests and that conflict is therefore an aberration. None the less, legacies of the older view remain. In particular it is still taken for granted that the relationship of the nobility and gentry to the crown was different, in that the gentry were inherently more responsive to the king's wishes. The underlying assumption is that the nobility could afford to be more selective in their obedience because they enjoyed greater independent power. There is an element of truth in this. The more an individual's power derived directly from the king, the more reliable he was likely to be – partly because he stood to lose more by disobedience, partly because he was likely to have some sense of

[62] *Stonor Letters* II p. 70, cited by McFarlane 1981, p. 109.

personal gratitude – but this distinction does not correspond neatly to the division between the nobility and gentry. In most generations there would be members of the nobility whose influence derived immediately from an exercise of royal favour. Conversely, many of the gentry were established, independent figures, for whom the benefits of royal service were attractive but certainly not essential. Both groups reveal a range of attitudes to the crown. Among nobles and gentry alike, some were regarded as particularly closely identified with the king, others were co-operative but hardly committed, some were frankly uninterested. There is, it is true, a difference in the types of service performed by the two groups. Nobles by and large were not interested in the *minutiae* of local affairs and would not expect to organize wood sales, for instance. But this is a difference in the manifestations of service, not its underlying assumptions. In both cases the king was seeking to utilize influence which existed independently of him, and the men concerned co-operated because it was in their interests to do so.

To see service in terms of the exploitation of existing influence is, however, only part of the picture. For the servant, one of the advantages of service was that it tended to enhance his standing: thus the lord was not only tapping into an existing network of influence but in so doing was modifying it as well. The result could be to set up a sort of spiral effect, where the more an individual was used, the more influential he became and the more he was used. This was to the advantage of both sides, and the effect could be achieved artificially by the use of patronage. In giving a servant office, or, in rare cases, land, a lord was both rewarding him and making him more useful in the future. In extreme cases, a lord might deliberately create a new sphere of influence for a trusted servant so as to have that influence at his disposal. Richard III resorted to this tactic when he 'planted' men in the south after Buckingham's rebellion. At first sight this policy offers considerable advantages. The more an individual had gained (or hoped to gain) from his lord, the more reliable he was likely to be, and a man whose influence derived solely from royal favour ought to be the most reliable of all. But there were also disadvantages. In creating influence royal *fiat* could do much, but it could not do everything. Local influence, resting as it did on a complex network of connections and mutual obligation, took time to develop fully. Exploiting existing connections would thus generally be more effective than building them up from scratch. Most reigns produced their share of new men, whose influence was created either as a mark of favour or to fill a political gap, but only the most insecure of kings would deliberately eschew existing influence in favour of his own creations.

There is another sense also in which the exploitation of existing influence is not the whole story. By its very nature such service could only be part-time. Varied and flexible as it was, it needed underpinning by some more permanent commitment in order to provide continuity of organization. It also failed to meet all the lord's needs. Although men of standing might be willing to serve the lord at table, for instance, he still needed men to buy, prepare and cook the food, let alone scour the dishes afterwards. There was thus a whole spectrum of service, of which the type discussed so far occupies only the upper end. At the other extreme were the full-time menial servants who provided the labour within the lord's estates and household and who are now largely invisible. The middle ground was filled by men whose role can loosely be called bureaucratic.[63] Some of them were themselves part-time, putting their professional expertise at the service of more than one master and so conforming very closely to the pattern of service already discussed. The leading common lawyers with flourishing consultancies are the most obvious example. Other bureaucrats worked mainly for one lord but took on occasional commitments elsewhere; while others, often humble figures, devoted all their time to the affairs of one master.

Within this spectrum of service there are two obvious lines of division. One is between the part- and full-timers which is in effect between those servants who offered influence and expertise of their own, and those of little or no personal authority whose importance, if any, derived from the master they served. That contemporaries were alive to this distinction comes across very clearly in a letter of c.1456 from William Worcester, amanuensis of Sir John Fastolf, to John Paston I. Paston was almost as much Fastolf's dogsbody, but distinguished by the crucial element of personal influence. As Worcester put it, complaining that Fastolf would not listen to him or his colleagues:

it sufficeth not our simple wits to appease his soul. But when he speaketh with Master Yelverton, you, or William Geney and such others as be

---

[63] Griffiths 1980, pp. 112–13.

authorised in the law and with abundance of goods, he is content and holdeth him pleased with your answers and motions, as reason is that he be. So would Jesus one of you 3 or some such other in your stead might hang at his girdle daily to answer his matters.[64]

The distinction is a real one, but it should not be over-drawn. As the tone of Worcester's letter makes plain, he and Paston occupied the same world. They also shared the same attitude to service. For Worcester, service was open-ended, a personal relationship rather than a defined set of responsibilities. Thus in a matter of weeks early in 1458 he can be seen attending to a transfer of land and assessing the property's state of repair; delivering letters; discussing the ransom of one of Fastolf's prisoners of war; pushing forward the matter of the Cromwell inheritance; gathering news; pricing grain and dried fruit; and acting as a collection point for Fastolf's revenues.[65] Even the specific tasks are not much different from those expected on an *ad hoc* basis from gentry servants, and in fact John Paston was associated with Worcester in the performance of several of them. It was the quantity of the work rather than its quality which separated the full-time servant from his part-time colleague. Worcester's performance of all these jobs one after the other is the mark of a man for whom his master's interests, rather than his own, are paramount.

This shared ethos suggests that the crucial division in the spectrum of service comes between the menial servants and the rest. Above this level service might take up widely varying amounts of time, but its assumptions were the same. Full-time bureaucrats, like their gentry colleagues, were expected to turn their hand to anything. Richard Tilles, controller first of Edward V's household and then of Richard III's works, found himself sent to investigate treason in the south west, for instance.[66] For both, too, service was honourable. By the mid fifteenth century service was a sufficient criterion of gentility for the professional bureaucrat; a tacit equation of his role with that of the gentleman-amateur.[67] The professional/amateur distinction is, indeed, something of an anachronism in this context. Numerous medieval families could trace their descent from a successful administrator.

[64] *PL* II pp. 156–7; McFarlane 1981, pp. 202–4.
[65] *PL* II pp. 531–4.
[66] *Harl. 433* I pp. 47–8, 154, II pp. 31–2.
[67] Storey 1982, pp. 92–3; Morgan 1986, pp. 24–7.

The Parrs of Kendale, for example, were apparently rather proud of their descent from a clerk of the kitchen to one of the lords Roos, who married his master's daughter.[68] Conversely, because administrative service was honourable, it was a proper career for someone of gentle birth. John Fitzherbert of Etwall (Derbs.), who made his career in the Exchequer, was the brother of Ralph Fitzherbert of Norbury, the head of an important Derbyshire family.[69]

Service was also honourable in a more personal sense. It was something to be proud of, and both eminent and humble included details of their service in their funeral inscriptions.[70] Alongside this went, in many cases, a respect and loyalty to their lord, a reminder of the personal dimension in service. The professional administrator Jacques Blondell asked in his will for prayers for his past lords and ladies, whom 'I sometimes served in household and had of them my living according to the degree that his grace called me to and better than I could deserve, God quit it them in heaven'. One of Edward IV's administrators, his clerk of the kitchen Nicholas Southworth, endowed prayers in the churches of his home country (St Peter's and St John's in Chester and St Winifred's at Holywell in North Wales) but wanted to be buried at Windsor, 'beside my old master king Edward'.[71] Although this study is primarily concerned with the men for whom service was only one part of their career, it would thus be unrealistic to try and exclude their full-time colleagues altogether. Full- and part-time servants were in any case complementary elements in royal government, together providing the continuity and influence which the effective exercise of the king's authority demanded.

In a very direct sense that authority rested on service: someone had to obey the king's command. Authority was also defined by service. A lord without servants was no lord, as contemporaries were well aware. The effect is to put the relationship of lord and man, or patronage and service, at the heart of medieval politics. To be sure of service the king had to demonstrate his good

---

[68] Leland, *Itin.* v p. 223.

[69] Cox 1875–9, III p. 236. Fitzherbert was first a teller, then king's remembrancer: PRO, E 404/76/4/24; C 67/51 m. 16.

[70] There are numerous examples in Weever 1631. Compare also the practice of portraying men in their livery collars: Tudor-Craig 1973, pp. 24–5 (and pl. 60); Griffiths 1981a, pls. 28, 34, 36.

[71] PRO, Prob 11/11 fo. 93v; 11/8 fo. 154v.

lordship. In part that was a national requirement, in that the king's good rule justified his claim on the support of his subjects. But it was also a requirement to be a good lord to his individual servants. This demanded the enhancement of their interests, whether by a direct exercise of favour, or indirectly, by the mere fact of their association with the great. These essentially selfish benefits were a major element in the relationship. But service was not only the mechanical pursuit of private advantage. Because it was a personal and honourable matter, service could also engage the emotions, and loyalty could on occasion override self-interest. Even when the two pointed in the same direction, respect and affection cannot entirely be ignored as motives. As a result, lordship could never be just an exercise in open-handedness. Thomas More recognized as much when, in a famous passage, he remarked of Richard III that 'with large gifts he got him unsteadfast friendship'.[72]

The career of Richard III provides a particularly good illustration of this crucial and complex relationship. As duke of Gloucester, Richard was the effective and trusted servant of his brother Edward IV, and their relationship is a copy-book example of the mutual advantages of good lordship, with Edward augmenting the power which Richard placed at his disposal. Gloucester was a linchpin of Yorkist royal authority, and his usurpation in 1483 posed a real dilemma for Edward's servants. Richard's apparent belief that he could call on the support of his brother's men was proved false, and the subsequent rebellions against him involved a significant number of royal servants. As a result, in much of the south he was forced to rebuild the nexus of service upon which his authority depended. But if the reign illuminates contemporary attitudes to service, the reverse is also true. For More, Richard's failure was a failure in lordship. Whether or not he was right, service provides an enlightening perspective from which to examine the reign.

[72] More, *Richard III* p. 8.

Chapter 1

THE CREATION OF AN AFFINITY

When Richard duke of Gloucester seized the throne in 1483 he did so at the head of the largest noble affinity of its day. The ducal retinue as it then stood was the creation of the previous fourteen years, during which Gloucester, with royal backing, had built up his power from negligible beginnings to become the acknowledged lord of the north. Gloucester did not, however, create a following out of nothing. Political society formed a complex network of lordship and service, in which all but a few misfits had some place. A newcomer to the political scene, whether lord or man, could not hope to operate outside this existing network, but had instead to find himself a place within it. For a lord this meant securing the service of men who were already the servants of others. To do this on a significant scale he had either to supersede another lord or outrank him so that the following of one lord became a component in the retinue of a superior lord.

The primary determinant of service was still land, in the sense that a lord normally drew the core of his following from the area where his estates lay, although the men who looked to him for lordship would not necessarily be his own tenants. Thus the Gowers of Stittenham (Yorks.) served the lord of nearby Sheriff Hutton, although they held Stittenham itself from the prior of Malton.[1] This strong territorial element meant that when a major estate changed hands, whether by inheritance or forfeiture, the affinity of the previous owner would tend to turn to his successor for lordship. But land ownership was not the only factor. National influence could give a lord a local following greater than his land alone would warrant, as Gloucester's own career was to demonstrate. The same was true of major office holding within a region. In the reign of Henry VII, Sir Thomas Lovell was able to raise a military contingent in Nottinghamshire,

---

[1] *Inqs p.m.* I nos. 556, 1005; Horrox 1986b, p. 83.

where he held no land, on the strength of his office holding in the county.[2] The size of a lord's following could also be determined by less tangible considerations. Personality evidently played some part. So could regional loyalties. A lord taking over a forfeited estate could not entirely take for granted the good will of the affinity, at least in the short term. This play of factors meant that a major retinue was never just the sum of its territorial parts. Gloucester's affinity can be characterized in terms of the political antecedents of its members, including, for instance, members of the de Vere, Neville and Clifford retinues. But these identifiable elements were blended into a new pattern, which owed its existence to Gloucester himself. He was responsible for shaping the material at his disposal into an effective unity, and the success with which he did so can be seen in the cohesion of the retinue in 1483.

Gloucester first came to prominence in 1469. Only eight at the time of his brother's accession in 1461, he spent the early years of Edward IV's reign in relative obscurity, overshadowed by his elder brother George duke of Clarence. There is no explicit reference to Gloucester's attainment of his majority, but Clarence was deemed to have come of age when he was sixteen and Richard's sixteenth birthday fell in October 1468. It was probably around this time that he left the household of his cousin Richard Neville earl of Warwick, where he had been placed in 1465. By February 1469 he was in the company of his brother the king and took an active role in the trial for treason of Henry Courtenay and Thomas Hungerford.[3] In the following May his new independence is reflected in his agreement with Margaret lady Hungerford, whereby Gloucester, the main beneficiary of the Hungerford attainders, promised to protect Margaret's dower rights and to be her good and gracious lord.[4] But although Gloucester was thus becoming politically visible for the first time, he was as yet of only limited importance. As the youngest royal brother, Richard had received a relatively modest endowment from Edward IV. His estates were, moreover, a heterogeneous collection, put together with an eye to providing him with an income rather than creating a political niche for him at a regional level. Unlike his

[2] Cameron 1974, p. 24.
[3] Ross 1981, pp. 7, 10–11, 14.
[4] BL, Cotton Julius BXII fos. 123–5; an abridged version is printed in *HMC, Hastings* I pp. 290–1.

brother Clarence, he acquired no ready-made affinity which he could exploit when he came of age.[5] The royal grant which had offered Richard the best chance of a viable power base had been that of the forfeited de Vere estates, made in August 1462, but these had been restored to the earl of Oxford at the beginning of 1464.[6] His other holdings included the lordship of Chirk in the Welsh marches and land forfeited by Henry Beaufort duke of Somerset, although this was encumbered by the claims of two dowagers.[7]

This rather unpromising collection was augmented with grants from the duchy of Lancaster. The first of these, which formed part of Gloucester's original endowment, was the manor of Kingston Lacy in Dorset, which he apparently held for the rest of the reign.[8] In 1465 he received the most valuable component of his early endowment, the duchy lordships of Bolingbroke (Lincs.), Pickering and Barnoldswick (Yorks.), to the annual value of £1,000.[9] This went some way towards closing the financial gap between Gloucester's endowment and that of his brother Clarence, but income is probably all that the grant was designed to provide. There is no suggestion that Gloucester enjoyed any influence within the lordships, where the royal officials remained unchanged. The grant was perhaps intended to give Gloucester a suitable income when he entered Warwick's household and it may be no coincidence that the sum involved was exactly that which Edward later granted the earl towards the duke's expenses.[10]

This emphasis on income rather than influence was appropriate in the endowment of a royal duke who was still a child, but once Gloucester came of age his lack of a suitable power base was less acceptable. Edward IV made a first attempt to remedy the situation within weeks of his brother's sixteenth birthday, when he gave Richard the land of Robert lord Hungerford, lying mainly in Somerset and Wiltshire. Alone among Gloucester's holdings this represented a coherent entity, but it was again

---

[5] Hicks 1980, p. 27.
[6] *CPR* 1461–7 p. 197; Ross 1981, pp. 9–10.
[7] *CPR* 1461–7 pp. 228, 292; Ross 1981, p. 10.
[8] *CPR* 1461–7 p. 197; there are apparently no subsequent grants from the lordship until Richard's own reign.
[9] BL, Cotton Julius BXII fo. 117.
[10] Ross 1981, p. 7n.

burdened with dower rights and other charges.[11] In May 1469 Edward tried again, turning once more to the resources of the duchy of Lancaster. Gloucester was given (during the king's pleasure) a major collection of duchy land in Lancashire and Cheshire, including Clitheroe, Liverpool and Halton. This time the grant specifically included all rights and offices in the lordships concerned.[12] It thus cut across existing interests in the region, notably those of the Stanley family, whose landed interests in the north west had been augmented by several key duchy offices. Their resentment at Gloucester's insertion into the area manifested itself in open rivalry with the duke and early in 1470 Edward was obliged to intervene in the quarrel.[13]

The episode spells out very clearly the difficulties in finding an appropriate niche for the duke. However generous Edward wished to be – and his willingness to challenge the Stanleys suggests that he saw Richard's endowment as a matter of some urgency – there was a limit to how much he could afford to do for his brother. It had been a recurrent problem of Edward's early years that he lacked the resources to reward all his leading supporters, and by 1469 he was left with very little room for manoeuvre. A major new endowment for Gloucester could only be achieved at the expense of existing interests, and this was politically unacceptable. It was only the office holding of the Stanleys which was threatened, but even that may have been enough to drive them into opposition to Edward by 1470.[14] In May 1469 the prospect of more large-scale gains for Gloucester was accordingly remote. It was a situation from which he was rescued by the rebellion of Clarence and Warwick in July 1469, an event which marked a turning point in his career. This was not primarily because their rebellion allowed Gloucester to demonstrate his usefulness to the king. Although the defection of Clarence, in particular, can only have enhanced Richard's standing in the king's eyes, the real contribution of the rebels to Gloucester's advancement lay in opening up the existing power structure by removing several of Edward's closest supporters.

The beneficiaries were, of course, intended to be Clarence and Warwick themselves. The two men had become increasingly

---

[11] *CPR* 1467–77 p. 139; Ross 1981, p. 10n.
[12] BL, Cotton Julius BXII fos. 115v–6v; PRO, DL 37/38 no. 7.
[13] *CCR* 1468–76 no. 535; and see note 34 below.
[14] Ross 1974, p. 143.

resentful of the circle around the king, and their rebellion was specifically directed against the 'covetous rule and guiding' of this group, identified in the rebels' manifesto as the family of queen Elizabeth Woodville, the earls of Devon and Pembroke, John lord Audley and Sir John Fogge.[15] On 26 July the rebels defeated part of the royalist forces at Edgecote and in the aftermath of the battle several of the king's allies were captured and executed, among them Devon and Pembroke and two of the queen's family, her father earl Rivers and her brother John. Edward IV himself fell into the rebels' hands and was sent prisoner first to Warwick castle and then to the Nevilles' northern stronghold of Middleham in Wensleydale. But although the rebels had thus far outmanoeuvred the king, they found themselves unable to translate their military success into long-term political supremacy. Their attempts to rule in the king's name were a failure and by the end of September, if not earlier, Edward had reasserted his freedom of action. In the middle of October he staged a triumphant return to London and set about rebuilding his position, a process from which Gloucester emerged as the main beneficiary.

The outbreak of trouble had found Gloucester with the king in East Anglia, on pilgrimage to the shrines of St Edmund at Bury and Our Lady of Walsingham. The first indication of danger was a growing unrest in the north of England. There had been trouble there as early as April, but that had been dealt with for the king by Warwick's brother John Neville. During June a more threatening outbreak developed under the leadership of 'Robin of Redesdale' (almost certainly Warwick's associate Sir John Conyers) and by the middle of the month Edward had decided to go north himself. On 18 June he wrote from Norwich to set preparations in train for equipping an army and he and his circle began to raise men locally. Their efforts were observed by John Paston III who, however, was watching events round the king almost entirely with an eye to how they might affect his family's dispute with the duke of Norfolk, and recorded the flurry of activity without noting its cause. His letter provides the earliest surviving evidence of Gloucester retaining men. Paston names four local men sworn to the duke's service, of whom the most important was William Calthorpe of Burnham Thorpe (Norf.).[16] The context makes it likely that Gloucester was offering a short-term military contract;

---

[15] Warkworth, *Chronicle* p. 46; Ross 1974, pp. 126–35.
[16] *PL* I p. 545.

in other words, that he was acting as recruiting officer for his brother's army rather than laying the foundations of a personal following in East Anglia where, at this date, he had no interests of his own. None of the four can be definitely linked with Gloucester in the 1470s, although the Calthorpes may have kept some connections with him.[17] If in this respect Gloucester was still very much his brother's agent, it is clear that his closeness to the king had already made him a person of some consequence. The decision to go north found the duke short of money and he wrote to Sir John Say for a loan of £100 to tide him over.[18] He added a postscript in his own hand: 'I pray you that ye fail me not at this time in my great need, as ye will that I show you my good lordship in that matter that ye labour to me for.' Say, the chancellor of the duchy of Lancaster, was a close associate of Edward IV and it is significant that he should already consider Gloucester's lordship valuable.[19] So did even more eminent figures. An undated letter from John Howard to the duke of Norfolk, which can probably be assigned to 1469, assured Norfolk of Gloucester's good will: 'I did remember your lordship to my lord, promising you I found my lord as well disposed toward you as any lord may be to another ... whereof I was right glad to hear it.'[20]

Gloucester's contribution to later events is obscure. If the Howard letter does belong to 1469, it shows that the duke was at Colchester on 21 July and was then planning to travel northwards to Bury St Edmunds. This may mean that he had remained in the region when the court set off for the midlands at the end of June. It is, however, more likely that he had accompanied the king to Nottingham and had then, like the Woodvilles, been sent away as the news grew more threatening. The queen's eldest brother, lord Scales, apparently returned to East Anglia, where his own land lay, and Gloucester may have accompanied him, perhaps (as the Howard letter seems to imply) with the intention of raising more men. There are, however, no more references to him until Edward's return to London in the autumn. In the interim

---

[17] See below, p. 78.
[18] BL, Cotton Vespasian FIII fo. 19; postscript printed by Tudor-Craig 1973, p. 66. The opening of the postscript printed as 'Sir I say I pray you...' should be read as 'Sir J[ohn] Say...' Say was also approached for loans by the king: PRO, DL 37/39 nos. 1, 6.
[19] Somerville 1953, pp. 390–1. Say was again associated with Gloucester in 1477: *Chron. S. Albani* II pp. 165–6.
[20] Turner, *Manners and Expenses* pp. 580–1.

Gloucester presumably continued his efforts on his brother's behalf, either in East Anglia or elsewhere. Polydore Vergil later claimed that Edward's chamberlain lord Hastings raised a force for the king in Lancashire. This was an area where, in theory, Gloucester now enjoyed considerable influence, and it may be, therefore, that he was also involved.[21] But whatever Gloucester's exact contribution, his part in the crisis had confirmed his emergence as a political force, and once Edward had regained power his brother's loyalty was duly rewarded. On 17 October Gloucester was made constable of England, an office formerly held by the executed earl Rivers with remainder to his son lord Scales, who must have waived his claim on Gloucester's behalf. Two days later, Gloucester's arrival in the inner court circle was further emphasized by the queen's grant to him of the stewardship of her land with an annual fee of £100. A month later the king gave him the castle and manor of Sudeley (Glos.).[22]

These grants, although valuable, were not much more than flourishes on an already diverse collection. Gloucester's major gain from the events of 1469 was his acquisition, for the first time, of a recognized sphere of action. This was in Wales, where royal authority had been dangerously undermined by the execution of William Herbert, earl of Pembroke. The exercise of that authority had proved a recurrent problem for late-medieval kings. Edward IV's solution had been to build up Herbert power until the family and their allies dominated most of Wales on the crown's behalf. The policy had aroused the hostility of the earl of Warwick, himself a landowner in the south march, where he held Glamorgan and Abergavenny in his wife's right. Within the south march the two men quarrelled over Newport, but their rivalry also had wider manifestations: Warwick felt threatened by Herbert's matrimonial ambitions, which had the backing of the king. Pembroke's execution, on Warwick's orders, has the air of a private act of revenge, as do the other executions which followed Edgecote.[23] As far as Wales was concerned, Warwick also took the opportunity offered by his control of Edward IV to help himself to some of Pembroke's key offices: justiciar of south

---

[21] Vergil p. 517. The strongest claims for Richard's involvement in his brother's rescue are made by Kendall 1955, p. 77 (and notes).

[22] BL, Cotton Julius BXII fos. 121v, 122–3; *CCR* 1468–76 no. 409; *CPR* 1467–77 pp. 19, 178.

[23] Griffiths 1972b, pp. 158–9; Pugh 1971, p. 198; Hicks 1980, pp. 38–40; Ross 1974, pp. 131–2.

Wales, constable of Carmarthen and Cardigan and steward of Cantrefmawr and Cardiganshire.[24] The scale of Herbert's power in Wales made his removal a major set-back to royal influence there, as was indicated by the immediate flare-up of trouble in the north and west of the region.[25] A rapid reassertion of royal authority was essential, and this provided Gloucester with an opening.

The first indication of the duke's new role was his appointment, at the end of October, to head commissions of array in the border counties of Shropshire, Gloucester and Worcester. On 7 November he was made justiciar of north Wales for life in place of Hastings to whom Warwick had given the office in the previous August. At the end of the month he was made chief steward, approver and surveyor of the principality of Wales and the earldom of March, and in mid December steward of Monmouth. The latter had been given only a month previously to John lord Dudley, and its transfer suggests that Gloucester's role in Wales was still evolving.[26] So far Edward had been careful to avoid any appearance of an attack on Warwick's own gains, but on 16 December Gloucester was authorized to subdue the rebels who had seized the castles of Cardigan and Carmarthen – castles of which Warwick was still technically constable. Finally, in February 1470, the king regranted the offices which Warwick had taken for himself in the previous August, with Gloucester again the main beneficiary. The duke was made justiciar of south Wales and steward of Cantrefmawr and Cardiganshire, which completed his collection of the major offices formerly held by the earl of Pembroke.[27]

Gloucester's position in Wales, however, was fundamentally different from that of Pembroke. Although Herbert's power had been enormously enhanced by royal backing, it was rooted in regional loyalties which Gloucester, as a newcomer, could not command. Moreover, the duke's authority was expected to be only temporary. William Herbert had held several of his key posts in tail male and they were accordingly only granted to the duke during the minority of the young earl of Pembroke, William Herbert II. In the event Edward was to have no qualms about

[24] *CPR* 1467–77 p. 165.
[25] Evans 1915, p. 189; *CPR* 1467–77 pp. 180–1.
[26] *CPR* 1467–77 pp. 179–80, 195; Somerville 1953, p. 648.
[27] *CPR* 1467–77 pp. 180–1, 185.

dismantling the power of the second earl in the 1470s, but in 1469 he wanted to keep his options open and, in particular, to keep the support of the surviving members of the Herbert connection. His aim was thus to keep the Herbert hegemony intact, while ensuring that it continued to be used in the royal interest. Gloucester's role was basically to preserve the status quo by taking on the temporary leadership of the connection, rather than to carve out a new power base for himself. A similar policy is evident in the disposal of the Herbert lands. They, together with the custody of the young earl, were given to the dowager countess and so remained under Herbert control. But the countess was the sister of the long-standing Yorkist servant Walter Devereux lord Ferrers, which no doubt helped to ensure that the patrimony was handled in ways acceptable to Edward IV.[28]

As far as the Herbert interest was concerned, therefore, Gloucester was put at the head of an existing connection which he was expected to do little to modify. He seems to have occupied the same position with regard to other royal servants in Wales, men like John Donne, Hugh Huntley and John Milewater, who were associated with the duke on a commission of 6 January 1470 to enquire into rebellion in south Wales.[29] Such men would inevitably develop links with Gloucester (Milewater was to die in his service at Barnet), but they were primarily the king's servants rather than the duke's. Among their other responsibilities, Donne was steward of Kidwelly and an esquire of the king's body; Huntley was one of the duchy of Lancaster receivers in Wales; and Milewater was receiver general of the duchy lands in south Wales and the march.[30] Such men gave continuity to royal activity in Wales and there was no question of their being superseded. Even had Gloucester wished to take a more independent line in Wales, it is doubtful how far he had the necessary connections. His own territorial base in Wales was relatively small, although in 1470 he was retaining men from his lordship of Chirk.[31] Nor did he yet have much of a following elsewhere which he could import into Wales, although he was probably responsible for the arrival in Wales of the Yorkshireman John

---

[28] *Ibid.* pp 174–5. Hicks 1980, p. 56 suggests that Ferrers may have acted as Gloucester's mentor in Wales.
[29] BL, Cotton Julius BXII fo. 120–v.
[30] Somerville 1953, pp. 640, 641n., 650; Griffiths 1972a, pp. 156–7, 187–8.
[31] W.W.E.W., 'Grant from Gloucester' p. 55; Lowe 1977, p. 279.

Pilkington, who served with the duke on the January commission.[32] Essentially, Gloucester was intended to provide a royal presence in Wales which could give weight and a focus to the activities of the king's servants and supporters there. This is not to belittle the importance of his role. Herbert's career had demonstrated how valuable it was to have a focus for royal efforts in Wales and the council of the prince of Wales was to serve the same purpose in the 1470s. Gloucester could not rival Herbert's local connections, but he did have the status to make an acceptable figurehead and he seems to have put considerable energy into the role. He probably left for Wales in November 1469 and may have spent most of the next few months there. He was certainly in Wales in mid June 1470 when, as justiciar, he presided at the Carmarthenshire great sessions.[33]

By this date Edward IV had faced, and apparently overcome, further opposition. Unrest had surfaced in Lincolnshire in late February and proved to have been fomented by Clarence and Warwick with the aim of placing Clarence on the throne. The Lincolnshire rebels were defeated near Stamford on 12 March and the two noblemen headed north in the hope of receiving support from the Neville affinity in the north east or Thomas lord Stanley in Lancashire. None was forthcoming, and the rebels fled south, escaping into exile in France. As in the previous year, Gloucester's contribution is unclear. On 26 March, at the height of the crisis, he was at Hornby (Lancs.). This was well north of any line of march from Wales to the north east, which suggests that Gloucester had business in Lancashire and was not just *en route* to join his brother, who was then at York. Hornby castle was part of the patrimony which the Harrington family was holding against strong opposition from the Stanleys, and this, coupled with a reference on the previous day to variance between Gloucester and lord Stanley, rather implies that Gloucester had made common ground with the Harringtons against Stanley influence in north Lancashire.[34] Gloucester may subsequently have joined the king in pursuit of

---

[32] Pilkington had conveyed seisin of the duchy estates from the king to Gloucester in May 1469: BL, Cotton Julius BXII fo. 116v. He is described as the duke's chamberlain in the early 1470s: PRO, C 263/2/1/6. For his later links with Gloucester: *CPR 1476–85* p. 34; *Plumpton Corresp.* p. 31; Steel 1954, pp. 4, 425; *Test. Ebor.* III pp. 238–41.

[33] Griffiths 1972a, p. 158.

[34] W.W.E.W., 'Grant from Gloucester' p. 55; *CCR 1468–76* no. 535. For a different interpretation: Kendall 1955, pp. 83–4 and notes; followed by Ross 1981, p. 17; Gillingham 1981, p. 175.

the rebels, but the next firm reference to his presence in his brother's company is not until July, when he accompanied the king into Yorkshire to deal with the rebellion of Warwick's kinsman lord Fitzhugh of Ravensworth.[35] As this demonstrated, the defection of Warwick had opened up gaps in the king's authority and Gloucester was again an immediate beneficiary. In August 1470 he was made warden of the west march towards Scotland, an office previously held by the earl of Warwick.[36] With hindsight, this can be seen as the first step in the transformation of Gloucester into the lord of the north, but this is to read too much into a single grant. Warwick's chief stewardship in the duchy of Lancaster went not to Gloucester but to Hastings and the implication seems to be that at this stage the king was more concerned to reward his allies than to undertake a major reconstruction of royal authority in the north.[37] However, his ultimate intentions must remain doubtful because in September Warwick and Clarence invaded with French backing and Edward and his brother had to flee into exile in the Low Countries.

This reverse proved short-lived. Edward returned to England in the following spring with Burgundian support and defeated first Warwick at the battle of Barnet and then the Lancastrian army at Tewkesbury. Gloucester fought in both battles and was later to endow prayers for those who had died there in his service.[38] The endowment gives a glimpse of Gloucester's retinue at this early stage in his career and reveals the blurring which existed between his affinity and his brother's servants. Of the five men commemorated by name, two were royal administrators who had been drawn into Gloucester's orbit by his activity in Wales. One, John Milewater, has already been mentioned. The other was John Harper, a royal auditor whose responsibilities included the duchy of Lancaster lands in Wales.[39] A third was a member of Edward IV's household, Christopher Worsley, a marshall of the hall, who had been sheriff of Somerset and Dorset in 1470 and whose links with Gloucester are unknown.[40] The other two were both northerners. One, Thomas Parr, was the brother of the king's servants William and John. Both the

[35] Dobson, *York Chamberlains' Rolls* p. 137; Ross 1981, pp. 17–18.
[36] BL, Cotton Julius BXII fos. 128–30.
[37] Somerville 1953, p. 422.
[38] Ross 1976, p. 3.
[39] Somerville 1953, p. 445; Wolffe 1971, p. 300.
[40] CPR 1461–7 pp. 200, 374; CFR 1461–71 pp. 128, 255, 268.

surviving brothers were to be linked with Gloucester in the 1470s, and Thomas (together with Milewater) was specifically described at the time of his death as Gloucester's esquire.[41] The remaining northerner was Thomas Huddleston, a younger son of Sir John of Millom (Cumb.). The family were to be closely associated with Gloucester in the 1470s, but in the 1460s they were Neville men, and Thomas and his brother William suffered forfeiture in 1470 for their support of Warwick and Clarence. Thomas seems to have reconsidered his allegiance by 1471, although it is possible that he actually died on Warwick's side and that his inclusion among those remembered springs from his father's later links with Gloucester. Sir John acted as Gloucester's attorney in a 1477 grant to Queens' College, Cambridge, and it was Queens' which was placed under an obligation to pray for Thomas and the rest.[42]

The royal background of so many of Gloucester's known associates at this date is to be expected. The duke's first establishment as a junior member of the royal family had probably been created by secondment from the royal household, as had also been the case for his brother Clarence.[43] The attainment of his majority would naturally have heralded a larger and more independent following, but Gloucester's early influence was in areas where there was an established network of royal servants and this shaped his developing retinue. His major territorial acquisition, the duchy of Lancaster estates in the north west, was already staffed by royal servants who would now look to the duke while retaining their links with the crown. In Wales also Gloucester was expected to set himself at the head of existing officials. It was only with the political readjustments which followed Edward IV's return from exile in 1471 that Gloucester can really be said to have acquired an independent power base. These readjustments, carried out between June and August, laid down in outline the areas where Richard was to be active for the rest of the reign. They also allowed a reconsideration of the duke's earlier endowment, some of which was surrendered. The massive duchy land grant of May 1469 was replaced by a more limited package of office, although even this was subsequently whittled down further, presumably under pressure from the Stanleys, and

[41] 'Register of sepulchral inscriptions' p. 288.
[42] *CPR* 1467–77 p. 218; *CPR* 1476–85 p. 34.
[43] Hicks 1980, pp. 20–4.

parts of the grant of 1471 seem never to have taken effect.[44] In Wales the second earl of Pembroke was allowed to enter his father's offices without proof of age in August 1471, which marked the end of Gloucester's overall authority.[45] Although the duke was later to acquire further interests of his own in Wales he never resumed the position of his brother's leading representative there.

Gloucester's major acquisitions in the reshuffle of 1471 lay in the north. This was a region which posed particular problems for medieval kings of England. As in the case of other peripheral areas, there was the practical difficulty of trying to exert authority at a distance; but this problem was compounded by the north's proximity to what was by this date England's only land boundary with another state. The north's position as a border region had contributed to the emergence and survival of a powerful nobility whose position was underpinned by strong regional loyalties. Given this background, medieval and Tudor kings recognized the necessity of accepting, and then attempting to exploit, the power of dominant local noblemen.[46] For Edward IV, however, this familiar problem had been given an additional twist by the Lancastrian sympathies of two of the leading northern families, the Percies and Cliffords. His response had been to build up the power of his supporters the Nevilles: Richard earl of Warwick and his brothers John, who was made earl of Northumberland, and George, who became archbishop of York. The defection and death of Richard and John Neville therefore reopened the question of how royal authority could best be exercised in the north, as well as raising the issue of what should be done with the Neville connection, which was now leaderless. Edward IV answered both questions by putting Gloucester into Warwick's place. The duke was to be heir both of the earl's own northern estates and of his 'public' role as the leading royal agent in the north. In the first capacity Gloucester was given, on 29 June, the key Neville strongholds of Middleham, Sheriff Hutton and Penrith. On 14 July this was superseded by a comprehensive grant of all the lands in Yorkshire and Cumberland entailed to Richard Neville and his heirs male: in other words, all the land in those

---

[44] PRO, DL 37/40 nos. 28, 46; BL, Cotton Julius BXII fos. 125v–6. For its erosion, see further below, pp. 67–9.

[45] *CPR* 1467–77 p. 275.

[46] Storey 1972, pp. 131–3.

counties which formed part of the Neville patrimony, as distinct from land which had come into Warwick's possession from his mother or wife, and which was held in tail general. This northern land was to remain in Gloucester's possession for the rest of his life, in spite of disputes over the descent of the rest of the Warwick inheritance, and formed the centrepiece of his influence in the north.[47]

In his second capacity, as heir of Warwick's public role, Gloucester took over the major royal offices which the earl had held in the north. He had already, in 1470, been given the wardenship of the west march. He was now made chief steward of the duchy of Lancaster in the north, an office which passed the duchy seal on 4 July, but which must have originated earlier since Gloucester was acting as steward early in June.[48] The stewardship constituted a significant extension of Gloucester's sphere of influence. In Yorkshire, the duchy estates included the lordships of Pickering and Tickhill, in the north and south of the county respectively. Another major block of duchy land lay along the Aire, from the soke of Snaith in the east, through Pontefract to Leeds and Bradford, with the forest of Knaresborough an outrider further north. Across the Pennines the duchy included the forest of Bowland (regarded as lying in Yorkshire), the county palatine of Lancashire and land in north Cheshire. There was a significant duchy interest in the north midlands, centred on Tutbury (Staffs.) and the High Peak (Derbs.), and estates in Lincolnshire, including Lincoln itself and land along the coast administered from Boling-broke. In addition, Gloucester was made master forester of the duchy forests in Lancashire, together with the forest of Bowland. He was also made surveyor of the forest of Galtres, to the north of York, which was not itself part of the duchy but included the duchy manors of Easingwold and Huby, of which the duke was also made surveyor. The manors were the natural complement to Gloucester's lordship of Sheriff Hutton and he was later to farm them both from the crown.[49]

In establishing himself in the north, Gloucester was able to build upon existing foundations. The events of 1470/1 had not

[47] *CPR* 1467–77 pp. 260, 266; Hicks 1979b, pp. 120–1. The extended grant had the effect of including the estates of the honour of Richmond in Richmondshire, for which see below, pp. 56–7.

[48] PRO, DL 37/40 nos. 28, 46; Somerville 1953, p. 493; Humberside RO, DDCL 16 m. 10 dorse. The grant was back-dated to Michaelmas 1470.

[49] PRO, DL 37/40 nos. 28, 46; BL, Cotton Julius BXII fos. 119–20.

entirely destroyed Edward IV's authority in the north. There remained a core of committed supporters who had accompanied Edward into exile or who rallied to him after his landing in Yorkshire in 1471. Among the former was the yeoman of the chamber Nicholas Leventhorpe of Bramham (Yorks.) who acted as go-between for the exiled king and Henry Percy, whom Edward had restored to the earldom of Northumberland in 1470.[50] On his return to Zeeland, Leventhorpe was accompanied by a servant of Sir Ralph Ashton, which implies that Ashton too was an ally of the king, as does his omission from all the Readeption commissions. Most examples of Yorkist support in the north, however, come from the period after Edward's landing. At Doncaster the king was joined by his esquire, Gloucester's associate John Pilkington, who lent him 100 marks. Ralph Snaith, a yeoman of the crown who was bailiff of Pontefract, lent £40 of his own and a further £30 from the revenues of his office.[51] At Nottingham Edward was joined by two more northern household men, Sir James Harrington of Brierly (Yorks.) and Sir William Parr of Kendal. Both men were presumably accompanied by their brothers, since Robert Harrington and John Parr were later knighted by Edward at Tewkesbury, and Thomas Parr died at Barnet. Other northerners knighted at the same time included two Westmorland men, Christopher Moresby of Windermere and Thomas Strikland of Sizergh.[52] Finally, the commissions appointed in July 1471 to arrest Warwick's associates provide the names of other northerners regarded as reliable by Edward IV, among them Ashton's son-in-law John Nesfield and Edmund Hastings.[53]

Some historians have been dismissive of this northern support. Edward IV himself was reputedly disappointed by the turn out, probably because he had hoped for the backing of the Percy connection, which the restored earl of Northumberland proved unable to mobilize.[54] In another respect, however, the king had grounds for satisfaction. The defection of the Nevilles could have

---

[50] PRO, DL 37/47A no. 2; C 67/50 m. 1. Leventhorpe had been receiver of Knaresborough since 1466; the honour's proximity to the Percy castle of Spofforth perhaps explains his selection as intermediary: PRO, DL 29/482/7777.

[51] PRO, DL 37/47A nos. 4, 7, 8.

[52] Pugh 1972, p. 109; Metcalfe 1885, p. 3. Another north-western family to support Edward IV were the Curwens: Cumbria RO, D/Cu/1/1.

[53] *CPR* 1467–77 pp. 286, 287; Baines 1888–93, II p. 397.

[54] Pugh 1972, p. 109; Ross 1974, pp. 163–4; *Historie of the Arrivall* p. 7.

done considerably more damage to the royal affinity which had developed in the north in the 1460s. In the event, although the affinity was perhaps slow to rally, it held up reasonably well. Some of it was in any case independent of the Neville influence, notably the element deriving from the duchy of York. At least two of the men mentioned above had links with the duchy. John Pilkington's home was near the duchy lordship of Wakefield and Ralph Snaith had close links with a leading duchy family, the Savilles of Thornhill.[55] But in other respects the royal affinity was potentially vulnerable. Several of its leading members had a background of service to the Nevilles. This was a consequence of the blurring of the two affinities in the early 1460s when Warwick was a loyal servant of the crown and when his men were in a sense the king's men at one remove, a relationship formalized in some cases by entry into the royal household. These double loyalties presented no problems as long as Warwick's interests and those of the crown were broadly in agreement, but as the earl moved into outright opposition such men had to decide where their loyalties lay and in 1470/1 some backed Edward. Ashton had been a servant of Warwick's father, the earl of Salisbury. The Harrington brothers had been feed by Warwick, and their father had been feed by Salisbury. Thomas Strikland's father Walter, who died in 1467, had also been retained by Salisbury.[56] Although Warwick's defection meant that the Neville connection as a whole was no longer at the king's disposal, Warwick was not able to carry all its members with him into opposition.

Warwick's defection also called into question the loyalty of royal retainers within the duchy of Lancaster. The duchy provided a rich fund of patronage which Edward tapped to provide fees and office for his northern supporters. Among the men who backed him in 1471 Pilkington was steward of Rochdale and James Harrington steward of Amounderness (Lancs.). Edmund Hastings and Ralph Snaith were bailiffs of Pickering and Pontefract respectively. Ashton was receiver and forester of Pickering.[57] At the same time the duchy administration had provided new recruits for Edward's service. Nicholas Leventhorpe came

---

[55] *Test. Ebor.* III no. 60.
[56] PRO, SC 6/1085/20; Pollard 1975, p. 57; Somerville 1953, p. 536; Bellasis 1889, p. 83. William Parr also had Neville links: Cumbria RO, D/Lons/L/MD/AS 61; Morgan 1973, p. 15.
[57] PRO, DL 29/500/8100; DL 37/47A no. 8; Somerville 1953, pp. 500, 506, 535, 536.

from a family active in the duchy since the beginning of the century.[58] The result was that, in Yorkshire and Lancashire at least, the duchy connection virtually was the royal affinity. Warwick's position as chief steward of the duchy in the north, and steward and constable of all the key Yorkshire lordships, meant that he stood in a position of authority towards all the other northern duchy servants and Edward IV would have been very seriously weakened if Warwick had managed to win them over.[59] This, however, he entirely failed to do. Leventhorpe and Ashton, receivers of Knaresborough and Pickering (where Warwick was steward), actively supported the exiled Edward IV. Even more telling is the example of Ralph Snaith, the bailiff of Pontefract. Warwick's brother John was based there in 1471 but Snaith was still able to join Edward IV, taking his revenues with him. John Neville's inactivity in the face of Edward's advance surely owed something to awareness that he could not rely on duchy support.[60]

In making Gloucester chief steward of the duchy of Lancaster in the north, Edward was thus effectively putting him at the head of the surviving royal affinity there. As chief steward, Gloucester had access to significant patronage. Although annuities and major office remained in the gift of the crown, with the issue of letters patent under the duchy seal warranted by royal signet or sign manual, these grants were the result of lobbying by interested parties and the chief steward was well placed to have his wishes heard. The same was true of farms and leases, which were generally authorized by the duchy council. Alongside this influence on others the chief steward could also make direct grants. Like any office holder, he could appoint his own deputy. He seems also to have had the right to appoint deputies to act for him in individual duchy lordships. Thus Gloucester made Hugh Hastings his deputy as steward in the soke of Snaith.[61] It is not clear how such appointments related to the right of the steward of a specific lordship to appoint his own deputy, but it is possible that two deputies coexisted. Thus in the lordship of Pickering the steward was William lord Hastings, confirmed in office by Edward IV for life in 1471. In 1476 there were two deputy

---

[58] Clutterbuck 1815–27, III pp. 206–7; Kerr 1935, p. 133.
[59] Ross 1974, p. 437.
[60] *Ibid.* p. 163; *Historie of the Arrivall* p. 6.
[61] Humberside RO, DDCL 16 m. 10 dorse.

stewards: Sir Edmund Hastings and William Chamberlain. The latter was a member of Gloucester's Sheriff Hutton connection and may be a ducal appointment, in which case it is likely that he was acting as deputy chief steward in the lordship.[62] Distinct from this was the chief steward's right to appoint the stewards of some lesser estates within the duchy. In 1474 William lord Hastings was made steward of Tutbury, Castle Donington (Leics.) and the Peak by Edward IV; but it was Gloucester who, by his own letters patent, made him steward of Ollerton (Notts.).[63] The right to that appointment was presumably an established perquisite of the chief steward. When, as king, Richard twice regranted the stewardships held by Hastings in the duchy, neither grant included Ollerton or the associated manors of Plumtree and Risley.[64] These are unlikely to have been the only offices in the gift of the chief steward and the total may have been substantial. In addition, he had the right to make grants at farm, although again the extent of the right is unknown. In 1473 Gloucester ordered Thomas Molyneux, the hereditary steward of West Derbyshire (Lancs.), to farm the park of Croxteth to William Molyneux.[65]

Access to such patronage gave Gloucester the possibility of rewarding his own men from the duchy. His deputy as chief steward, for instance, was his councillor Miles Metcalfe.[66] But far more valuable was the chance it gave him of widening his sphere of influence. It gave him a role in parts of the north where he held no land of his own. In 1472, for instance, Robert Bolling of Bradford turned to Gloucester for help in achieving the restoration of his land.[67] It also made his good lordship attractive to men outside his immediate circle. The Molyneux grant is a case in point. Thomas Molyneux of Sefton, who was probably the prime mover on William's behalf, was a leading figure in south Lancashire. He was an esquire of the king's body and had links with other lords in the north west and north Wales, including the Stanleys and Anthony earl Rivers, for whom he acted as deputy

[62] PRO, DL 5/1 fo. 93; DL 37/51/5; Somerville 1953, p. 534.
[63] Lancs. RO, DDTo O/12/126.
[64] *Harl. 433* 1 pp. 69, 174.
[65] Lancs. RO, DDM 26/1.
[66] Somerville 1953, p. 426; *Yorks. Deeds* III, no. 417 (the corresponding bond is Lancs. RO, DDHe 56/5).
[67] PRO, SC 8/29/1426 (endorsement).

of Beaumaris.[68] He was thus never exclusively Gloucester's man, but by 1480 had developed sufficiently close links with the duke to stand surety with other ducal retainers for Gloucester's associate John Huddleston.[69] This was a connection which would almost certainly not have developed but for Gloucester's duchy office. However, it should not be forgotten that Molyneux was also a royal servant, and that in securing patronage for his kinsman in 1473 he was receiving a reward appropriate to his position as a leading local member of the king's household. A similar ambiguity is apparent in the grant in the same year to Sir John Pilkington of the farm of a messuage and vaccary in the forest of Rossendale (Lancs.). The duke's influence is clear. He was himself master forester of Rossendale, and Pilkington was his chamberlain. Significantly, two out of three sureties for Pilkington's payment of the farm were leading ducal retainers. But it would be unrealistic to leave out of account the fact that Pilkington was a knight of the king's body and one, moreover, owed a favour for his support of Edward in 1471.[70] The duchy resources were still used on behalf of the royal retinue and it is striking that most of the best offices and farms went to the king's household. As a result, those of Gloucester's associates who gained most from duchy patronage were those who were also royal servants, men like John Pilkington's brother Charles, an usher of the chamber, or the king's knights John Huddleston and Ralph Ashton.[71]

As these examples suggest, it becomes increasingly difficult to disentangle royal and ducal retinues. Because of Gloucester's influence in the duchy, royal servants naturally looked to him for lordship. Less obvious, perhaps, is the other side of the equation. Because Gloucester was the king's man, his own associates, whether promoted through the duchy or elsewhere, were in effect part of the royal affinity. This integration benefited both sides. The advantage to Gloucester is obvious. His position within the duchy had brought him the support of men who would otherwise

---

[68] Lancs. RO, DDM 3/4–5; PRO, C 244/116/55.

[69] PRO, C 244/129/20D. It may not be coincidence that within a matter of months Huddleston had yielded the farm of a valuable group of duchy manors to Molyneux: PRO, DL 41/34/1 fo. 1v; DL 42/19 fos. 20–1; Lancs. RO, DDX 621/3.

[70] PRO, DL 41/34/1 fo. 1v. An earlier reward to Pilkington had been abortive: DL 37/47A no. 9. For his links with Gloucester see note 32 above.

[71] Charles Pilkington: PRO, DL 42/19 fo. 29v; Lancs. RO, DDTo O/12/130; *CPR 1476–85* p. 158. Huddleston: PRO, DL 41/34/1 fo. 1v; DL 42/20 fo. 38–v. Ashton: Somerville 1953, p. 535; PRO, DL 37/47A no. 1; and below, note 78.

have been outside his sphere of influence, as well as making him the better lord for his own servants. The king gained because Gloucester's power was at his disposal and therefore any enhancement of the duke's position strengthened royal authority.[72] This basic premise also dictated Edward's policy elsewhere. In the 1460s it lay behind his development of the Herbert hegemony in Wales and his consolidation of Neville power in the north. In the 1470s the closest parallel is to be found in the north midlands, where Hastings' possession of the key duchy of Lancaster offices put him at the head of the royal connection in the region. Here one can see the same assumption that Hastings' power is the king's power, with a consequent blurring of the two retinues.[73] But, with hindsight, Gloucester's position within the duchy seems to differ from that of Hastings or Warwick in one important respect. It is clear that neither of them could call on the personal loyalty of the royal servants in the duchy. In 1471 Warwick failed to turn the duchy servants against Edward IV and in 1483 Hastings' death was followed immediately by the transfer of the royal connection to his successor in office.[74] In both cases loyalty was owed to the crown rather than the steward. When Gloucester deposed Edward V, by contrast, he apparently carried his brother's servants with him.

To some extent this distinction is illusory. The usurpation of 1483 happened so quickly that many of the duchy servants were presented with a *fait accompli*, whereupon as usual they backed the crown (which now happened to be worn by their erstwhile chief steward). But this is not the whole story. By 1483 some at least of the royal servants were sufficiently committed to Gloucester to play an active role in his coup. One who did so was Charles Pilkington, who was involved in the arrest of Hastings. Pilkington, the brother of Gloucester's retainer John, had been a royal servant since the early 1460s and had been rewarded with land in the north midlands, bringing him within the duchy connection. As a result he developed links with Hastings as well as Gloucester, but it was the latter which dictated his actions in 1483.[75] Also involved in the arrest was the duchy official Robert Harrington, whose brother James was one of Edward IV's knights. Both

---

[72] For a more critical assessment of this policy compare Loades 1986, p. 136.
[73] Rowney 1984a, p. 141; Wright 1983, p. 88.
[74] Rowney 1984b, p. 42.
[75] Hanham 1975, p. 167; Lancs. RO, DDTo O/12/126, 130; K/32/60.

brothers had chosen to back Edward rather than Warwick in 1471, in spite of their Neville links, but by 1483 their connection with Gloucester was uppermost.

Gloucester's lordship was thus, at least in some cases, attractive enough to displace that of the crown. An obvious explanation is the patronage which he had at his disposal as chief steward, for although this derived from the crown its exercise was a manifestation of the duke's own good lordship. However, both Warwick and Hastings had access to duchy patronage without, it seems, managing to create a strong personal following within the duchy connection. Gloucester's success implies a more effective use of the patronage at his disposal, and there are some suggestions that he was running the duchy in his own interests. In 1482 the duchy council complained that Gloucester and his subordinates were wasting the assets of the duchy.[76] Support for the accusation comes from two cases where associates of the duke were dismissed by the council for failing to render account, but then remained in post. Sir John Pilkington's removal as escheator of Lancashire was ordered in 1476, but no replacement is recorded until after his death three years later.[77] Sir Ralph Ashton, the receiver of Pickering, was dismissed in 1480, but remained in office until after Richard's death.[78] Their survival in office challenged efficient management of the duchy and may have entailed actual financial loss if they had been keeping revenue in their own hands. But such cases were not, as the council claimed, the result of slack administration by the chief steward. Gloucester was, on the contrary, exercising his good lordship. 'Waste' usually meant profit in someone's pocket. What really lay behind the council's complaint was Gloucester's willingness to put the maintenance of an affinity before financial considerations.

Gloucester was thus strengthening his grip on the duchy connection, but it was also in the interest of the crown for him to preserve the connection: an ambiguity emphasized by the fact that Ashton and Pilkington were royal as well as ducal servants. As long as Gloucester was the loyal servant of the crown, what was good for him was good for royal authority, and Edward's acceptance of that fact enormously strengthened the duke's hand.

---

[76] Somerville 1953, p. 254.
[77] *Ibid.* p. 466; Myers, 'Official progress' p. 27.
[78] Somerville 1953, p. 249; PRO, DL 29/500/8100–2. The existence of these accounts suggests that Ashton mended his ways.

It is unlikely that Gloucester could have flouted the council's wishes without at least tacit royal approval, and it is this which distinguished the duke from his predecessor as chief steward. For his final years in office, Warwick was known to be out of favour with the king, something which must have reduced his authority within the duchy. Gloucester, by contrast, kept the king's full confidence. He could thus rely on royal backing while he used the duchy as an arena in which to demonstrate his own good lordship. This is not to say that Gloucester was consciously building up his own authority at the expense of the crown – the distinction is meaningless in Edward IV's lifetime – but by 1483 the duchy connection was Gloucester's as well as the king's.

The strength of Gloucester's hold on the duchy connection cannot, however, be explained only by reference to the situation within the duchy itself. His influence there was underpinned by territorial interests elsewhere in the north. The importance of these becomes obvious by comparison with Hastings, whose claim on the loyalty of the duchy servants in the north midlands was weakened by the fact that in much of the region his authority rested only on duchy office. It is also significant that Gloucester's hold on the duchy servants in Lancashire, where he had no land, was weaker than in Yorkshire. The main component of Gloucester's landed influence in the north was the former Neville land centred on Middleham, Sheriff Hutton and Penrith. Here, as in the duchy of Lancaster, Gloucester was able to draw on existing loyalties. In the course of the previous two generations the junior branch of the Nevilles, Warwick and his father Salisbury, had established an important northern affinity within the three lordships. That connection was now leaderless and it was in the interests of both the affinity and Gloucester to come to a rapid agreement. The former Neville men wanted a new lord, a need particularly acute for those who had supported Warwick in 1470/1 and who therefore faced possible recriminations. Indeed, the low level of northern attainders after the Yorkist victory of 1471 is itself in part testimony to the successful take-over of the Neville connection by Gloucester.[79] The duke himself, meanwhile, wanted to establish himself in the north as quickly and as fully as possible, and control of the Neville affinity offered one means to

---

[79] *Rot. Parl.* VI pp. 144–9. Lander 1976, pp. 137–9, suggests that the low figures were due to Edward's decision not to attaint Warwick and his brother, which would have made the attainder of their followers unjust.

that end. He had begun retaining from Middleham (the only one of the three lordships for which evidence survives) by August 1471, when he feed the earl's auditor and councillor Thomas Metcalfe, and further indentures followed in the course of the autumn and winter. These reveal that Gloucester already had the backing of the linch pin of the Middleham connection, Sir John Conyers of Hornby (Yorks.). He was related, through his immensely prolific family, to many of the northern gentry and the Conyers family tree is virtually a roll call of the Neville retinue. When Gloucester took Sir John into his service he acknowledged his importance by doubling his wages: the knight was confirmed as steward of Middleham with his fee increased from £13 6s 8d to £20 and he was also made constable of the castle with a fee of £16 13s 4d. The money was well spent. Conyers evidently formed a bridge between the Middleham affinity and its new lord: the first men whom Gloucester retained there were virtually all kinsmen of Sir John.[80]

Given the pressures on both sides it is not surprising to find considerable continuity between Gloucester's affinity and that of the Nevilles. Again, Middleham is the best documented of the three lordships, with lists of fees extant for both Neville earls as well as Gloucester himself.[81] Many examples are to be found among local families, who probably had little practical alternative to accepting any change of lordship at Middleham. Two Wensleydale families, the Conyers and Metcalfes, feature in all three lists. Another, the Wycliffes of Wycliffe, provided retainers for Salisbury and Gloucester, while the Burghs of Catterick served both Warwick and Gloucester. Middleham, however, was not only a focus for local families. It was also a source of fees for more distant associates and although such relationships were more vulnerable to dynastic change, because less bound up with the territorial dominance of the lord of Middleham, some did nevertheless survive the transfer of power in 1471. Gloucester continued, for instance, to fee Thomas Talbot of Bashall (Yorks.). If one looks beyond the surviving lists of fees to less formal evidence of affiliation, more instances of continuity are to be found. The Mountfords of Hackforth (Yorks.) provided feed retainers for both Neville earls, and although no fee is recorded

[80] PRO, DL 29/648/10485; Pollard 1979, pp. 38, 48, 53–4; Pollard 1983, p. 5.
[81] PRO, DL 29/648/10485; SC 6/1085/20; Pollard 1975. For analysis see Pollard 1979, 1983; Coles 1961.

from Gloucester they had links with him also. Thomas Mount-ford, Warwick's retainer, acted as guarantor of an arbitration by Gloucester and was given an annuity by him after his accession, while his kinsman John was one of the duke's chaplains.[82] Conversely, Gloucester inherited the services of the Tunstalls of Thurland (Lancs.) from Warwick, although the first formal record of a fee is apparently that granted by Gloucester to Thomas Tunstall in autumn 1471. Thomas had received a royal pardon in the previous April, just one week after Barnet, which implies a Neville connection. So, probably, does the fact that his concubine of several years' standing, whom he subsequently married, was the illegitimate daughter of archbishop George Neville.[83] His two brothers, Richard and William, followed him into Gloucester's service. Sir Richard, the eldest, was probably the 'master Tun-stall' who was one of the duke's councillors and William was one of Gloucester's feoffees.[84]

In the other two Neville lordships indirect evidence of this kind is now all that is available and continuity is accordingly harder to prove, although there is no reason to believe that it was any less marked. At Sheriff Hutton, as at Middleham, the core of the affinity consisted of men whose own estates lay close to the castle and it is among these that continuity is likely to have been strongest. Within a radius of three miles were the Withams of Cornborough, the Gowers of Stittenham, the Leptons of Terring-ton and the Hardgills of Lilling; a few miles further away were the Constables of Barnby by Bossall, a cadet branch of the Flam-borough family.[85] All had probably served the Nevilles, although firm evidence survives only for the Withams, Gowers and Constables. The Gowers had backed Warwick in 1470/1 and were still in opposition in June 1471, when a commission of arrest was issued for the head of the family, Thomas, and his uncles Robert and George.[86] It was probably not long after this that they made their peace with the Yorkists and entered Gloucester's service. Thomas Gower became a leading figure in the Sheriff Hutton connection and was almost certainly constable of the castle itself, although this is nowhere explicitly stated. Thomas Witham

---

[82] Pollard 1978, p. 162; *Harl. 433* 1 p. 158; *Cal. Papal Regs.* xiii part ii p. 792.
[83] *Cal. Papal Regs.* xiii part ii p. 524; *CPR 1467–77* p. 258; Chippindall 1928, pedigree facing p. 304.
[84] Essex RO, D/DQ 14/124/3/40; BL, Cotton Julius BXII fo. 241v.
[85] For this and what follows see Horrox 1986b.
[86] *CPR 1467–77* p. 286.

became one of the duke's councillors. For the other families, however, association with the duke can be inferred only from grants made after his accession. Beyond this cental group evidence of continuity is even more fragmentary. Among Gloucester's known associates in the area, only one, Ralph Bulmer, can be linked to the Nevilles with any confidence. His family took their name from a manor near Sheriff Hutton and held land within the lordship.[87]

Slightly more evidence survives from the north west, although here again there was probably more continuity in 1471 than is now apparent. The centre of the Neville interest was the lordship of Penrith, including land to the east of the town, along the Eden, and Plumpton Park within the forest of Inglewood to the north.[88] The only formal evidence of continuity comes from this area in the shape of grants of an annuity to Thomas Hoton of Hutton John by both Warwick and Gloucester.[89] But other local families are likely to have served both lords, among them the Musgraves of Edenhall. Richard Musgrave, the head of the family under the Yorkists, had been retained by Salisbury as a young man. There is no specific reference to his serving Gloucester until after the duke's accession (when he became an esquire of the body), but his brother John was given land by the duke, which implies a close connection.[90] Penrith also served as a source of reward for more scattered retainers. There had been an important group of Neville associates further south, centred on Sir William Parr of Kendal. In 1471 Parr declared for Edward IV and carried his brothers-in-law Christopher Moresby and Thomas Strikland with him. They subsequently turned to the duke, and by the following year Moresby was installed as Gloucester's steward at Penrith, with his younger brother James acting as bailiff.[91] Other examples of continuity in the north west include the Redmanes of Levens, who also held land in Yorkshire and were feed by both Warwick and Gloucester from Middleham, and probably the Dogets of Grayrigg who fought for Warwick in 1469 and subsequently provided Richard with a chaplain.[92] Another family to serve both lords was the Huddlestons of Millom on the

[87] *Inqs p.m.* I no. 108.
[88] Longleat ms 563; Hutchinson 1794, I pp. 477, 490.
[89] Cumbria RO, D/Hud/18/3, 4; printed by Blair, 'Two letters patent'.
[90] Cumbria RO, D/Mus/H/123; Hutchinson 1794, I pp. 273–4; *Inqs p.m.* I no. 471.
[91] Cumbria RO, D/Mus/P/14.
[92] Duckett 1869, p. 18; Ross 1981, p. 134.

Duddon estuary. The head of the family, Sir John, was related by marriage to Warwick's allies the Fitzhughs of Ravensworth, and two of his sons married Neville wives. The eldest, Richard, married Warwick's illegitimate daughter Margaret, and the earl endowed the couple with his manor of Blennerhasset (Cumb.) and land in Penrith. His brother, William, married the daughter of Warwick's brother John.[93] The family was later to be among Gloucester's closest associates.

Such continuity was valuable to Gloucester, but it is important not to exaggerate the extent to which he simply took over a ready-made connection. Although former Neville men were predisposed to look to the duke, Gloucester still had to work at being a good lord in order to give substance to the relationship. Nor was Gloucester's northern connection ever just that of the earl of Warwick. Noble affinities were in any case constantly evolving as their members came of age, married and died, but Gloucester's lordship brought other changes. As he acquired further land and office in the north, the affinity inevitably widened. Not only were men from other areas drawn into Gloucester's circle but, by a cumulative process, the duke's new interests made him a more attractive lord within the Neville lands themselves.

The 1471 grant of Middleham, Sheriff Hutton, Penrith and their members did not give Gloucester control of all the northern estates formerly held by Warwick. One notable omission was Barnard Castle in County Durham, which Warwick had acquired by his marriage to the Beauchamp heiress Anne. The descent of her inheritance was the object of intense rivalry in the early 1470s between Clarence, who had married one of Warwick's coheiresses, and Gloucester, who married the other. In the case of Barnard Castle their struggle was complicated by the involvement of a third party, bishop Bothe of Durham, who claimed the lordship as part of his palatinate. Edward IV had conceded this claim in 1470, at a time when he was willing to limit Warwick's northern influence, but the question was inevitably reopened once Gloucester had taken Warwick's place. Exactly how the matter was resolved is obscure, but there is no doubt that Gloucester took possession of the lordship, presumably with royal backing.[94] The castle became one of the duke's main northern

[93] Hampton 1979, nos. 40, 41, 92, corrects the pedigree in *Visit. Camb.* p. 27.
[94] Pollard 1986, pp. 110–11.

residences and local families turned naturally to him for lordship. These included the Brackenburys of Denton, a younger son of whom, Robert Brackenbury of Selaby, became Gloucester's treasurer of the household.[95] The Brackenburys' near neighbours, the Hansards of Walworth, probably also had links with Gloucester although, as with many northern families, this can only be inferred from Richard's willingness to use them in sensitive assignments after his accession. Richard Hansard was then one of a group of northerners sent to restore royal authority in Hampshire. Among his colleagues there was his feoffee John Hoton of Tudhoe, who should probably also be numbered among Gloucester's Durham associates.[96]

Once Gloucester was established in the south of County Durham, his influence began to reach further into the bishopric. By 1474 the prior of Durham, Richard Bell, could refer to Gloucester as the convent's *dominus specialissimus*.[97] This enthusiasm was not, however, shared by the bishop, Laurence Bothe, who was clearly unhappy at the arrival of so powerful a neighbour. Only in the last few months of his pontificate, before his promotion to York, did Bothe recognize the duke's local interests by appointing ducal servants to office within the bishopric, not only at Crayke (which lay within the duke's sphere of influence in the forest of Galtres), but within County Durham itself, where Gloucester's retainer John Redmane was made bailiff of Bishop Auckland.[98] This cool relationship between duke and bishop was, however, transformed by the arrival of William Dudley as Bothe's successor in 1476. Dudley, a trusted royal servant, was prepared to see an expansion of ducal influence in the county. Immediately after Dudley's elevation, Gloucester was appointed to the commission of the peace, where he played an active role.[99] Dudley also proved more willing to appoint ducal servants to offices in his gift and to employ them in his own administration. Richard Hansard, for instance, was made constable of Durham castle, while the commission Dudley appointed to survey his land included numerous ducal associates, among them Sir William Parr, Thomas Witham and Thomas Metcalfe.

[95] PRO, DL 29/639/10387; Surtees 1816–40, IV pp. 17–20.
[96] *Dep. Keeper, 35th Report* p. 139; Hampton 1985a, p. 6; for further examples see Pollard 1986, p. 114.
[97] Dobson 1965, p. 207.
[98] PRO, DL 29/648/10485; *Dep. Keeper, 35th Report* pp. 96, 103.
[99] Pollard 1986, p. 116.

Metcalfe, one of Gloucester's councillors, was to become one of the key financial administrators in the bishopric.[100] Durham had thus become another sphere in which Gloucester could exercise his good lordship and, with Dudley's backing, the duke seized the opportunity with both hands. By the end of the decade it was Gloucester, not the bishop, who dominated the region and contemporaries knew it. When Gerard Salvin wanted redress against the men who had attacked his house at Croxdale, just a few miles south of Durham itself, it was Gloucester to whom he appealed.[101]

Barnard Castle was Gloucester's major gain from the division of the Beauchamp inheritance, but it was not the only one. His other direct gain in the north was part of Cottingham in the East Riding, which was in his hands by 1472.[102] The final partition of the inheritance in 1474 also brought him Chesterfield and Scarsdale (Derbs.) and Bushey (Herts.) which in the following year he exchanged with the crown for more land in Yorkshire: a further piece of Cottingham; the royal castle and lordship of Scarborough; and land in Falsgrave, with the fee farm there.[103] The meat of the grant was Scarborough, which formed a useful complement to Gloucester's duchy interests. It was an enclave within the duchy lordship of Pickering, which came down to the coast at Filey Brigg in the south and at Scalby, just north of Scarborough, before continuing along the coast towards Whitby.[104] The grant was part of a consolidation of Gloucester's position around this time, which may have been linked with plans for Gloucester to lead a raid into Scotland.[105] In February 1475 the duke's standing in the north west was strengthened by his appointment for life as sheriff of Cumberland. In the following June the terms of the grant were amplified.[106] Gloucester was to have the right to appoint his own deputy, an office he is said to have given to Sir John Huddleston.[107] He was also to enjoy all issues of the shrievalty, the demesne lands of the castle of Carlisle

[100] *Ibid.* p. 117; *Dep. Keeper, 35th Report* pp. 139, 140.
[101] Surtees 1816–40, IV pp. 114–5.
[102] Horrox 1986b, p. 85.
[103] BL, Cotton Julius BXII fos. 208v–10v; *Rot. Parl.* VI pp. 125–6.
[104] Leland, *Itin.* I p. 64.
[105] Macdougall 1986, pp. 157, 159.
[106] *CPR* 1467–77 pp. 485, 556.
[107] Hutchinson 1794, I p. 528; although the other offices reputedly given to Huddleston are less plausible.

and the city's fee farm. The grant explicitly excluded the royal forest of Inglewood, but this was probably only to avoid setting a precedent for future sheriffs. Gloucester seems already to have had control of the forest, and granted a fee from two closes there in 1473, which suggests that it may have been assigned to him as warden of the west march, although this is nowhere explicitly stated.[108]

The summer of 1475 brought one other addition to Gloucester's northern land. In June the duke and the heirs of his body were granted the Clifford barony in the West Riding, consisting of Skipton and Marton in Craven and associated land.[109] The Cliffords had forfeited their estates at the beginning of the reign for their adherence to Lancaster. In 1462 their land in Westmorland, including Brougham and Appleby, had been granted to Warwick and the Yorkshire estates to William Stanley. In 1475 Stanley surrendered his share to the crown, receiving in lieu the castle and lordship of Chirk, in the march of Wales, and the manor of Wilmington (Kent). Chirk had been held by Gloucester and although it is not stated in the grant the king was evidently promoting, or at least sanctioning, an exchange of interests. Chirk was now peripheral to Gloucester's main concerns but complemented Stanley involvement in Cheshire and Flint. Wilmington, also part of the Beaufort lands, seems to have been included as a makeweight.[110] As with the Scarborough grant, Gloucester was surrendering land of little value to himself in return for a significant acquisition. Skipton and its members rounded out his trans-Pennine duchy interests, as well as giving him his first territorial stake in the West Riding. It is clear that the duke took his interest in Skipton seriously. He is known to have resided there and in 1480 he extended his Craven estates by buying the manor of Carleton in Craven and associated land from William Singleton.[111]

Among the local families who had dealings with the duke were the Ratcliffes of Bradley near Skipton, one of whom was retained by Gloucester for service in the Scottish campaign of 1480.[112] He may also have developed some connections with the Tempests of

[108] Cumbria RO, D/Lons/L/Deeds/D65.
[109] *CPR* 1467–77 p. 549.
[110] *CPR* 1461–7 pp. 115–6, 186, 189, 474; *CPR* 1467–77 pp. 179, 505. The Clifford barony in Westmorland went to the Parrs: *CPR* 1467–77 pp. 264, 423.
[111] *Test. Ebor.* III p. 239; *CCR* 1476–85 nos. 598, 602.
[112] Whitaker 1878, p. 221.

Bracewell. The third brother, Nicholas, is described as of Marton in Craven in 1478 and had married the sister of Gloucester's associate Sir John Pilkington.[113] But Gloucester's acquisition of Skipton was as much a matter of strengthening existing connections as of creating new ones. Although Warwick had not held Skipton itself, he had had connections with some of the local families (perhaps through his possession of the Clifford estates elsewhere) and these Gloucester seems to have taken over. Thomas Talbot of Bashall was among those feed by both Warwick and Gloucester from Middleham. The Hertlingtons of Hartlington, previously Clifford associates, may have been inherited by Gloucester from Warwick. Their first recorded connection with Richard is after his accession, when the second son Roger became a yeoman of the crown. He was unusually well rewarded and this, coupled with the fact that he was employed to seize rebel lands, strongly suggests that he had been associated with Richard before 1483. An earlier Neville connection is implied by the marriage of Roger's sister Alice to Thomas Metcalfe, a match which must have taken place by the mid 1460s.[114] But the clearest evidence that Gloucester's links with the Clifford connection preceded his possession of Skipton is his grant of a fee to one of the surviving Clifford brothers, Robert, in 1471. In spite of this, Gloucester's links with the Cliffords themselves do not seem to have been close. Robert's interests shifted to Hertfordshire in the late 1470s when he married the widow of Sir Ralph Josselin, but even before this he is never recorded as acting with the duke in the north, and after Richard's accession he was to move into opposition, along with his brother Roger.[115]

Gloucester again relinquished peripheral holdings in exchange for the last addition to his Yorkshire estates in March 1478, shortly after the execution of Clarence. This time he received the castle and fee farm of Richmond, the manors of Harome and Carlton by Helmsley, and the reversion of Helmsley itself, in exchange for Sudeley (Glos.), Farleigh Hungerford (Wilts.) and

[113] PRO, C 244/126/77; Pilkington 1893, pedigree facing p. 159; this corrects the usual claim that Tempest's wife was Pilkington's daughter.

[114] *CPR 1476–85* pp. 482, 507; *Harl. 433* I p. 103, II pp. 86–7, 116–7; Whitaker 1878, pp. 515–16. The date of the marriage is based on the likely age of James, the eldest son, who seems to become active in the early 1480s: PRO, PSO 1/56/2869; BL, Harleian ms 793 fo. 67.

[115] PRO, DL 29/648/10485; Hampton 1979, no. 122. For their opposition to Richard see below, p. 279.

Corfe (Dorset).[116] The Yorkshire land had all been held by Clarence and the scale of the alienations made in exchange suggests that Gloucester set considerable store by its acquisition. The castle of Richmond filled an obvious gap in Gloucester's domination of Richmondshire, although the lack of it had made little practical difference to his position there, since Clarence seems to have played no part in northern affairs after 1471. Clarence had been given the honour of Richmond in 1462; or, more strictly, had been given the two thirds then in the crown's possession and the reversion of the remaining third on the death of the dowager duchess of Bedford. But this grant cut across the claims of the Nevilles, who already held two thirds of the honour's land in Richmondshire in tail male and had the reversion of the other third. In practice, Clarence's grant was a dead letter in Richmondshire, although it gave him extensive interests elsewhere, notably in Lincolnshire and East Anglia. In 1471 the Neville share passed to Gloucester, with Warwick's tail male lands, and he also took possession of the remaining third in 1472 when the reversion fell in. This gave him all the honour's lands in Richmondshire except, it seems, the castle itself, a deficiency made good in 1478.[117] The remaining land had come to Clarence by the forfeiture of Thomas lord Roos, although dower rights had prevented him enjoying Helmsley itself. Gloucester was more fortunate, the dowager dying within days of the grant.[118] Again, the grant consolidated existing ducal interests, rounding out Gloucester's influence in the honour of Pickering further east. It may also have brought some families into his service for the first time, among them the Pulleys (or Pullowes) of Helmsley, whose head, Henry, was to be one of Richard's yeomen after his accession.[119]

Although it is convenient to treat Gloucester's northern acquisitions separately, the affinity they produced was a unity. This can be seen most clearly in the case of men who entered Gloucester's service in one context and were then employed or rewarded in another. The Metcalfes of Nappa near Askrigg in Wensleydale were members of the Middleham connection, holding numerous offices within the lordship. Under Gloucester they

---

[116] *CPR* 1476–85 p. 90.
[117] *CPR* 1441–6 p. 429; *CPR* 1446–52 p. 281; *CPR* 1461–7 pp. 212–3; *CPR* 1467–77 p. 483. Clarence's share of the honour is listed by Hicks 1980, appendix II.
[118] Ross 1981, p. 25.
[119] York, Prob. Reg. 5 fos. 515v–16v; *CPR* 1476–85 p. 440.

expanded into other parts of the north east. Thomas Metcalfe was Gloucester's auditor of Richmondshire and became, with ducal backing, one of the auditors of the bishop of Durham. His brother Miles, one of the duke's legal counsel, was Gloucester's deputy as chief steward of the duchy of Lancaster in the north. He also became recorder of York, an appointment made on the king's recommendation but probably owing more to Gloucester.[120] At a more modest level, the office of clerk of the works at Middleham was filled by a Westmorland man, Michael Wharton of Kirkby Thore, whose home lay a few miles from Gloucester's lordship of Penrith.[121] A Cumberland man, Richard Ratcliffe, was made constable of Barnard Castle and also acquired land in Richmond-shire by his marriage (probably achieved with the duke's support) to the widowed sister of John lord Scrope of Bolton.[122] The Huddlestons of Millom were active on Gloucester's behalf throughout Cumbria, but their own land led them to look rather to north Lancashire, where they had dealings with the Harringtons.[123]

The coherence of the retinue was not, however, just a matter of ducal *fiat*. It was underpinned by the interests and aspirations of its members themselves. Only the least significant of retainers would fit neatly into a single sphere of ducal influence. Many had wider tenurial interests. The Redmanes of Levens held land in both Westmorland and Yorkshire, while several ducal associates, including the Harringtons, held land in Lancashire and Yorkshire. At the same time, personal connections naturally developed between individual members of the affinity. These are most visible when ducal retainers stood surety for each other. When John Pilkington farmed land in Rossendale (Lancs.) his sureties were John Huddleston of Millom, William Plumpton of Plumpton and William Hopton of Swillington (Yorks.).[124] Sometimes other hints of friendship between men from different elements of the connection survive. The two lay founders of a chantry in

---

[120] PRO, DL 29/648/10485; *Dep. Keeper, 35th Report* p. 141; Somerville 1953, p. 426; Raine, *York Records* I p. 19. The chapter of York also made Miles their steward: Dobson 1986, pp. 138–9.

[121] *Harl. 433* II p. 25; Campbell, *Materials* I p. 445; compare Plantagenet-Harrison 1879, p. 256.

[122] Surtees 1816–40, I p. 32; Pollard 1978, p. 165.

[123] Lancs. RO, DDFz (unnumbered) a group of Harrington deeds of the 1460s, witnessed by Sir John Huddleston.

[124] PRO, DL 41/34/1 fo. 1v.

Richard's honour at Riccall on the Ouse were James Charleton of
Riccall, feed from Sheriff Hutton, and Richard Bank of Allerton
Bywater in the duchy of Lancaster honour of Pontefract.[125] For
the duke's servants, as for Gloucester himself, there was a single
connection of which they were all part.

Several of the examples quoted above emphasize the extent to
which each of Gloucester's acquisitions, as well as bringing new
families into his orbit, consolidated his influence elsewhere. Thus
his possession of Barnard Castle gave him the service of Robert
Brackenbury, but also the means to reward Richard Ratcliffe. As
Gloucester's power grew, it made him a better lord for the affinity
as a whole. This development also had a wider dimension. By the
mid 1470s, Gloucester's lordship was attracting men outside his
immediate circle. One example is provided by the extension of
the duke's influence into south Yorkshire, an area where he held
no land of his own. The major landowners were the duchy of
York, with which Gloucester had no formal connection, and the
earls of Shrewsbury. The latter were represented after 1474 by a
minor in the custody of William lord Hastings, who does not
seem to have played much part in south Yorkshire. This may
have strengthened Gloucester's hand in the region, but it is not in
itself an adequate explanation of his arrival there. In part it is due
to the proximity of the duchy of Lancaster lordships of Pontefract
and Tickhill, which provided an additional source of reward for a
number of royal servants in south Yorkshire. The most influential
family to hold office in both duchies, of York and Lancaster, was
the Pilkingtons, but lesser families shared the spread of interest,
including the Snythales of Barnby on Don.[126]

The duchy of Lancaster affiliations of such families brought
them within Gloucester's orbit and gave him a point of contact
with other duchy of York families, such as the Savilles and
Wentworths. But the mere existence of such contacts did not
mean very much. Given the interrelationships of medieval gentry
families, any lord could claim a range of connections shading
away from his immediate circle, most of which were, for all
practical purposes, irrelevant. Gloucester does, however, seem to
have been in a position to activate his links with south Yorkshire.
In some cases, again, his links with the local gentry can be inferred

[125] Horrox 1986b, p. 90.
[126] PRO, DL 5/1 fo. 34v; DL 42/19 fos. 36, 101; SC 6/1088/24–5; York, Prob. Reg. 5 fo.
120v, 6 fos. 233v–4.

only from his readiness to use them on sensitive business after 1483. The head of one of the leading duchy of York families, John Saville of Thornhill, was put in charge of the Isle of Wight by Richard as king.[127] But in at least one case it can be shown that Richard was retaining in the area in the 1470s. An undated ducal warrant survives ordering William Fitzwilliam of Sprotborough to meet Gloucester at Doncaster with eight horses and accompany him to London.[128] Fitzwilliam's brothers-in-law also seem to have had ducal connections, although these are more tenuous. Gloucester headed the feoffees of one, Richard Wentworth of Bretton, in 1476.[129] The other brother-in-law, Sir Thomas Wortley, was linked with Gloucester after his accession, and the contact had probably been made by 1479 when Wortley married as his second wife the widow of Gloucester's ally Sir John Pilkington. He was later to repudiate her but not, significantly, until after Richard's own death.[130]

Fitzwilliam's initial link with Gloucester can be traced. He had married one of the daughters of Sir John Conyers, the central figure of the Middleham connection.[131] However, the fact that Gloucester was able to forge a real link with Fitzwilliam, in an area where the duke's territorial influence was minimal, is testimony less to the strength of the Conyers bond than to Gloucester's own growing dominance in the north as a whole. His lordship was attractive enough to give substance to otherwise tenuous connections. This was only partly explained by Gloucester's territorial interests in the north, which by their very nature gave him authority only in defined areas. More important in establishing his general dominance was his closeness to the crown. The duke's role as the leading royal agent in the north brought a merging of his connection with that of the crown, not only within the duchy of Lancaster but also, to some extent, in the areas where Gloucester had less direct interests. This helps to explain his involvement in the duchy of York, where John Saville, for instance, was a royal esquire in the late 1470s.[132] In the north west the Parrs came into Gloucester's circle through royal service as well as former Neville links, and gave him an influence

---

[127] *CCR* 1476–85 no. 1417, and see further below, p. 195.
[128] Hunter 1823–31, I p. 339.
[129] *Ibid.* II p. 245; this implies a merging of the Shrewsbury and Gloucester connections.
[130] *Ibid.* II pp. 311–3.
[131] *Ibid.* I p. 339.
[132] Wrottesley, 'Plea rolls' p. 125.

in Westmorland greater than he might otherwise have enjoyed. In more general terms, too, Gloucester's local standing was enhanced by his court connections. It is often claimed that a lord on the spot was of more immediate relevance to local men, especially in outlying regions, than the king at Westminster. But although many of the expectations of the gentry could indeed be met locally, others could not, and men were alert to the advantage of a reliable line of communication with the king. Gloucester was ideally placed to satisfy this need – something which has been underemphasized since Kendall's romantic portrait of him as an isolated northern figure.[133] For his contemporaries, Gloucester clearly filled a double role, as is illustrated by his dealings with the city of York. His help was called for in purely local matters, such as the corporation's attempts to clear fishgarths from the Ouse, but he also pressed the city's claims at court, and in 1476 was credited with the preservation of York's liberties by his great labour to the king.[134]

It was this royal backing which turned Gloucester's territorial influence into a regional hegemony. One manifestation of his dominance was his ability to draw other local noblemen into his own orbit, which he could hardly have achieved on the strength of his landed interests alone. The most striking example is Henry Percy, earl of Northumberland.[135] He had been restored to the earldom in 1470 as part of Edward's measures against Clarence and the Nevilles, who had been the main beneficiaries of the Percy forfeiture. The Percy connection had taken no part in the events following Edward's return from exile in 1471 – an inactivity which, given their Lancastrian background, was probably regarded as tantamount to support for Edward IV. Certainly Percy was not penalized and his restoration was allowed to stand. In spite of this, his position in 1471 was rather different from that in 1470. Then, his restoration had been intended as a counterbalance to Warwick's influence in the north, but in 1471 the Nevilles had been replaced by Gloucester. This was to tip the balance of power decisively against Northumberland. Gloucester was the king's trusted supporter and brother. Moreover, although both men faced the job of rebuilding their followings, Percy had

[133] Kendall 1955, *passim*, especially pp. 110, 127, 144, 146–7.
[134] Palliser 1986, p. 55.
[135] For Percy's career see in general: Reid 1921, pp. 41–3; Weiss 1976, pp. 501–9; Hicks 1978, pp. 78–107.

the harder task since his family's traditional support had fragmented in the previous decade. Whatever Edward IV had initially envisaged as the relationship between the two men, Gloucester gained the upper hand almost immediately. This is confirmed by the only formal record of their relationship: an indenture drawn up between the two men in 1474, but embodying an agreement made in the previous year before the king and his council.[136] In the indenture, Gloucester undertook to be the earl's good and faithful lord and promised not to claim any office or fee granted to the earl by the king or others and not to take into his service any men retained by the earl. Clearly Percy had felt himself seriously threatened by Gloucester's position in the north. Of the two promises made by the duke, it is the second which has received most attention, implying as it does that the duke had been poaching the earl's retainers. But the first is also significant, suggesting that the duke had had designs on some of the earl's patronage. Together, they point to aggressive empire-building by the duke in the north.

The agreement was designed to protect Northumberland from direct encroachment and to defuse a potentially dangerous rivalry. In the latter, at least, it seems to have succeeded. For the rest of the reign the two nobles apparently co-operated, and were in particular careful to avoid being drawn into disputes between their men. William Plumpton, cultivating Gloucester and his retainer John Pilkington in the hope of bringing pressure to bear on Northumberland over a Knaresborough office, was firmly warned off by a more sophisticated associate.[137] But this harmony was not the *modus vivendi* of two equals. It rested unmistakably on Gloucester's superiority and recognition of that fact was the price Northumberland paid for his protection. Contemporaries recognized it too, and although after 1474 there is no suggestion of outright ducal poaching, men from families with Percy affiliations did apparently continue to enter the duke's service. One clear example comes from near the forest of Knaresborough, where Gloucester had influence through the duchy of Lancaster and where Northumberland held land. Among the earl's possessions there was the lordship of Spofforth, the home of the Middletons of Stokeld, who as a result naturally looked to the Percies for lordship. By 1480, however, one of the younger brothers,

---

[136] *HMC, 6th Report* pp. 223–4; the salient points are reprinted in Hicks 1978, p. 83.
[137] *Plumpton Corresp.* pp. 31–2; Hicks 1978, p. 88.

Richard, was in Gloucester's household.[138] Another example is provided by Richard Ratcliffe, whose father and brother were both feed by Northumberland.[139]

Such examples testify to the attractiveness of Gloucester's lordship. They are also a reminder that although the 1474 agreement had forbidden the two nobles to retain the same men, this left open the possibility of other forms of shared allegiance. Different members of one family could have links with both lords. An individual could have formal links with one but still keep informal connections with the other. Sir Hugh Hastings of Fenwick seems to have been primarily Northumberland's man, but his land in south Yorkshire had brought him into contact with Gloucester as early as 1471, when the duke made him his deputy steward of Snaith, and to judge by his choice of feoffees Hastings maintained links with the duke's circle.[140] This was hardly surprising in an area where both lords were influential. Only families whose own interests were limited to a single area of ducal or comital influence could afford to ignore the other lord. As a result there was in practice considerable blurring between the two retinues. This most frequently benefited Gloucester, as the dominant lord, but this was not invariably the case and the ducal councillor Edmund Hastings of Pickering placed one of his sons in Northumberland's household.[141]

As the agreement of 1474 had made clear, Gloucester was Percy's lord. It followed that Northumberland's men were in a sense Gloucester's men, even though the duke could not retain them directly. This sanctioned the informal merging of the Percy retinue into Gloucester's, and it is likely that these examples of men with a Percy background entering Gloucester's service owed as much to Northumberland's good lordship as to private enterprise. The evidence for Richard Middleton's membership of Gloucester's household comes from his marriage licence, which shows that he was marrying within the Percy connection. His

---

[138] *Reg. Thomas Rotherham* p. 1. Another Knaresborough recruit for Gloucester was Robert Percy of Scotton, a gentleman tenant of the forest: PRO, DL 5/1 fos. 94v, 96v, 113. His mother was a Metcalfe: Hampton 1985b, p. 184. Kendall's version of his early career rests on no evidence: Kendall 1955, pp. 46, 72 and notes.

[139] Cumbria RO, D/Lec/302, D/Lec/29/8.

[140] PRO, C 244/122/49, 54; E 405/71 m. 5 dorse; Humberside RO, DDCL 16 m. 10 dorse; *Test. Ebor.* III p. 274.

[141] Dobson, *York Chamberlains' Rolls* p. 152 ('Edward', but Edmund is clearly meant); *Test. Ebor.* III p. 348.

wife was a kinswoman of the earl's councillor Sir John Pickering, which implies that Middleton did not see service to Gloucester as an alternative to Northumberland's lordship. Ratcliffe's position is comparable. His mother was a Parr, which may have given him an independent *entrée* into Gloucester's service, but he could equally well have come to the duke's attention through the Percy connection. His marriage, too, although it presumably owed much to Gloucester, also allied him with the Percies, since his new brother-in-law lord Scrope was not only a neighbour of the duke but also a Percy retainer.[142]

The retinues of other northern lords can also be seen as components of the ducal connection. The most explicit example is that of Thomas lord Scrope of Masham and Upsale, who inherited the title in 1476, when he was about sixteen. The affiliations of his father are not known, but Thomas was immediately committed to the duke's 'rule and guiding' by his mother. In an indenture drawn up in January 1476 Gloucester undertook to be a good and loving lord to Thomas and his mother. Thomas was to be retained by the duke, and all the servants, tenants and inhabitants of the Scrope estates were to be the duke's men.[143] The relationship is unusual in that Scrope's men were set directly under the duke. Normally the duke's lordship was exercised at one remove although, as in Northumberland's case, some blurring of the two retinues might ensue in practice. This last pattern is also found in Gloucester's relationship with the Lovell/Fitzhugh connection. The Fitzhughs of Ravensworth were a North Riding family closely linked with the Nevilles. Richard Fitzhugh did not take seisin of his lands until 1480 and did not become politically active until after 1483, but it is clear that he was already a satellite of his cousin the duke.[144] Fitzhugh was the brother-in-law of another of Gloucester's close associates, Francis lord Lovell, whose inheritance included land in the North Riding and who had been a Neville ward in the 1460s. Both lords also had interests further south, along the Ouse valley, which formed an extension of Gloucester's Sheriff Hutton connection. The ducal retainer James Charleton of Riccall was probably introduced to Gloucester's service by the Fitzhughs, while Geoffrey Franke of Escrick (later Gloucester's receiver in

[142] Hicks 1978, p. 89n.
[143] Attreed 1983, pp. 1018–25.
[144] *CPR* 1476–85 p. 178; Ross 1981, pp. 48–9.

the northern Neville lands) belonged to a family which had Lovell as well as Neville links.[145]

As this suggests, Gloucester's relationship with other northern lords not only endorsed his authority in areas where he was already influential, but allowed an extension of that authority. It is therefore significant that by the late 1470s most northern lords can be linked with the duke. Ralph lord Greystoke was a member of the ducal council and probably contributed to the extension of ducal influence across the Derwent into the Wolds, where he held land and where the ducal associate Ralph Bigod had Greystoke connections.[146] Humphrey lord Dacre of Gilsland acted as Gloucester's deputy on the west march, while in Durham Gloucester retained George Lumley, heir of lord Lumley, whose father had once been a retainer of the earl of Salisbury.[147] Meanwhile, his relationship with Northumberland brought other nobles into his orbit, most notably John lord Scrope of Bolton. Scrope was feed by Northumberland, and his heir Henry married the earl's sister, but after 1483 lord John and his brothers emerge unequivocally as Richard's close allies.[148] The most striking recruit to Gloucester's circle, however, was Ralph lord Neville, nephew and heir of the elderly earl of Westmorland. Ralph was associated with Gloucester by 1477, possibly after an earlier flirtation with Northumberland, and his arrival in the duke's service marks the end of a feud which had split the Nevilles for over forty years. The first earl of Westmorland had married twice and had dismembered his patrimony to provide for his family by his second wife, Joan Beaufort, granting them the lordships of Middleham, Sheriff Hutton and Penrith. Gloucester was thus territorially the heir of the junior line, and the willingness of lord Neville, heir of the senior line, to ally with him is eloquent testimony to Gloucester's domination of the north.[149]

That domination brought a unity to the north which had been notably lacking since the end of the previous century. Gloucester had not only ended the division within the Neville family but, through his relationship with Northumberland, had called a halt to the long-standing hostility of Neville and Percy. The north,

[145] Horrox 1986b, pp. 84–5.
[146] Dobson, *York Chamberlains' Rolls* p. 152; *Test. Ebor.* III p. 226 and notes.
[147] Hicks 1978, pp. 85, 86; Pollard 1975, p. 57.
[148] Hicks 1978, p. 89n.
[149] *Ibid.* p. 86; Hicks 1971, table III i; Storey 1966, pp. 112–4.

moreover, was not only united but united behind the king since Gloucester was pre-eminently the king's man. This was a major achievement, and can be considered the outstanding success of Edward IV's regional policy. Edward's contribution to that success was obvious. He gave Gloucester the Neville lands which formed the core of his influence, and then continued to augment his holdings of land and office. Even more important was Edward's tacit approval of the use his brother made of his northern power. Without this continuing endorsement Gloucester could not have maintained so wide a hegemony. But the duke's own contribution, although less tangible, was no less crucial. One obvious element was his willingness to work at being a good lord. This was not only a matter of saying yes to petitioners and having the resources to say yes often, although Gloucester was well placed in this respect. Effective lordship was, rather, a matter of judging when yes was the right answer; of balancing his own needs against those of others; and of deciding between competing claims. Such decisions must have been the daily stuff of lordship, but they are now usually only visible in the formal context of legal disputes. Gloucester was much in demand as an arbiter and as a source of legal redress, and it is clear that he took the matter seriously. In one dispute he is twice quoted as saying, on different occasions, 'we intend, nor will none otherwise do at any time, but according to the king's laws' – and there is no reason to suppose that he did not mean it. On another occasion he was prepared to decide against one of his own retainers.[150] As this suggests, the duke recognized a wider responsibility than to his own servants. His lordship was regional, not simply territorial. The examples are also a reminder that lordship had a personal dimension. A good lord brought to the role his own abilities and charisma which are now impossible to quantify but which were vital to his success. In this intangible sense also, Gloucester's lordship clearly succeeded. Even after his death, when most of his servants had come to terms with the new regime, several remembered him with respect and affection. William Malyverer bequeathed to Our Lady of Walsingham a little ring with a diamond which Richard had given him. More striking is the example of Ralph Bigod who, safely transferred to the service of Henry VII and his mother, still refused to criticize his old

[150] Essex RO, D/DQ 14/24/3/40; Pollard 1986, p. 120. See also Sutton 1976.

master.[151] Even when due allowance is made for the material advantages of Gloucester's lordship, there is no doubt of his personal attraction.

The duke's success, however, could not have been foreseen in 1471. In spite of his enthusiastic involvement in Wales, he must then have been something of an unknown quantity and it is possible that his role in the north was originally envisaged as that of one among equals. The additions to his power in the course of the 1470s may have constituted a reassessment of his position, with the king's perception of his role developing as the duke matured.[152] But whatever the exact chronology of Gloucester's emergence as lord of the north, by the end of the decade the process was in effect complete. Either in his own right, or through his links with other lords, Gloucester dominated the entire north east and the north-western counties of Cumberland and Westmorland. In these areas Gloucester's appointment in 1480 as the king's lieutenant in the north did not do much more than recognize existing realities. The grant was made specifically in the context of a projected campaign against Scotland and was designed to avoid damaging disputes over military authority by setting Gloucester firmly above the other northern peers.[153] It thus formalized the inclusion of other noble retinues within Gloucester's affinity but probably conferred little additional authority. The king's own influence in the north rested primarily on the support of local men, and the appointment of a lieutenant could do little more than seek to transfer that support, something which had already been largely achieved through recognition of Gloucester's role as his brother's agent in the north. But the commission did clarify Gloucester's position in one area of the north where it had previously been somewhat equivocal. This was in Lancashire, where Gloucester's authority in the duchy of Lancaster confronted the influence of Thomas lord Stanley and his brother William.

Stanley interests had first been brought into conflict with Gloucester by Edward's grant of extensive Lancashire land to the duke in 1469. After his return in 1471 Edward tried to limit the damage to the Stanleys by modifying Gloucester's grant. On 4 July the duke was made chief steward of the duchy of Lancaster in

---

[151] *Test. Ebor.* IV, p. 182n.; Warnicke 1984, p. 300.
[152] Although compare Hicks 1986a, p. 14, who suggests that the initiative was Gloucester's.
[153] Ross 1981, pp. 44–5.

the north; steward of Rochdale and Tottington in the county palatine; of Clitheroe and Penwortham (Lancs.) and of Halton (Ches.); and master forester of the Lancashire forests, together with the forest of Bowland, then regarded as lying in Yorkshire.[154] This still, however, posed a threat to Stanley influence. Thomas lord Stanley had held the stewardship of Halton since 1461. He had also been made steward of Tottington, Rochdale and Penwortham just two weeks before the grant to Gloucester. Edward apparently intended the later grant to stand, and on 7 July ordered Stanley and his servants to cease meddling in the offices granted to Gloucester.[155] After the Stanleys' ambivalent behaviour in 1469–71 Edward may have seen his brother's presence in the region as a useful counterbalance, but it is unlikely that he wanted to see the Stanleys totally eclipsed. In the next few years, as Gloucester's power elsewhere in the north grew, his influence in Lancashire became more narrowly defined. To some extent this may have been due to the Stanleys' own efforts, since they had the firmer territorial base in the region, but it must also reflect the king's wishes. Gloucester's position in the north east reveals how greatly his standing was enhanced by royal backing, and his failure to achieve similar dominance in Lancashire strongly implies that the king had chosen to support the Stanleys instead.

The exact chronology of this development is unclear, although it is likely that the erosion of the duke's power began immediately, with some of the provisions of his 1471 grant a dead letter from the outset. In Halton, where lord Stanley was receiver, the duke never received his fee as steward, and Stanley continued to pay himself the fee as both constable and steward on the authority of the 1461 letters patent. He may also have kept the stewardship of Tottington and Rochdale, in spite of Edward's orders to the contrary. Gloucester was more successful in asserting his claims to the stewardship of Clitheroe and its members. The honour was historically linked with the honour of Pontefract and together they formed a single trans-Pennine power bloc. The reality of Gloucester's influence there is also reflected in the fact that, of all the master forestships he had been granted in 1471, the only two he seems to have exercised were those which best complemented this trans-Pennine interest: Bowland to the north and Rossendale further south. The forests further west remained in the control of

---

[154] PRO, DL 37/40 nos. 28, 46.
[155] *Ibid.*; DL 37/47A no. 15; Somerville 1953, p. 511.

the Stanleys and others.[156] In effect, therefore, Gloucester's offices were concentrated in the east of Lancashire, where they formed an extension of his West Riding interests, and elsewhere he yielded place to the Stanleys. This is the arrangement formalized in Edward's territorial reordering of 1473–5, which saw Lancashire as the northern end of a Stanley power bloc stretching through Cheshire into north Wales, rather than as one more component in Gloucester's northern hegemony. Part of that reordering was Gloucester's exchange of Skipton in Craven for Chirk in 1475, endorsed if not actually organized by the crown, which was a tacit acknowledgement of the division of power between the Stanleys and Gloucester.

The most sensitive touchstone of effective influence in Lancashire was, however, the dispute over Hornby castle, which was also finally settled in 1475, probably under the impetus of Edward's planned invasion of France.[157] The dispute had its origins in the battle of Wakefield, at which Sir Thomas Harrington of Hornby and his eldest son John were killed on the Yorkist side. John's heirs were his two daughters, whose wardship passed to Edward IV after his accession. That of the eldest girl, Anne, was granted to Geoffrey Middleton, the head of a Lonsdale family. But Geoffrey proved unable, or unwilling, to resist the claims of the girls' uncles, James and Robert Harrington. The brothers seized both heiresses and hung onto the family lands themselves. Their action was not seriously challenged until 1468, when the king's attorney called them into chancery to answer the charges against them. This long immunity undoubtedly owed something to their impeccable Yorkist background, and its termination may, conversely, be partly explained by the fall from favour of their other patron, the earl of Warwick. Edward IV now gave the girls' wardship to the Stanleys, a family powerful enough to resist the Harringtons' claims. The Stanleys promptly married the girls into their own family, but in the short term they were unable to dislodge the Harringtons from Hornby, and the dispute dragged on into Edward's second reign. By this time the Harringtons had a further hold on Edward's gratitude, having joined him promptly on his return in 1471, and they had also secured a new and influential patron in the person of the duke of Gloucester, who may already have intervened on the Harringtons' side in 1470.

[156] PRO, DL 29/17/241–2, 29/90/1653, 29/119/1964; Holt 1982, pp. 102–4.
[157] For what follows, see M.K. Jones 1986a, pp. 37–40; Ross 1974, pp. 408–9.

The king, however, also had reason to conciliate the Stanleys and in 1472 the matter went to arbitration. The decision went against the Harringtons, but they still refused to capitulate, presumably confident of ducal backing, and the matter was not finally settled until 1475, when Hornby was confirmed to the daughters and hence to the Stanleys.

By 1475, therefore, the Stanleys had in effect been confirmed as the leading royal agents in Lancashire. Gloucester's immediate influence was mainly restricted to the edges of the county: to the lordship of Clitheroe in the east and to Furness in the north – both areas where his influence was in a sense overspill from more substantial interests elsewhere. Gloucester's reaction to this arrangement is unknown, but Lancashire was the one area of the north where Edward failed to endorse his power and the duke may well have resented his exclusion; recent work has emphasized that he never entirely abandoned claims to grants which he had once held.[158] There was a local tradition that Gloucester and the Stanleys came to blows over the division of authority, and their continuing rivalry may lie behind a royal command in 1476 that the tenants of Congleton should attend 'only upon the king's highness and in his absence upon the lord Stanley'.[159] It is significant that there was little overlap between the ducal and Stanley affinities, although some royal officials necessarily had dealings with both lords. There was, however, overlap between the Stanley connection and the royal household, which confirms that the Stanleys were seen as part of the royal affinity rather than as part of Gloucester's.[160] This identification was emphasized in 1483 when Gloucester took the precaution of arresting lord Stanley as a prelude to his usurpation. Stanley was thus distinguished from Gloucester's other northern satellites, several of whom, including Northumberland, apparently co-operated in his coup. The growing hostility between Richard and the Stanleys after 1484 can be explained in terms of the king's policies, but it may also have owed something to the frictions of the previous fifteen years.

Even without Lancashire, Gloucester's domination of the north is impressive. It is also unique in the late Middle Ages, and the novelty of the duke's position is reflected in the creation, in the

[158] Hicks 1986b, pp. 7–9.
[159] Bennett 1985, p. 76; Myers, 'Official progress' p. 7.
[160] e.g. John Savage junior: *CPR 1476–85* p. 94.

parliament of 1482–3, of a northern county palatine for him – the first since Lancashire was made a county palatine in 1351. It was to consist of as much land as Gloucester was able to win in the Scottish dales along the west march. At the same time his wardenship of the march was confirmed and made hereditary, and to support the office he was given specified royal lands and rights in Cumberland together with 10,000 marks. The grant has led one historian to question Edward's mental state, but this is an over-reaction.[161] The creation of a new county palatine was indeed a grand gesture, and a notably archaic one, but on examination the gesture is more than the substance. Palatine status was restricted to former Scottish territory, where Gloucester's chances of carving out a significant holding for himself were at best uncertain. The duke's campaign of the previous season, which had won Berwick for the crown, may have whipped up enthusiasm for future conquests, but it had also been a lesson in the expense and difficulty of winning a small piece of land and the cost of keeping it thereafter.[162] For most practical purposes, therefore, the meat of the grant lay in the clauses relating to Cumberland, and these were more modest. To some extent they were also a confirmation. As well as warden, Gloucester was already sheriff of Cumberland for life and had possession of Carlisle and its fee farm. The grant of 1482/3 made these hereditary, and also gave the duke and his heirs all other royal land in the county, together with the right to appoint the escheator. This represented a significant increase in Gloucester's power in the region, but not necessarily a corresponding decrease in royal authority. The remoteness of the county must always have meant that kings remained particularly dependent on local good will. In the short term, with the loyal Gloucester in control, Edward IV may even have felt that the grant would strengthen royal authority in the region rather than diminish it. In the longer term, of course, this would not necessarily have been true, simply because the loyalty, and the ability, of Gloucester's successors were an unknown quantity, but it is significant that the terms of the Cumberland grants were less generous than those north of the border. In his planned county palatine Gloucester was to hold in

<hr/>

[161] *Rot. Parl.* VI pp. 204–5; Scofield 1923, II p. 359.
[162] Ross 1974, p. 290. For a contemporary estimate of the cost of defending Berwick see Horrox, 'Financial memoranda' p. 225.

fee simple, in Cumberland the grants were to him and the heirs male of his body.

This grant was to be Edward's final contribution to his brother's northern empire. It forms an appropriate conclusion, not only in its scale, but in its embodiment of the principle that what was good for Gloucester was good for royal authority. This assumption shaped Edward's policy of establishing regional hegemonies and it was vindicated by Gloucester's control of a notoriously difficult region. It is only with hindsight that Gloucester can be seen as another overmighty subject, wilfully created by a king who should have known better. At the time he probably seemed instead a manifestation of resurgent royal authority. Although the heart of his empire was the Neville land, it would be wrong to cast Gloucester in the role of hereditary northern magnate, whose estates made him an independent regional force. The land alone cannot account for the size of the region Gloucester came to control; that derived from royal office and royal backing.

It is in the north that Richard's power was greatest and he is now usually regarded as a northern figure. But his interests were never exclusively northern. Although there was no other region which he dominated for the king, he did have other land which allowed him to exercise lordship on a more modest scale. The most important of these subsidiary holdings lay in East Anglia where, as in the north, the centrepiece of Gloucester's influence was the land of a single family, in this case the de Veres, the earls of Oxford. Their Lancastrian sympathies had resulted in the forfeiture of their land early in the 1460s, when much of it was granted to Gloucester, but the de Veres had subsequently reached an accommodation with the new regime and had regained their land before Gloucester came of age. The de Veres' change of heart, however, proved short-lived and by the end of the decade the family was again involved in opposition to Edward IV, this time in support of the earl of Warwick, whose sister Margaret had married the thirteenth earl of Oxford, John de Vere. Oxford was an active supporter of the Readeption of Henry VI in 1470/1, and on Edward IV's return the family lost their estates for a second time. The beneficiary was again Gloucester. He received a formal grant of the land in December 1471, although he had perhaps been promised it earlier, since one of his associates was promoted to a benefice within the estate in the previous October.[163] This time the land remained in the duke's possession. Oxford had fled into exile in 1471 but was arrested after his involvement in the unrest of 1473 and sent prisoner to Hammes, one of the Calais fortresses, where he remained until his escape in 1484.

The 1471 grant gave Gloucester the lion's share of the forfeited property, including all the Cambridgeshire land, all but one of the Suffolk manors and all but four of those in Essex.[164] The land in the king's gift, however, did not include the estates held in her own right by the countess Elizabeth, widow of the twelfth earl, which included substantial further holdings in Suffolk and Essex.[165] Gloucester opened negotiations with the dowager almost immediately, apparently claiming that he had been given custody of her and her land by the king, and by January 1473 the countess and her feoffees had agreed to make an estate to Gloucester in all the dower lands. The countess' heir, the attainted thirteenth earl, had the transaction annulled after his restoration by Henry VII and later brought witnesses to depose that the countess had submitted under duress.[166] According to one deponent, the duke had threatened to remove the countess to Middleham, at which she yielded, 'considering her great age, the great journey, and the great cold which then was of frost and snow'. Although the depositions must be somewhat suspect, it is likely that the countess did feel herself under pressure to agree, and it may be significant that her feoffees, after agreeing in principle to the transfer, then dragged their feet over finalizing it and had to be sued in chancery by Gloucester and, nominally, the countess. Gloucester's petition embodies the only surviving details of his side of the agreement, which are, however, too vague for one to be sure how hard a bargain he had driven.[167] The main provision was that he would pay the countess an annuity of 500 marks for her life – an open-ended commitment which in the event did not prove particularly onerous since the countess died soon after

[163] Thomas Barowe was made rector of Castle Camps: Emden 1963, p. 40; Horrox 1986b, pp. 85–6.

[164] *CPR* 1467–77 p. 297; *Cal. Inq. post mortem sive Escaetarum* IV p. 370.

[165] The land in question was Howard land; the countess was the daughter of John Howard (the half-brother of Robert, father of the 1st duke of Norfolk). I am grateful to Dr Roger Virgoe for advice on this point. The relevant documents have now been printed by Hicks, 'Last days of the countess'.

[166] PRO, C 263/2/1/6; BL, Cotton Julius BXII fos. 227–9; *Rot. Parl.* VI pp. 281–2, 473–4; *CCR* 1468–76 no. 1214.

[167] PRO, C 4/2/51; BL, Cotton Julius BXII fos. 315–6.

Christmas 1475.[168] Gloucester undertook to settle the countess' debts to a total of £240 and to give her unspecified sums for the performance of her last will. He also promised to promote her son, then studying at Cambridge, to appropriate benefices and to make other benefactions. Finally, he agreed to meet various costs and charges of the countess' children and grandchildren at her request. None of these elements is specified, and only one can be identified with any confidence. In April 1477 the duke's feoffees granted the countess' manor of Fowlmere (Cambs.) to Queens' College, Cambridge, for prayers for the good estate of the king and queen and of Gloucester, his wife and son, and for the souls of John de Vere late earl of Oxford and Elizabeth his consort.[169]

The de Vere lands were not Gloucester's only East Anglian acquisition. The grant of 1471 also included land in the region forfeited by Lewis Fitzjohn, John Darcy and Robert Harleston, as well as estates in Lincolnshire forfeited by Sir Thomas de la Laund and Sir Thomas Dymmoke. This diffuse collection was, however, considerably pruned in 1475, when the de Vere estates held by the duke were also reordered. Of the subsidiary grants, Gloucester lost all but the de la Laund estates, although this grant was widened to include the reversion of the land held by the knight's widow Katherine Tempest. By this date Darcy's attainder had been reversed and Gloucester had surrendered his estates.[170] The Fitzjohn land went to the queen, who was also the main beneficiary of the readjustments to Gloucester's holdings of de Vere land, enshrined in new letters patent of August 1475. Gloucester gave up all the Suffolk manors which he had been granted in 1471 and individual manors elsewhere, including Castle Hedingham and Earl's Colne (Essex), receiving in return further de Vere land scattered over five counties. Of the land he had surrendered, all the Essex land and Lavenham (Suff.) went to the queen and her feoffees, with the rest of the Suffolk land going to John Howard. Lesser pickings from the reorganization went to William Stanley and Walter Devereux lord Ferrers.[171]

This revision was a further stage in the territorial reordering which Edward undertook between 1473 and 1475.[172] As far as

---

[168] *CP* x pp. 238–9.

[169] *CPR* 1476–85 p. 34.

[170] *Rot. Parl.* VI p. 131; Hicks 1986b, p. 18.

[171] *CPR* 1467–77 pp. 538, 545, 547, 556, 560, 565, 566–7.

[172] Morgan 1973, pp. 17–19

Gloucester was concerned, it was a recognition of the fact that the north had now emerged as his main sphere of interest, and his surrender of land in East Anglia was to some extent the corollary of the consolidation of his northern interests which was taking place in the same year. It did not entail the abandonment of his eastern interests. He still kept a significant share of the forfeited de Vere lands in Cambridge and Essex as well as the lands of the countess Elizabeth which, as a private acquisition, were unaffected by the reordering. But the reorganization does seem to have marked the end of any assumption that East Anglia might become another major sphere of ducal influence. The land which Gloucester surrendered included the main centres of de Vere influence in the region, which suggests that Gloucester was resigning any political role, while preserving his financial position. This change of emphasis is also reflected in his receipt of other patronage. Initially Edward had been prepared to augment Gloucester's landed interest with further grants and had given him the custody and marriage of two local heirs, Henry Marney and William Walgrave. It was also Gloucester, rather than Clarence, who received most of the Warwick inheritance in the region.[173] After 1475, however, Gloucester made no further acquisitions, either through royal grants or private enterprise. On the contrary, he was prepared to consider alienations. In about 1479 he offered to sell a de Vere property in London to the royal servant John Risley. The property had been part of the countess' lands, and when Risley asked the king's advice on the matter Edward warned him off: 'Risley, meddle not ye with the buying of the said place, for though the title of [it] be good in my brother of Gloucester's hands or in another man's hands of like might, it will be dangerous to thee to buy it and also to keep it and defend it.'[174] Gloucester had more success with John lord Howard, who in 1480 bought Wivenhoe (Essex) and other lands for 1,100 marks.[175] After his accession Richard parted with all his East Anglian estates to Howard, an indication that he regarded them as a peripheral part of his power base.

---

[173] *CPR* 1467–77 pp. 329, 338; Hicks 1980, appendix IIC. Gloucester promptly sold the Marney wardship to Robert Tyrell and Thomas Green: *Cat. Anc. Deeds* VI A6298.

[174] PRO, C 263/2/1/6; the comment reveals Edward's awareness that Gloucester's title to the land was suspect.

[175] Collier, *Household Books* p. 18; *CCR* 1476–85 no. 735. Given the family connection, John Howard was probably confident of resisting any challenge to his title: Crawford 1986, pp. 7–9.

East Anglia may have been peripheral, but it was not ignored. No lord could afford to turn his back on an opportunity to demonstrate good lordship and extend his connection, particularly as lordship was cumulative, with each sphere of influence strengthening others. The nature of Gloucester's involvement in East Anglia was, however, profoundly different from that in the north. He never developed a major following there – even, as far as can be seen, in the early 1470s when there was still a possibility that he might take on a political role. The obvious core of such a following would have been the de Vere supporters, and there was a degree of continuity within the estates, with former de Vere associates like John Coke of Beaumont continuing to farm manors.[176] But in a wider context Gloucester failed to establish himself as the heir of the earls of Oxford. The Pastons, who had been associated with the earl during the Readeption and renewed the connection after 1485, did not turn to Gloucester in the interval. Edmund Paston, it is true, was retained by the duke in 1475, but this was specifically for the campaign against France, and his letters give no hint of a more extended relationship with the duke.[177] This lack of continuity can partly be explained by the characteristically flexible patterns of association in the region, where the existence of several major landowners with overlapping interests militated against the formation of long-standing connections. Gloucester thus did not, as in the north, have the benefit of traditional loyalties as a foundation upon which to build. But much of the explanation lies in the duke's own position. Gloucester was simply not sufficiently involved in the region to maintain a large-scale connection against competition from local lords. It was clearly his national eminence, rather than any claim to be a natural arbiter of local affairs, which made his lordship attractive. Significantly, the one recorded local dispute in which he was concerned (a violent struggle over the manor of Gregories in Theydon Garnon) shows him drawn in as a political heavyweight to counterbalance strong support on the other side. Although some ducal servants were heavily involved, Gloucester emerges from the mass of evidence as a fairly distant figure, who settled immediately

---

[176] PRO, DL 29/637/10360A. Coke was a feoffee of the dowager countess: BL, Cotton Julius BXII fo. 228.
[177] *PL* I no. 396.

once he realized that the dispute had pitted him against his mother.[178]

The fact that Gloucester's role in the region was that of a national rather than local figure is also reflected in the fragmentary nature of his following. His most important retainer was Sir James Tyrell of Gipping (Suff.), although Gloucester employed him mainly elsewhere. At first sight Tyrell looks like an example of continuity from the de Vere connection since his father had been executed for his involvement with the de Veres in 1462. But the family were also linked tenurially with the house of York, and after William Tyrell's execution it was the dowager duchess of York who had custody of James and his land, although she granted both to William's widow and her feoffees.[179] James Tyrell had evidently committed himself to the Yorkists by 1471, when he was knighted at Tewkesbury, and it may have been links with the crown which eased his passage into Gloucester's service. The same was probably true of Gloucester's steward in the region, Sir Robert Chamberlain of Capel and Gedding (Suff.), who had been a knight of the king's body since the mid 1460s.[180]

But Gloucester's contacts were not only with his brother's men. He is said to have feed Thomas Heveningham, son and heir of Sir John Heveningham, and the Heveninghams had probably been drawn into Gloucester's circle through their kinship with the Hoptons.[181] William Hopton, the son of John Hopton of Blythburgh (Suff.), was one of Gloucester's most active associates. A ducal esquire by 1475, when the London mercers thought him a man worth cultivating, he was also the duke's feoffee and after Richard's accession became treasurer of the royal household.[182] His connection with Gloucester was probably rooted in the north rather than Suffolk. The family was an illegitimate branch of the Yorkshire Hoptons, being descended from Sir Robert Swillington by his mistress Joan Hopton. They accordingly had interests in the north as well as East Anglia, and the Yorkshire lands were probably the particular responsibility of William, who is regularly described as 'of Swillington'. The manor, in the Aire valley just

[178] The material relating to this dispute is to be found in two collections in the Essex RO: D/DQ/14/124, D/DCe. It is summarized in part in Waller 1895a, 1895b, 1898.

[179] *PL* II p. 593; *Great Chron.* p. 199; BL, Add. Ch. 16564.

[180] PRO, DL 29/637/10360A; E 101/412/2 fo. 36.

[181] Blomefield 1739–75, III p. 61; Richmond 1981a, pp. 238–40.

[182] BL, Cotton Julius BXII fo. 241v; PRO, E 404/78/2/25; *CCR* 1476–85 no. 650; *CPR* 1476–85 p. 34; Imray 1969, p. 166.

outside Leeds, was held of the duchy of Lancaster, which may first have brought William to Gloucester's notice.[183] In Norfolk Gloucester had links with the Boleyns. Thomas Boleyn had acted for the duke in 1469, and his brother and heir William witnessed a ducal charter in 1480 in company with known retainers of the duke. In 1483 John Howard duke of Norfolk made William Boleyn his deputy as admiral for the coasts of Norfolk and Suffolk, and it is possible that Boleyn had initially held the post as Gloucester's deputy.[184]

Apart from these men, only one East Anglian can definitely be identified with Gloucester: William Harmer, esquire, of Bee-chamwell (Norf.), who was a gentleman of the duke's house-hold.[185] Beyond this the composition of the retinue can only be inferred, in itself evidence of the low level of ducal involvement. The Hoptons could have introduced other local families to the duke. They were particularly closely linked with the Calthorpes and Wentworths. Sir William Calthorpe had been retained by the duke in 1469, while the Wentworths were another family combining Yorkshire and Suffolk interests, so both were plausible ducal associates in the 1470s but there is no hard evidence in either case. Also involved with the Hoptons was Philip Bothe of Coddenham (Suff.) a second generation emigrant from the north west who suddenly rose to local prominence after 1483 – which seems to imply an earlier connection with Richard.[186] The same argument can be used to add a few more names to the list, but the total is still not large. Nor does the list display much unity, apart from the suggested group around the Hoptons. The geographical background of the men concerned does not even correspond particularly closely with the duke's territorial interests in the region. Even allowing that the list is incomplete, East Anglia seems to have contributed individuals rather than a connection to the ducal retinue.

Given this apparently patchy local following, it is not surprising to find signs of a steady drift of members of the duke's northern connection into the region. Gloucester seems to have turned to his northern allies in first asserting his possession of the land. Early in

[183] PRO, DL 41/34/1 fo. 1v; *Inqs p.m.* 1 no. 480; *Reg. Thomas Rotherham* 1 p. 35; Richmond 1981a, chap. 1.
[184] BL, Cotton Julius BXII fo. 123; North Riding RO, ZRC/17503 (a reference I owe to the kindness of Dr Hicks); Blomefield 1739–75, II p. 511.
[185] PRO, C 1/67/106.
[186] PRO, C 244/133/15; Axon 1938, p. 36.

1472 Arthur Pilkington, the illegitimate son of Sir Thomas, head of the Lancashire Pilkingtons, was described as of Hedingham (Essex).[187] It is significant, too, that at around this time a royal commission of arrest in Essex was headed by a Yorkshireman, John Nesfield, who was probably already a ducal associate.[188] The de Vere lands remained a source of reward for northern servants of the duke. Gloucester's bailiff of Newton, for instance, was Edmund Carre, who in 1474 is described as of Earl's Colne, one of the de Vere manors then still in Gloucester's hands. But Edmund was almost certainly one of the northern Carres, since the 1474 reference is to his acting with Ralph Burnant of Yokefleet (Yorks.) as surety for Sir Thomas Markenfield, one of Gloucester's Middleham retainers.[189] Another outsider who probably arrived in the area under Gloucester's aegis was Ralph Willoughby, a younger son of the Willoughbys of Wollaton (Notts.), who acquired landed interests in East Anglia through marriage to the widow of Henry Castell of Raveningham (Norf.).[190] Willoughby witnessed a ducal charter in 1480 and was Richard's first sheriff of Norfolk and Suffolk. Such examples could be taken to demonstrate the homogeneity of the ducal retinue, except that there is no firm evidence of movement in the opposite direction. To some extent the East Anglian lands seem to have been exploited for the benefit of the northern retinue, and the same attitude can be seen in the use of some of the de Vere lands to endow Gloucester's new college at Middleham.[191]

The duke's local supporters in East Anglia appear not only disparate but also relatively insignificant. As a group they are eclipsed not only by the connections of local magnates, but by the affinity which developed around the queen and her brother earl Rivers. Rivers, through his marriage to the heiress of the Scales barony, held a significant block of land in Norfolk. The core of the connection, however, was provided by the queen's possession of the duchy of Lancaster estates in much of the south, including East Anglia.[192] With the estates came the service of the existing duchy officials, but the queen was also able to establish her own

[187] PRO, C 244/114/118; Foster 1874, I *sub* Pilkington.
[188] *CPR* 1467–77 p. 318.
[189] PRO, C 244/119/60; DL 29/637/10360A.
[190] He was the son of Sir Hugh Willoughby: PRO, Prob 11/14 fos. 174v–5v; *HMC, Middleton* p. 507 ('Rodolphus'); Blomefield 1739–75, IV p. 268.
[191] North Riding RO, ZRC/17503.
[192] Somerville 1953, pp. 238–9.

connection there, and several of her servants and kinsmen were subsequently rewarded from the duchy.[193] The territorial re-adjustments of 1475 suggest that by then the queen's interest in East Anglia was regarded as the main instrument of royal authority there. The connection received a further boost early in 1478, when the heiress of the last Mowbray duke of Norfolk married the king's second son, Richard duke of York. This allowed an amalgamation of the Mowbray retinue with the royal interest in East Anglia and the result was an immensely influential grouping. It was also a notably cohesive one, since ties of kinship linked its leading members with the queen's family and with each other. The nexus embraced, for instance, the Brandon, Wingfield, Darcy, Haute and Fitzlewis families, and was further strengthened by the marriage of Rivers to Mary Fitzlewis.[194] But in spite of this personal dimension, the connection was never exclusively the queen's, nor even the Woodvilles'. Many of its members, particu-larly within the duchy of Lancaster, were men with a tradition of service to the crown, compared with which their Woodville connection was only transient. Conversely, the queen's servants were *ipso facto* the king's men (many in the literal sense of being also members of the king's household) and it would be unrealistic to ignore this dimension of their loyalty. It is more accurate to see the East Anglian affinity as a *court* connection rather than a narrowly Woodville one. This becomes obvious in 1483, when the usurpation of Richard III split the connection into those whose loyalties remained with the crown and those prepared to back Woodville opposition to the new regime.

It is important, however, not to project this split back into the 1470s. There is no evidence that the court circle in East Anglia, including those elements most closely identified with the queen, was inimical to Gloucester, or that the duke regarded them as rivals for power in the region. On the contrary, ducal influence in East Anglia should probably be seen as another component of this influential court connection. There were certainly points of contact between members of the two circles. The Tyrells of Gipping, for instance, were closely related to the Darcies and through them with other members of the court group.[195] The

---

[193] Myers, 'Household of Queen Eliz.', pp. 207–35, 443–81.
[194] She was the niece of the attainted Lewis Fitzjohn (otherwise Lewes Fitzlewes or Lewes John): Elliot 1898, pp. 36–7.
[195] Berry 1840, pp. 58–9; amplified by King 1864, pp. 75–94; King 1869, pp. 1–24.

most intriguing example, however, comes from the surviving receiver's account for Gloucester's land in the region, in which the only annuity, other than fees to ducal officers, was one of £5 to Katherine Haute, a kinswoman of the queen.[196] Her connection with the duke is not explained, but it is possible that she was his mistress since Gloucester's illegitimate daughter bore the same Christian name. Other members of the queen's family were also associated with the duke in the 1470s, among them Richard Haute junior, who was knighted by Gloucester on the Scottish campaign of 1482. He was sworn in as one of the duchy of Lancaster council in February 1483, presumably with Gloucester's support. His wife Eleanor Roos, meanwhile, was in the queen's service – a clear demonstration that the two circles were not incompatible.[197]

It is only viewed in retrospect that such dual loyalties seem strange: in the context of Edward IV's reign they made very good sense. In Wales, too, Gloucester can be seen as part of a wider court interest. The duke's initial influence in the region had rested on his role as caretaker of the Herbert hegemony and had ended with the readjustments which followed Edward's return in 1471. But in the partition of the Warwick and Salisbury lands which was finally achieved in 1474 it was Gloucester who secured the Welsh estates. The most important of these were Abergavenny and Glamorgan, which together gave Gloucester a significant interest in the south of the country. In the 1477/8 parliament his position there was further strengthened by the exchange of Elfael, which had come to him with the Neville land but which was peripheral to his main Welsh interests, for the duchy of Lancaster lordship of Ogmore, which complemented his holdings in Glamorgan.[198] It is not clear who initiated the exchange, which benefited both sides, but the transaction demonstrates that the king was willing to strengthen Gloucester's hold on the region, and the result was a compact power base. Ducal influence in the region has, however, been judged remote and ineffectual, a verdict based largely on Gloucester's inability to get to grips with the problems caused by the decaying system of local office holding.[199]

---

[196] PRO, DL 29/637/10360A.
[197] PRO, DL 5/1 fo. 70; Metcalfe 1885, p. 7; Myers, 'Household of Queen Eliz.' p. 467n.; Lambert 1933, p. 83.
[198] BL, Cotton Julius BXII fos. 204–5; *Rot. Parl.* VI p. 170.
[199] Pugh 1971, pp. 202–3; Lowe 1981, p. 549. Both also adduce Gloucester's administrative inefficiency in the duchy of Lancaster, but this was probably politically inspired, see above, p. 47.

Certainly, by the time Gloucester secured these Welsh estates, the north had emerged decisively as his main sphere of activity. Whereas East Anglia might have become a second power base in the early 1470s, Gloucester's Welsh lands were never expected to be more than peripheral.

How far Gloucester built up a local following is unclear. His key agent in the region, Sir James Tyrell of Gipping, was an outsider, as were at least two more of his officials: his constable of Ogmore, William Houghton of Birtsmorton (Worcs.), and his constable of Caerphilly, Nicholas Spicer of Bristol, who was to become one of Richard's leading administrators in Wales after 1483.[200] However, this was a commonplace in Wales and the fact that Tyrell received numerous grants from local landowners anxious to have his good will implies that he at least was a force to be reckoned with.[201] There are a few apparently local men in the ducal retinue, such as the Richard ap Robert ap Ivan Vaughan who was rewarded as a ducal servant in 1478 and who may be the Richard Vaughan who held office on the duke's Buckinghamshire estates.[202] Presumably, like Warwick before him, Gloucester developed connections with local families like the Stradlings of St Donat's. John Stradling was receiver of Ogmore when it came into Gloucester's hands and, unlike the steward and constable, was kept in office by the duke.[203] Beyond this, one can add as likely members of the retinue a few men who suddenly became visible after Richard's accession, such as David ap Guillim Morgan or, at a humbler level, David ap Jenkins who migrated to England to become a yeoman of the crown and hold office in Pontefract.[204] The list, however, is hardly impressive and, as in East Anglia, it looks as though Gloucester was acquiring the service of individuals rather than building up a coherent connection – although, in the absence of receivers' accounts for the duke's Welsh lordships, this can only be inference.

Gloucester's connection in no way compares with that of the prince of Wales, whose council at Ludlow was the focus for royal

[200] PRO, DL 29/593/9505; WAM 4110 m. 1. Houghton appears acting with Tyrell in East Anglia as early as 1472: PRO, C 244/114/118.
[201] Pugh 1971, p. 201.
[202] Hicks 1980, p. 151; PRO, DL 29/637/10360A.
[203] *Cartae de Glamorgancia* v no. 1220 (p. 1690); Somerville 1953, p. 644; PRO, DL 29/593/9505; E 101/412/3 fo. 2v.
[204] PRO, C 67/51 m. 26; DL 42/20 fos. 10v–11, 39v–40; Prob 11/16 fo. 62; *CPR* 1476–85 p. 485.

servants in Wales from the mid 1470s. But rather than seeing Gloucester as a weak independent power eclipsed by a strong court connection, one should probably, as in East Anglia, think of him as part of that connection. He was himself a member of the prince's council, and although he is unlikely to have played much part in its activities this is only to be expected from a nobleman of his rank and does not mean that he remained aloof from the king's plans for the region. As the loyal brother of the king, his possession of Glamorgan and Abergavenny formed a useful pendant to royal possessions in Wales and the march. This explains why Clarence was forced to disgorge the Neville lands in Wales, which he had held since 1471, in favour of his brother. The assumption that Gloucester would be a more satisfactory component of royal authority in Wales proved justified, and on the rare occasions for which evidence survives he does seem to have co-operated with the council.[205] He also seems to have developed connections with the circle around the prince. He was on sufficiently good terms with the prince's chamberlain, Sir Thomas Vaughan, for Vaughan to lend him his London house in the 1470s, and although this relationship did not survive Richard's usurpation, other servants of the prince transferred to Richard's household after his accession. The most important was Richard Mynours, who had been a gentleman usher of the prince's chamber in the mid 1470s and entered Richard's household in the same capacity. He had been active in south Wales under Edward IV, being made chamberlain there in 1479, and it may have been this which brought him to Gloucester's attention. He held the same office under Richard III (apart from a few months when it was held by the duke of Buckingham) and as the main financial officer in south Wales was largely responsible for funding royal servants such as Tyrell and Richard Newton.[206] At least two of Mynours' colleagues in Richard's chamber were also inherited from the prince's circle, the gentleman usher Walter Harvard and the yeoman usher Robert Jenkin.[207]

The pattern of lordship to be found in Gloucester's dealings with East Anglia and Wales is repeated, on a still smaller scale,

---

[205] Hicks 1980, p. 122; Lowe 1981, p. 571.

[206] PRO, C 263/2/1/6; *CPR* 1467–77 p. 451; *Harl. 433* II p. 114; Griffiths 1972a, pp. 160, 189.

[207] Harvard: PRO, E 404/76/4/131; *CPR* 1476–85 p. 470; Griffiths 1972a, p. 392. Jenkin: *Harl. 433* I p. 225; Lowe 1977, p. 283.

within his holdings elsewhere. All made some contribution to the ducal retinue. Most offered rewards for Gloucester's servants. At Sudeley (Glos.), for instance, which Gloucester held between 1469 and 1478, the key offices went to John Huddleston junior of Millom, initiating a family connection with the county which endured for several generations.[208] But land also brought new men into the duke's orbit. Lesser offices remained the preserve of local men, although they were usually people of limited importance. Thus Gloucester's possession of Chesham (Bucks.) gave him the service of the Wedons, who had held land in the manor since the thirteenth century and who acted as his bailiffs there.[209] More valuable, and usually more visible, were the regional gentry attracted to the duke's service. Outside the north these rarely constituted a coherent connection, but as individuals they provided a necessary point of contact with the area concerned, through which the duke could take action. The duke's Lincoln-shire land, for instance, brought him into contact with Robert Ratcliffe of Tattershall, who acted as his steward in the county.[210] At a humbler level, it gave him the service of Richard Barnby of Great Gonerby, whom Richard was to add to the Lincolnshire commission of array in winter 1484.[211] It probably also explains why the brothers Alexander and Richard Quadring entered his household after he became king.[212]

The duke's lordship cannot, however, be discussed only in terms of his land. His power had a wider dimension. Throughout his brother's second reign, Gloucester was constable and admiral of England and was active in both capacities. The constable's traditional competence lay in military and chivalric matters, and thus in 1478 it was Gloucester, 'in his own person', who dealt with the refusal of four new knights to pay the customary fees to

---

[208] Leland, *Itin.* II p. 56; *CPR* 1476–85 p. 93 which is likely to be a confirmation of an earlier, ducal appointment.

[209] PRO, DL 29/637/10360A; Longleat ms 516 m. 3; *CPR* 1476–85 p. 485; *VCH Bucks.* III p. 213.

[210] PRO, DL 29/639/10386–7. This was the Robert Ratcliffe, son of Sir Thomas, who married Joan Stanhope, lady Cromwell (hence the Tattershall connection) and then, after 1485, Katherine Drury, the widow of Henry le Strange of Hunstanton: PRO, Prob 11/11 fo. 184v. Most pedigrees confuse him with his namesake, the son of Sir John of Attleborough, who married Margaret, widow of lord Dymmoke.

[211] Rogers 1968, p. 45, a reference I owe to W. E. Hampton.

[212] PRO, Prob 11/14 fo. 194–v; *CPR* 1476–85 pp. 388, 435. The family was of Friskney: *Lincs. Pedigrees* III p. 803.

the officers of arms.[213] As an extension of this military competence, the constable was by this date the established authority in
cases of treason which had involved raising war against the king.
Edward IV also seems to have been interested in broadening the
constable's jurisdiction to cover other forms of treason and
disaffection. This first became apparent in the 1460s, under John
Tiptoft, but was continued under Gloucester. In 1473 the king
ordered him to look into a dispute between two members of the
goldsmiths' company. After lobbying by the company (the only
extant reference to the matter) Gloucester found that it was a
matter of mutual rancour, of no danger to the crown, and
remitted it to the goldsmiths.[214] He was equally active as admiral,
and in the previous year admiralty business had taken him along
the south coast, where his presence was noted at Southampton
and Lydd.[215] These two offices, coupled with the less formal
influence Gloucester derived from his closeness to the king,
ensured that for contemporaries the duke's importance was
national rather than purely regional.

This did not mean that Gloucester developed a nation-wide
affinity. Given the value attached to a lord's maintenance of his
servants' local interests, national eminence could not, in itself,
create a significant connection in areas where the lord had no
other influence. Lordship without a local dimension was not
particularly attractive and the lord himself would not be as
interested in service outside his immediate sphere of activity. The
effect of Gloucester's national importance was thus largely to
reinforce his regional connection. But, like any major retinue, his
affinity did have a non-regional component. The dependence of
service on mutual local interest was true only of the gentry service
discussed so far in this chapter. Full-time menial servants could
presumably be drawn from anywhere. So could men offering
other professional service. Gloucester's receiver in East Anglia and
the east midlands, Richard Pole, was from none of the duke's
land. He came from Wilton (Wilts.), although the family's
residence there was itself the result of a career move by an earlier
professional administrator; they had come originally from the

---

[213] Metcalfe 1885, pp. 7–8. In general: Keen 1965, chaps. III–IV.
[214] Reddaway 1975, p. 152; Bellamy 1970, pp. 160–3.
[215] Southampton RO, SC 5/1/14 fo. 30; *HMC, 5th Report* p. 525.

north west.[216] Another of the duke's professional servants was the victualler and purveyor Richard Forthey of Faversham (Kent), while one of Gloucester's physicians was a Nottingham man.[217]

Among a lord's professional servants the lawyers formed an important category. Common lawyers tended to develop regional specialisms, however, and there was thus often some correlation between a lord's areas of interest and those of the lawyers who advised him. Gloucester's legal council accordingly displayed a marked northern bias, including among its members Guy Fairfax, Robert Danby, Richard Pygot, Miles Metcalfe and John Vavasour.[218] The Thomas Molyneux feed from the duke's Lincolnshire lands was probably the lawyer of Haughton (Notts.) rather than his kinsman and namesake of Sefton (Lancs.).[219] Lincolnshire also provided a fee for William Huse, later one of the royal justices, while Gloucester's East Anglian lands supported the Suffolk lawyer John Suliard of Wetherden.[220] For all these men, service to the duke was only one of a number of consultancies. Fairfax, for instance, was also retained by the earl of Northumberland, the dowager duchess of Norfolk, the duke of Buckingham and the city of York.[221] Lawyers for whom ducal service constituted a major part of their career were more likely to have been drawn from outside the duke's regional orbit. Morgan Kidwelly, the duke's attorney, seems to be in this category; he was in Gloucester's service by August 1471 and stayed there until Bosworth forced him to find a new master. Morgan came from a family of professional administrators who took their regional colouring from the location of their service, but the family came originally from Wales and one of Morgan's uncles, Owain ap Cadwgan, still held office in the lordship which gave the Anglicized members of the family their surname. The Welsh connection may have brought Morgan to the duke's notice during his control of the Herbert lands, but it was Morgan's legal expertise rather than any regional pull which Gloucester valued. Only after

[216] Thorpe 1928, pp. 200–01; a few extra details are added by Wedgwood 1936, pp. 690–1. For the family's interests in the north: Lancs. RO, DDFz 22.

[217] PRO, C 1/64/907; *HMC, 11th Report* p. 102; *Records of Nottingham* II p. 330.

[218] PRO, DL 29/648/10485; C 81/1640/39–42; Essex RO, D/DQ 14/124/3/43; *Yorks. Deeds* III no. 417.

[219] PRO, DL 29/639/10386–7; Wedgwood 1936, p. 599. He was also of Altcar (Lancs.): PRO, C 67/51 m. 14.

[220] PRO, DL 29/637/10360A.

[221] Lancs. RO, DDK/1746/15 m. 2 dorse; *Test. Ebor.* III p. 306; Dobson, *York Chamberlains' Rolls* p. 151; Rawcliffe 1978, p. 226.

his accession did Richard seek to exploit Morgan's Welsh connections, and by then Morgan's private interests had shifted firmly to the south of England, where marriage had brought him land in Dorset and Hampshire.[222]

Once one looks away from the north, Gloucester's connection appears to fragment. But the disparate elements which made up his southern affinity were linked, both to each other and to the northern retinue, by the same bonds of ducal patronage and personal relationship which gave internal cohesion to the northern retinue itself. Ducal servants from all areas acted together. When John Armourer, from Robert Chamberlain's manor of Gedding (Suff.), needed sureties, he found them in James Tyrell (himself from Suffolk but active in Wales), Robert Fiennes (also of Suffolk), Arthur Pilkington (from Lancashire but then resident in Essex) and William Houghton (of Worcestershire).[223] In the 1480 Scottish campaign, Gloucester's ship the *Anne* of Fowey was captained by the northerner William Blakeston and victualled by the duke's Hampshire servant Thomas Greenfield.[224] For outsiders, too, there was one ducal connection, not several. When Thomas Clifford, acting for John Prince in the dispute over Gregories, approached Gloucester in the matter, he found himself dealing not only with the East Anglian, Tyrell, but with Pilkington, Tunstall and Harrington (all northerners) and with Kidwelly.[225] The same unity can be seen after Richard's accession. In his search for loyal men to reassert royal authority in the aftermath of Buckingham's rebellion Richard did not, as is often implied, turn to northerners as such. He looked to the former ducal retinue, including such non-northerners as Pole, Tyrell and Houghton.

That retinue was one of the great affinities of the Middle Ages, both in scale and cohesion. Traditionally its importance is demonstrated by the fact that it underpinned Gloucester's usurpation and his brief reign. But to see it from this perspective is to distort it.

---

[222] PRO, Prob 11/7 fos. 68v–9, 11/14 fos. 239v–40; *CPR 1467–77* p. 275; *Harl. 433* III p. 205. Morgan's father was made receiver of Kidwelly in 1469: Somerville 1953, p. 642. For Morgan's Welsh role after 1483 see below, pp. 210–11.

[223] PRO, C 244/114/118.

[224] PRO, E 405/69 m. 1 and dorse. Blakeston was presumably a kinsman of the Thomas retained from Middleham, but it is not clear whether he should be identified with the alderman and merchant of Newcastle: PRO, DL 29/648/10485; Blair 1937, p. 53. Greenfield was of Southwell in the parish of Romsey, which was for a time owned by Gloucester: Putnam, *Proceedings* p. 249; Hicks 1986b, p. 36 (n. 43).

[225] Essex RO, D/DQ/14/124/3/40.

Because Richard usurped the throne, his retinue is inevitably seen as inimical to the crown and therefore in an important sense independent of royal authority. In the context of Edward IV's reign, in which the retinue was created, neither assumption is true. The development of the retinue would have been impossible without royal backing and reflected, rather than negated, the king's authority. Within the north itself, Gloucester's connection subsumed that of the crown. Elsewhere, in East Anglia and Wales, that focus for royal servants was provided by others, but Gloucester was still part of the royal connection, not remote from it. In the rest of England, as constable and admiral, he had contributed to the enforcement of royal authority. When he seized power in 1483 he did so not from outside the prevailing political structure but from its heart.

Chapter 2

THE USURPATION

On 9 April 1483 Edward IV died at Westminster. Until the onset of his final illness, some ten days before his death, there is no evidence that his health was failing.[1] His death was, on the contrary, so unexpected that it found several of the key political figures away from court. Gloucester was in the north. The prince of Wales, with his uncle Anthony Woodville, earl Rivers, was at Ludlow. Whatever one's interpretation of the events of the next two and a half months, there can be little doubt that they represent an improvised response rather than a matured plan. It is unlikely that anyone had seriously anticipated a minority. At Edward's death his heir was aged twelve and the king would only have needed to live a few more years to have handed power to an adult heir. As it was, the prince's age could hardly have been more awkward. Too young to rule effectively in person, he was too old to make a minority an attractive prospect. Although conventional wisdom sees a long royal minority as the most daunting prospect any medieval state might face, in many respects a short minority posed more intractable problems. Any distribution of power could be only temporary and everyone involved knew it: a situation which brought its own tensions. In addition, an adolescent king needed to be taken into account in a way that an infant did not. Even if the king himself did not press for an early political role, others might well do so on his behalf as a way of strengthening their own position. Control of an almost adult king was a potent political weapon.

Edward IV's own solution to this problem is unclear – the first difficulty in a notoriously controversial period. It is likely that he did express a preference, for although his collapse was dramatic enough for premature reports of his death to reach at least two

---

[1] The apparently contemporary reference to a deterioration in the king's health noted in *HMC, 9th Report* p. 145 is an editorial interpolation, compare Canterbury RO, FA 6 fo. 32. It was accepted as genuine by Wood 1975, p. 248.

cities, he then rallied sufficiently to add codicils to his will.[2] Whether or not these actually related to the disposition of his kingdom, the implication is that Edward was in a position to make his wishes known. However, no formal record of those wishes now survives. Edward's only extant will is that made before the French expedition of 1475, and on internal evidence it had been modified, if not superseded, by 1483.[3] The only references to Edward's intentions are thus to be found in the various chronicle accounts of the period, of which the most nearly contemporary is that of Dominic Mancini, an Italian visitor to England in 1483 who recorded his impressions shortly afterwards. Mancini also gives the most circumstantial account of Edward's wishes and their reception, and it is his version (with slight modifications) which has become the standard treatment since the rediscovery of his manuscript earlier this century.

Mancini believed that Edward IV had designated his brother Gloucester as protector – a statement which he first introduces with a cautious 'as they say', but which then becomes the cornerstone of his argument. In the absence of formal evidence, this claim cannot be checked, but it has always been recognized that the choice of Gloucester to head the government was an obvious possibility for the dying king. If Edward wanted a protector, the duke was, indeed, the inevitable candidate. Gloucester's position as sole surviving brother of the king, coupled with his outstanding record of service to the crown, would have made it impossible to pass him over, even in a society aware of the dangers which guardianship by a paternal uncle posed to the interests of the heir. But Mancini does not leave the story there. He claims that the council chose to ignore Edward's wishes, preferring the immediate coronation of the young king to a formal minority. Their decision was prompted by fears that the protector might usurp the throne, although Mancini adds that it was supported by the queen's family, who wanted to prevent power passing to Gloucester.[4] Having carried this initial point, the Woodvilles

---

[2] York certainly received early news of the king's death: Palliser 1986, p. 56. Exeter began dating by year of grace on 7 April, suggesting that it had also had premature news of Edward's death: Devon RO, Exeter mayor's court roll, 22 Edw. IV – 1 Ric. III. Codicils: *Crowland* pp. 152–3.

[3] Bentley, *Excerpta* pp. 366–79. The 1475 executors were not the same as those acting in 1483: *Reg. Thome Bourgchier* p. 54.

[4] Mancini pp. 60–1, 70–1. For the question of how far a king could impose his will on his successors, see Roskell 1953, pp. 216–19.

then proceeded to dig in militarily and financially. Mancini records the council's decision to put the queen's brother, Sir Edward Woodville, at the head of a force to be sent against Philippe de Crèvecoeur, who had started an informal war in the Channel. He also notes that the late king's treasure was divided between the queen, Sir Edward and the marquis of Dorset, the queen's eldest son by her first marriage.[5] The picture is thus one of overt factions, with the Woodvilles manipulating the majority of the council against Gloucester and the small group of councillors who supported the idea of a protectorate – an element usually identified with the dead king's friend and chamberlain William lord Hastings, who had personal reasons for fearing an increase in Woodville power and therefore for backing Gloucester. The stability which had characterized Edward IV's last years had thus collapsed, almost overnight, into a struggle for control during the minority which was in the end to lose his son the throne.

At first sight, Mancini's account appears to be supported by other evidence. It is clear, for example, that the council was planning an immediate coronation, with 4 May the chosen date.[6] Sir Edward's military appointment is confirmed by an extant financial memorandum, which also reveals that, alongside Edward's force of 2,000 men, his nephew Dorset was paid for keeping the sea with 1,000 men. There is no way of telling how many of these men were actually raised, but Sir Edward certainly went to sea with a fleet at the end of April, and Dorset was thought to have accompanied him. The same memorandum shows that these measures, costing £3,670, absorbed all Edward IV's cash reserves, and this is likely to be the origin of Mancini's story of the Woodvilles' raid on the king's treasury.[7]

Mancini's emphasis, which implicitly accuses the Woodvilles of theft, is particularly interesting in the light of More's comment on the same episode. Describing Gloucester's subsequent attack on the Woodvilles, More continues: '[Gloucester and Buckingham] said that the lord marquis had entered into the Tower of London and thence taken out the king's treasure and sent men to the sea. All which things these dukes wist well were done for good

---

5 Mancini pp. 80–1.

6 *Crowland* pp. 154–5; Sutton and Hammond, *Coronation* pp. 14–16.

7 Horrox, 'Financial memoranda' p. 220. There is no evidence that the queen received any share of the treasure. For her hand-to-mouth existence after Gloucester's arrival in London, see BL, Harleian ch. 58.F.49.

purpose and necessary by the whole council at London.'[8] There are other indications that Mancini's account, for all its overt criticism of the duke, may be based on a version of events originating in the circle around Gloucester. It casts the Woodvilles as the aggressors and Gloucester as the victim of circumstance. The duke was virtually forced into some sort of counter-offensive to protect his own interests, and his seizure of prince Edward at the end of April could even be justified, although Mancini does not say so, as a return to Edward IV's original wishes.

This raises the interesting possibility that Mancini's insistence that Edward IV wanted his brother to be protector also derives from a version of events put about by the duke after he had seized the prince and was seeking recognition as protector. Certainly one of the shakiest parts of Mancini's account is his attempt to explain why, if Edward wanted a protector, the council sought to overturn his wishes. His suggestion that the council feared a usurpation displays the hindsight to be expected from someone writing after June 1483, when Gloucester had indeed used the protectorship as a stepping-stone to the throne. It is difficult to believe that anyone in April seriously feared that Gloucester had designs on the crown. The duke had a record of close co-operation with the Yorkist establishment, something at least as important in the context of 1483 as his much-emphasized loyalty to his brother. He was not an alien, northern magnate from whom anything might be expected, but a key figure in the reconstructed royal authority which now needed to be preserved for the young king.

This weakness in Mancini's argument has, however, gone unremarked, largely because most commentators have chosen to emphasize Mancini's second point and argue that the real reason for what happened was Woodville hostility to Gloucester. Mancini himself is clear that there was long-standing rivalry between the duke and the queen's family, and this has been accepted by almost every subsequent writer. A clash of interest was therefore inevitable once Gloucester had been chosen protector. But Mancini is here guilty of reading back into Edward IV's reign the tensions which he observed after the king's death. There is no contemporary evidence of hostility earlier than the end of April 1483. Although the personal attitudes of the protagonists are unknown, it is clear that their working relationship was one of co-operation. In particular, Gloucester apparently acquiesced in the Woodville attack on Clarence in 1477/8, the very issue which is usually seen as grounds for their animosity.[9] This does not preclude the possibility that the Woodvilles turned against their former ally in 1483 and cynically excluded Gloucester from the protectorship in order to secure more power for themselves. But this would make nonsense of events at the end of April, when Gloucester was able to seize possession of the prince from an unsuspecting earl Rivers. The earl, who had apparently dispersed his men before meeting the duke, clearly expected no trouble from Gloucester – confidence which would be incredible if Gloucester had just been the victim of a Woodville coup.

Doubts about Mancini's version are reinforced when it is compared with the account produced early in 1486 by the anonymous continuator of the Crowland chronicle. The author was a councillor of Edward IV and is in general a far more reliable source than Mancini. His facts (although not always his glosses) cannot usually be faulted, and he was ideally placed to give the definitive account of events after Edward's death.[10] Although he evidently knew what the king had planned, he nowhere states it explicitly, and his silence has left the field to Mancini's version. But this very silence casts doubt on Mancini's central point that the council actually voted down the king's expressed wishes. As a councillor himself, the author would surely have drawn attention to such a reversal. Instead, he allows it to be assumed that the council's plans for the coronation of Edward V were in line with the king's *sagax dispositio* as embodied in the codicils to his will. This makes it unlikely that Edward had sought a protectorate. The implication instead seems to be that Edward's 'wise ordering' did not envisage a formal minority at all, but entailed the immediate accession of his heir – for which there was a precedent in 1377, when the eleven-year-old Richard II had succeeded his grandfather. This is perhaps also implied by the chronicler's comment that all the councillors 'fully desired the prince to succeed his father in all his glory'.[11] The remark could be no

---

9 Hicks 1980, pp. 150–2, 155–6; see also Lowe 1981, p. 571. Their relationship is discussed further below, p. 121.

10 *Crowland* pp. 80–3 sums up the pointers to authorship. Wood 1986, p. 164 discusses the different quality of facts and glosses, although his explanation of the contrast in terms of John Russell's authorship is unconvincing.

11 *Crowland* p. 152 (my translation).

more than a pious platitude, but the context allows a more specific reading: that the council had agreed to accept the nominal rule of the young king.

This is not a possibility which seems to have been considered seriously hitherto, perhaps because the 1377 precedent was such a disastrous one. But in the circumstances of 1483 an immediate accession may have seemed to offer real advantages. Edward IV's last years (unlike those of Edward III) had seen a return to political stability. His territorial reordering of the 1470s had apparently been a great success, creating a nexus of trusted associates prepared to work in the crown's interests, while those outside the charmed circle seemed, by the end of the decade, to have acquiesced in their exclusion. Against this background, it is likely that Edward's ordering of his kingdom aimed above all to secure continuity. This was already an element in the 1475 will, in which Edward left instructions for the continuance of grants made to 'divers of the lords as well of our blood as other, and also knights, squires and divers other our true loving subjects and servants'.[12] This was in part an act of Yorkist *pietas*, since those who had suffered on the king's behalf are particularly remembered, but it was also a plea for political continuity. That continuity, however, demanded some focus and in 1483 Edward may well have felt that the most effective focus would be provided by his son. This implied no criticism of Gloucester, who, as the recent grant of a palatinate had shown, was still high in his brother's favour. Any elevation of Gloucester to a position of supreme authority during the minority would, however, have destroyed the very continuity which, on this interpretation, Edward was seeking. What was needed was someone outside and above the territorial nexus, requirements fulfilled only by the young king.

This reading of events gains some support from what little is known of the council's role during April, before Gloucester and the prince reached London. Whereas Mancini's version assumes a council increasingly split by faction, as the Woodvilles manipulated it against Hastings and other supporters of Gloucester, the council seems in fact to have been successfully holding a balance between the various elements in government. This can best be seen in the appointment of commissions to assess the subsidy on aliens granted in Edward IV's last parliament, one of the few cases

---

[12] Bentley, *Excerpta* p. 377.

where the council took positive decisions about personnel rather than (as with the sheriffs, for instance) simply confirming Edward IV's appointments.[13] The commissions were not of much political importance themselves, but each of the thirty-two county commissions was headed by a national figure whose selection gives some idea of the balance of power. A distinctively 'conciliar' feature of the commissions is the number headed by leading Yorkist bureaucrats, notably John Russell, bishop of Lincoln and keeper of the privy seal, and John Alcock, bishop of Worcester and president of the council in the march of Wales. Gloucester does not feature at all, something which has been read as a sign of Woodville control of the council. But his omission is because no northern commissions were appointed – something more likely to reflect a readiness to wait for Gloucester's advice than an intention to snub him.[14] That the council had not come under factional control is suggested by its careful regard to the interests of William lord Hastings and the Woodvilles. These were the only elements on the council between which there is any contemporary suggestion of hostility and it is thus significant how evenly they were balanced on the commissions. Hastings headed seven (the highest individual total), while the Woodvilles jointly managed eight, of which Rivers headed three and Dorset five.

On the available evidence, the council's policy after Edward's death can best be summed up as a strenuous effort to preserve the balance of power established in the king's second reign, and this was surely (*pace* Mancini) in response to the dead king's own wishes. The policy thus ensured the Woodvilles, and indeed Gloucester, a continuing place in government and makes it unnecessary to see the events of April 1483 in terms of an immediate power struggle. This does not mean, however, that there were no political tensions. Although the council might have been prepared to accept the Woodvilles' present position, its desire for continuity would have made it unwilling to see Woodville influence extended. It was recognized that the young king was particularly close to his mother's family, and there was therefore a danger that the coronation of the young king would be followed by an increase in the family's power. Anxiety over this question surfaced almost immediately in a dispute about the size

---

[13] *CFR* 1471–85 nos. 692–5, 728–32.
[14] *CPR* 1476–85 pp. 353–5. For the contrary interpretation see Kendall 1955, pp. 168–9; Ross 1981, pp. 67–8.

of retinue to accompany the king from Ludlow to his coronation. As any retinue would be under the command of the prince's governor, earl Rivers, a large force might tilt the balance of power too far in the Woodvilles' favour. Demands for a modest retinue were led by Hastings, who, as the Crowland chronicler makes clear, feared for his own position if the queen's family were allowed to dominate the government. But he had the backing of what the chronicler calls the 'more foresighted' part of the council, and this tacit approval suggests that the argument was not simply that of an 'anti-Woodville' faction, but represented a genuine attempt to avoid rocking the political boat – an attitude in line with what is known of council policy.[15]

In the short term, the squabble was resolved, although the seriousness of the issue is indicated by Hastings' threat to withdraw to Calais, where he was captain, if his demands were not met. According to the Crowland chronicler, the settlement was the result of an initiative by the queen and there is no reason to doubt this. Even if (as seems likely) the Woodvilles were anticipating an increased role after the coronation, it was still important not to alienate the council in the meantime. The queen's apparent reasonableness does indeed seem to have paid off, and the granting of military commands to Dorset and his uncle met with no recorded opposition. But the fears of Hastings and his allies are unlikely to have been entirely removed. Although the council had so far managed to hold a balance, its ability to do so once the king was crowned was more doubtful. It is even possible that a few councillors were sufficiently worried by the prospect for them to advocate a protectorate as a way of blocking Woodville pretensions. There is no hint of this in the Crowland chronicle, but it would correspond with Mancini's picture of a minority on the council wanting a protector, while the majority backed an immediate coronation and conciliar authority. Mancini's account is an inversion of that suggested here, but it is possible that he had the spectrum of conciliar opinion right and then misread its implications.

Whatever the council's response to Edward IV's death, it was soon overtaken by events. At the end of April Gloucester took possession of the young king. The episode is described by all the chroniclers and although their accounts differ in detail, the

[15] *Crowland* pp. 152–5.

outlines are clear.[16] Gloucester, travelling south from Yorkshire, proposed a rendezvous with the prince and his escort so that they could enter London together, and the prince's route was modified accordingly. The duke was also in contact with Henry Stafford, duke of Buckingham, and the two men entered Northampton together on 29 April. They were joined there by earl Rivers, who had left the prince at Stony Stratford and ridden north to greet the dukes, having first dispersed his men among neighbouring villages to ensure accommodation near the prince for the new arrivals. Rivers was warmly received by the dukes, but was arrested early the next morning before the party set off to join the prince. Gloucester and Buckingham then rode to Stony Stratford to take possession of Edward V. His escort was dismissed and some of his closest associates arrested, among them his stepbrother Richard Grey and his chamberlain Sir Thomas Vaughan. The prince himself was taken back to Northampton, where he remained while Gloucester consolidated his position. An extant letter of 2 May, written from Northampton nominally by the prince, requests the archbishop of Canterbury to see to the safe-keeping of the great seal, the royal treasure and the Tower of London. Steps were also taken to postpone the coronation on 4 May, the day on which Gloucester and the prince entered London.

The events at Stony Stratford clearly took the political community by surprise, and their reaction makes it likely that the seizure of the prince was a pre-emptive strike by Gloucester rather than (as Mancini's scenario would suggest) a retaliation for his exclusion from power. The episode should, in other words, be seen as a new departure rather than one more stage in a faction struggle initiated by the Woodvilles, and this places responsibility firmly on Gloucester's shoulders. His action could simply be explained by ambition: his career in the north had shown that he was a man who liked and understood power. But his motives cannot be viewed in isolation from the contemporary situation. Gloucester may well have shared the current anxieties about how the Woodvilles' role would develop after the coronation. A marked increase in their power would challenge what he surely considered his rightful position within the Yorkist polity. It would also threaten the stability of the polity itself, and Gloucester's public pronouncements in this period consistently

[16] For what follows see *Crowland* pp. 154–7; Mancini pp. 74–83 (and notes). There is a useful chronology in Sutton and Hammond, *Coronation* pp. 13–25.

present him as the defender of his brother's achievements against the machinations of the Woodvilles.

It was thus the disruptive potential of the queen's family which Gloucester chose to stress in justifying his action. Before reaching London, Gloucester apparently wrote to the council and to the city's mayor, explaining that he had taken possession of the prince because the circle around the boy had been inimical to the safety of king and kingdom. He gave visual expression to the same point during his entry into the city, when the procession included cartloads of weapons which criers identified as having been captured from the Woodvilles. Gloucester claimed that the weapons had been intended for use against him, a story that he was later to use in an attempt to have the captured Woodvilles executed, although Mancini comments that no one took it seriously.[17] The underlying message of the weapons, that the Woodvilles, by planning a resort to force, threatened the political stability which the council had been struggling to maintain, may, however, have been more persuasive. When news of Stony Stratford reached London, the Woodvilles had tried to whip up resistance to Gloucester.[18] The attempt had failed, and the queen had withdrawn to sanctuary with her youngest son, the duke of York. But the fact that the attempt had been made at all must have given credibility to Gloucester's claim that the Woodvilles were prepared to use force in pursuit of their ends.

Gloucester's justifications for his actions were, however, less important than the underlying realities of the situation. By the time he entered London he was in a commanding position. He and Buckingham had a significant force behind them, and they also had control of the young king. The only way to reverse the situation was by force, and the failure of the Woodvilles' efforts in that direction had demonstrated that no one wanted to risk a slide into civil war. The council thus had little choice but to accept Gloucester's claim to be protector. A few of its members may already have persuaded themselves that a protector was the most reliable counterweight to Woodville influence. Hastings, at least, was reported to be delighted with the turn of events.[19] The rest of the council, whatever their reaction to the initial seizure of the

[17] Mancini pp. 82–3; echoed by More, *Richard III* pp. 23–4.
[18] *Crowland* pp. 156–7 paints a less dramatic picture than Mancini pp. 78–9 (who may again be influenced by views emanating from Gloucester's circle).
[19] *Crowland* pp. 158–9.

prince, must have recognized that Gloucester now offered the best hope of stability in a difficult situation. No formal record of Gloucester's appointment survives, but his title of protector was in use by 8 May, confirming Mancini's claim that the duke took immediate steps to have his position formalized.[20]

Once the council had recognized Gloucester as protector, the duke set about consolidating his position by dismantling the power of the Woodvilles and their allies. His first move was to try and persuade the council to agree to the execution of the imprisoned Rivers and Grey on the grounds that their alleged plan to murder him constituted treason. The tactic, however, failed. The council apparently argued that as Gloucester had not been protector at the time, any attempt on his life could not be construed as treason.[21] The duke therefore had to be satisfied with rather less permanent methods of limiting the Woodvilles' power. From around the middle of May he began to order the confiscation of the family's land, although there were no legal grounds for its forfeiture. The questionable legality of the move may explain why two of the earliest confiscations were authorized by Gloucester personally rather than in the king's name.[22] These are stray survivals, but it is likely that other forfeitures were authorized in the same way. There is, for instance, no recorded order to seize Rivers' land, but its forfeiture was effective by 28 May (when money from it was paid into the exchequer) and on the following day a steward was appointed for the earl's Norfolk land.[23] With the exception of the queen herself and her brother, Lionel bishop of Salisbury, the whole family apparently suffered forfeiture. On 19 May Gloucester ordered Robert Pemberton to seize Wymington (Beds.), the land of Rivers' brother Richard, and on 21 May the tenants of Thorpe Waterville (Northants) were notified that the manor had been granted to Gloucester's ally Francis viscount Lovell. The casualty in this case was Richard Grey, the queen's youngest son by her first marriage. The lordship had been settled on him in Edward IV's final parliament, together with other manors of the duchy of Exeter, as part of a distribution of the duchy lands among the queen's family. The main bene-

---

[20] *Harl. 433* III p. 16, the main series of signet enrolments began on the next day, *ibid.* p. 1; Mancini pp. 82–5.
[21] Mancini pp. 82–5.
[22] *Harl. 433* III p. 216.
[23] PRO, E 401/949; *Harl. 433* I pp. 51, 55.

ficiary had been Grey's brother Dorset, whose heir had been married to Anne, the daughter of the dowager duchess of Exeter by her second husband. Gloucester was clearly intent on over-turning the settlement, and as well as seizing Richard Grey's share, he ordered the young duchess to be handed over to his leading supporter the duke of Buckingham, presumably as a preliminary to resuming the whole duchy.[24]

Some of the Woodvilles' associates also came under attack. The only one to suffer the loss of his land seems to have been the queen's cousin Richard Haute, who was among those arrested at Stony Stratford. Gloucester ordered the seizure of Ightham Mote (Kent) on 14 May and the doubtful legality of the move is suggested by the duke's use of one of his northern associates, Sir Thomas Wortley.[25] Several men connected with the queen's family lost office. The most eminent was Thomas Rotherham, archbishop of York, who was replaced as chancellor on 10 May by John Russell, bishop of Lincoln. This prompt removal suggests that he was identified with the Woodvilles, although More is alone in the story that Rotherham had delivered the great seal to the queen when she went into sanctuary. The archbishop remained out of favour. He was one of those arrested in June, when Richard was moving towards the throne, and this was apparently accompanied by some more or less official seizure of his temporalities. In September Richard wrote to the tenants of the archbishopric ordering them not to withhold their duties from Rotherham: 'We not willing any of his said rents and duties so to be withholden from him for any thing displeasing us.' At the least, the order suggests that the archbishop was so out of favour in high quarters that his tenants had risked withholding their money.[26]

Among others who lost office at this time were two of the sheriffs inherited from Edward IV, who were replaced on 13 May. In Southampton, Robert Poyntz was replaced by William Berkeley of Beverstone (Glos.). Poyntz had married the illegitimate daughter of earl Rivers and was clearly suspect as a result, although the choice of Berkeley, a kinsman, to replace him perhaps implies a wish not to antagonize Poyntz's associates.

---

[24] *Harl. 433* III pp. 3, 216; *Rot. Parl.* VI pp. 217–8. For the duchy of Exeter see further below, pp. 122–3.

[25] *Harl. 433* III p. 2.

[26] More, *Richard III* pp. 21–3; *Crowland* pp. 158–9; Leathes, *Grace Book A* pp. 172–2; *Harl. 433* II pp. 17–18.

Berkeley had earlier, on 9 May, replaced Poyntz as constable of Carisbrooke castle – a politically sensitive office at a time when Sir Edward Woodville's fleet was lying in Southampton Water. Finally, on 21 May, the office of constable of St Briavel's (Glos.) which Poyntz had held with Rivers and Thomas Baynham was regranted to Baynham and Richard Williams. Baynham was a local man, of Westbury (Glos.), and his survival in office again suggests that Gloucester was anxious to avoid upsetting local interests unnecessarily.[27] In Kent, Edward IV's sheriff had been William Haute, brother of the arrested Richard Haute, and he was now replaced by Sir Henry Ferrers of Peckham, a former servant of Edward IV and a nephew of William lord Hastings. Another Haute, Edmund, lost an annuity to Walter Hungerford, who petitioned for it at the end of May: an indication that the family's gains from royal service were recognized as being available for redistribution.[28]

At this stage, however, only a small number of men were so closely identified with the Woodvilles that they were perceived as a threat by Richard. Most of Edward IV's servants had accepted Gloucester's appointment as protector and were prepared to acquiesce in his attack on the Woodvilles. The new chancellor, John Russell, traditionally seen as no friend to Richard, was prepared to make pointed and hostile references to earl Rivers in his draft speech for the opening of parliament.[29] Former servants of Edward IV, and of the queen herself, were among the beneficiaries of the Woodvilles' disgrace. Robert Pemberton, used by Gloucester to seize Woodville land, had been one of Edward IV's ushers of the chamber (a post he was also to hold under Richard III) and had been appointed by the queen as parker and warrener of Higham Ferrers (Northants) in 1468. John Reynsford, made parker of Dorset's forfeited manor of Woodham Ferrers (Essex) on 22 May, was the son of one of the queen's annuitants.[30] The use of such men probably again reflects a desire

---

[27] *CFR* 1471–85 nos. 694, 730; *Harl. 433* I pp. 26–7, III p. 1; *CPR* 1476–85 p. 261; Maclean 1887, p. 151. Poyntz's stepfather was Sir Edward Berkeley, the uncle of William Berkeley.

[28] *CFR* 1471–85 nos. 696, 732; *Harl. 433* I p. 48; Hampton 1979, no. 410. The summary of the Haute pedigree in Sutton 1982, pp. 54–5, corrects Conway 1925, p. 120.

[29] Nichols, *Grants from the Crown* pp. xl, xli. For Russell's reservations see *Stonor Letters* II p. 161; Rous, *Hist. Regum Angliae* p. 213; Knecht 1958, pp. 123–4.

[30] PRO, SC 6/342/5560–1; *CPR* 1467–77 p. 590; *Harl. 433* I p. 36; Somerville 1953, p. 423; Myers, 'Household of Queen Eliz.' p. 467.

to minimize local upheaval and, more specifically, to avoid alienating the circle of royal servants beyond the immediate Woodville group. But the appointments were presumably also made on the assumption that the men concerned could be relied upon to obey Gloucester rather than the Woodvilles, an assumption which, during the protectorate, seems to have been vindicated.

This can be seen particularly clearly in the measures taken against Sir Edward Woodville, who, according to Mancini, had left London the day before news of Rivers' arrest reached the city. Gloucester immediately recognized the threat posed to his own position by Woodville and his fleet, and the first recorded actions of the new regime include an overhaul of the officials in strategically important castles around the Solent. On 9 May William Berkeley was put in charge of the Isle of Wight, and the lieutenant of Porchester, of which Woodville was constable, was ordered to deliver the castle to William Ovedale. But Woodville had the council's authority for his command of the fleet and there are signs that Gloucester at first felt the need to move cautiously. On the next day Sir Thomas Fulford and John Halwell were ordered to sea with all haste, 'to go to the Downs among Sir Edward and his company'. The phrasing is ambiguous, perhaps deliberately so, but suggests that for the moment only surveillance was intended. Not until 14 May did Gloucester come into the open, and Edward Brampton, John Welles and Thomas Grayson were ordered to take Woodville. William Berkeley, William Ovedale and Roger Kelsale were made responsible for victualling the ships, and were also authorized to receive all those prepared to make their peace with the new regime except Woodville himself, Dorset (the only indication that he might have joined his uncle) and Robert Ratcliffe, a former associate of Rivers at Calais.[31] Ironically, on the same day an unsuspecting Woodville, describing himself as 'uncle unto our said sovereign lord and great captain of his navy', was signing an indenture with the patron of a carrack lying in Southampton Water. Woodville had seized £10,250 in English gold coin from the vessel on the grounds that it was forfeit to the

---

[31] Mancini p. 81; *Harl. 433* III pp. 1–2. Dorset's actual whereabouts are unknown. For Ratcliffe see Ives 1968, p. 221; he was porter of Calais and held land there: PRO, DL 42/19 fo. 23–v; Anderson, *Letters* p. 26; *Cely Letters* pp. 259, 283–4. He was the son of John of Attleborough (Norf.) and should not be confused with his namesake in Richard's service.

crown, and by the indenture bound himself to give the patron its value in English merchandise if that proved not to be the case.[32]

Gloucester's move against Sir Edward proved only partially successful. Most of the fleet surrendered, but Woodville himself, with two ships, managed to make good his escape, presumably with the gold coin, of which nothing more is known. The interest of the episode lies in Gloucester's ability to command his brother's men, even in controversial assignments. With the possible exception of Fulford and Halwell, all the men concerned had been in Edward IV's household. Grayson was a Plymouth merchant and yeoman of the crown, who had recently been involved in maritime activity against pirates in the south west.[33] Brampton was a gentleman usher with extensive mercantile interests, and Welles another yeoman of the crown. The men made responsible for victualling were all active in and around Southampton. Berkeley, an esquire of the body, was constable of Southampton itself. Ovedale, another esquire of the body, was from Wickham, a few miles to the east, while Kelsale, a yeoman usher, was customer of Southampton. Gloucester also employed Kelsale on another sensitive task around this time, sending him to Beaulieu abbey in case the marquis of Dorset should seek sanctuary there.[34] The apparent willingness of such men to support Gloucester casts doubt on Mancini's claim that the fleet only deserted Woodville because they were tricked by the Genoese crews of the commandeered vessels.[35] Although the story is probably a fair reflection of the Italians' unwillingness to find themselves in the middle of an English war, most Englishmen seem to have acknowledged Gloucester's authority.

The attacks on the Woodvilles should not be taken as typical of Gloucester's approach as protector. In most other respects he seems to have been anxious to preserve the status quo, and there was relatively little reshuffling of office. The major change in the central administration was the removal of Rotherham as

[32] Horrox, 'Financial memoranda' p. 216.

[33] Grayson: *ibid.* p. 219; PRO, C 67/51 m. 28; E 404/78/3/25; E 405/71 m. 2. Fulford, of Fulford (Devon), had been given the keeping of the sea in the west country in 1481: PRO, C 81/1390/10; C 67/51 m. 2. Halwell was also a Devonian, from Bigbury.

[34] Brampton: Collier, *Household Books* p. 4; Roth 1920. Welles: *CCR 1476–85* no. 816. Berkeley: *CPR 1467–77* p. 447; *CPR 1476–85* pp. 35, 88, 105, 135. Ovedale: *Archaeol.* 1 p.352; Wedgwood 1936, p. 901. Kelsale: *Archaeol.* 1 p. 353; Horrox, 'Financial memoranda' p. 233; Southampton RO, SC 5/1/18 fo. 24v.

[35] Mancini pp. 84–7.

chancellor. Russell, who replaced him, had been keeper of the privy seal, and that office was in turn filled by John Gunthorpe, clerk of parliament and dean of the late king's household. This amounted to little more than a regrading of established Yorkist bureaucrats, and the same can be said of the exchequer, where the office of treasurer, left empty by the death of the earl of Essex, was filled by the earl's former deputy John Wood.[36] Gloucester's commitment to continuity can most clearly be seen in the signet office. Royal secretaries were notoriously vulnerable to dynastic change, since they were so close to the king, but Edward IV's secretary, Oliver King, remained in office until mid June.[37] Another confidential royal servant, however, fared less well. Edward's treasurer of the chamber, Sir Thomas Vaughan, had been arrested at Stony Stratford in his capacity as chamberlain of the prince of Wales and was apparently not replaced.[38]

At a local level, Gloucester's changes were largely confined to filling gaps left by the removal of the Woodvilles. In the duchy of Cornwall (part of the patrimony of the prince of Wales), Rivers' office of receiver went to John Sapcote, one of Edward IV's esquires of the body, who had been active in the Fitzwarin estates in the south west since at least 1477. The stewardship of the duchy was given to John lord Dynham, who had been one of Edward IV's leading associates in the south west and as such had already had dealings with the duchy.[39] The office of controller of the coinage of tin, previously held by Sir Thomas Vaughan, passed to another of Edward IV's household men, Avery Cornburgh, who had been feodary of the duchy and occupier of the mines in Devon and Cornwall.[40] In the prince's earldom of Chester there were even fewer changes. Thomas Fouleshurst of Crewe replaced Richard Grey as constable of Chester. At a lower level, the portership of Beeston went to William Brenner after the death of the previous holder. Brenner was the prince's man rather than

[36] Storey 1958, p. 87; Emden 1963, pp. 275–7; *Harl. 433* I p. 15; Kirby 1957, pp. 674–5; Roskell 1959a, pp. 24–6. There is no record of the appointment of another under-treasurer until Wood's death, when lord Audeley became treasurer and Avery Cornburgh his deputy: PRO, E 404/78/3/63; *Harl. 433* I p. 280.

[37] Otway-Ruthven 1939, pp. 66–7. The last extant warrant signed by King is 9 June, but there is then a break in the series until September: PRO, PSO 1/56/2848–9.

[38] *Crowland* pp. 156–7; Vergil p. 540. For Richard's later revival of the office see below, p. 301.

[39] *Harl. 433* I pp. 18, 20; *CCR 1476–85* no. 264; *CPR 1467–77* pp. 173, 176; *CPR 1476–85* pp. 218, 228; Chope 1918, pp. 437–58.

[40] *Harl. 433* I pp. 41–2; *CPR 1476–85* p. 41.

Gloucester's, and was to be removed from office after Richard's accession.[41] His appointment is a further indication that Gloucester was not indulging in a witch-hunt outside the immediate Woodville circle. Other servants of the prince who continued to hold office in the earldom were his steward of the household, Sir William Stanley, and Robert Roo, his gentleman of the pantry.[42]

In all these appointments Richard was choosing men who were acceptable to Yorkist opinion and probably to the prince himself. The same attitude can be seen in the matter of Edward V's household. When Gloucester had taken control of the young king he had dismissed the boy's personal attendants and arrested at least two of them: Vaughan, the chamberlain, and Richard Haute, the controller.[43] But this was not the prelude to surrounding the new king with the duke's own men. In the period before Edward V's deposition only a handful of references to his household survive, but all the men named were former servants of Edward IV. Among those assigned a specific household office, rather than loosely designated as 'our servant', are the esquires of the body John Norreys and Walter Hungerford, and the usher of the chamber Edward Hardgill. All three had attended Edward IV's funeral in the previous month, as had several other former royal servants who can be associated with Gloucester in this period.[44] The implication is that the dead king's household had stayed together more or less formally and that these were the servants into whose care Edward V was given – an approach consonant with Gloucester's apparent desire to preserve the status quo.

One corollary of that desire was that, apart from the Woodville forfeitures, little patronage became available for redistribution. With so little at Gloucester's disposal, it is striking that most of his grants went to former servants of his brother. It has to be assumed that the recipients were at least acceptable to Gloucester, and some can be shown to have had dealings with him in the previous reign. Cornburgh, for instance, had organized the finances of the 1481 expedition against the Scots, which had been led by the duke. Also involved on that occasion was John lord Howard, whom

---

[41] PRO, SC 6/782/8–9; *Harl. 433* I pp. 44–5.

[42] PRO, SC 6/782/8. Roo later transferred to the service of Richard's queen: DL 42/20 fo. 45–v.

[43] *Crowland* pp. 156–7; Orme 1984, p. 124.

[44] *Harl. 433* I pp. 21–2, 48, III pp. 8–9; *Archaeol.* I pp. 350–3.

Gloucester now made chief steward of the duchy of Lancaster in the south in place of the dead earl of Essex.[45] But, as a key figure in his brother's polity, Gloucester probably knew most of his brother's leading servants. It is more significant how little patronage was going to men who were primarily the duke's own servants. Among those who did receive grants, moreover, most received them in areas where they already had influence. Gloucester's associate Francis viscount Lovell, whose estates included land in Oxfordshire along the Thames valley, replaced Richard Grey as constable and steward of the duchy of Cornwall honour of Wallingford (Oxon.), with the right to appoint officers there. In the north west, Richard Huddleston, the heir of the Huddlestons of Millom, was made receiver of Dorset's estates in Lancashire and Cumberland.[46] Gloucester showed no desire to unleash a northern invasion of the south, although a few northerners did receive minor pickings there. William Tunstall, kinsman of Richard's councillor Sir Richard Tunstall, was made water bailiff of Winchelsea early in the protectorate, for instance.[47]

This judicious and modest distribution of patronage is, however, overshadowed by the massive grants made to Richard's leading supporter, Henry Stafford duke of Buckingham. Chroniclers are undecided as to who took the initiative in joining forces, but all are clear that once the two dukes had met at Northampton, Buckingham became Gloucester's *alter ego*. The Crowland chronicler, in his discussion of events at Stony Stratford, makes no distinction between the contribution of the two dukes. Mancini is more concerned to emphasize Gloucester's role, but adds that Buckingham 'was always at hand ready to assist Gloucester with his advice and resources'.[48] This equality technically came to an end when Gloucester was made protector, but Buckingham's importance continued to be recognized and his reward was on a commensurate scale. Indeed, 'reward' is a rather weak description

[45] Collier, *Household Books* p. 4; *Harl. 433* I p. 7; Somerville 1953, p. 429.
[46] PRO, SC 6/1302/1 m. 5; *Harl. 433* I p. 39, III p. 3.
[47] *Harl. 433* I p. 7.
[48] *Crowland* pp. 154–7; Mancini p. 83 (Armstrong's translation). On the question of who approached whom, the Crowland chronicler and Vergil avoid the issue, Mancini and the Great Chronicle of London give the initiative to Gloucester, More cannot decide: *Crowland* pp. 154–5; Vergil p. 540; Mancini pp. 74–5; *Great Chron.* p. 230; More, *Richard III* pp. 42–3, 88.

of something which has the appearance of a deliberate partition of authority. Gloucester was protector, but Buckingham was given an independent satrapy consisting of Wales, the March and three southern English counties.

The series of grants which implemented this transfer of power began on 15 May. Buckingham was made constable and steward of all the royal land in Shropshire, Herefordshire, Somerset, Dorset and Wiltshire and was given power of array in the same counties. He was made justiciar and chamberlain of both north and south Wales and was to take over the offices of constable and steward of royal lands in Wales as they fell vacant. The grant specifically included the right, during the royal minority, to exercise the king's patronage throughout the area concerned. The Welsh estates put under Buckingham's control in this way included the earldom of March and, in case there should be any doubt about Buckingham's quasi-regal status, the chancellor of the earldom was told to take his orders from the duke. On the next day, 16 May, a separate grant gave Buckingham the offices of constable, steward and receiver of the duchy of Lancaster honour of Monmouth. A warrant issued on the same day makes it clear that Buckingham's authority extended over the duchy of York lordship of Ludlow, not specifically mentioned elsewhere. In the following ten days a series of warrants authorized payment for these various responsibilities, including a fee of 1,000m as justiciar. Finally, on 26 May, the duke was granted the rule of the Gower lands, the Mowbray estates in Wales, previously controlled by Thomas Vaughan and Richard Haute junior.[49]

In political terms, the grants to Buckingham can be partially justified by the need to replace the council of the prince of Wales which, apart from the attack on its Woodville members, had lost its focus with the accession of Edward V. But the scale of the grants leaves no doubt that the primary aim was the aggrandizement of Buckingham. Power which under Edward IV had been distributed through a network of royal servants would now gradually become concentrated in one man. The abnormality of these grants in the context of the protectorate is not, however, only a matter of scale. They are the first indication that Gloucester was willing to make significant changes in the power structure

---

[49] PRO, PSO 1/56/2834–5, 2840–5; *Harl. 433* I pp. 8–13, 16–17, 28–34, 47, III p. 2; *CPR 1476–85* pp. 222, 288.

inherited from Edward IV. The wholesale nature of the grants also threatened the interests of men not recognized as opponents of the regime, something which Gloucester was careful to avoid elsewhere. Although Buckingham was to take possession in most cases only as offices fell vacant, the existence of such a powerful reversionary interest could only be seen as a threat by existing office holders. Their fears are unlikely to have been eased by the outright grant of office in Monmouth to Buckingham, which dispossessed the holder, John Mortimer. He was one of Edward IV's servants and went on to become an esquire of the body of Richard III, but he never regained office in Monmouth and deserted Richard before Bosworth.[50]

The distribution of patronage and the related question of internal security were not the only problems exercising the protector during May and early June. Edward IV's financial legacy was not as healthy as is usually assumed and the administration seems to have found itself juggling income and expenditure with more than usual anxiety.[51] At the root of the problem were the Scottish campaigns of 1480–2, which had not only been expensive in themselves but had brought continuing expenditure on defence, notably through the acquisition of Berwick. This border town, captured by Gloucester and clearly close to his heart, was reckoned by the exchequer to cost £700 a month in defence – a charge which brought relatively little by way of increased security in return. On top of this recurrent expenditure, Gloucester was pressing for a major rebuilding programme, to include not only repairs to the castle and town walls, but the construction of 120 new houses at an estimated cost of £1,600. Before his death Edward IV had also initiated military activity against France, following Louis XI's renunciation of some of the key terms of the 1475 treaty of Picquigny. By the time Gloucester arrived in London the council had already committed a considerable amount of money. The fleet sent against de Crèvecoeur, together with arrangements to send an expeditionary force to France, cost around £3,670 – money which was probably wasted since the duke disbanded the fleet as part of his measures against the

---

[50] *Harl. 433* I pp. 16–17; Somerville 1953, pp. 648–9. Household status: *Rot. Parl.* VI p. 201; *CPR* 1476–85 p. 502.

[51] Unless otherwise stated all the financial details which follow are taken from Horrox, 'Financial memoranda'.

Woodvilles. The council had also sent an extra 300 men to Calais immediately after Edward's death, pushing the monthly wages bill there up to £627.[52] On top of this military expenditure, the government had to find the cost of Edward IV's funeral (£1,886) and the cost of Edward V's coronation, now rescheduled for 22 June.

By the time Gloucester took control, the cash left by Edward IV had been absorbed by these military costs and there was relatively little money coming in. There are signs that the system of chamber finance had collapsed following the death of the king and the arrest of his treasurer of the chamber, and this may have meant that in the short term royal receivers were retaining issues in their own hands until the situation clarified. Edward's parliamentary grant of tonnage and poundage had automatically lapsed at his death, although the government attempted to go on collecting it, apparently on the assumption that it would be regranted in the next parliament, summoned for 25 June. The London mercers petitioned the council against collection of the subsidy and Gloucester sent word to the treasurer of the exchequer that collection should be halted.[53] The king's death had not, however, cancelled the grant of a tax on aliens granted in his last parliament and this fell due at Midsummer, although £400 was already assigned to the household and the remainder apparently earmarked for the coronation. Against this background of financial strain it is not surprising that one of Gloucester's first recorded actions as protector was to summon convocation in the hope of raising money from the clergy of the southern province. In fact the meeting was forestalled by the deposition of Edward V, but by then the government had raised some £1,680 from the bishops in anticipation of a grant.[54] Gloucester was also to some extent underwriting the costs of government himself. He received no payment for his attendance on the young king and he also paid £800 towards the king's expenses, including the cost of the royal household – a contribution which must have enhanced his political prestige.

This period of about five weeks, in which Gloucester and the

---

[52] PRO, E 405/71 m. 2 dorse.

[53] Lyell and Watney, *Acts of Court* pp. 149, 152–4. For the assumption that the next parliament would renew the grant: Horrox, 'Financial memoranda' p. 217.

[54] *Harl. 433* I p. 16. A tenth was not granted until 1484: McHardy 1984, p. 188.

council governed in apparent harmony, provides an unfamiliar perspective from which to view Gloucester's subsequent usurpation. It is a period almost entirely ignored by the chroniclers, whose emphasis on the dramatic has the effect of telescoping these weeks. In Mancini, for instance, the removal of York from sanctuary in the middle of June follows immediately upon the measures taken against Sir Edward Woodville in mid May, with the events seen as consecutive steps by Gloucester towards the throne. The result is to make more plausible Mancini's claim that from the seizure of the prince at the end of April some men were suspicious of Gloucester's ultimate intentions. But this version is shaped by hindsight. It is more likely that by mid May contemporaries had recovered from any anxieties prompted by the seizure of the prince and were prepared to accept Gloucester's protectorship at face value.[55] Certainly Polydore Vergil seems to have fallen victim to his own condensed chronology when he argues that it was the events at Stony Stratford which caused Hastings to mistrust Gloucester and so led to Hastings' opposition and execution.[56] Apart from the inherent illogicality of this version, when all the available evidence suggests that Hastings had wanted Gloucester to take a major role, it ignores the weeks of apparently good relations between the two men which followed Gloucester's arrival in London. It is true that Hastings' own gains in this period were modest, consisting only of the mastership of the mint, but his interests were respected. One of the two new sheriffs was his nephew, while two of his feoffees received royal patronage: Thomas Kebell was made attorney of the duchy of Lancaster and William Chauntry replaced John Gunthorpe as dean of the king's chapel. The grant of the chancellorship of the earldom of March to William Catesby may also have owed something to Hastings, although, given the location of the office, probably more to another of Catesby's patrons, the duke of Buckingham.[57] As late as 5 June, the candidates for knighthood at the impending coronation included a number of Hastings' men and that this was in response to Hastings' own wishes is suggested

---

[55] Mancini pp. 82–9. By mid May towns such as Southampton and Exeter, which had been dating by year of grace since Edward IV's death, had reverted to dating by regnal year, with the earliest examples 13 and 19 May respectively: Southampton RO, SC 7/1/9; Devon RO, Mayor's court roll 22 Edw. IV – 1 Rich. III.

[56] Vergil pp. 540–1.

[57] CPR 1476–85 p. 348; *Harl. 433* I pp. 6, 8, III pp. 6–7; Ives 1983, pp. 63, 94–5.

by the fact that most were not subsequently knighted at Richard's coronation.[58]

This peaceful interlude between Gloucester's assumption of the protectorship and the events which culminated in his accession challenges those historians who see his usurpation as a panic response to growing insecurity.[59] By mid May the duke had been accepted as protector by most of the Yorkist establishment. The support of his brother's men gave him a nexus of servants throughout the country, the value of which can be seen in his measures against Sir Edward Woodville. Gloucester's strength is also reflected in the choice of knights of the shire for the county of Cornwall, one of the few elections to the planned parliament of Edward V for which returns survive. Gloucester had had some links with the county through the former de Vere estates, but he does not seem to have been particularly active there and his influence was overshadowed by the duchy of Cornwall interest. In spite of this, one of the knights chosen in 1483 was Gloucester's close associate Sir James Tyrell. The other, John Beaumont, may also have been to some extent Gloucester's man since he and his putative father Sir Henry Bodrugan went on to become supporters of Richard III in the region.[60] Gloucester's influence may also have been at work in the selection of a duchy of Lancaster lawyer as the new recorder of London in June 1483, although the man concerned (Thomas Fitzwilliam of Mablethorpe, Lincs.) preserved a studied neutrality when, only days after his appointment, he found himself in the middle of the deposition crisis.[61]

All this is not to say that Gloucester faced no problems, but none of them seems to have threatened his tenure of the protectorship. Finance was clearly an anxiety, but it may even have strengthened Gloucester's hand. The queen's presence in sanctuary with her second son, the duke of York, was an embarrassment and one which the council, at least, probably wanted to resolve. Towards the end of May the leading figures in

---

[58] *Harl. 433* II pp. 11–12; Metcalfe 1885, p. 8. The only Hastings men in both lists were Gervase Clifton (a royal servant active in the duchy of Lancaster) and John Babington of Chilwell: Dunham 1955, p. 188 (although it is possible that the Hastings retainer was John Babington of Dethick).

[59] A view succinctly expressed by Loades 1974, p. 89: 'Richard's *coup* showed every sign of hasty contrivance, and of the ruthlessness of chronic insecurity.'

[60] Somerset RO, DD/Wo 37/8/unnumb.; printed in *Trevelyan Papers* pp. 87–8; *CPR 1461–7* pp. 539–40; *CPR 1467–77* p. 297. Tyrell had previously been returned for Cornwall in 1478: Wedgwood 1938, p. 434.

[61] Horrox 1984, pp. 324–5.

government, headed by Gloucester, published an oath to respect the queen's safety if she came out of sanctuary. Their offer was, however, refused and Gloucester may not have been sorry. The queen dowager would probably have been considerably more of an embarrassment at large, and the Crowland chronicler implies that Gloucester did not really want to resolve the question.[62] The other potential problem was what would happen to Gloucester's authority after the young king's coronation, but even this seems to have been settled to the duke's advantage and John Russell, in his draft speech for the opening of parliament, assumed that Gloucester would remain in overall control – although he clearly also felt that this was a departure from precedent which needed to be justified.[63] Given the apparent strength of Gloucester's position, it is difficult to argue that he was panicked into seizing the throne. Throughout May the protectorship had seemed viable. It was Gloucester who chose to put an end to it.

The date by which that choice had been made can be defined fairly precisely, although the motives behind the decision remain obscure. Government was still proceeding as normal on 9 June. The council meeting on that day tackled the question of how to pay for the coronation and the longer-term problem of household expenses. Later the same day, a London correspondent could write to William Stonor that he had nothing new to report.[64] On the next day, 10 June, Gloucester wrote to York under his own signet for military help. He evidently also wrote to the earl of Northumberland for the same purpose since the earl was raising men in the East Riding on 16 June (the day after the duke's letter reached York). He also approached Ralph lord Neville and perhaps others.[65] Only the York letter, however, offers any explanation for this sudden burst of activity. In it Richard appealed for help:

against the queen, her blood, adherents and affinity, which have intended and daily doth intend to murder and utterly destroy us and our cousin, the duke of Buckingham, and the old royal blood of this realm and, as is now openly known, by their subtle and damnable ways forecasted the same, and also the final destruction and disinheritance of you and all

---

[62] Corporation of London RO, Journal 9 fo. 23v; *Crowland* pp. 158–9.
[63] Nichols, *Grants from the Crown* pp. xlvii–xlix; Ross 1981, p. 75.
[64] Horrox, 'Financial memoranda' pp. 216–18; *Stonor Letters* II pp. 159–60.
[65] Kingston upon Hull RO, Bench Book 3A fo. 133v; Raine, *York Records* I pp. 73–5; Kendall 1955, p. 206.

other the inheritors and men of honour, as well of the north parts as other countries that belong [to] us.[66]

Whether Richard had really uncovered a Woodville plot against himself is doubtful. The family, as the main sufferers under his regime, clearly had every reason to seek his overthrow, and it would hardly be surprising if they had been hopefully dabbling in witchcraft – although this was a standard late-medieval smear. What is difficult to believe is that they had suddenly become a real threat to Gloucester. Their attempt to whip up opposition to him when news of Stony Stratford reached London had proved abortive and since then they had apparently been a spent force. Even Gloucester's attack on their inheritance, usually a sensitive issue with the political community, does not seem to have met with resistance. If they had now become dangerous, the only plausible explanation is that they had received significant new support. For many writers this is indeed what had happened, and they point to the execution of Hastings on 13 June as evidence that Hastings (and perhaps by implication other members of the Yorkist establishment) had made common ground with the Woodvilles against Gloucester.

This argument has received wide currency, in part because it again presents Gloucester as the victim of circumstances rather than their manipulator.[67] If there really was a conspiracy against Gloucester, his subsequent actions can be seen as a matter of self-defence, culminating in his seizure of the throne as the only way of achieving long-term security from Woodville recriminations. But this interpretation is open to criticism on two main grounds. One is the difficulty of explaining Hastings' apparent *volte-face*. Most authors who accept the conspiracy also accept Vergil's argument that Hastings was alienated by the manner in which Gloucester made himself protector.[68] This then presents the entire period from May to mid June as a slippery slope down which Gloucester plunged, his attempts to achieve security committing him to progressively more desperate measures. But Vergil

---

[66] Raine, *York Records* I pp. 73–4. Forecasting the duke's death may have had overtones of witchcraft to contemporaries. The first chronicler to claim that Gloucester accused the Woodvilles of using witchcraft against him is Vergil p. 543.

[67] Kendall 1955, pp. 204–8 is the strongest exponent of the conspiracy theory. Others include: Myers 1967, pp. 127–8; Loades 1974, p. 89; Keen 1973, p. 484; Wood 1986, pp. 156–9. Dissenting voices include Wolffe 1974, pp. 842–3.

[68] Vergil pp. 540–1. Even James Gairdner rather grudgingly accepted Vergil's testimony on this point: Gairdner 1898, pp. 61–2.

is here, as argued above, the victim of his own telescoped chronology. It is clear that if Hastings did become disenchanted with his erstwhile ally, the split did not develop until later and therefore, presumably, for other reasons. There are various possibilities. One is that Hastings was unhappy with Gloucester's wish to extend his power as protector beyond the coronation, but this seems illogical when the available evidence suggests that Hastings had earlier welcomed Gloucester as a bulwark against the increase in Woodville power likely to follow the young king's nominal assumption of authority. Somewhat more plausible is the possibility that Gloucester had decided to proceed to the execution of the captured Woodvilles (as his letter to York perhaps implies) and that Hastings, while willing to see Woodville power limited, was not prepared to countenance their execution. Finally, Hastings may have got wind of Gloucester's designs on the throne. This is the most likely, in so far as the threatened deposition of Edward V would provide the strongest reason for Hastings to switch sides, but in that case any conspiracy becomes the result, and not the cause, of Gloucester's decision to take the throne.

A more fundamental difficulty in the way of accepting the conspiracy, whether as cause or effect, is the complete lack of contemporary evidence. No contemporary, except Gloucester himself in his letter to York, mentions a revival of Woodville opposition, and not even Gloucester links it with Hastings.[69] The first writer to make the connection was Polydore Vergil, whose version became, with flourishes, the standard Tudor account. According to Vergil, Gloucester announced to a meeting of the council that the Woodvilles were using witchcraft against him and then formally denounced Hastings for his involvement before calling in men at arms to arrest him.[70] This is broadly the version adopted by proponents of the conspiracy theory. But Vergil's presentation of the episode makes it clear that he thought the accusation had no validity and was merely an excuse for Hastings' execution. The more nearly contemporary Mancini shares this view of Hastings' removal as an unprovoked attack, but presents it without any reference to the Woodvilles. In his version, Gloucester met with Hastings and his allies in the Tower, and

---

[69] Mancini pp. 88–93; *Crowland* pp. 158–9; Green, 'Hist. notes' p. 588. Simon Stallworth, whose letter to William Stonor is the most strictly contemporary account, is also silent on the issue: *Stonor Letters* II p. 161.

[70] Vergil p. 543; More, *Richard III* pp. 47–9.

cried out that he had been ambushed, whereupon waiting soldiers rushed in and cut down Hastings on the spot. This has usually been rejected, on the grounds that other sources suggest that Hastings was executed rather than murdered – Armstrong going so far as to suggest that such a murder would be un-English and that Mancini has been led astray by Italian precedents.[71] But Mancini's basic point – that Gloucester had set up a fake attack on himself as an excuse to deal with Hastings – seems eminently plausible. It was the very tactic which he had tried to use against the Woodvilles after Stony Stratford and which had then failed because the council refused to sanction their execution. For Gloucester to go one step further and actually stage the ambush so that his enemies could be dealt with there and then would seem a logical refinement of the earlier scheme.

The exact mechanism of Hastings' fall is, however, less important than the motives behind it. The most likely explanation of the episode is that it was a pre-emptive strike, designed to smooth Gloucester's way to the throne. But if Gloucester chose to act against Hastings, rather than being stampeded into it by his discovery of a conspiracy, why did he choose to show his hand before his troops reached London and before he had control of the other possible claimants to the throne?[72] Edward V was in his hands, and so probably by this date was Clarence's son, Edward earl of Warwick, who was barred by his father's attainder, but whose title was otherwise better than Richard's own.[73] But that still left Edward IV's second son, Richard duke of York, who was in sanctuary with his mother and did not emerge until 16 June. One recent solution to this apparent illogicality was an attempt to reorder the two key events, so that the removal of York from sanctuary preceded the execution of Hastings. But this, although attractively tidy, is also clearly incorrect. For all its problems, the traditional order must stand.[74] It is this which strengthens claims that Richard's usurpation was a series of panic responses rather

---

[71] Mancini pp. 90–1 and notes.

[72] Wood 1986, p. 157 sums up the argument: 'if Richard himself had fabricated this crisis, he could have afforded to wait; but if he did not, he could not – and he didn't.'

[73] Mancini pp. 88–9. If his statement that Warwick was placed in the household of Anne Neville is taken literally, the earl must have reached London after her arrival on 5 June: *Stonor Letters* II p. 160.

[74] Thomson 1975, pp. 28–30. The debate was opened in Hanham 1972. For subsequent contributions, see the list in Ross 1981, p. 84 (n. 62), plus Sutton and Hammond 1978; Green, 'Hist. notes' p. 588; Wood 1986.

than a coherent scheme. But this is not the only explanation. It is possible that Richard's letter to York did mark the beginning of a planned chain of events but that something then forced his hand and he found himself having to deal with Hastings before his plans had matured. What the 'something' was can only be speculation. News of Richard's letter to York may have leaked out and alerted Hastings. Or perhaps Gloucester had simply discovered that Hastings' distaste for Woodville authority would not, after all, extend to the deposition of Edward V. Mancini, as well as later sources, has references to Gloucester sounding out the loyalty of Hastings and others, and a clumsy enquiry may have alerted Hastings to the duke's intentions as well as warning Gloucester that Hastings would not co-operate.

Whatever one's interpretation of these events, however, attempts to explain away the chronological oddity of the attack on Hastings should not be allowed to obscure the fact that in practice it did not stop Richard taking control of the duke of York. It is even possible that Gloucester's claims of another plot against him were intended not only to justify Hastings' removal but to impress the council with the gravity of the situation and make them more disposed, not less, to back Gloucester's leadership as the one hope of stability in a worsening political climate. With hindsight, the Crowland chronicler goes further and sees Hastings' death as a cynical move *pour encourager les autres:* 'with the rest of [Edward IV's] faithful men expecting something similar these two dukes thereafter did what they wanted'.[75]

But if the death of Hastings was a sign that Gloucester had made up his mind to take the throne, this was not yet something which could be admitted. In public, the duke continued to make plans for the coronation of Edward V, still scheduled for 22 June. At some point over the weekend of 14–15 June, Gloucester persuaded the council that the presence of York was needed for the coronation. On Monday 16 June the council, including Thomas Bourgchier, archbishop of Canterbury and John Russell of Lincoln, duly waited on the queen at Westminster and persuaded her to hand over York. Neither Gloucester nor Buckingham put in an appearance until the surrender was safely accomplished, and the inference is that the business had been left to Bourgchier, a respected elder statesman, as a demonstration of Gloucester's good

[75] *Crowland* pp. 158–9.

faith.[76] That Elizabeth Woodville submitted is therefore perhaps not very surprising. She was probably prepared to trust the cardinal archbishop when he undertook to guarantee her son's safety and, even if she had doubts, she may have preferred an arrangement involving Bourgchier to the risk of forcing Gloucester into unilateral action. It is more surprising that Bourgchier accepted the role of go-between. Mancini suggests that it was to prevent Gloucester breaking sanctuary, and there are other indications that the duke was prepared to resort to force if negotiation failed. The Crowland chronicler goes further and states bluntly that Bourgchier was compelled to play his part.[77] Either may be true. But it is possible that both views were influenced by hindsight and that matters seemed less clear-cut at the time. Since Gloucester's arrival in London he had seemed to offer the stability which the council wanted. They may simply not yet have accepted that Gloucester now had his own ambitions beyond the preservation of his brother's polity. Even if the unwelcome possibility was beginning to dawn on them, they may not have wanted to be the first to break the consensus. Bourgchier may well have thought, as Mancini implies in a narrower context, that to co-operate with the duke rather than opposing him still offered the best hope of warding off disaster.[78]

If this were the case, the council must have been rapidly undeceived. Later the same day, Gloucester issued writs of *supersedeas* cancelling the parliament summoned for 25 June. He also postponed the coronation of Edward V until 9 November.[79] From this point contemporaries recognized that Richard was moving to take the throne. Business began to wind down as men tacitly awaited the new regime. In the signet office, the last dated document to survive was issued on 11 June. Here business was likely to have been dislocated by the arrest of the king's secretary Oliver King on 13 June, but departments without that problem show a comparable running down of business. The last grants to pass the great seal (although others were in the pipeline) were the appointments of the chief baron of the exchequer and two

[76] *Stonor Letters* II p. 161.
[77] Mancini pp. 88–9; *Crowland* pp. 158–9.
[78] Mancini pp. 88–9; compare also his comment (p. 93) that even after the death of Hastings men hoped for the best: 'because he was not yet claiming the throne, inasmuch as he still professed to do all these things as an avenger of treason and old wrongs'.
[79] Corp. of London RO, Journal 9 fo. 25v; Sutton and Hammond, *Coronation* p. 22 (and notes).

serjeants at law on 14 and 15 June – a last attempt by the establishment to pretend that it was business as normal.[80] This prompt response to political crisis reflects the fact that the progress of grants through the system relied on the initiative of the recipients, who must have realized that grants from Edward V would shortly become worthless.[81] In other departments business ran down more slowly. In the exchequer, 16 June was an average business day but 21 June saw only two small receipts from the customs recorded. The last extant chancery bond is dated 21 June.[82] The next day, Dr Ralph Shaw publicized Richard's claims to the throne in a sermon at St Paul's Cross.[83]

The justification for Gloucester's assumption of power confused contemporaries and has continued to arouse controversy. The fullest version of Gloucester's arguments is to be found on the parliament roll of January 1484 and purports to be the petition presented to Gloucester when he was asked to take the throne in June.[84] It is, however, doubtful whether this genuinely represents the ideas circulating in 1483. The 1484 act is scathing about the misrule of Edward IV:

the prosperity of this land daily decreased, so that felicity was turned into misery and prosperity into adversity and the order of policy, and of the law of God and Man, confounded; whereby it is likely this Realm to fall into extreme misery and desolation, which God defend, without due provision of couvenable remedy be had in this behalf in all goodly haste.[85]

Such attacks on the corruption of the previous regime were the stock in trade of usurping rulers, but it is not the line Richard took in 1483. He was then anxious to win the support of the Yorkist establishment and, both as protector and during his early weeks as king, represented himself rather as the only hope for the continuance of the *good* government of Edward IV. It was only after the rebellion of autumn 1483 had demonstrated that Richard had lost the support of a significant number of his brother's men, that it made political sense to indulge in general criticism of Edward IV's

[80] *Harl. 433* I p. xxii; Green, 'Hist. notes' p. 588.
[81] Although kings often honoured their predecessor's grants, they regarded themselves as under no obligation to do so, particularly after a deposition. Many recipients of grants from Edward IV and V took the precaution of securing a regrant from Richard III.
[82] PRO, E 401/949; C 244/133/15.
[83] Sutton and Hammond, *Coronation* p. 24.
[84] *Rot. Parl.* VI pp. 240–2.
[85] *Ibid.* p. 240.

reign. In June 1483, to judge by Mancini (the only chronicler writing without hindsight in this respect), Gloucester preferred instead to emphasize that he was the legitimate heir of York.

According to Mancini, the sermons preached on 22 June declared that Edward IV himself was illegitimate. This argument seems, however, to have been soon dropped, and in the 1484 act survives only in the oblique remark that Richard, unlike his brothers, had been born in England.[86] It was apparently replaced with the claim that Edward's children were illegitimate, because Edward, before his marriage to Elizabeth Woodville, had been betrothed to another woman.[87] The promulgation of this version seems to have been largely in the hands of Buckingham, who lectured the lords and the mayor and aldermen of London on the subject – the latter for a 'good half hour' according to the Great Chronicle.[88] Mancini reported that the woman in question was a foreigner whom Edward had married by proxy on the orders of the earl of Warwick, a reference perhaps to Bona of Savoy. Mancini may be guilty of garbling the story here, since the woman who later emerged as Edward's betrothed was Eleanor Butler (née Talbot), the widow of Thomas Butler of Sudeley.[89] But it is possible that the details took time to be formulated. Certainly, when Richard himself wrote to the Calais garrison on 28 June, setting out his title, his claim was vague to the point of invisibility. He simply announced that although Edward V had been recognized as the rightful heir, this was only because men were 'then ignorant of the very sure and true title which our sovereign lord that now is, king Richard III, hath and had the same time to the crown of England'.[90] The details of that title are nowhere given, beyond a statement that they were set out in the petition of the three estates which besought Richard to take the crown. This, as suggested above, is probably not the petition enshrined in the 1484 act, but instead, as the Crowland chronicler claims, a straight-forward statement of the pre-contract story.[91]

Whatever the validity of the various claims advanced in 1483–4, they were surely justifications for a decision taken on other

---

[86] *Ibid.* p. 241; Mancini pp. 94–5.
[87] If true, this would indeed have rendered the children illegitimate: Helmholz 1986 pp. 91–103 is the definitive discussion.
[88] Mancini pp. 94–7; *Great Chron.* p. 232.
[89] Mancini pp. 96–7; *Crowland* pp. 160–1; *Rot. Parl.* VI p. 241; Griffiths 1981a, pp. 803, 841.
[90] *Harl. 433* III p. 29.
[91] *Crowland* pp. 158–61.

grounds. Contemporaries certainly regarded them in this light. By the time Shaw preached his sermon, informed opinion recognized Gloucester's accession as inevitable, and this helps to explain the apparent lack of interest with which the most nearly contemporary chroniclers treat the grounds for Edward V's deposition. They are equally brief when it comes to the details of Richard's accession, Mancini in particular treating Gloucester's actual assumption of the throne as something of a tailpiece to the real story. The constitutional issues thus become not much more than flourishes to a *fait accompli.*[92] Gloucester's justification is presented as the armed force at his disposal, and it is against this background that he was petitioned to take the throne by the three estates. To this petition Gloucester agreed and on 26 June, in a ceremony consciously modelled on his brother's accession, he took his seat at Westminster and began his reign.[93]

Within three months of Edward IV's death, therefore, his brother had deposed his son and taken the throne for himself. It is a dramatic reversal and one unparalleled in English history. The reasons behind it, however, and the related issue of where responsibility lies, have still not been entirely explained. Traditional accounts place the blame squarely on Gloucester's shoulders, assuming in effect that his own ambition is an adequate explanation for what happened. Most modern historians, by contrast, have argued that Edward IV himself must take much of the responsibility for the deposition of his heir.[94] The king's willingness to build up the power of his trusted allies, it is argued, set up tensions not only between the beneficiaries and those excluded from power, but within the circle of royal supporters itself. These tensions were held in check by Edward IV but he did nothing to resolve them, and after his death they erupted into the faction struggle which cost Edward V his throne. The interpretation is a valuable reminder that the crisis of 1483 did not exist in a vacuum. Inevitably it had its roots in the previous reign and some of Edward IV's actions made their contribution to events after his death. But the exact nature of the contribution is perhaps less straightforward than is now often assumed.

[92] For an attempt to return them to the centre of the stage: Wood 1975, pp. 269–86; Dunham and Wood 1976, pp. 756–61.
[93] Armstrong 1948a, pp. 51, 67.
[94] The definitive exposition of this view is Ross 1974, pp. 423–6.

Modern discussion of the issue has normally centred on the role of the Woodvilles, who are identified as the cause of a split within the ruling group which lay at the root of the crisis. Their contribution is perceived as threefold: they were long-standing rivals of Gloucester, which virtually guaranteed a power struggle in 1483; the favour shown them by the king had made them unpopular with the rest of the Yorkist establishment; and they were so closely identified with the young king, Edward V, that any limitation of their power could only be made permanent by his deposition. Taken to its logical conclusion, this would present the deposition as a side-effect of the political community's attempt to rid themselves of an unpopular group of upstarts. There are, however, difficulties with this interpretation, some of which have already been mentioned. There is no contemporary support for the suggestion that Gloucester and the Woodvilles were rivals before Edward IV's death, and that the king should therefore have taken steps to remedy the situation. The argument to the contrary is largely an argument from silence, but the silence is suggestive. The local interests of the duke and the Woodvilles coincided at several points, notably in Wales and East Anglia, but also (briefly) in Richmondshire, where the queen's mother, the dowager duchess of Bedford, held one third of the honour until 1472. Had the two interests been hostile, one would expect some evidence of local friction, but there is none. It was only the circumstances of the minority which brought them into conflict, and even then the rivalry should probably not be seen as inevitable. Rivers, by all accounts no fool, apparently still expected co-operation from Gloucester as late as the end of April.

Similarly, it is difficult to accept that hostility towards the Woodvilles from the rest of the political community was a major issue at the time of Edward's death. This is not to deny that they had enemies. They seem to have been an unscrupulous family, willing to exploit their closeness to the crown.[95] But this is a long way from arguing that they were such political pariahs that the deposition of Edward V could seem preferable to a regime dominated by them. It is doubtful whether they had ever been such a serious liability to the Yorkist regime. Their emergence in the mid 1460s had alienated Clarence and Warwick, and for a time, in 1469–70, hostility to the family had become a political

---

[95] For Woodville self-help, see Hicks 1979a.

issue. But most of the Yorkist establishment had remained loyal to Edward IV and the rebels ultimately achieved a precarious viability only by looking outside the realm for support: to Louis XI of France and the exiled Lancastrians whom he harboured. After Edward IV's restoration in 1471 opposition to the Woodvilles became even less effective as a rallying cry, as Clarence's isolation and ultimate downfall suggest. This is not because the family had become less powerful. On the contrary, the birth of sons to the queen in 1471 and 1473 had given her and her kinsmen a more secure political status. But this in itself had made overt opposition less likely.

The Woodvilles' assimilation into the political community was further eased by a less aggressive manipulation of royal patronage on their behalf. There is nothing in the second reign to compare with the king's exploitation of the marriage market as a means of endowing the queen's siblings in the first reign. In part this was simply no longer necessary, but it also represents a shift of royal policy, and members of the family without an adequate endowment did not have the deficiency made good. The only major royal intervention in the land market on the family's behalf was the parliamentary act which allowed the Holland estates to be used as a patrimony for younger generations of the family. The queen's eldest son by her first husband, Thomas Grey, had in the first reign married the king's niece Anne Holland, the daughter and heiress of Henry Holland duke of Exeter by Edward's sister Anne. Anne Holland died without issue by Grey, who remarried the Bonville heiress and had a son, another Thomas. Anne Plantagenet, meanwhile, had divorced Exeter and married Thomas St Leger, by whom she had a daughter, also called Anne. This second Anne was betrothed to the younger Thomas Grey and the bulk of the Exeter lands settled on them, with some reserved to endow the queen's second son, Richard Grey.[96] The arrangement was of dubious legality, as the resort to an act of parliament implies, but it did not challenge other interests. Exeter had been a committed Lancastrian who had suffered forfeiture of his estates to the crown, so that in effect the endowment of the Greys was being made out of the royal lands. Although Richard III later reversed the settlement, he apparently did so only as part of his dismantling of Woodville influence and not out of any sense

[96] *Ibid.* p. 68; *Rot. Parl.* VI pp. 215–18.

that the disposal of the lands had been inequitable. In particular, he did not take the opportunity to restore the land to the heir general, his close ally Ralph lord Neville, but simply added it to his fund of patronage.[97]

There was thus little in the second reign to stir up renewed animosity towards the Woodvilles. They may not have been popular, indeed subsequent events suggest that they were not, but they were tolerated, and there is no evidence that Edward IV's death was followed by an attempt to dislodge them. The council was prepared to give significant military commands to members of the family, and blocked Gloucester's attempts to have Rivers and Richard Grey executed. The only council member who can be seen to be motivated by hostility to the family is William, lord Hastings. The ill feeling between him and the Woodvilles apparently had its roots in the previous reign and it is significant that even those chroniclers who emphasize the Gloucester/Woodville animosity, consider that it was the Hastings/Woodville feud which was worrying Edward IV on his death bed. Mancini claimed that the king then tried to reconcile Hastings and Dorset, and this is echoed by Tudor sources.[98] The story does not appear in the Crowland chronicle, which confirms the existence of ill will between Hastings and the Woodvilles, but without offering any explanation. Mancini, as usual, sees the situation in exclusively personal terms, and explains the animosity between Hastings and Dorset as rivalry over mistresses. There may have been personal antipathy involved, although Mancini's account reads rather like an attempt to rationalize a hostility which he could not explain – as does More's bland assertion that women commonly hate their husband's best friends. In the non-chronicle sources there are suggestions of rivalry over Calais, where Hastings had replaced Rivers as lieutenant in 1471, and there may also have been some friction over the Ferrers inheritance, although this does not seem to have been a major issue.[99] Indeed, the evidence in general is so slight that it implies that any animosities had been held in check by Edward IV and only surfaced fully after his death. The speed with which they then became an issue, however,

---

[97] Compare Pugh 1972, pp. 111–12; Ross 1974, pp. 336–7. Neville did receive land from Richard III, but forfeitures from the 1483 rebellion: CPR 1476–85 p. 427.

[98] Mancini p. 68 (and notes); More, *Richard III* pp. 10–11.

[99] Ives 1968, pp. 221–2. I am grateful to Dr Christine Carpenter for discussing the Ferrers dispute with me.

shows that they were real enough. What is less clear is their effect on the situation. According to Mancini, it was Hastings who stirred up Gloucester against the Woodvilles by sending him letters in which he stressed the pretensions of the queen's family. He also outlined what action the duke should take, providing what was in effect a blueprint for events at Stony Stratford.[100] It is unlikely that Gloucester needed Hastings to prod him into action, although if Mancini is even partially correct it would be significant that the duke's view of events in London was coming from so biased a source. Hastings' contribution more probably consisted of stirring up others by articulating anxieties about the future role of the Woodvilles and, perhaps, by canvassing the possibility of a protector as a viable alternative.

Hastings apart, the degree of opposition to the Woodvilles is difficult to gauge. Although the political establishment apparently accepted that the family was entitled to some role during the minority, its closeness to the young king gave rise to anxiety about how that role would develop. It is significant that whenever Gloucester took a controversial step, such as seizing the prince or sending north for reinforcements, he justified it by reference to a Woodville plot to subvert the state. This was, of course, intended to give him grounds for proceeding against the family, which was potentially his main rival for power during the king's youth, but it was necessary that the accusations be taken seriously and Gloucester presumably thought the Woodvilles plausible scapegoats. Even if, as Mancini thought, not all the details of these 'plots' commanded belief, the Woodvilles' background of aggressive opportunism must have given credibility to the claim that they intended to dominate the young king. Mistrust of the family's ultimate intentions may also explain the ease with which Gloucester was able to dismantle their power. His illegal confiscation of their estates was the sort of action to which the landed classes were normally extremely sensitive but, in the short term, it met with no resistance. This, however, is not necessarily a fair test of the family's unpopularity. By this stage Gloucester was securely in control, while the Woodvilles' influence had collapsed with their loss of the prince. Support for the family against Gloucester must have seemed at best futile, at worst likely to precipitate the

---

[100] Mancini pp. 70–3.

slide into factional conflict which the political community was most anxious to avoid.

The completeness of the Woodville collapse casts doubt on any suggestion that Edward IV had deliberately built up their power as a bulwark for his son – something which would have been tantamount to a conscious factionalization of politics.[101] The family had certainly enjoyed the king's favour, and their identification with the prince of Wales and his brother had brought them a recognized political role. The main beneficiary in both cases was the head of the family, Anthony earl Rivers. His own estates lay mainly in Northamptonshire, but his marriage to the Scales heiress had brought him a group of manors in East Anglia, a regional connection maintained by his second marriage, to Mary Fitzlewis. His influence in those areas was complemented by the queen's possession of the duchy of Lancaster estates in the east midlands and by the marriage of his nephew Richard duke of York to the Mowbray heiress, which gave Rivers a substantial role in the duchy of Norfolk. His strongest formal links were, however, with the prince of Wales. Rivers was the prince's governor and, by the end of the 1470s, steward and receiver general of his estates. This gave him authority not only in Wales but in the earldom of Chester and duchy of Cornwall.[102] Other members of the family were found niches in this empire. Richard Grey, for instance, was made constable of Chester and of the duchy of Cornwall honour of Wallingford, as well as being given the castle and lordship of Kidwelly.[103]

On paper, the Woodville empire is impressive, but it is doubtful whether it can be considered an independent power base. Much of the family's influence derived not from land, but from office holding within the royal demesne, and the implications of this tend to be overlooked. Discussions of Woodville influence usually start from the premise that men with whom the family had dealings were *ipso facto* members of a Woodville affinity, an equation which puts the family at the head of a very impressive connection within the royal government. Thus in Wales, men active within the prince's council are categorized as Woodville associates, as are the officials of the duchy of Lancaster estates held by the queen. Sometimes this is valid. Robert

[101] Ives 1968, p. 224.
[102] *Ibid.* pp. 222–3; Lowe 1981, pp. 555–6.
[103] PRO, DL 42/19 fo. 27v; SC 6/782/8; SC 6/1302/1 m. 5.

Ratcliffe, who was given office in Sheen (Surrey) by the queen, can be identified with the Woodville interest.[104] But many of the men concerned were primarily royal servants, whose independent connections with the Woodvilles were very tenuous. As long as the Woodvilles were identified with the crown this distinction was unimportant, but if the two interests split, as they did in 1483, the loyalties of such men would tend to remain with the crown. John Bardfield is a case in point. He was of Margaretting (Essex) and in 1470 was made receiver of the duchy of Lancaster lands in the south west. This brought him to Rivers' attention, and he became the earl's deputy as receiver of the duchy of Cornwall. In 1483 it was the royal connection which held firm. Under Richard III he was made receiver of the Lancaster lands formerly held by Elizabeth Woodville and was granted the farm of valuable land within the duchy.[105]

The Woodvilles' personal following was thus smaller than is sometimes assumed. In fact, rather than talking of an explicitly 'Woodville' affinity, it is probably more realistic to see the family as part of the royal connection. This, of course, could be said of any of Edward's leading associates, since it was their relationship to the crown which allowed them to draw lesser royal servants into their service. Hastings' retinue was essentially the duchy of Lancaster connection in the north midlands. Gloucester drew on the support of the northern duchy servants. There are, however, differences of emphasis. Gloucester's possession of the northern Neville lands meant that if Edward had withdrawn his favour the duke's power would have been much reduced, but he would still have had a following. The duke, in other words, contributed to the royal connection as well as providing a focus for existing royal servants. The Woodvilles' power, by contrast, was almost entirely derivative, so much so that their identification with the prince was more of a bulwark for them than vice versa. It was perhaps their awareness of this, rather than their arrogance, which led them to emphasize the relationship so strongly after Edward IV's death.[106] When they could no longer claim to act with royal backing they were dangerously vulnerable. The commission of

---

[104] PRO, DL 29/59/1127; and see note 31 above.

[105] Somerville 1953, p. 623; PRO, SC 6/1302/1 m. 5 dorse; DL 29/59/1128; DL 41/34/1 fo. 107.

[106] e.g. in the commissions to levy the subsidy on aliens (*CPR 1476–85* pp. 353–5) and in Sir Edward Woodville's indenture of 14 May (Horrox, 'Financial memoranda' p. 216).

array authorizing Rivers to raise men in the marches, for instance, would have become valueless once it became known that he was out of favour.[107] Similarly, Edward Woodville's fleet posed a threat to Gloucester only as long as the duke's own position was uncertain; once he had been recognized as protector the matter could be dealt with. It was not until Gloucester had seized the throne, and the Woodvilles could again claim to be acting in Edward V's interests, that the family, at least in some circles, regained their political credibility.

It is impossible to make a final assessment of the Woodvilles' contribution to the crisis. Given Mancini's scenario, their role is clear: they selfishly overturned Edward's wishes and set in motion the train of events which led directly to Edward V's deposition. But if it had been Edward IV who wanted the immediate accession of his heir, the events after his death say relatively little about the Woodvilles' intentions. In the short term it was in their interest to co-operate with the rest of the council, and the real test of their ambitions would come after the coronation, when they would be in a position to exploit their closeness to the new king. Any plans they may have had, however, were forestalled by Gloucester's seizure of the prince at Stony Stratford. In taking this action, the duke showed himself to be several jumps ahead of the rest of the political community. Although doubts may have been growing about the Woodvilles' ultimate intentions, there are no signs that anyone else was contemplating direct action against them – or that the family had yet done anything to warrant it. The Woodvilles, in short, may constitute a potential weakness in Edward's scheme of things, but it was Gloucester who actually dictated events, first by seizing the prince and then by taking the throne, and the Woodvilles' importance becomes a question of how far it was they who triggered Gloucester's actions.

The duke's motivation is one of the most controversial aspects of the period. One explanation, at least, can be dismissed: Gloucester was not reacting against his position in the previous reign. Kendall's influential picture of Gloucester as the outsider, alienated from a Woodville-dominated court, will not do. Gloucester was very much an insider, and the rest of those inside, including the queen and her family, were his allies and associates. He was arguably the most powerful man in England after the king

107 Ives 1968, p. 224. For the importance of royal endorsement in raising men see also Williams 1928, p. 183.

and his influence over Edward IV, whether employed on his own behalf or that of others, is beyond question. Given this power, it is possible that Gloucester simply yielded to temptation in 1483, first to dominate the minority and then, when that proved easy, to make himself king. Both his coups began with a ruthless pre-emptive strike from a position of strength. The Woodvilles had given no grounds for complaint when he moved against them at the end of April, and the protectorate was still viable in mid June when he chose to end it.

Gloucester may also have feared that the accession of Edward V would bring a diminution of the power he had enjoyed hitherto. Although he was more powerful than the Woodvilles, they were closer to the prince. This had not been an issue as long as Edward IV was in good health, and his death was so unexpected that it was not preceded by a political regrouping around the heir. It inevitably became an issue, however, after the king's death, and Gloucester's vulnerability was further increased by the death of his kinsman George Neville on 4 May – something which immediately converted the duke's title to the northern Neville lands into a life interest only.[108] Once Richard had launched his attack on the Woodvilles, moreover, he exposed himself to recriminations should Edward V come to power, and this in turn may have played some part in deciding him to take the throne.[109] But his actions were perhaps not entirely a matter of cynical expediency. He may well have believed that the factionalization inherent in Woodville control of the heir posed such a threat to political stability that his own rule was preferable – he may have persuaded himself, in fact, that he was acting for the good of the realm. This was the line he took in his propaganda, but this does not necessarily mean that he did not believe it himself. Which motive was dominant can only be a matter of opinion, but it is in any case unrealistic to grade them too rigorously. Probably they were all present to some degree.

Gloucester's actions after his brother's death are traditionally seen as the triumph of an over-mighty subject, and it follows that Edward IV had been making a rod for his own back when he allowed Gloucester to become lord of the north. There is an element of truth in this. Gloucester's power was largely his

---

[108] Hicks 1986b, pp. 26–30.
[109] The precedent of the previous protector, another duke of Gloucester, was hardly encouraging: Griffiths 1983, p. 38.

brother's creation and that power underpinned his success in 1483. It was, not surprisingly, to members of his own affinity that Gloucester turned for the performance of sensitive tasks. The men arrested at Stony Stratford were sent north for safekeeping. Rivers was taken to Sheriff Hutton, where Sir Thomas Gower and other ducal retainers later witnessed his will.[110] Gloucester used his own men in the arrest of Hastings and the confiscations which followed.[111] It was a northern servant of the duke, John Nesfield, whom More credits with stage-managing Richard's acclamation by the citizens of London.[112] Alongside these individual contributions, Gloucester's northern connection also provided the muscle behind his coup. He wrote north for reinforcements on 10 June and the army assembled at Pontefract a fortnight later, where it witnessed the execution of Rivers, Vaughan and Grey before moving south under the command of Northumberland and Sir Richard Ratcliffe.[113] In the event they were never called upon to fight, reaching London only after Richard had been declared king. But the army's approach was already public knowledge when Gloucester advanced his claim to the throne, and the threat, as Mancini suggests, may have helped to ensure that Richard's usurpation met no overt resistance.[114] Richard himself was certainly grateful for the northern backing, and several of his grants as king were made 'for service done at great labour and charge, in particular about the acceptation of the crown and royal title of this kingdom'.[115]

Richard's coup cannot, however, be presented simply as the achievement of a powerful and independent northern magnate.

---

[110] Bentley, *Excerpta* pp. 246–8. The Richard 'Lexton' among the witnesses is Richard Lepton, a kinsman of the ducal retainer John Lepton of Terrington.

[111] *Stonor Letters* II p. 161; Hanham 1975, p. 167; compare More, *Richard III* pp. 48–9. Rotherham, arrested at the same time, was reputedly given into the custody of Sir James Tyrell (Vergil p. 544), perhaps as an intermediate stage between his initial imprisonment in the Tower (*Stonor Letters* II p. 161) and full freedom, although compare *Crowland* pp. 158–9.

[112] More, *Richard III* p. 76.

[113] *Ibid.* pp. 57–8; *Crowland* pp. 160–1; Rous, *Hist. Regum Angliae* pp. 213–14. Northumberland raised men in his own territory, including the East Riding, and then seems to have taken overall command: Hull RO, Bench Book 3A fo. 133v; Raine, *York Records* I pp. 73–5.

[114] Mancini pp. 96–7; Guth 1986, pp. 188–9.

[115] A paraphrase of PRO, DL 42/20 fo. 8v: a grant to William Evers, a Percy servant who probably joined the northern army. Such details are not always given in *CPR*, e.g. a grant to Thomas Tunstall, calendared as being for help against the 1483 rebels, was also for 'promoting our right and title': *CPR 1476–85* p. 479; Humberside RO, DDCC 114/1.

His own connection may have given him military credibility, but his political credibility derived from his role as a central figure in his brother's polity. This made him an acceptable candidate as protector and, once he held that office, helped to ensure that he could call on the backing of the Yorkist establishment. Although he turned to his own men for a number of controversial assignments, he was able to use his brother's servants for hardly less sensitive duties. Royal household men were sent against Edward Woodville and to search for Dorset. Even when Gloucester was apparently exploiting his own connection, his hand was strengthened by his status as representative of the young king. The northern reinforcements were thus not strictly a private army, but were summoned to aid the protector against insurrection, although there may have been contemporary doubts about the validity of the distinction. York seems to have hesitated over raising men, probably for this reason since it decided that its contingent should wear the city's badge until they reached Pontefract, and then Gloucester's as well.[116] It is, indeed, doubtful how much help Gloucester could have commanded explicitly in order to take the throne: some, almost certainly, but much (if not most) of the backing he enjoyed was given to the protector for the maintenance of stability – a distinction of which Gloucester himself seems not to have been fully conscious.[117]

Although Gloucester's power, both in the north and more generally, derived ultimately from Edward IV, it is difficult to argue that the king was wrong in what he did. His advancement of Gloucester can be criticized only by those who believe that the only good nobleman is an impotent nobleman. Medieval kings did not think in those terms. Gloucester's power was valuable because it ensured royal control of a significant and troublesome part of the country. Nor can Edward be blamed for not foreseeing the ends to which Gloucester might put his power. The duke had been a loyal upholder of the house of York, a central figure in Edward's polity; there was no obvious reason why he should not occupy the same role under Edward V. In this respect, precedent was on Edward's side. Previous minorities had seen squabbles over the distribution of power, but no young king had ever been deposed. Even royal uncles traditionally drew the line at that, something which explains why Gloucester's action seemed so

[116] Palliser 1986, p. 72.
[117] Hicks 1986a, pp. 20–1.

shocking to contemporaries and, perhaps, why he got away with it so easily in the short term.

In an immediate sense, Gloucester must take final responsibility for what happened in 1483. However one explains the motives behind his actions, things happened because he chose that they should: there is nothing in the previous reign which compelled him to act as he did. But although earlier events cannot be said to have caused the crisis, they did have some bearing on how it developed. Like any reign, Edward IV's had produced its share of the disgruntled and disenchanted hoping for better times. There was a legacy of forfeitures from the conflicts of the 1460s. Edward had created a further group of dispossessed by his readiness to manipulate property descents, either to endow his family or to advance the creation of regional hegemonies for trusted supporters. The latter policy could also entail a drastic withdrawal of royal favour from those who did not fit into Edward's plans. The Herbert influence in Wales, for instance, was ruthlessly dismantled in favour of the prince's council at Ludlow.[118] In practice, few grievances against Edward IV became an issue in May–June 1483. This owed something to the thoroughness with which Gloucester outmanoeuvred the opposition, which meant that he did not need to hunt for extra support. But Gloucester also insisted throughout that he stood for the continuance of Edward IV's regime, an emphasis which inevitably played down the political significance of the 'outs'. It is possible to identify something of a backlash against Edward's policies, but it occurred in October, rather than May, 1483 and was subsumed in the rebellion against Richard III.

There are, however, two cases in which Edward's actions may have created allies for Gloucester. One is the king's treatment of the Mowbray inheritance. Edward IV's second son, Richard duke of York, had married the only daughter of the last Mowbray duke of Norfolk in 1478. The bride died without issue in 1482, at which stage the land should have reverted to the heirs general, since a widower had no title in his wife's land unless there were children of the marriage. Edward IV, however, was unwilling to see it go. He had already persuaded one of the heirs, William Berkeley, to release his claims in return for the cancellation of his debts to the Talbots, and York's hereditary title to that moiety

---

[118] Lowe 1977, pp. 292–4; and see further below, pp. 207–8.

was embodied in an act passed by Edward IV's last parliament in 1483. The same act gave the prince a life interest in the remaining moiety, so deferring the inheritance of the other heir, John lord Howard.[119] As the prince was still only nine, and Howard in his fifties, this meant that Howard himself, and probably his son, Thomas, stood relatively little chance of ever acquiring the property. This disendowment of a loyal servant is reminiscent of Edward's shabby treatment of John Neville in 1470 and had similar consequences: Neville rebelled at the first real opportunity and the Howards backed Gloucester in 1483.[120] There is no way of knowing at what stage the Howards discovered that they were supporting a usurpation, but there are no signs of second thoughts. John Howard received his dukedom, supported Richard against rebels later the same year, and died with him at Bosworth. His descendants continued to regard Richard III as the founder of the family fortunes and the fourth duke kept a portrait of him in the long gallery at Kennington.[121]

The other ally whom Gloucester gained as a result of Edward IV's policies was to prove an altogether more dubious asset. This was Henry Stafford, duke of Buckingham, who had come of age in 1473 but had been refused any political role by Edward IV. The areas of traditional Stafford influence, the Welsh march and north midlands, had been otherwise provided for during the duke's minority but there was a degree of political reorganization in both areas in 1473, which could have been exploited to allow the duke a role there had the king wished. In Wales, the prince's council, established in 1471, was expanded in 1473 by the appointment of ten new councillors. Neither then nor later was Buckingham made a councillor or involved in the council's activity.[122] In the north midlands, the dominant figure in the 1460s had been the king's brother Clarence, who had been granted the important duchy of Lancaster estates in the region centred on the honour of Tutbury (Staffs.). He had drawn into his orbit John Talbot, earl of Shrewsbury, whose retinue constituted a significant part of the

[119] *Rot. Parl.* VI pp. 205–7; Ross 1974, pp. 248–9; Crawford 1985. The debts ($£34,000$) were the consequence of the great Berkeley/Talbot feud and may have been largely forfeited recognizances. Edward also used debts to put pressure on William Herbert, see below, p. 208.

[120] Thomas Howard was involved in Hastings' arrest: Hanham 1975, p. 167. For Neville see Ross 1974, pp. 144–5, 152–3.

[121] Williams 1964, p. 43

[122] Lowe 1981, pp. 556, 563.

ducal connection. In 1473 both nobles were removed from the scene. Talbot died in June, and in December all Clarence's royal grants were resumed – a resumption which was to prove permanent in the case of the north midlands estates.[123] The beneficiary was, again, not Buckingham but William lord Hastings, who was given the wardship of the Talbot heir and all the major offices within the Lancaster estates. It is clear that Buckingham's exclusion was a matter of deliberate royal policy, although Edward's motives are uncertain. He may have mistrusted Buckingham's proximity to the throne, although this is unlikely to have been a major issue given Edward's own apparent security at this stage. It is more likely that he was doubtful of the duke's ability. But whatever the reason, for the rest of Edward's reign the duke enjoyed only ceremonial duties and received markedly little patronage.

Buckingham also suffered from Edward IV's unwillingness to disgorge land. He could claim a significant part of the duchy of Lancaster lands in the south. The duchy lands were those which had come to the crown on the accession of Henry IV, and consisted of the land of his father, John of Gaunt, duke of Lancaster, and the land which Henry himself had acquired through his marriage to Mary, the coheiress of Humphrey de Bohun, earl of Hereford (d. 1373). Mary's elder sister, Eleanor, had married the youngest son of Edward III, Thomas of Woodstock. Eleanor's ultimate heir was the daughter of that marriage, Anne, the wife of Edmund Stafford, and the Staffords thus had half the Bohun estates while the Lancastrian kings, as heirs of Mary de Bohun, had the rest. Mary's direct line came to an end with the death of Henry VI and his son in 1471, leaving Henry Stafford the residual heir of the Lancastrian share of the inheritance. This claim was blocked by the attainder of Henry VI and the consequent forfeiture of his land to the crown, an arrangement which Edward IV showed no inclination to overturn for Buckingham's benefit – not surprisingly, when it would have deprived the crown of a valuable source of patronage.[124]

Buckingham was Gloucester's closest ally in the weeks after Edward IV's death. He appears acting with or for Gloucester at all the key points in the crisis, as well as providing additional military

[123] Hicks 1980, pp. 122–6; *CP* XI p. 706.
[124] Ross 1974, p. 335; Rawcliffe 1978, pp. 28–31.

backing.[125] So ubiquitous is he, that some writers have been tempted to cast him as the dominant partner.[126] This seems improbable, but there can be no doubt how highly Richard valued his support. The patronage showered upon him was exceptional not only in its scale, but in its implications. Gloucester stood for continuity, but the presence of Buckingham among his supporters threatened significant changes to Edward IV's polity. Stafford had been excluded from both Wales and the north midlands. Reassertion of the Stafford presence in Wales did not pose too many problems: the accession of Edward V had inevitably reopened the question of royal authority in Wales now that the council at Ludlow could no longer be represented as the prince's council. Even so, the insertion of Buckingham into Wales went far beyond any readjustment to Edward's arrangement, threatening to replace the existing nexus of royal servants with a single dominant nobleman. Matters were not so simple in the north midlands. Influence there was in the hands of another of Gloucester's allies, William lord Hastings, and at first Gloucester was careful not to challenge his position, giving such little local patronage as became available to Hastings' retinue.[127] Buckingham was, however, dissatisfied with the situation, and it is possible that his territorial jealousies contributed to the fall of Hastings in June. Mancini makes Buckingham responsible for sounding out the loyalty of Hastings. More gives this role to William Catesby, but the two accounts are not incompatible. Although More sees Catesby as a servant of Hastings who betrayed his master, he also had links with Buckingham, which would have made him an obvious choice as intermediary. Mancini also gives Buckingham the main role in stage-managing Hastings' arrest.[128] Although it would be going too far to suggest that Buckingham fabricated the case against Hastings, he did have every reason to discredit him and Buckingham's jealousies may help to explain why Hastings was executed, while the other servants of Edward IV arrested with him were simply imprisoned and subsequently released. Certainly Buckingham was the main beneficiary of Hastings' fall.

[125] Rawcliffe 1978, pp. 29–30.
[126] Kendall 1955, pp. 175–6, 219. Other defenders of Richard have developed this, e.g. Potter 1983, p. 37.
[127] Nicholas Knyveton was made bailiff of Chesterfield and Scarsdale: *Harl. 433* 1 p. 36; Dunham 1955, pp. 118–9; Wright 1983, pp. 89–90.
[128] Mancini pp. 90–1; More, *Richard III* pp. 45–6; Roskell 1959b, p. 156; Rawcliffe 1978, p. 226.

He did not formally receive the key duchy of Lancaster offices in the north midlands until after Richard's accession, but the reality of the change of power had been recognized within days of Hastings' death, when his servants were reported to be looking to Buckingham for lordship.[129]

In alienating Buckingham and Howard, Edward IV may have contributed to the deposition of his heir. The same could be said of his willingness to see the Woodvilles become identified with his son or to allow Gloucester to develop his northern hegemony. But all this needs to be kept in perspective. None of these issues was perceived as a problem in Edward's own lifetime. It was his death, leaving an adolescent heir, which transformed the situation. Thus Gloucester's suspicion of the Woodvilles was a product of the minority, not of any existing hostility: the rivalry between them was a consequence of the duke's actions rather than their cause. If Edward IV can be blamed for what happened, it is not because he refused to deal with tensions which were already apparent. The real question is whether, given the tensions likely to be generated by an immature heir, Edward's disposition of his kingdom was the best way to limit the risk. The difficulty here is to be sure what Edward intended. The traditional answer, a protectorate, is normally criticized on the assumption that it enflamed an existing animosity between Gloucester and the Woodvilles, but given that their record was in fact one of co-operation it might have been a reasonable solution. To have made Gloucester protector, while leaving Rivers as governor, could have achieved a viable balance of power.

Instead, Edward seems to have opted for an immediate accession. It is important not to see this as a factional decision. It was not tantamount to snubbing Gloucester and handing control to the Woodvilles – and Edward IV had no reason to see it in these terms. For him, his leading supporters formed a unity, something which can easily be forgotten in the modern emphasis on the regional power blocs which he created for his allies. His servants, whether nobles of Gloucester's standing or the household gentry, were interlinked, and even where there were personal rivalries among them they generally co-operated in the crown's interests. It was this unity and co-operation which Edward IV wanted to keep intact for his son, by preserving the existing balance of power. But

[129] *Stonor Letters* II p. 161.

his heir was still a child, who at best lacked the personal authority of his father and at worst might prove susceptible to manipulation. The success of Edward IV's wishes thus relied on the willingness of the Yorkist establishment to maintain the status quo and, in particular, to eschew any attempt to exploit the situation. That reliance proved misplaced. In part, Edward may have been unduly optimistic about the goodwill of his allies. He may also have underestimated his own importance within the polity which he had created. Because internal politics had functioned so smoothly in his second reign he assumed that this would continue under his son, in spite of the fact that the boy signally lacked his father's authority.

Complete continuity was probably not possible. But if Edward had misjudged the situation, his basic assumption was sound. Most of the political community did want continuity, at least in the sense that they wanted stability and an avoidance of factional conflict. This explains how the council was able to hold a balance of power until its efforts were overtaken by Gloucester's seizure of the prince, and one cannot assume that it would have failed to hold the same balance had Edward V been crowned. It is significant that Gloucester's strongest card as protector was his claim to represent continuity and a peaceful transition from Edward IV to Edward V. The speech which John Russell prepared for the opening of Edward V's parliament takes up this theme, equating Gloucester's continuing protectorate with security and the queen's family with dissension: 'Then if there be any surety or firmness here in this world, such as may be found out of heaven, it is rather in the Isles and lands environed with water than in the sea or in any great Rivers.'[130] Contemporaries may have accepted this reading of the situation, particularly as Gloucester was, on the whole, prepared to practise what he preached and to keep his brother's men in office. But even if they had reservations, it was obvious that to displace Gloucester would be to put an end to stability, which explains why, even after the execution of Hastings, the council was still prepared to go along with the duke's plans.

Gloucester exploited this desire for continuity to good effect, but he may also have shared it. The circumstances of his accession and his policies as king were modelled on those of his brother, and

[130] Nichols, *Grants from the Crown* p. xl. 'Rivers', of course, is a pun, which suggests that 'Isles' might be as well, but if so the double meaning is now lost.

although this may be no more than pragmatism (they had, after all, been shown to work), it may reflect Richard's perception of himself as the upholder of Yorkist traditions. But whatever his own views, he misread contemporary opinion. As protector, his emphasis on continuity ensured him almost complete support, and this was surely a factor in his decision to take the throne: he believed that he would be able to call on the same support as king. His actions in mid June were, in essentials, a repeat of those which had made him protector. In both cases he obtained a commanding position by an unexpected attack on potential rivals, which he then justified by claiming a conspiracy among his opponents to subvert the Yorkist polity. But on the second occasion it did not work – although this was not to become obvious for several weeks. Gloucester's self-identification with stability was acceptable when he was acting on behalf of Edward V, but not when it entailed deposing him. Although in June he moved too quickly for his coup to meet overt resistance, a significant element in the political community acquiesced only for as long as it took to concert opposition.

Chapter 3

REBELLION

The coronation of Richard III on 6 July 1483 was a ceremonial and public expression of the new king's claim to represent the continuance of his brother's government. Although there was a northern element among those attending, particularly among the servants of queen Anne, it was a Yorkist occasion, not the celebration of a factional triumph. Virtually all the English nobility were present. So were over seventy knights, of whom more than a third had been in Edward IV's household, a far higher proportion than those who had formal associations with Richard himself.[1] Surveying the attendance, the new king must have been encouraged in his belief that his brother's servants, having backed him as protector, were now prepared to support him as king.

That assumption lies behind the almost complete continuity of office holding to be found in the early weeks of the reign. Such continuity offered substantial advantages. It allowed the new king to call upon expertise developed under his predecessor, a consideration which had made continuity of tenure the norm in many areas of central government. A more specific advantage for Richard III was that in taking over his brother's local servants he was acquiring a ready-made following in areas where his own influence was slight. Although his interests as duke of Gloucester had not been exclusively northern, the geographical spread of his affinity was inevitably more limited than that of the king. But continuity was not just the temporary expedient of a king unfamiliar with parts of his new kingdom. Armed with lists of existing royal office holders, Richard was quick to remove men whom he regarded as suspect, and where he retained men in office it can be assumed that it was because he regarded them as reliable.[2] Nor was continuity an attempt to win the officials'

[1] Sutton and Hammond, *Coronation* pp. 84, 168–70, 270–4.
[2] *Harl. 433* I pp. xxxii–xxxiii, III pp. 191–206, 213–4.

138

goodwill by keeping them in office. The support of his brother's men was undoubtedly valuable to the new king, but it was not something he perceived himself as having to buy, and the pattern of patronage in these early weeks gives no support to Tudor claims that Richard indulged in the wholesale bribery of Yorkist servants.[3] It was only retrospectively, when the real weakness of Richard's support among his brother's servants had become apparent, that such tactics could be thought necessary. At the time, confidence rather than insecurity dictated Richard's policies.

Continuity was most marked within the central administration. At its middle and lower levels continuity between reigns was standard practice, and therefore says relatively little about royal policy. But survival in office could not be taken for granted by leading officials, whose importance and closeness to the king left them vulnerable to political change. This was particularly true of the king's secretary, and Edward's secretary Oliver King had been one of the casualties of the crisis of mid June. His place was taken by Richard's own secretary John Kendale, who was himself to conform to the usual pattern when he was attainted by Henry VII after Bosworth.[4] Otherwise Richard III made remarkably few changes, and most of the grants of government office recorded in this period were in fact confirmations, even where this is not explicitly stated. The reshuffling of high office during the protectorate was allowed to stand, with Gunthorpe verbally confirmed as keeper of the privy seal on 27 June and Russell formally receiving the great seal on the same day.[5] The lack of movement in government circles is confirmed by the fact that it was not until September that a niche was found for Richard's chancellor Thomas Barowe, who was then made master of the rolls of chancery in place of Robert Morton. Morton was the nephew of John bishop of Ely, who had been arrested with Hastings at the Tower, and his survival in office until September emphasizes Richard's reluctance to initiate change.[6]

The same desire for continuity can be seen in Richard's treatment of another sensitive area, Calais. William lord Hastings had been in command there, and his execution cast doubt on the

---

3 Vergil pp. 544, 554. The leading modern exponent of this view is Lander 1980, p. 317.
4 *Rot. Parl.* VI p. 276; Sutton 1981b, pp. 441–3.
5 *CPR 1476–85* p. 460; *Foedera* XII p. 189.
6 *CPR 1476–85* p. 462; Leathes, *Grace Book A* pp. 171–2; Hutchins 1861–74, II pp. 594–5.

reliability of the officials associated with him – doubt which must have been strengthened when John lord Dynham, Hastings' deputy, wrote to Richard to ask how the officers were to square his accession with their previous oaths of loyalty to Edward V. In spite of this somewhat tactless enquiry, Dynham was put in charge of Calais, although the clerk who made out the warrant for the grant deleted the usual clause that Dynham was to hold the office as fully as its previous holders, which implies some royal reservations.[7] Most of Hastings' former colleagues were also confirmed in office, but his brother Ralph (who had a reputation for outspokenness) was evidently felt to be too much of a risk and was replaced as lieutenant of Guisnes.[8] The office was given to John Blount lord Mountjoy, a choice which emphasized Richard's avoidance of major upheaval since Blount (like his brother James, the constable of Hammes) had been a Hastings retainer.[9] The only other casualty was the treasurer, William Slefeld, who was replaced by Thomas Thwaites, Edward IV's chancellor of the duchy and county of Lancaster. Thwaites' duchy office would have brought him into contact with Gloucester and he had existing interests in Calais, which made him an ideal candidate for the job. It is not, however, clear whether the object of the exercise was to replace Slefeld, or to move Thwaites out of the duchy – where his office went to Richard's auditor and councillor Thomas Metcalfe.[10] The northern duchy estates had been central to Gloucester's power and he was clearly unwilling to lose direct control as king. The appointment of Thomas Metcalfe, and Richard's refusal to appoint a replacement for himself as chief steward (which left day-to-day control in the hands of Thomas' brother Miles), meant that the northern duchy lands would continue to be run as a virtual appendage of Richard's own estates.

The king showed himself slightly more willing to make changes at a local level, although again most of his brothers' grants were allowed to stand. There was most scope for change in the duchy of Lancaster lordships held by Elizabeth Woodville, where her

---

[7] *Harl. 433* III pp. 28–31; PRO, C 81/1529/18.
[8] *Harl. 433* III pp. 31, 38–9. In May 1483 Ralph could comment, 'my lord [i.e. William lord Hastings] saith I write always so plainly to him that it feareth him': *PL* II p. 440.
[9] *Harl. 433* III p. 31; Dunham 1955, pp. 118–20.
[10] Somerville 1953, pp. 391–2; Colvin, Brown and Taylor 1963, I pp. 430–1.

grants were later treated as void.[11] But even here relatively few
offices changed hands in the early weeks of the reign, except for
those held by recognized Woodville supporters. Robert Ratcliffe,
for instance, lost his Sheen offices to Henry Davy, Richard's
serjeant tailor.[12] Other Woodville associates lost office elsewhere,
including Robert Poyntz, who had already lost several offices
during the protectorate and was now replaced as steward of
Sodbury (Glos.) by Nicholas Spicer, Richard's constable of
Caerphilly.[13] Such changes, however, had little effect on the
distribution of political influence within the shires, and at this
level Richard was, again, disinclined to interfere. Edward IV had
built up a good working relationship with the local gentry, partly
reflected in an increased household presence among them. Leading
local figures had been taken into the king's service and, conversely,
royal servants had been given the local influence to put them into
the front rank of county society. Richard's belief that he had the
support of his brother's servants therefore had as its corollary the
assumption that he had inherited the power base which Edward
had built up in the shires. As a result, Richard felt it necessary to
make only a few changes to the commissions of the peace after his
accession. The Woodvilles and their immediate allies were
dropped, but several men associated with them were allowed to
remain on the bench. As in the case of royal grants, this low level
of change cannot be ascribed to ignorance or inertia. Richard
made additions, turning usually to former servants of his brother
although he also added some of his own men with appropriate
local connections, and in one county (Hertfordshire) undertook a
thorough overhaul of the commission.[14] The implication is that
where no changes were made, it was because Richard believed the
men reliable.

Two counties can stand as illustrations of Richard's attitude.
Kent had been a centre of Woodville influence under Edward IV,
and the commission of the peace issued on 26 June was the first
since November 1481, but relatively few changes were made.
Gloucester himself was of course deleted, as was the earl of Essex,
who had died in April 1483, and the executed earl Rivers.

---

[11] PRO, DL 29/59/1127. Annuities (but not offices) in the duchy lands dominated by
Hastings were treated similarly: DL 29/404/6475.

[12] PRO, DL 29/59/1127; *Harl. 433* I pp. 78, 89, 90. The low level of change may be partly
due to the promise of much of this land to Buckingham, see below, p. 143.

[13] *Harl. 433* I p. 76; *CPR* 1476–85 p. 99; WAM 4110 m. I.

[14] The Hertfordshire commission is discussed below, pp. 198–9.

William Haute, the brother of the imprisoned Richard Haute, was also dropped, although other Woodville associates remained. Among them was Sir John Fogge, a leading local ally of Edward IV whom Richard was making efforts to conciliate.[15] One of Fogge's local associates, Richard Lee of Maidstone, was deleted, but this seems to have been an error and he was reinstated in the following month.[16] Richard added the bishop of Rochester, the dukes of Norfolk and Buckingham, John Broke lord Cobham (an associate of Howard who had been active against Edward Woodville) and two members of the local gentry.[17] One of these, Richard Page of Horton, had been a receiver and annuitant of Edward IV. The other, Sir John Guildford of Rolvenden, was a kinsman of the Woodvilles and was to play a prominent part in the rebellions later that year.[18] Two further commissions were then named in quick succession at the end of July, to allow the reinstatement of Lee and the addition of two more newcomers: Robert Rede and Sir Ralph Ashton. Rede was a local lawyer, from Chiddingstone. Ashton, by contrast, was a northern retainer of Gloucester, who had arrived in Kentish society only a few weeks previously with his betrothal to Elizabeth Chicheley, the widow of John Kyriel.[19]

Wiltshire reveals a similar approach. There, too, Richard's first commission of 20 July needed to take account of some natural changes since 1481. Richard Beauchamp, bishop of Salisbury, had died in the interval, and was replaced by his successor as bishop, Lionel Woodville: a striking demonstration that at this stage Richard III was still prepared to allow a sense of what was due to Lionel as bishop to override his mistrust of the family. Another natural casualty was probably John Whiteoaksmede, one of the local members of the commission. There was some shuffling of the legal element, and Gloucester himself was dropped, but there were only three 'political' deletions. Thomas Grey, marquis of Dorset, was a predictable omission. John Cheyne was also dropped. He had been an addition by Edward IV to the local

---

[15] Fogge's career is summarized by Bolton 1980, pp. 202–9; see also More, *Richard III* pp. 81–2; Gairdner 1898, pp. 98–100.
[16] PRO, C 67/51 m. 27; C 244/136/132. He should not be confused with his namesake of Quarrendon (Bucks.), one of Richard's yeomen of the crown.
[17] Canterbury RO, FA 2 fo. 207v; Crawford 1986, p. 15.
[18] Page: PRO, C 67/52 m. 3; *CPR 1476–85* p. 477. Guildford: Conway 1925, pp. 107, 120.
[19] Rede: *CCR 1476–85* no. 1323; Ives 1983, pp. 474–5. Ashton: *CCR 1476–85* no. 1113; and see further below, pp. 199–200.

gentry, and was one of the very few men outside the immediate Woodville circle whom Richard treated with suspicion from the outset. His fall from favour may explain the temporary removal from the commission of his stepson, John lord Stourton, who was reinstated in the following December.[20] In their place Richard added, apart from the new bishop, the dukes of Norfolk and Buckingham and one local man, John Seymour. The changes left six men on the commission, a third of the total, who were to rebel against the king in the following autumn.[21]

The royal emphasis on continuity meant that, just as during the protectorate, relatively few grants became available for redistribution. The execution of Hastings provided the only significant addition to the supply, and even then Richard only seized his royal grants, confirming his family lands and two major wardships to his widow, Katherine Neville.[22] The lion's share of the available patronage continued to be absorbed by Buckingham. He took over Gloucester's former offices of great chamberlain and constable of England, as well as Hastings' offices in the north midlands. He also dispossessed Hastings' retainer Nicholas Knyveton of the Derbyshire offices which he had been given during the protectorate. His greatest triumph, however, was to secure Richard's agreement to the dismemberment of the duchy of Lancaster on his behalf. In a signet letter of 13 July, Richard conceded the Lancastrian share of the Bohun inheritance to the duke as if the act of attainder against Henry VI had never been made.[23] The agreement was to be ratified by an act of parliament, now the usual method of confirming major territorial readjustments, but in the meantime the duke was authorized to enter the manors concerned and receive their revenues from the previous Easter. An attached schedule shows the scale of the alienation, including some thirty-eight manors lying mainly in East Anglia and the south of England. Their value was set at £1,100, but their surrender did not only represent a financial loss to the crown. The estates had provided a rich source of reward for royal servants, accounting in particular for much of the available patronage in Essex and Hertfordshire.

---

[20] Sutton and Hammond, *Coronation* p. 321; *CP* XII part 1 p. 303.
[21] Buckingham, Lionel Woodville, Roger Tocotes, Richard Beauchamp, William Collingbourne, Walter Hungerford.
[22] *Harl. 433* II pp. 4–5.
[23] *Ibid.* I pp. 65, 69, 72, II pp. 2–4.

The only grants to approach these in value were made to the Howards. During the protectorate John Howard had already been made chief steward of the duchy of Lancaster in the south. Now he added Richard's former office of admiral, and was made duke of Norfolk with a moiety of the Mowbray inheritance. This, however, was heavily encumbered by the claims of two dowagers, and Richard augmented Howard's endowment with further land grants, including land forfeited by Rivers but mainly consisting of the de Vere land and other property in the south held by Richard himself as duke of Gloucester.[24] The inclusion of this land demonstrates the king's limited resources, but it must also mean that Richard was prepared to see Howard take over his own former sphere of influence in East Anglia. Howard's son Thomas was given Rivers' office of steward of the duchy of Lancaster lands in Norfolk and was made earl of Surrey, at first with no further endowment, although in the following year he was given an annuity of £1,100 during his father's lifetime.[25]

The scale of these grants is exceptional. The relative scarcity of patronage meant that even close associates of the king usually had to be content with modest gains. Francis viscount Lovell was confirmed as butler of England and steward of Wallingford, both offices which he had received during the protectorate, and received nothing more, although he was able to secure patronage for others. The grant of the bailiffship of Pattingham (Staffs.) to Richard Rugge, for instance, was probably Lovell's doing.[26] But the quantity of patronage was not the only problem the king faced in meeting his obligations to his supporters. Most of the available grants lay in central and southern England, while many of Richard's allies came from north of Trent. Whatever the king's own attitude towards giving local office to 'outsiders' (and his emphasis on continuity may have made him unwilling, at this stage, to do so), would-be recipients were generally more interested in grants which complemented existing interests, unless the grant were sufficiently valuable to be attractive in its own right. As a result, relatively few northerners received patronage in the south. The major exception was Robert Brackenbury, who was

---

[24] *Ibid.* 1 pp. 72, 74, 80–1; *CPR* 1476–85 pp. 358, 359, 363, 365.

[25] *Harl. 433* 1 pp. 75, 206, 213; *CPR* 1476–85 p. 479. This was the approximate value of the land grant to Norfolk, which yielded £1,013 in 1483–4: BL, Add. Roll 16559.

[26] *CPR* 1476–85 p. 365. Lovell made him one of his deputy butlers, *ibid.* p. 375, and he was later involved with other Lovell associates: *CFR* 1471–85 no. 789.

put in charge of the Tower of London.[27] For the rest, a few northerners were able to extend existing southern interests. Thomas Otter, for instance, was one of the Neville retainers inherited by Gloucester, and his family had acquired Warwickshire interests during their service with the earl of Warwick. Thomas was now made bailiff of two Warwickshire manors and an Oxfordshire hundred.[28] Those northerners who did not look to the south found the scope for patronage limited. Sir John Conyers was rewarded by Richard alienating some of his own northern land – a unique favour and a measure of the importance attached to this dominant figure of the Middleham connection now that Richard himself was no longer based in the north.[29] In two cases a northerner was given an annuity until suitable office should become available, but it is indicative of the shortage of northern patronage that in neither case did an office materialize.[30]

As this suggests, although Richard's own men are a new, and therefore noticeable, element in the patronage of July–September, they form only a minority of recipients. Most grants continued to go to men with a background of service to Edward IV. In part this was because many of Richard's early grants simply renewed his brother's appointments, although this was not always stated. William Langley, for example, who was given the portership of Northampton, was a long-standing Yorkist servant who had held the same office under Edward IV.[31] But even among the new grants, Edward's men seem to have been holding their own. The patronage granted at this time was in any case only a fraction of the total, and the overall continuity was largely to the benefit of Edward's servants. As far as royal office was concerned, Richard's accession, far from prompting a take-over by the former ducal retinue, was followed by the placing of a small number of new men within an existing power structure.

Something similar may have happened within the royal household, although in the complete absence of household records for Richard's reign this can only be a matter of speculation. Knowledge of household membership has to be gleaned from casual

[27] *CPR 1476–85* p. 364.
[28] *Ibid.* p. 369; *CPR 1467–77* pp. 215, 291–2; Carpenter 1976, pp. 165–6.
[29] *CPR 1476–85* p. 450 (March 1484). It was made under the signet in September 1483: *Harl. 433* I p. 92; PRO, C 81/886/41.
[30] John Egremont and Henry Pullowe: *CPR 1476–85* p. 440; *Harl. 433* I pp. 89, 91. Egremont was later given land: *CPR 1476–85* p. 428.
[31] *CPR 1461–7* p. 143; *CPR 1476–85* p. 364.

references in other sources, of which royal grants are one of the richest. As a result, knowledge of Richard's household is much fuller after the rebellion of 1483, when forfeitures generated a flood of royal grants, than in the lean weeks immediately after Richard's coronation. One consequence of this imbalance is that it is easier to identify those of Edward's servants who entered Richard's service and remained loyal than to trace how many of them crossed into Richard's household in June or July 1483 and later rebelled. It seems probable, however, that Richard's readiness to trust and employ his brother's servants in central and local government was paralleled by almost complete continuity within the household. At the lower levels of the household, continuity between reigns was in any case the norm by this date. Certainly five of Edward IV's yeomen who subsequently rebelled had entered Richard's household before doing so, for they are described as his yeomen of the crown in the act of attainder.[32]

Above this level the question is less straightforward, since continuity cannot be so readily assumed. By this date, however, there was very close link between membership of the household and the enjoyment of office on the royal estates, so that where a member of Edward's household kept his grants, or received more, there is a strong presumption that he had transferred to Richard's household.[33] On this basis, continuity even at the upper level of the household seems to have been almost complete in 1483. Of Edward IV's known knights, twenty-nine were alive at Richard's accession. Fifteen certainly continued in Richard's household and another was one of his councillors. A further eight received patronage commensurate with household status. The remaining five were all rebels, for whom evidence after October 1483 is not available. Three of them had been active in local government before October 1483, which leaves only two who failed to make the transition: Edward Woodville and Thomas St Leger, widower of the king's sister Anne and closely involved with the Woodvilles in the south west. With possible continuity of this order, it becomes more appropriate to think of Richard III putting himself at the head of his brother's household, and augmenting it with some of his own servants, than to envisage him taking selected servants of his brother into his own retinue.

[32] *Rot. Parl.* VI pp. 245–6 (Potter, Fisher, Strode, Knight, Cruse). This is an underestimate, see n. 117 below.
[33] The household is discussed more fully in chap. 5 below.

No doubt the king's closest supporters entered the household straight away. William Catesby, for instance, was an esquire of the body by the time of the coronation and John Nesfield by August.[34] More northerners may have joined them while Richard was in Yorkshire in September. The visit seems to have been intended as a celebration of Richard's northern links, during which he was attended by the local gentry and made generous gifts to local religious houses. It would have been an appropriate occasion to recognize the strength of his northern connection by taking some of its members into the royal household.[35] John Huddleston, for example, is mentioned as an esquire of the body in September and Geoffrey Franke early the following month.[36] Neither Richard nor his contemporaries, however, would have expected all the ducal retinue to transfer to the household as a matter of course, and it was probably only after the 1483 rebellion had demonstrated the shakiness of Richard's support within his brother's household that large numbers of the retinue did make the transition. Until then, the loyalty and service of most of the retinue remained focussed on the northern household of the king's son.

The traditional view of Richard III's reign, that he came to the throne at the head of a northern affinity through which he proceeded to rule England, derives from the aftermath of the rebellion of October 1483. Richard's immediate intention was very different. As king, he sought to put himself in Edward IV's place, not merely in a symbolic sense but directly and literally by setting himself at the head of the nexus of servants built up by his brother. His own estates provided a reservoir of loyal servants upon whom he could draw as necessary, and members of the retinue were rewarded and found places in the household, but most were probably destined for a continuing local role. Richard, in effect, was filling two separate but concurrent roles: those of king of England and great northern magnate. In practice they overlapped, but there was no intention that they should merge, or that one should supersede the other. There is a parallel here with Henry IV's position as king and duke of Lancaster and, like him, Richard III may have planned to keep his own northern estates as a separate administrative unit. Certainly he was not prepared to

34 Sutton and Hammond, *Coronation* p. 155; PRO, C 81/886/25; *Harl. 433* I p. 87.
35 *Harl. 433* II pp. 10–11; compare Halle, *Union* (Reign of Richard III) fo. 5–v.
36 PRO, C 81/886/30; *Harl. 433* II p. 29.

see them dismembered and during his admittedly brief reign they seem to have kept their organizational identity. This separation of roles was, however, feasible only as long as the king could call on the backing of a national following – something Richard III believed that he had achieved in taking over the servants of his brother. It was not until October that he was proved wrong.

In July 1483 Richard still had every reason to feel satisfied with his achievements. He had apparently established himself on the throne with a minimum of opposition, and the continuity of his brother's men in key positions is one measure of his confidence. Another is his willingness to disband his northern army and embark, in mid July, on a progress designed to demonstrate his success to a wider audience.[37] Fifteenth-century kings were far less peripatetic than their predecessors, and such formal progresses were therefore valuable opportunities for the king to see and be seen. Communities along the way would demonstrate their loyalty and obedience, while the king might respond with some mark of favour. Little evidence survives of the civic pageantry which greeted Richard III, although it is known to have existed.[38] Far better documented is the royal desire to please. Richard's progress was marked by grants to towns and religious houses along his route. At Woodstock he disafforested land which Edward IV had annexed to Wychwood forest. Gloucester had its liberties confirmed and new grants made. At Oxford the Franciscans were given an annuity of 50m and at Worcester the same order was granted a meadow. The monastery of Tewkesbury was promised the repayment of a debt of 560m owed by the king's dead brother Clarence.[39] More modest grants accompanied the king's entry into Yorkshire. The Augustinians of Tickhill were given an annuity of 5m in honour of St Ninian, to whom Richard had a special devotion. In Pontefract the Dominicans were given £5 p.a. for the continuance of an obit for Richard's father, and the anchoress was granted £2 p.a. York itself was rewarded with a remission of its fee farm and royal backing for its claims that the Ainsty should bear part of a rent which the York weavers paid to the exchequer.[40] Richard also made a point of refusing the

---

[37] His movements are charted by Edwards 1983, pp. 4–9.
[38] Raine, *York Records* I pp. 78–9 contains a reference to civic pageants elsewhere. For the pageantry which greeted Henry VII see Anglo 1969, pp. 23–35.
[39] *Harl. 433* I pp. 78, 88, II pp. 7, 9–10; Gairdner 1898, p. 112.
[40] PRO, DL 42/20 fos. 8, 9; *Harl. 433* I pp. 88, 89, II pp. 22–3; Attreed 1981, pp. 30–2. For St Ninian see Palliser 1986, pp. 60–1.

customary gifts of money offered to him by the towns he visited. After this assiduous courting of local opinion, one of Richard's councillors was able to report that the king 'contents the people where he goes best that ever did prince'.[41]

Alongside this public success, however, Richard's progress was punctuated by news of gathering opposition. Shortly after leaving London Richard had granted the duke of Norfolk sole power of array throughout the south east and East Anglia, and he was probably half expecting trouble from the Woodvilles.[42] By the end of the month the danger was beginning to take shape. On 29 July Richard wrote to his chancellor ordering the appointment of a commission to try unnamed men arrested for an 'enterprise'.[43] No further details are given, but the enterprise was almost certainly the attempt to rescue Edward IV's sons described by John Stow. The scheme entailed starting fires in the city of London and then rescuing the princes under cover of the resulting confusion. According to Stow, whose phrasing suggests that he had seen the relevant indictments, four men were executed for their part in the plot: Robert Russe, serjeant of London; William Davy, pardoner, of Hounslow; John Smith, groom of the stirrup of Edward IV; and Stephen Ireland, wardrober in the Tower.[44] The contemporary French chronicler Basin, who is apparently the only other author to mention the episode, believed that in all fifty Londoners were involved but that the city failed to follow their lead.[45]

Although the conspiracy failed, it had disturbing implications for the new king. The involvement of two royal servants, one based in the Tower, not only gave the plan some feasibility but was an ominous foretaste of what was to become the major weakness in Richard's position: the fact that opposition came from among his own servants as well as from outside. Moreover, although none of the named conspirators was very important, there were more influential figures in the background. Smith's head of department under Edward IV had been John Cheyne,

[41] *Christ Church Letters* p. 46; compare Canterbury RO, FA 7 fo. 13v.

[42] PRO, C 81/1529/20; *CPR* 1476–85 p. 362.

[43] PRO, C 81/1392/1; printed by Tudor-Craig 1973, p. 98.

[44] Stow, *Annales* p. 762; for another possible use of indictments by him see below, pp. 155, 156. Of the four men named only Smith can be traced; he is listed among the grooms of the stable in 21–22 Edw. IV: PRO, E 101/107/15 fo. 18.

[45] Basin, *Histoire de Louis XI* III pp. 234–5. I owe this reference to the kindness of Dr M. K. Jones.

master of the king's horse until Richard's accession, and Cheyne may well have been involved. The men executed were also accused of sending letters to the earls of Richmond and Pembroke in Brittany – the first mention of Henry Tudor, earl of Richmond, in the context of opposition to Richard III. This Tudor dimension strongly suggests that Margaret Beaufort, Henry's mother, was active somewhere behind the scenes. The advancement of her son, who had been in exile throughout Edward IV's second reign, was her overriding concern.[46] At this stage, with the princes still assumed to be alive, there was no question of Tudor claiming the throne. Lady Margaret presumably hoped that a grateful Edward V would restore her son to political life and to the earldom of Richmond. But her involvement in this early conspiracy meant that she and her son were well placed when opponents of Richard III were faced with finding an alternative candidate for the throne.

The London conspiracy was just the first manifestation of growing unrest. Around the same time the Crowland chronicler notes attempts to remove the daughters of Edward IV from sanctuary at Westminster and send them overseas. Richard countered the threat by putting an armed guard around the abbey under the command of John Nesfield, with orders to watch everyone going in and out – a policy which not only kept the princesses secure but resulted in Nesfield netting a number of minor malefactors.[47] On 13 August the land of John Welles, who was specifically described as the king's rebel, was put into the custody of John lord Scrope of Bolton.[48] Welles was the half-brother of Margaret Beaufort, and the forfeiture may mean that he had been involved in the conspiracy of the previous month or it may be a pointer to further opposition. Four days later Richard ordered 2,000 Welsh bills to be sent to him in all haste.[49] On 28 August a strong commission of *oyer et terminer*, headed by the king's 'dearest kinsman' Henry duke of Buckingham, was appointed to enquire into treasons and felonies in London, Surrey, Sussex, Kent, Middlesex, Oxfordshire, Berkshire, Essex

[46] PRO, E 101/107/15; Sutton and Hammond, *Coronation* p. 321; M. K. Jones 1986b, pp. 27–30. For other possible disaffection around Cheyne at this time see Sutton 1981a, p. 4.
[47] *Crowland* pp. 162–3; PRO, KB 9/366/16, 9/950/24.
[48] *Harl. 433* II p. 7.
[49] *Ibid.* pp. 8–9.

and Hertfordshire.[50] These counties were to be central to the October risings and Richard had clearly got word of gathering trouble. The rebels' preparations were in hand as early as this, for on 20 August one of their leaders, Giles Daubeney, set in train the process of settling two of his manors on himself and his wife jointly, presumably in the hope of saving them from forfeiture in the event of failure.[51]

At this stage the aim of the rebels was probably still the restoration of Edward V, and the growing disaffection provides the most plausible context for Richard's putative murder of his nephews. Faced with the possibility of serious opposition, Richard may have hoped to cut the ground from under the rebels' feet by having his nephews killed and, equally important, allowing it to be known that they were dead.[52] If that was his intention, the plan failed. But it is a measure of its near success that the rebels had to resort to such an implausible alternative candidate. Henry Tudor's own claims to the throne were virtually non-existent and it is clear that it was only his promise to marry Elizabeth of York which made him acceptable to much Yorkist opinion. In the short term, Richard may have believed that his tactic had been successful. There are no further indications of opposition for about a month, then on 22 September Thomas Barowe replaced Robert Morton as keeper of the rolls of chancery, and on the following day Richard ordered the seizure of the temporalities of Lionel Woodville, bishop of Salisbury.[53] The bishop's immunity hitherto had been striking and this sudden fall from favour suggests that news of some specific treasonable activity had reached the king; but if so, no other evidence appears to survive. It is, however, suggestive that Buckingham was later to be accused of inciting Tudor to invade in letters written on 24 September 'and many other times before and after'.[54] Although it is unlikely that Richard yet knew of Buckingham's involvement,

---

[50] *CPR* 1476–85 pp. 465–6. The description of Buckingham is not calendared, see PRO, C 66/556 m. 7 dorse.

[51] *Inqs p.m.* III no. 529. The tactic failed (*CPR* 1476–85 p. 479) although the act of attainder nominally excluded land held to the use of rebels and their wives: *Rot. Parl.* VI p. 248.

[52] Vergil p. 547. The princes appear to conform to the pattern established by earlier deposed kings, who remained alive until a rebellion in their favour demonstrated that they were still a threat.

[53] *CPR* 1476–85 p. 462; *Harl. 433* II pp. 23–4. Compare also Thomson 1986, pp. 132–3.

[54] *Rot. Parl.* VI p. 245.

he probably had become aware that the rebels had got into their stride again, with the intention now of putting Henry Tudor on the throne.

More specific news had reached the king by the second week of October, as he moved south through Lincolnshire. On 11 October he wrote from Lincoln to order a general mobilization of forces against his erstwhile ally the duke of Buckingham, who 'traitorously is turned upon us'.[55] It is likely that Richard knew of the duke's defection earlier than this. On 12 October the king wrote to his chancellor (who was then at Westminster) asking for the great seal to be sent to him, since Russell was too ill to bring it in person, and the context makes it clear that Richard had already been in touch with Russell on the subject. The letter refers to the king's advance against Buckingham 'as lately by our other letters we certified you our mind more at large'. This may just refer to the letters of the previous day, but the implication seems rather to be that Richard had already asked Russell to bring the seal in person, and that Russell's plea of illness was in response to this earlier request.[56] A correspondence lasting several days would support the claim of both the Crowland chronicler and Vergil that Richard dissembled his knowledge of Buckingham's involvement (provided by an informer) until he had had time to make his preparations.[57]

Whenever Richard first became aware of Buckingham's defection, from this point events moved swiftly. Within only a day or so of the mobilization of his forces, word must have reached the king of a rising in the south east. This, indeed, is what is usually said to have alerted Richard to Buckingham's defection, but the timing seems too tight. At the very latest, the king had news of Buckingham's involvement by 11 October, whereas news of trouble in the Weald only reached London on 10 October. The duke of Norfolk, who was then in the city, took immediate action to contain the trouble, sending men into Kent to resist the

---

[55] Raine, *York Records* I pp. 83–4; a similar letter was sent to Hull: Hull RO, Bench Book 3A fos. 135v–6. See also *Stonor Letters* II p. 163.
[56] PRO, C 81/1392/6. If Russell was dragging his feet, it gives additional significance to Richard's postscript insisting that he would have no trouble dealing with the rebels.
[57] *Crowland* pp. 162–5; Vergil pp. 548, 551. Gairdner 1898, pp. 131–2 rejects this possibility on the grounds that Richard's bitter postscript to Russell's letter shows that the news had taken him unawares, but the news was then at least one day old and may, therefore, have been older.

rebels and taking steps to defend London.[58] He presumably also sent word to the king, but it can hardly have reached Lincoln by the next day. Nor, if Norfolk took action as soon as he heard of the rising, is it much more feasible that the news reached Lincoln independently by 11 October. It is more likely that the two issues were separate, and that Richard had already committed himself to action against Buckingham when news reached him of the Kentish unrest. Faced with two threats he may have hesitated. The army was due to assemble at Leicester on 20–1 October, and the king's obvious route to join it from Lincoln was straight down the Fosse Way. Instead, he was at Grantham on 19 October which may suggest that he had decided to return to London. If so, however, he thought better of it, and turned west again, through Melton Mowbray, arriving at Leicester on 22 October, having presumably decided to leave the Kent rebels to Norfolk and march against Buckingham himself.[59]

From this point most modern accounts of the chronology of the rebellion are based on the act of attainder passed in the parliament of January 1484. This presents the official, and retrospective, view of the affair and as such needs to be treated with caution. It portrays the rebellion as an integrated series of risings in separate parts of southern England. In the south east there were risings at Maidstone, Rochester, Gravesend and Guildford. Newbury served as the focus for the rebels of Oxfordshire and Berkshire; Salisbury for Wiltshire, Hampshire, Somerset and Dorset; Exeter for the south west. There was also a small circle around the duke of Buckingham at Brecon. These scattered centres were given cohesion by Buckingham, to whom the act assigns responsibility for stirring up rebellion in each of the areas mentioned, as well as for inviting Tudor to invade. The centres were also united by links between the rebels assigned to each sector, something which is most marked in the case of the Woodvilles, who almost seem to have been parcelled out between the various regions.[60] As well as this cohesion of personnel, the

---

[58] *PL* II no. 799; Ross 1981, p. 116. On average, urgent messages could be carried at sixty miles a day: Armstrong 1948b, pp. 444–54 (although Armstrong accepts that news of the Kent rising did reach Lincoln on 11 October: pp. 450–1).

[59] This interpretation is strengthened by Richard's apparent presence at Nottingham on 18 October, suggesting that he may have set off down the Fosse Way before turning east. The reference is, however, problematical: Edwards 1983, p. 8.

[60] *Rot. Parl.* VI pp. 244–51: Richard Haute (Kent), Richard Woodville (Newbury), Lionel Woodville (Salisbury), Thomas Grey (Exeter).

act gives the rising a chronological unity. All the risings are said to have occurred on 18 October, although this is slightly modified in the south east, where the Maidstone rising is assigned to that day and the other centres are said to have followed on 20, 22 and 25 October; 18 October is also given as the date on which Henry Tudor set sail from Brittany. The impression conveyed is of a tightly organized conspiracy linking the southern counties and emanating from Brecon. How closely this corresponds to reality is, however, another matter.[61]

The act's emphasis on 18 October has normally been taken at face value, although in no case does it receive independent support. The Kent rebels were certainly in arms over a week before their nominal starting date, something which, on the strength of the act, is usually explained as their having rebelled too early. But this is to give undue credence to the act's chronology. Buckingham himself was in arms before 18 October. On that day Edward Plumpton, writing to Sir Robert Plumpton, had heard that the duke had already raised an army.[62] The departure date of Tudor from Brittany is a matter of some controversy, but it was certainly not 18 October.[63] The act's emphasis on the date thus begins to look like a legal fiction. As the act itself makes clear, the date had been adopted as the point from which the rebels were deemed to have forfeited their possessions, regardless of the actual date of confiscation. Thus the three attainted bishops were all considered to have forfeited their temporalities then, although Lionel Woodville's had been seized on 23 September, Piers Courtenay's probably not until November and John Morton's arguably as early as 13 June. The choice of 18 October may have been dictated by some feature of the rebellion, but it is just as likely that, as a major feast day (St Luke), the date had been adopted for ease of reference. Certainly, the insistence of the act's draftsmen on working it explicitly into every aspect of the rebellion gives the risings a temporal coherence which is clearly spurious.

Extra-parliamentary sources suggest that trouble began in Kent early in October and then spread westwards, with the south west

---

[61] Gillingham 1981, p. 228 is another critic of the act's chronology.

[62] *Plumpton Corresp.* pp. 44–5.

[63] Vergil, usually well informed about Tudor's exile, suggests 6 Ides October (10 Oct.) for the crossing: p. 553, but unless this represents a first, abortive, attempt it is too early. For attempts to reconstruct Tudor's movements: Kendall 1955, pp. 482–3; Griffiths and Thomas 1985, pp. 102–3; Antonovics 1986, p. 171.

not seriously involved until the beginning of November. The Weald was in revolt by 10 October, and on the following day Norfolk sent men to Gravesend and Rochester. At Gravesend the rebels were responsible for an affray in the fair, that is, on 13 October, the translation of St Edward.[64] By 15 October one of the Kent rebels, William Clifford of Iwade, had already been arrested, but the unrest continued.[65] Early in November Canterbury was still paying for men riding with lord Cobham, and Stow believed that the trouble did not finally collapse until news of Buckingham's execution (on 2 November) reached the county.[66]

Further west the timing of the revolt is even less certain. There was trouble in Wiltshire by 17 October, when a servant of the sheriff of Cornwall, on his way to the exchequer with a file of returned writs, met the rebel Walter Hungerford and others at Warminster and had his documents stolen.[67] By 23 October the king, who was then at Leicester, was aware of trouble in the Newbury and Salisbury sectors, as well as Kent, for men assigned by the act of attainder to those three areas were included in his proclamation against the rebels. The proclamation includes no rebels from the south west, however, apart from Thomas Grey, marquis Dorset, whose inclusion was probably inevitable. This, together with the absence of Courtenay of Exeter from the list of implicated bishops, suggests that Richard was unaware of disaffection in Devon and Cornwall.[68] This was apparently still the case at the beginning of November, when the king, then at Salisbury, issued commissions to seize the goods of named rebels. They included men from Somerset (whom the act of attainder was later to assign to the Salisbury sector) but no one from further west.[69] News of the west's involvement must, however, have reached the king soon after this, for when he left Salisbury (probably on 4 November) he headed south west into Dorset and then continued to Exeter, arriving there by 8 November. By then the rebellion

---

[64] Collier, *Household Books* pp. 470–1; Stow, *Annales* p. 775; Kilburne 1659, pp. 113–4.

[65] Collier, *Household Books* p. 472. Clifford, who was subsequently executed, is often confused with the Roger Clifford executed by Richard at Southampton later in the reign. London sources, however, get the identification correct: Green, 'Hist. notes' p. 589; *Great Chron.* pp. 234–6.

[66] Canterbury RO, FA 7 fo. 10. Cobham was acting as Norfolk's representative, compare Collier, *Household Books* pp. 471–2.

[67] PRO, E 207/21/16/12.

[68] *CPR 1476–85* p. 371.

[69] *Harl. 433* II pp. 31–2. The commissions themselves are undated, but are at the head of a group of warrants of 2–3 November.

was effectively over. The last episode which can be identified was the proclamation of Tudor at Bodmin on 3 November.[70] Richard remained in Exeter for about a week, probably in the hope of capturing Tudor, whose fleet was off the south coast. A royal fleet put to sea under John lord Scrope of Bolton, who commandeered the *Grace Dieu* of Dartmouth and other vessels for the purpose. Men were also set to watch the coast. Sir Thomas Malyverer was put in charge of Plymouth. At Southampton, as well as a naval guard off the Isle of Wight, there were royal soldiers in the New Forest – supplied with beer, fish and oysters by the city.[71] Tudor, however, escaped safely to Brittany and on 15 November Richard began his journey back to London, arriving there on 25 November.

The act's stress on 18 October thus masks a rebellion which lasted for almost a month. But its simplification of events is not only chronological. Its division of the rebellion into sectors is also misleading. In fact, each sector represents the findings of the regional commissions appointed by Richard to enquire into the rebellion. On 13 November such commissions were appointed for Devon/Cornwall, Oxfordshire/Berkshire, Dorset/Somerset and Southampton/Wiltshire.[72] None is recorded for Wales or the south east but some judicial process must have been set in train there also. The findings of the commissions do not survive among the royal records, but there are some references to them elsewhere. Stow, for instance, may have taken his circumstantial account of the trouble at Gravesend from an indictment. The fullest evidence, however, relates to the south west and casts considerable light on the compilation of the act of attainder.

Hooker, the historian of Exeter, incorporated into his commonplace book a list of the rebels indicted before lord Scrope at Torrington, and the details were used by Holinshed in his chronicle account. There is also an extant indictment of the Bodmin rebels before Scrope, Edward Redmane, Halneth Malyverer and Piers St Aubin, the commissioners appointed by Richard on 13 November.[73] Together these two indictments

---

[70] Borlase 1888, pp. 29–30. The original has been traced by Nicholas Kingwell to the Royal Institution of Cornwall, where it is ms BV. 1/4. I am extremely grateful to Dr Oliver Padel for supplying me with a copy of the ms.

[71] PRO, E 404/78/3/25, 40; Southampton RO, SC 5/1/19 fo. 26–v; *Harl. 433* II pp. 34–5.

[72] *CPR* 1476–85 p. 371.

[73] Devon RO, ECA Book 51; Holinshed, *Chronicles* III p. 421. For Bodmin see note 70 above.

account for nine of the eighteen men who were subsequently attainted and whom the act assigns to the Exeter sector, as well as supplying the names of further men who escaped attainder. Of those attainted the Torrington list includes Dorset, Piers Courtenay bishop of Exeter, Thomas St Leger, Robert Willoughby, Thomas Arundel, Walter Courtenay and John Halwell. The bishop and Arundel were also indicted at Bodmin along with Edward Courtenay of Boconnoc and John Trefry of Fowey. The other attainted rebels in the Exeter sector were presumably indicted elsewhere in the region. There must, for instance, have been an investigation into Exeter's own involvement. Apart from the cathedral clergy, who largely escaped attainder, four of the known rebels are described as 'of Exeter' and a fifth, Richard Cruse, held office nearby.[74]

The implication that Exeter was the centre of rebellion in the south west is thus seriously misleading. The compilers of the act simply used Exeter as an umbrella for those attainted as a result of indictments presented to the royal commissioners in Devon and Cornwall. The same is likely to be true of the other sectors. Indeed the act itself implies as much in its treatment of the south east, where several centres are mentioned but their rebels are again conflated. The Newbury sector thus represents the findings of the Oxfordshire/Berkshire commissioners, and Salisbury those of the Dorset/Somerset and Wiltshire/Southampton commissioners – these last amalgamated, perhaps, because of the degree of overlap among the rebels involved. Once this is recognized, it becomes possible to suggest further centres hidden by the act's division into sectors. Southampton was certainly one. It was an obvious focus for several of the gentry involved, men like William Ovedale of Wickham and William Berkeley of Bisterne. The city itself was also drawn in, perhaps at the instigation of Berkeley, the constable, whose presence is recorded there on 8 and 21 October. The mayor, Walter Williams, was later attainted for his part in the rebellion and it is hardly surprising that on 8 November, when the rebellion had visibly failed, the city thought it prudent to send a tun of wine to the king. Richard later imposed an oath of fealty on the townsmen, itself suggestive of

---

[74] *Rot. Parl.* vi p. 246; *CPR* 1476–85 p. 473. Since Exeter seems not to have been the rebels' home in all cases, the designation must derive from their involvement in the rebellion there.

heavy local involvement, and may have suspended the city's liberties.[75]

The south east sector, as represented in the act, is particularly misleading. Although at first sight the act seems more than usually informative about this area, listing four centres as opposed to one, examination suggests that it still underestimates the spread of disaffection. It is clear, for instance, that there was unrest in Sussex. Only two Sussex men are listed in the act of attainder: Thomas Lewkenore of Trotton and Thomas Fiennes of Herstmonceux. Several others, however, took out bonds for good behaviour later in the reign or were bound to appear before the royal council, including various members of the Fiennes family.[76] The Sussex contingent may initially have joined the Kentish rising, but if so, as the tide turned against them, they fell back on Lewkenore's castle of Bodiam, where they were besieged in November.[77] A more interesting omission is East Anglia. Although the act has no East Anglian sector, several local men were attainted or can be shown to have been involved. William Knyvet of Buckenham (Norf.), who had married Buckingham's aunt, is listed under Brecon, although he managed to buy his way out of attainder. Thomas Lovell of Beechamwell (Norf.) is included in the Exeter sector, perhaps because he was acting with Dorset, whose life he had, according to Tudor accounts, preserved during the period between Richard's accession and the rebellion.[78] The most significant group of East Anglians is, however, to be found among the Kent rebels, including the Brandons, John Wingfield and Robert Brews. Some of the Kent and Sussex rebels also had East Anglian interests. Richard Haute of Ightham had been a candidate for the shrievalty of Essex in the last year of Edward IV's reign. Thomas Fiennes had been given land and office in the region by Edward IV and, perhaps on the strength of it, had married an Essex widow.[79] Given this community of interest, it is not surprising that one of John Howard's first moves on hearing of the trouble in Kent was to secure the Thames crossings. He probably did not manage to confine the rising to the

[75] Southampton RO, SC 5/1/19 fos. 28-v, 31-v. A similar oath was imposed on Kent: *Harl. 433* II pp. 75-7.

[76] PRO, C 244/134/29, 244/136/27-8; *CCR* 1476-85 no. 1456.

[77] *CPR* 1476-85 p. 370.

[78] Knyvet: *Rot. Parl.* VI p. 298; Rawcliffe 1978, p. 227. Lovell: Holinshed, *Chronicles* III p. 416; Hardyng, *Chronicle* p. 529 ('Rowell'); Vergil p. 551 ('Rouell').

[79] PRO, C 81/1391/19; *CPR* 1476-85 pp. 180, 261, 543.

south bank, however, for the Crowland chronicler puts Essex third in his list of rebellious counties.[80] First place was taken by London, which also contributed men to those attainted without being mentioned specifically in the act. Perhaps in this case the omission is justified, for although trouble was feared in the city London sources give no indication that it materialized. This may have been due to Howard's prompt action in defending the city. Most of the men described in the act as 'of London' were not native Londoners but were linked with the East Anglian and Kentish rebels, which perhaps suggests that the rebel forces from those areas had planned to converge on the city.[81]

The existence of additional centres of unrest, hidden in the act of attainder, does not necessarily imply that the rebel effort was fragmented. As the Torrington and Bodmin indictments show, men might be involved in more than one place – which suggests that, were more indictments to survive, the various centres might prove to represent different chronological stages of the rebellion rather than discrete elements. It is likely, for instance, that many rebels fell back into the south west as the rising began to collapse further east. Thus the 'Salisbury' rebels John Cheyne and Giles Daubeney made their escape to Brittany with the 'Exeter' rebel John Halwell in a boat belonging to Stephen Calmady of Calmady (Devon).[82] As this implies, there was probably also more overlap between the sectors of the rebellion than the act of attainder would suggest. It presents each sector as entirely self contained, with each rebel assigned to only one sector, but this was an over-simplification. In October the customer of Poole, John Kymer, was summoned to account at the exchequer but to his dismay found that the rebels William Norreys and John Cheyne with other rebels 'in great number' lay between him and the palace of Westminster.[83] According to the act of attainder Norreys was active in the Newbury centre and Cheyne at Salisbury, but if Kymer is to be believed they had joined forces. Such co-operation is also implied by the distribution of the Cheyne brothers between three of the act's sectors. John and the two brothers who were attainted with him were assigned to the

[80] *Crowland* pp. 162–3.
[81] Horrox 1984, pp. 326–7; Prideaux 1896–7, I p. 27. One London source described the rebellion as affecting 'Kent to St. Michael's Mount': Green, 'Hist. notes' p. 588.
[82] PRO, C 82/55/6, a reference I owe to the kindness of Miss Margaret Condon. See also *Harl. 433* II p. 37.
[83] PRO, E 208/17/unnumb. Kymer sent a substitute, who was robbed by Norreys.

Salisbury sector, but their brother William (who escaped attainder) was implicated in Kent and another brother was pardoned 'of Newbury' in the aftermath of the rebellion.[84]

As this example suggests, there is another sense in which the act of attainder presents only a partial picture of the rebellion. Although the number attainted was unusually high, it was still only a fraction of those involved. The rank and file were largely excluded. So was anyone who had managed to make his peace with the crown before the act was finally passed. The list of rebels provided by the act can be augmented considerably from other sources. Additional rebels were named in the commissions of arrest issued after the rising and in the extant indictments. Some were penalized in other ways by the crown, by loss of office or exclusion from commissions. Others entered bonds for good behaviour or felt it advisable to seek a general pardon. These additional names often do no more than reinforce elements present in the act of attainder. Thus suspicion fell on the close kinsmen of some attainted rebels, such as Bartholomew St Leger and Anthony Brown, brothers of the executed rebels Thomas St Leger and George Brown.[85] But some of those suspected of complicity were more independent figures. The possible involvement of Sir Thomas Bourgchier of Barnes called into question the loyalty of a major Yorkist family.[86] The Audleys also came under suspicion. Thomas Audley was listed among the Dorset rebels in November but secured a pardon in February 1484 and was not attainted. His brother John lord Audley and John's son James were pardoned at the same time and were presumably thought to have been implicated since lord Audley was dropped from commissions of the peace in the immediate aftermath of the rebellion, although he later recovered the king's confidence.[87] In such cases it is not possible to be sure of the degree of complicity. In a few cases the crown may simply have got it wrong. Sir John Donne, the brother-in-law of lord Hastings and his associate at

---

[84] 'Pedigrees of the blood royal' p. 314; *Harl. 433* II p. 48; PRO, C 67/51 m. 14. Another brother, Alexander, was also implicated, probably at Newbury since his land lay in Berkshire: *Harl. 433* II p. 43; *CPR 1476–85* p. 417; PRO, C 244/134/67.

[85] St Leger: Holinshed, *Chronicles* III p. 421; PRO, Prob 11/18 fo. 122–v. Another brother, James, was pardoned at the same time as Bartholomew and may also have been implicated: PRO, C 67/51 m. 27; Prob 11/16 fo. 224v. Brown: *Harl. 433* II p. 48; *CPR 1461–7* p. 88.

[86] *Harl. 433* II p. 32; *Reg. Thome Bourgchier* p. xxii.

[87] *Harl. 433* II p. 31; PRO, C 67/51 m. 1.

Calais, was thought to have rebelled and Richard ordered the confiscation of his land. But Donne was evidently able to clear himself and by autumn 1484 was sufficiently trusted to be pricked as sheriff, although he never regained his Calais office, regranted in the aftermath of the rebellion.[88] The extent of royal suspicion is, however, significant, since it was this (as much as 'real' complicity) which determined the king's response to the rebellion.

The 1483 risings were thus a more serious prospect than the act of attainder alone might suggest: in size, geographical extent and duration. The composition of the rebels was also particularly threatening. On the whole they were not outsiders but insiders: men whom the king had believed he could trust and who had the resources of royal favour behind them. This meant that the rebellion was a profound shock to the king, and the blow to his confidence was to shape royal policy for the rest of the reign. It also, more immediately, meant that his efforts to deal with the rebellion were flawed. The royal household was the obvious spearhead for any move against the rebels – most of the men sent by John Howard into Kent, for instance, were royal servants.[89] A significant proportion of household men in the south were, however, in sympathy with the rebels. Howard himself may have suffered from this. The 'Bownteyne' whom he sent to Gravesend on 11 October could well be the John Bounteyn who was with the rebels at Gravesend on 13 October (where he murdered master Mowbray) and who was subsequently attainted.[90] When Richard III ordered troops to be raised in October, Francis viscount Lovell wrote to William Stonor asking him to raise the Lovell retinue as well as his own men.[91] But Stonor joined the rebels, and may even have taken Lovell's men with him.

Given this weakness within his own ranks, Richard III was fortunate to come out of the rebellion as well as he did. In the event, the risings collapsed without coming to battle and this makes it easy to play down the danger they posed. But the

---

[88] *Harl. 433* II p. 32; Griffiths 1972a, pp. 187–8; McFarlane 1971, p. 2. For Calais see below, pp. 290–2.

[89] Collier, *Household Books* p. 471: Wotton, Nortriche, Passe, Richmond, Cartmail, Leader, Danyell, Scopham, Dobson and Middleton. PRO, E 101/412/10 fo. 36; *CPR 1467–77* pp. 293, 570; *CPR 1476–85* pp. 70, 199, 344, 346; Nicolas *Wardrobe Accounts* p. 164.

[90] *Rot. Parl.* VI p. 245; Stow, *Annales* p. 775. Howard's man may, however, have been the yeoman of the crown *Richard* Bounteyn.

[91] *Stonor Letters* II p. 163.

rebellion was far from negligible. Many of the leading gentry in the southern third of the country were in arms for a month, and their opposition would surely have gained further momentum had events once begun to swing in their favour. Tudor chroniclers were conscious of this apparent contradiction and were in no doubt of the explanation. With varying degrees of bluntness they asserted that the rebellion failed because when it came to the point Buckingham would not give battle.[92] Modern opinion, by contrast, has tended to play down Buckingham's significance. Although the Crowland chronicler thought him the principal captain of the rebels, and the preamble to the act of attainder stresses his central role, this does not seem to be borne out by the lists of those attainted. The number of rebels listed under Brecon is not only tiny by comparison with the other sectors, but suggests that the duke had won no local support. Only four men are named: the bishop of Ely (whom most chronicle sources credit with persuading the duke to rebel), William Knyvet, John Rushe and Thomas Nandyke. Rushe was a London merchant who owned land in East Anglia and had links with the Woodvilles.[93] Nandyke was a Cambridge master of arts, described in the act as a necromancer, but more properly, to judge from other sources, an astrologer and physician.[94] Moreover, few of the rebels elsewhere had close links with the duke. The Salisbury sector included Nicholas Latimer of Duntish in Buckland (Dorset), the duke's chamberlain. In Kent the Pympe brothers were Stafford tenants and John Pympe had been the ward of Buckingham's parents, but their involvement could also be explained by their relationship to the leading Kent rebels, the Guildfords.[95] In short, the Brecon sector, and by implication Buckingham himself, seems not fully integrated into the rebellion, but peripheral in a political as well as a geographical sense.

The act, however, reflects Buckingham's failure. His intended role may have been considerably more important. There is evidence that the duke was lobbying for support from the Stanleys, and there must have seemed a good chance that he would win it, given that Thomas lord Stanley was the husband of

[92] e.g. *Great Chron.* p. 234; Vergil p. 552; Stow, *Annales* p. 775. *Crowland* pp. 164–5 gives more weight to Richard's countermeasures.

[93] *Crowland* pp. 162–3; *Rot. Parl.* VI p. 245; *Harl. 433* II p. 115; Ives 1968, p. 222.

[94] PRO, Prob 2/48; Leathes, *Grace Book A* p. 116 shows that he studied medicine.

[95] Rawcliffe 1978, pp. 33–4; Ball 1909, pp. 165–7.

Margaret Beaufort.[96] Another family which might have backed a rising along the Welsh march was the Talbots. During the minority of the young earl of Shrewsbury the effective head of the family was the earl's uncle Gilbert, who seems to have been out of favour with Richard III from the beginning. He was dropped from the Shropshire commissions of the peace immediately after the king's accession, possibly because of the family's strong Hastings links, although Richard seems on the whole to have been well disposed towards the Hastings connection. Gilbert remained out of favour for the rest of the reign, finally leading the family's forces against the king at Bosworth. If Buckingham had succeeded in joining with the Talbots and Stanleys, his sector of the rebellion, far from being peripheral, would have constituted one arm of a pincer movement which, with the rebels in the southern counties as the other, would have come near to encircling the king as he marched west.

This may well have been the rebels' intention, and would make sense of Buckingham's movements in October 1483. Only two chroniclers are at all explicit about the duke's route: the Crowland chronicler, who states that he delayed at Weobley (Herefs.), and Hall, who has the duke advancing through the Forest of Dean but then failing to cross the Severn and fleeing northwards. The two versions were conflated by Gairdner into a single account which strains credibility but has been widely followed. This has Buckingham going first to Weobley, and then down into the Forest of Dean. If the two accounts are to be combined, the reverse order makes better geographical sense, but it is more likely that the Crowland chronicler's version is correct and that when Buckingham left Brecon he simply headed north east on the Leominster road, advancing as far as Weobley. There, according to a family source, he called the local gentry to him and, when he had spoken with them, departed. Before doing so he gave his heir into the protection of Sir Richard de la Bere and his departure is thus probably a euphemism for his decision to take flight, as *Crowland* suggests. When he was finally arrested it was in Shropshire, which suggests that Weobley marked the effective end of his advance and that he then fled north.[97]

Given the potential importance of the Brecon sector, it

[96] *Plumpton Corresp.* pp. 44–5.
[97] *Crowland* pp. 164–5; Halle, *Union* (Richard III) fo. 15; Gairdner 1898, p. 138; Owen and Blakeway 1825, p. 241.

becomes less surprising that its collapse should undermine the whole rebellion. That collapse, however, was not simply a matter of ducal cowardice. Buckingham failed to give battle because he had no support. The local gentry were clearly unwilling to back him.[98] The bald account of the Weobley meeting suggests that the duke sought help from the Herefordshire gentry and that they refused it. His own tenants were no more enthusiastic, some even sacking Brecon behind him. Buckingham also failed to mobilize the potential noble opposition to Richard III. The Stanleys may have hesitated, but in the end they backed the king. The Talbots, as far as one can tell, did nothing. The interests of both families had been challenged by the duke's sudden arrival on the political scene. The Stanleys are unlikely to have welcomed a major new influence on the borders of their own power base in north Wales and Cheshire.[99] The Talbots were ducal rivals not only along the march but in the north midlands. Neither family had any reason to support a change of regime which was likely to endorse the duke's empire-building. The same feelings were almost certainly at work among the lesser Yorkist servants in the region, who had seen their role undermined by the sweeping grants to Buckingham. The Brecon sector, significantly, was the only one to contain no local servants of Edward IV. John Mortimer, displaced at Monmouth by the duke, showed no sign of involvement in 1483 but joined Tudor in 1485. If Buckingham had remained loyal to Richard, his ascendancy might have fuelled a major rebellion in Wales and along the march. As it was, his decision to join the rebels removed any possibility of coherent opposition there, and without it the southern wing of the rebellion faltered and collapsed.[100] Tudor writers were thus probably right to see Buckingham as the major flaw in the rebellion. Paradoxically, Richard's betrayal by his leading ally may have rescued the king from the full consequences of the rebellion.

This still leaves unanswered the most intriguing question of all, which is why Buckingham should have rebelled in the first place. As far as one can judge, Richard had refused him nothing, unless Buckingham had had his eye on the two wardships confirmed to

[98] Pugh 1963, pp. 240–1; Rawcliffe 1978, p. 34; Griffiths and Thomas 1985, p. 115.
[99] The question of Stanley opposition to Buckingham is explored further in M. K. Jones 1988, pp. 18–19.
[100] If, as all the Tudor sources claim, Buckingham was suborned by John Morton, the bishop must take some responsibility for the resulting *débâcle*.

164

lady Hastings.[101] Despite claims to the contrary, Buckingham had been given effective possession of the coveted Bohun inheritance.[102] Vergil's subsidiary suggestion, that Buckingham's claim to the inheritance had alerted Richard to the duke's 'Lancastrian' title to the throne, leading to a cooling of relations between the two men, is implausible.[103] The duke's title to the estates derived not from any Lancastrian descent but through his descent from Eleanor Bohun, which conferred no title to the throne. It is true that Buckingham had a double royal descent, from Thomas of Woodstock and from the Beauforts, but both descents were inferior to Richard's own. There is also no evidence to support Hall's claim that the duke had been alienated by Richard's tactics in taking the crown and in particular by the murder of the princes. On the contrary, Buckingham had been involved in each stage of the usurpation, and a persistent rumour credits him with advising the death of the princes.[104] Faced with so many negatives, it is hardly surprising that some modern writers have felt that Buckingham's aim in rebelling must have been to make himself king, that being the only step which would actually improve his position. On this interpretaion, the duke entered the rebellion after the death of the princes had left the rebels without a claimant for the throne, although it is then an open question whether he subsequently deferred to Tudor's claims (perhaps in the expectation of being able to dominate him) or whether he continued to hope for the crown – in which case Brecon's isolation could be explained by its being ideologically distinct from the rest of the rebellion. Both contemporary and Tudor sources stress the duke's endorsement of Henry Tudor, but it is not impossible that this was a deliberate attempt to slur over the sensitive question of the duke's title to the throne.[105]

This interpretation of events, however, probably starts from the wrong premise. It assumes that the duke must have had a positive reason to rebel, a view based on the tacit belief that the rebellion was a rather forlorn hope. But it is unlikely to have seemed so to contemporaries, and Buckingham (who had already shown himself an opportunist in his support of Gloucester) may

---

[101] See note 22 above.
[102] For the contrary view see (e.g.) Lander 1980, p. 318.
[103] Vergil pp. 548–9.
[104] Halle, *Union* (Richard III) fos. 9v–10; Green, 'Hist. notes' pp. 587–8; Hammond 1974, pp. 16–17.
[105] Rawcliffe 1978, pp. 31–2; Chrimes 1972, pp. 20–1.

well have felt that if the rebellion had a good chance of succeeding, the best way to safeguard his new eminence was to switch sides.[106] If plans for the rebellion did include a rising along the march Buckingham had no hope of avoiding the issue by remaining uncommitted, and any hesitation over which was the stronger side was perhaps finally removed when the presumed death of the princes failed to check the rebels' plans.

By contrast with the controversy over Buckingham's motives, those of Margaret Beaufort are eminently straightforward. She wanted the advancement of her son: first to a place among the English nobility under a restored Edward V, and then to the crown itself. Her success in persuading the rebels to accept Tudor as their rival to Richard III was a major contribution to the shape of the rebellion. But she was able to give relatively little practical support. The act of attainder accuses her only of supplying financial help. Even Tudor sources, which were anxious to emphasize her role, credit her with little more than backstairs lobbying on her son's behalf. She failed to bring in the Stanleys, although it may have been the expectation of her doing so which persuaded the Woodvilles and others to accept Tudor's candidature. She might have succeeded if Buckingham had not become involved, or if Richard III had not been shrewd enough (or angry enough) to march straight towards the duke without being deflected by the risings on his flank. The Stanley brothers are famous for always backing the right side, and the sight of Buckingham failing to win enough local support to cope with the advancing royal army would have removed any lingering doubts about which was the right side. It is a measure of the king's delight, and relief, at this development that lord Stanley was among the first to benefit from the duke's fall, receiving Buckingham's lordship of Kimbolton (Hunts.) on 2 November, the day of the duke's execution.[107] The Stanleys' loyalty also dictated the leniency with which Margaret Beaufort was treated. Tudor chroniclers indulge in heavy irony at Richard's expense over his failure to treat her more severely, but it is difficult to see what other course was open to him.[108] Much as she might deserve punishment, any penalties imposed on her would have material repercussions for her husband. The rebellion had, moreover,

[106] Ross 1981, p. 115; Richmond 1986, p. 180.
[107] *Harl. 433* II p. 30.
[108] M. K. Jones 1986b, pp. 31–2; Halle, *Union* (Richard III) fo. 18.

demonstrated that without Stanley support the Beaufort interest was negligible, and if leniency towards Margaret was part of the price of continuing Stanley loyalty, Richard probably thought it worth paying.

The involvement of Margaret Beaufort and the choice of her son as alternative candidate for the throne may seem to give the 1483 rebellion something of a Lancastrian flavour. It is, however, doubtful whether such labels have much validity by this date. Twenty-three years of Yorkist government had resulted in most of the former opponents of the regime making their peace and being absorbed into the political establishment. Although some of the rebels could be said to have a Lancastrian background, all (except the Tudors) had been reconciled and would have been perceived as supporters of the house of York in April 1483, something which makes it difficult to interpret their rebellion six months later in purely factional terms. This is exemplified by the case of Sir Nicholas Latimer, who had been attainted after the battle of Towton in 1461. He made his peace with the Yorkists in 1463 and set about redeeming his forfeited land, buying back the manors of Duntish and Dewlish from John Howard in 1464. This rehabilitation nearly came to an abrupt end in 1470, when he followed Clarence into opposition, but he returned to the fold with the duke in 1471 and was made a banneret at Tewkesbury. By 1475 he had become associated with the Staffords, a connection which resulted in the second attainder of his career when he backed Buckingham's rebellion. He entered into a bond for his good behaviour in May 1484 and again set about rebuilding his fortunes. In December 1484 Richard granted Latimer's land to four trustees including Latimer's son-in-law John Mordaunt.[109] Latimer's career suggests that he may have been something of a political misfit, but it cannot be explained simply in terms of Lancastrian loyalism.

The example of Latimer suggests the dangers in totting up past Lancastrian affiliations as a guide to the motivation of the rebels in 1483. A number did have personal grievances which were a legacy of the dynastic conflict of the 1450s and 1460s, but this was not incompatible with a record of service to the house of York, as the career of Walter Hungerford indicates. He was of Heytesbury

[109] Turner, *Manners and Expenses* pp. 176–7, 468; *CCR* 1476–85 no. 1243; *CPR* 1476–85 p. 527; Rawcliffe 1978, p. 227; Hampton 1979, no. 404. For Mordaunt: McGregor, *Bedfordshire Wills* pp. 68–71; Ives 1983, pp. 468–9.

(Wilts.), the second son of Robert lord Hungerford who had remained loyal to Henry VI in the early 1460s and had been executed after the battle of Hexham in 1464. Walter's elder brother Thomas had been involved in the abortive Lancastrian conspiracies of the late 1460s and was hanged early in 1469. Walter, by contrast, had chosen to make his peace with the Yorkists, a not uncommon example of a family keeping contacts open with both sides. By 1465 he had entered the service of Edward IV and in 1483 he was one of the esquires of the body who carried the dead king to burial. The death of Thomas left Walter as the Hungerford heir male, since Thomas' only surviving child was a daughter. Walter was later to claim that much of the Hungerford land was held in tail male, so that any reversal of the attainders of his father and brother would have benefited him substantially. Such a reversal was not, however, forthcoming, in spite of Walter's service to Edward IV and in spite of the fact that the other potential beneficiary, Thomas' daughter Mary, was married in the late 1470s to the heir of Edward IV's close friend William lord Hastings.[110] This must have been because the chief beneficiary of the Hungerford attainders had been Gloucester and the duke was not prepared to lose the land. In 1483 Richard parted with the land to his ally John Howard, another recipient whose closeness to the king made his hold on the estates secure.[111] This further demonstration that royal service was unlikely to be rewarded with a restoration of the Hungerford land may have triggered Walter's decision to rebel.

A rebel with a similar background was Edward Courtenay of Boconnoc, the heir of the Lancastrian earls of Devon. The senior Courtenay line, the holders of the title, had died out without direct heirs in 1471, leaving as their heirs general their kinsmen of Boconnoc who, like the senior line, had remained Lancastrian in sympathy. Edward's father Hugh had supported the Readeption and was executed after the battle of Tewkesbury. Edward himself was subsequently pardoned but, unlike Hungerford, did not develop links with the crown, and there was no reason why Edward IV should have considered restoring the earldom in his favour.[112] The estates went towards the endowment of Clarence and, after his fall, formed a useful source of reward for royal

[110] Wiltshire RO, 490/1471 fos. 1–7v; *CP* VI p. 618–23.
[111] BL, Cotton Julius BXII fos. 123–5; *CPR* 1476–85 p. 359.
[112] Thomson 1972, pp. 230–5; Hicks 1980, pp. 72, 188.

servants. Courtenay's rebellion was thus a straightforward piece of opportunism which ultimately paid off: he got the earldom from Henry VII two months after Bosworth. Another west country family in search of an inheritance was equally successful. The Lutterells had lost their estates with the attainder of Sir James in 1461. Like other disenchanted families, they had been associated with Clarence in the 1470s but the duke lacked the political muscle to secure the restoration of their land. In 1482 Edward IV granted Hugh Lutterell, the surviving son of Sir James, the reversion of a moiety of one of the family's Suffolk manors – hardly a very substantial carrot. Hugh joined the rebels in 1483 but escaped attainder. The first parliament of Henry VII subsequently reversed Sir James' attainder and cancelled the Yorkist grants from the estates.[113]

This quasi-Lancastrian group among the rebels is completed by John Welles, whose claim to the Welles barony had been blocked by Edward IV. His father, Lionel lord Welles, had been attainted in 1461, after his death on the Lancastrian side at Towton. Lionel's son by his first marriage, Robert, had gradually achieved the restoration of the family land and title in the course of the 1460s, but he and his son Richard were then implicated in the 1470 Lincolnshire rising and executed. Neither was attainted and the barony was allowed to pass to Robert's sister Joan, the wife of Richard Hastings, the brother of Edward IV's chamberlain. Joan died without heirs in the mid 1470s, leaving as her heir general her half-brother John, Lionel's son by his second marriage. Edward IV, however, blocked this descent by attainting Robert and Richard Welles in the parliament of 1475 and by granting a life estate in the property to Richard Hastings.[114] In theory, therefore, John Welles' reasons for rebellion in 1483 look thoroughly 'Lancastrian', particularly as he was the half-brother of Margaret Beaufort. But on closer examination Welles' motives, like those of Hungerford, become less straightforward. By 1483 he was securely established in Edward IV's household. He is also known to have been in rebellion sufficiently early for his initial aim to have been the restoration of Edward V. Similar information is lacking for the other rebels, but one cannot assume that men like Lutterell or Courtenay wanted a specifically Lancastrian revolu-

---

[113] *Rot. Parl.* v p. 479, vi p. 297; Hicks 1974, p. 374; Holinshed, *Chronicles* III p. 421; Lyte 1882, pp. 62–3.

[114] *CP* XII part II pp. 443–8; *Rot. Parl.* VI pp. 144–5, 148–9.

tion. Although they had hitherto done badly from the Yorkists, their role in the rebellion might have earned them their reward as readily from a restored Edward V as from the Tudors. Their contribution to the rebellion, in other words, owed nothing to dynastic idealism and everything to the realization that for the first time in over a decade rebellion in pursuit of personal aims could be a feasible tactic.

The argument against regarding the 1483 rebellion as another outbreak of dynastic rivalry does not rest only on the difficulty of defining a Lancastrian in the context of the 1480s. Even if Courtenay and the rest are allowed Lancastrian motives, the complexion of the rebels as a whole still remains overwhelmingly 'Yorkist'. That is to say that fundamentally the rebellion came from within the Yorkist establishment as it had existed in 1483. Some of the rebels were associates of Edward IV who had lost heavily by Richard's accession. The Woodvilles and Hautes are the obvious examples. They had not only been shouldered from power but had seen their family lands seized. Their motive for rebellion was straightforward and Richard must have been expecting trouble from that quarter. But they were the exception. The risings cannot be interpreted simply as a rebellion of 'outs' chafing under their exclusion from the new regime. Most of those implicated were men whom Richard had been prepared to keep in favour. Thirty-three of the rebels were justices of the peace at the time of their rebellion and ten of those had been added to the bench by Richard himself. Three were sheriffs.[115] Many held other royal office which the king had shown no sign of regranting. A few even received grants from Richard in the weeks before the rebellion broke, including Walter Hungerford and Thomas Arundel.[116] An unknown, but probably significant, number had transferred from Edward IV's household to that of the new king. Five of Richard's own yeomen were attainted, and the rebel John Bounteyn, described as 'late' yeoman of the crown in the act of attainder, may also have entered Richard's service. A seventh, Robert Brent, was pardoned before parliament rose in terms which make it clear that he was in the household at the time of his rebellion. London sources state that four yeomen of the crown were hanged

[115] John Trefry (Cornwall): *Trevelyan Papers* p. 87. John Wingfield (Norf./Suff.) and William Berkeley (Southants): *CFR* 1471–85 no. 764. Richard de la Bere, who rescued Buckingham's son, was sheriff of Hereford.
[116] *Harl. 433* 1 pp. 87, 88.

at Tyburn, and these are perhaps additional since most of the attainted yeomen appear to have survived the reign.[117]

The degree to which opposition came from within the establishment suggests that Yorkist sensibilities had been outraged by the circumstances of Richard's accession, and any interpretation of the rebellion has to take this into account. But moral indignation is not the whole story. The majority of the Yorkist establishment was prepared to serve Richard III, or at least to refrain from overt opposition. Unless one is to categorize such men as time-servers and the rebels as men of principle, other factors have to be taken into account. One of the most important was simply opportunity: men were drawn into rebellion because kinsmen and friends were involved, or because the district in which they lived was affected. Thus John Cheyne, who can be categorized as one of the 'outs', drew in his five brothers and also William Bampton of Faulstone (Wilts.), a Cheyne manor. Similarly Giles Daubeney involved six of his servants and William Case of South Petherton (Som.).[118] Roger Tocotes and his stepson Richard Beauchamp lord St Amand were both involved. A similar relationship probably explains the involvement of Sir George Brown, the stepson of the executed Sir Thomas Vaughan, while Brown in turn drew in his own stepson, Edward Poynings, and his brother Anthony Brown.[119] The episcopal rebels had the backing of some of their lesser clergy as well as their kinsmen. Thus at Exeter Piers Courtenay was supported by his brother Walter and also by the dean, John Arundel, the archdeacon, David Hopton, and the registrar, Thomas Eliot.[120]

These examples are relatively straightforward. More difficult to evaluate are the looser family relationships linking many of the rebels. The best-known example is to be found in Kent and Sussex, where a group of interrelated families was drawn into rebellion by their relationship with the Woodvilles.[121] A similar nexus, again with Woodville links, can be traced in East Anglia.

---

[117] *Rot. Parl.* VI pp. 245–6; *CPR* 1476–85 p. 418; *Great Chron.* p. 235; Fabyan, *Chronicles* p. 671; Green, 'Hist. notes' p. 589. Only the latter mentions a name, Richard Poynch. He has not been identified.

[118] *Rot. Parl.* VI p. 246.

[119] *CPR* 1461–7 p. 88; Wedgwood 1936, pp. 121–2. The Brown/Poynings involvement may also owe something to their dispute with Richard's ally Northumberland: Jeffs 1961, pp. 148–62.

[120] Holinshed, *Chronicles* III p. 421; *CPR* 1476–85 p. 458.

[121] Conway 1925; the author's pedigrees are inaccurate in detail but her general conclusions stand.

The pivot here was the Fitzlewis family. Mary Fitzlewis was the second wife of Anthony earl Rivers. Her aunt Elizabeth had married into the Wingfields, and the two John Wingfields who rebelled were Mary's cousins. So was Catherine Wingfield, the wife of the rebel Robert Brews, and Thomas Wingfield, who is not known to have been involved in 1483 but reputedly died on Tudor's side at Bosworth. The Wingfields also had links by marriage with the Brandons, who headed the rebellion in Essex and in turn probably drew in the rebel William Loveday. The connection can also be extended, although more tenuously, from the Brandons through the Darcies to the Hautes and so back to the Woodvilles.[122] In the west, a number of the leading rebels formed a family group around John Cheyne. He married Margaret, the widow of William lord Stourton (d. 1478), which gave him links, through the Stourtons, with the Berkeleys of Beverstone and, through Margaret herself, with the rebels Thomas Arundel and Giles Daubeney.[123]

Such interrelationships can be suggestive, particularly if it can be shown that the men concerned co-operated on other matters, but they need to be kept in perspective. All the rebels can equally well be linked with men who remained loyal, and it is not usually possible to say why one family relationship pulled more strongly than another. Some men followed their in-laws into rebellion. Robert Brews chose to join his wife's family, the Wingfields, rather than staying loyal like his half-brother William, who was in turn related by marriage to Richard's allies the Hoptons.[124] The Pympe brothers, in a similar position, both rebelled, in effect preferring Reginald's links with the Woodvilles to John's links with the Whetehills, who remained the king's men.[125] Thomas Arundel was accompanied into rebellion by one brother-in-law, Giles Daubeney, while another, John lord Dynham, stayed loyal to Richard. Two Trefry brothers, John and William, rebelled, a third apparently did nothing and their brother-in-law John Trevanion remained an active member of the royal circle in

---

[122] The pedigree can be reconstructed from: Elliot 1898; King 1869; Wingfield 1925, pp. 18–37.

[123] *CP* XII part I pp. 302–5; 'Pedigrees of the blood royal' pp. 306–7.

[124] Above, n. 122; *Inqs p.m.* I nos. 648, 654, 1025; Richmond 1981a, pp. 142–3.

[125] *Inqs p.m.* I no. 1235; Conway 1925, p. 120. John Pympe's will make it clear that it was his St Leger and Cheyne connections which he valued, and which he wanted commemorated: PRO, Prob 11/11 fo. 21–v. Adrian Whetehill, his wife's brother, was an esquire of Richard III's body: PRO, E 207/21/22/3.

Cornwall.[126] Such divisions are the inevitable result of a much intermarried society, and on the whole they were useful rather than otherwise. Thomas Lewkenore of Trotton found his rehabilitation after attainder eased by the fact that his brother-in-law was John Wood, Richard's treasurer of the exchequer.[127] Indeed some of the most striking family divisions may have been a deliberate attempt to keep a foot in both camps. The attainted rebels include a number of men whose fathers or brothers remained loyal. Edmund Hampden was the second son of Thomas Hampden of Hampden (Bucks.). He was probably drawn into the rebellion by his father's cousin, William Stonor, but Thomas himself and his eldest son kept their distance.[128] Of the Courtenays of Powderham (Devon), two brothers, Piers and Walter, rebelled while the other four entered the king's service. Even the Hautes kept connections open with the new regime. James Haute co-operated with the king against the rebels and was given the land of his brother Richard senior – the ultimate justification of such tactics.[129] But even in these cases it is not usually obvious why a family divided as it did. James Haute may have had existing links with the king if, as seems possible, he was the husband of the Katherine Haute paid an annuity by Gloucester in the 1470s.[130] But why was it Edmund Hampden, rather than one of his four brothers, who joined the rebels?

Sometimes the division of loyalist/rebel parallels a division on some other issue, although again it is important not to read too much into a single episode. Local politics were not an affair of immutable 'parties' and men who co-operated on one issue might find themselves rivals in another context. Two of the leading rebels in the south west, Thomas St Leger and Thomas Fulford, had been in conflict in 1477, when Fulford paid compensation to one of St Leger's servants who had been beaten up by his men.[131]

---

[126] PRO, Prob 11/14 fos. 164v–5v; Vivian 1887, pp. 459, 501. Trevanion received land from Richard III and was added to the bench in December 1483. He was also Tyrell's deputy as bailiff of the duchy of Cornwall, in which capacity he was attacked while holding the manor court of Stoke Climsland: PRO, KB 9/367/4.

[127] *Inqs p.m.* II no. 629; *CCR 1476–85* no. 1242.

[128] *Inqs p.m.* III no. 614; *Visit. Bucks.* p. 70; *Stonor Letters* I p. xix.

[129] In the grant James is described as *dilectus ligeus et serviens noster*: PRO, PSO 1/57/2942; *CPR 1476–85* p. 458; Davis 1955, pp. 170–1 (I am grateful to Anne Sutton for a copy of her notes on this book).

[130] PRO, Prob 11/16 fo. 28v.

[131] *CCR 1476–85* no. 222. Fulford was indicted before Scrope but secured a pardon and was not attainted: Holinshed, *Chronicles* III p. 421; PRO, C 67/51 m. 2.

But there are cases where the battle lines in 1483 may have been influenced by existing rivalries. It is possible that it was a land dispute, rather than a desire to hedge their bets, which divided the Brews brothers. In June 1483 Thomas Hansard, William Brews' son-in-law, had entered into a bond not to harm Robert Brews or any of his people. This suggests that Robert may have been drawn into a dispute between his mother (William's stepmother) and his half-brother over land settled on William by his father.[132]

Rather better documented is the dispute in the south west over the Arundel inheritance. Sir John Arundel of Lanherne (Corn.) had married twice. By his first wife he had had a daughter, Anne, who married Sir James Tyrell.[133] By his second wife, Katherine Chidiok, he had a son, Thomas, and five more daughters. Katherine's executor was one of her sons-in-law, Giles Daubeney, and at the end of Edward IV's reign Tyrell sued Daubeney over his wife's dowry. Tyrell claimed that John Arundel had promised him £200 on the accomplishment of the marriage, but had died without making the payment. His widow Katherine had settled land on Daubeney and others for the payment of her husband's debts and her own, but Daubeney had refused to pay the £200.[134] This dispute was relatively minor, but behind it lay a more far-reaching quarrel. John Arundel's first wife, the mother of Anne, was Elizabeth, the daughter of Thomas lord Morley. Elizabeth's uncle, William de la Pole duke of Suffolk, had settled on her extensive lands in Devon and Cornwall, which had subsequently passed to John Arundel's son by his second marriage, Thomas. Anne evidently claimed the land as Elizabeth's heiress, but by the end of Edward IV's reign she and Tyrell had recovered only three of some twenty-five manors.[135] The accession of Richard III, Tyrell's patron, thus threatened the Arundels not only with the loss of £200 but of a substantial group of manors – something which may have prompted Thomas Arundel's rebellion. In the event Arundel backed the wrong side and on 9 November, while Richard was at Exeter, Piers St Aubin was ordered to seize the disputed land and hand it all to Tyrell, a decision which was subsequently ratified in parliament.[136]

---

[132] PRO, C 244/133/15; and refs. in n. 124 above.
[133] Yeatman 1882, p. 261.
[134] PRO, C 1/53/3.
[135] *Rot. Parl.* VI pp. 255–6, which, however, only gives Tyrell's version of events.
[136] *Ibid.*; *Harl.* 433 II p. 34.

For Arundel, the dispute with Tyrell may have constituted his primary motive for rebellion. Usually, however, such disputes were only one element in a more complex situation. In the south east it was on the cards from the beginning of the reign that Sir John Fogge would oppose the new regime. He was closely linked with the Woodvilles and Hautes, and the trouble Richard took to try and conciliate him suggests that his defection was anticipated. But by the time of the rebellion Fogge was also in dispute with Richard's ally Sir Ralph Ashton, who had, at the very beginning of the reign, arranged to marry Elizabeth Chicheley, the widow of John Kyriel of Stockbury (Kent). Fogge's own first wife had been Alice Kyriel, the coheiress of John's brother Thomas, through whom he had acquired a share of the Kyriel inheritance. The dispute with Ashton, however, appears to have arisen from Fogge's role as feoffee of John Kyriel. Kyriel had settled his manors of Westenhanger, Great Mongeham and Walmer (Kent) on Elizabeth for life, but Fogge apparently refused to hand over the deeds to Elizabeth and her new husband.[137] Most of the evidence for this dispute comes from the beginning of the next reign, when tempers had no doubt been further inflamed by Fogge's attainder and the subsequent grant of much of his land to Ashton.[138] It is likely, however, that as early as summer 1483 Fogge was unhappy with the arrival of one of Richard's close associates in his sphere of influence – particularly, perhaps, one with Ashton's bad reputation.[139]

Although the exact motives which drove an individual into rebellion cannot be reconstructed, some broad trends can be identified. The original nucleus of rebels was probably those who had suffered by Richard's accession, notably the Woodvilles. They in turn drew in friends and kinsmen, with the result that it is easy to present the rebellion as a Woodville rising. This, however, is a misleading emphasis. Few of those involved were so closely linked with the family that they had been prepared to back them in May–June. The situation had been transformed by Richard's accession, and the extent of the transformation is reflected in the fact that almost all the men whom Gloucester had used against Sir

---

[137] PRO, C 1/76/3–5, 1/79/2; Dunlop 1927, pp. 257–9, a reference I owe to W. E. Hampton; *CFR* 1471–85 no. 668; *CCR* 1476–85 nos. 1013, 1113; *Christ Church Letters* p. 47.

[138] *Harl. 433* I p. 137, II pp. 55–6, 77.

[139] In his native north west Ashton passed into legend: Axon 1870; Briggs 1971, part B vol. I pp. 47–9.

Edward Woodville in May chose to join the rebels in October.[140] The rebellion was essentially a Yorkist affair, although this is too sweeping a definition. Not all of Edward IV's servants were drawn in. Many refrained from opposition and several gave active support to the new king. Inevitably personal motives or pressure of circumstance shaped the way men decided. But there remained an underlying sense in many minds that Richard had acted improperly in seizing the throne. For some, including those closest to Edward IV, this may have been coupled with the fear that although Richard had so far been conciliatory, he might take a harsher line once he was established.

Although the rebellion was primarily against Richard III, it also contained elements of reaction against Edward IV. For the previous twelve years, overt opposition to the crown had not really been feasible – as Clarence's isolation shows. Richard's usurpation changed all that. By destabilizing the political situation he restored rebellion as a viable option, and the 1483 risings reflect this. As well as involving those who specifically wanted to see Richard III deposed, they also attracted men like Lutterell and Courtenay who saw the chance of achieving territorial ambitions. This could have been a weakness in the rebellion, but in practice the two elements did not seriously clash. The restoration of the dispossessed would mainly have affected the Howards, William Herbert (who held the Lutterell lands) and Richard Hastings. The Howards were already closely identified with Richard's regime. Herbert, who had done badly under Edward IV, is sometimes seen as another early convert to Richard's cause, but he does not become politically visible until November 1483 and it may have been the rebellion itself which showed him where his best interests lay.[141] Hastings too failed to back the rebels and was subsequently rewarded by Richard III, although in his case it is impossible to tell whether this was a matter of conviction, or whether his actions were dictated by Welles' presence on the other side.[142]

There was, however, one discordant element among the rebels. The arrival of Buckingham put paid to any hope of raising the

[140] *Harl. 433* I pp. xxiii–xxiv.
[141] Ross 1981, pp. 37–8, 158; *CPR 1476–85* p. 367; *Harl. 433* II pp. 31–2; and see further below, pp. 207–9. He was in Richard's company during part of the progress of summer 1483: Hairsine 1985, pp. 309, 326.
[142] *CPR 1476–85* pp. 453, 525.

Welsh march against Richard, and the duke's failure undermined the rebellion elsewhere. The completeness of the rebels' collapse is reflected in the low number of casualties on their side, with most men able to make good their escape before the royal army arrived. Buckingham was betrayed by one of his servants and executed at Salisbury. Thomas St Leger and two others were executed at Exeter. Sir George Brown, William Clifford and a group of royal yeomen were put to death at London. A few others were captured subsequently, including Sir John Guildford and Richard Haute.[143] Some took to sanctuary; several, it seems, at Beaulieu.[144] Others, particularly among the west country rebels, escaped abroad. Many set about making their peace with the crown, itself an indication of the thoroughness of Richard's victory. But although the king had triumphantly overcome this first major challenge to his reign, the rebellion had left two uncomfortable legacies. It had demonstrated the failure of Richard's attempt to take over the power structure built up by Edward IV, and so faced him with the problem of reasserting royal control almost from scratch in the counties most badly affected. It also meant that there was, for the first time since 1471, an acknowledged alternative to the Yorkist dynasty, with all that that implied for the continuing instability of Richard's reign.

[143] Guildford: *Rot. Parl.* VI p. 251; *CPR* 1476–85 p. 465. Haute: Canterbury RO, FA 7 fo. 10; he was one of those arrested at Stony Stratford but had presumably been released after Richard's accession.

[144] PRO, C 81/1531/48; C 67/51 m. 10 (pardon to Robert Poyntz as late of Beaulieu). On 15 December 1483 Richard was enquiring urgently about the status of the sanctuary at Beaulieu: *Harl. 433* II p. 59; Thomson 1986, pp. 134–5.

Chapter 4

THE REASSERTION OF
ROYAL AUTHORITY

It was the rebellion of October 1483, rather than Richard's usurpation, which proved the decisive break in the continuity of Yorkist government. This is reflected in the act embodying Richard's title to the throne, which was passed by the parliament of January 1484. The act begins with a sweeping attack on the corruption of Edward IV's regime. It is often assumed that the main targets here were the Woodvilles, but the act does not say so, and tacitly encourages a more general interpretation by criticizing the servants of the regime at some length before turning to an attack on Edward IV's marriage and its unfortunate consequences. The act also explicitly accuses the king himself: it was 'therefore no marvel that the sovereign lord and head of this land being of such ungodly disposition and provoking the ire and indignation of our lord God, such heinous mischiefs ... were used and committed in the realm among the subjects'.[1] This outburst needs to be read in the context of the act of attainder of the 1483 rebels which follows. Of the ninety-eight men mentioned in the main body of the act, just over one third are known to have been in Edward's service and the true proportion is probably nearer a half. The attack on the corruption of Edward's government makes clear Richard's loss of confidence in his brother's men as the basis of his own authority. This lies behind the radical change in royal policy which followed the rebellion. Richard was to show himself consistently more willing to rely on members of his ducal affinity than on former servants of his brother. Exceptions can be found, and the rebellion had to some extent demonstrated which of Edward's servants could be trusted as well as which could not, but the shift in attitude is unmistakable and was to colour Richard's policies for the rest of the reign.

The king's most pressing problem in November 1483 was the

[1] *Rot. Parl.* VI p. 241.

restoration of royal authority in the areas affected by the rebellion. This was a problem posed by any insurrection, but Richard's difficulties were particularly acute. The rebels of 1483 had not, on the whole, been disaffected outsiders but the very men to whom the king would normally look for local support. The scale of the problem can be illustrated by the case of Hampshire. Seven of the attainted rebels came from the county or had landed interests there.[2] This does not, of course, account for all the men active in local government. Taking the gentry members of the commission of the peace as a convenient sample, two rebelled and six did not, and another local man was raised to the bench in the aftermath of the rebellion. But this simple calculation ignores a significant difference in status among the men concerned. None of the 'loyal' justices held other major office in the county, while the seven rebels account for an impressive number of key posts. Among them are to be found the sheriff of the county, the mayor of Southampton, the supervisor and one of the customers in the port there, and the custodians of the royal castles of Southampton and Portchester. The rebels also account for the element in local society which had the strongest court connections. Of the seven rebels, four were household servants of Edward IV, which accounts for all his known household men in the county. Even if one defines court connections in a looser sense, only one of the loyal justices qualifies: Edward Berkeley of Stapley (in Odiam, Hants), who was the brother of a former knight of the body and the uncle of the rebel William Berkeley. The latter connection clearly aroused the king's suspicions, and although Edward Berkeley kept his place on the commission of the peace, he lost at least some of the patronage he had secured under Edward IV.[3]

Not all the counties involved in the rebellion were as badly affected as this. In the band of counties stretching roughly from East Anglia to Gloucestershire the king could still call on a reasonable number of servants after the rebellion. But in most of the southern counties involved, that is from Kent and Surrey in the east to Devon and Cornwall in the west, the Hampshire pattern is repeated. What it meant in practice was that there were still plenty of local gentry who had escaped overt involvement –

---

[2] Ovedale, Kelsale, Williams, Overy, Fesaunt, Knight, Berkeley.
[3] The office of bailiff of Burley (Hants): *CPR 1467–77* pp. 52, 88; *CPR 1476–85* p. 195; *Harl. 433* I pp. 115, 185, 243. Berkeley regained it from Henry VII: *CPR 1485–94* p. 45.

the type of men who staffed royal commissions and the like – but that the king had lost the group of acknowledged servants to whom he would normally turn for particularly sensitive tasks. Thus of Edward IV's knights known to have remained in Richard's household after the rebellion nine came from south of the Humber but only two from south of the Thames: John Elrington of Hoxton (Middx.), who died soon after the rebellion, and William Petche of Lullingstone (Kent).[4] The esquires show a similar imbalance. Only lower down the household, among the yeomen, does the proportion of southerners increase, but men at this level had a more limited political role. This explains their higher survival rate but at the same time made their survival less useful to the king. Even where some of Edward's men had apparently remained loyal, the king might still view them with suspicion. Thus, in spite of Richard's need for allies in Kent, he apparently made no use of Petche, who is invisible in local affairs. In the short term, at least, the counties where Richard most needed local support were also those where he was least willing to use what was available.

It was this sense that the court circle within a given region was fundamentally unreliable which explains the dilemma confronting Richard III. He not only had to assert royal influence, but had first to find new channels through which that could be achieved. One obvious answer was to follow Edward IV's lead and create a new network of royal servants among the local gentry who had escaped involvement in the rebellion, incorporating such fragments of Edward IV's political structure as survived. This was arguably the only long-term solution, but in the short term it presented difficulties. Although the rebellion had collapsed without coming to battle, its scale and the standing of many of those involved made it crucial that the king repair his undermined authority quickly, particularly as the very lack of a military conclusion had meant that most of the rebels had escaped to fight another day. If Tudor's new significance was to be minimized, Richard had to demonstrate that he was securely in control. The creation of a new affinity, however, could not be achieved overnight. Nor could it be achieved by an exercise of the royal will alone. It was essentially a two-way process. Potential recruits

---

4 Elrington: PRO, Prob 11/7 fo. 59–v; *CPR* 1476–85 pp. 367, 515. Petche: *CPR* 1476–85 p. 416 (confirmation of fee as carver).

had to find royal service attractive, and at the same time the king needed to be convinced that he wanted the service being offered.

Both sides of this equation had been upset by the 1483 rebellion. On the gentry side the extent of the damage will always remain obscure. There is no way of telling how the southern gentry regarded the king in the aftermath of the rebellion. The prevailing attitude could have been anything from uncooperative resentment to eagerness to benefit from the shake-out of local political society. Relatively few gentry from the rebel counties seem to have entered the royal household after 1483, but this could reflect the king's wishes as much as their own. What is clear, however, is that the rebellion had broken one of the main lines of communication between the king and the counties affected. The obvious method of approach for an intending royal servant was through an existing household man, often, naturally, one from his own region. The dislocation of the household element among the southern gentry thus directly attacked the household's ability to renew itself in the areas concerned.

The same break in communications had a bearing on the king's position. One of the primary functions of the royal household was to provide the king with information, and the loss of this intelligence-gathering service can only have compounded Richard's problems. The rebellion seems to have left the king with a marked reluctance to trust any local men in the counties most badly affected. The involvement of men whose loyalty Richard had taken for granted was a profound shock and there is a distinct note of hysteria in the royal order that the land and goods of *all* household men and gentry in Wiltshire and Hampshire should be seized.[5] But if this was an over-reaction, Richard was nevertheless faced with a real difficulty. Although the leaders of the risings may have been identified, there was no way of telling how far support for the rebels had penetrated the rest of local society. This did not, perhaps, matter very much as far as routine local administration was concerned. In the south west men could still be found to enquire into the complaints of foreign merchants, for instance. But for more sensitive issues the king needed men whose loyalty was assured. Even if some of the gentry could be relied on, how were they to be identified? A few had identified themselves by co-operating against the rebels, like the Somerset

[5] *Harl. 433* II p. 32

yeoman of the crown William Bracher.[6] But in the absence of such specific demonstrations of loyalty the king was dependent on local information, and this was largely lacking. To be sure of loyal support the king had little choice but to turn to men with whom he had already had dealings and this, in many cases, meant men whose primary interests lay in other parts of the country.

This policy was made practicable by the forfeitures incurred by the 1483 rebels. These gave the king the means of endowing the men to whom he now turned and who were, in effect, to take the rebels' place in local affairs. The resources released were immense. Not only were the rebels' own lands involved, but the high proportion of royal servants among them meant that they had collectively absorbed much of the most important local office, which now became available for redistribution. In the four south-western counties alone, Cornwall, Devon, Somerset and Dorset, some nine constableships changed hands after the rebellion. Such offices could, it is clear, be redistributed without formality, regardless of the terms of the original grant. Even life grants seem in practice to have remained dependent on the king's goodwill, something tacitly recognized by those office holders who took the trouble to secure a confirmation at a change of reign. This was a consequence of the very close links which existed under the Yorkist kings between service to the crown and the grant of local office. If that service was withheld the royal patronage associated with it was likely to be granted elsewhere, as a dispute over the office of keeper of the armoury of Pontefract demonstrates. The office had been held in the 1460s by George Gower of Westow (Yorks.), a servant of John Neville, the brother of the earl of Warwick. After the restoration of Edward IV in 1471, Robert Pilkington, the illegitimate son of Sir John Pilkington, one of Edward's leading northern retainers, obtained the office on the grounds that Gower had supported Henry VI during the Readeption. In seeking redress, Gower denied the charge, adducing in support of his loyalty to the Yorkists the fact that he had actually been thrown out of office under Henry VI in favour of another Neville supporter. The implication is that the enjoyment of royal patronage depended on continuing loyalty to the crown, and it was on this basis, rather than on the primacy of his grant, that Gower was demanding reinstatement.[7]

---

[6] *CPR* 1476–85 p. 390; and see further below, p. 261.

[7] PRO, DL 5/1 fo. 4v. Gower's appeal apparently failed: *Harl. 433* III p. 201

The Pontefract example suggests that the only requirement for the resumption of office was a failure of loyalty or commitment on the part of the holder. This was certainly Richard III's understanding of the situation. While he was still protector he began to redistribute the offices of Robert Poyntz, whose only offence was too close an identification with the Woodvilles. In the aftermath of the 1483 rebellion confiscation of office was used against men who had escaped attainder but who had been linked with the rebels. As well as Edward Berkeley, who lost a life office, John lord Audley was stripped of most, if not all, of the Dorset offices he had been given by Edward IV.[8] As these examples show, there was only a narrow line between loss of office justified by disloyalty and confiscation as a political expedient. It was, of course, open to the ejected official to challenge his supplanter, as Gower did, but the king was likely to stand by his new candidate. The only exception was where a demonstrable royal mistake had been made. Thus Edward IV cancelled a grant of the stewardship of Bradford to John Pilkington in 1471 because he had forgotten that it had already been granted to James Harrington for life.[9] Harrington, like Pilkington, had made an early commitment to Edward IV on the latter's return from exile in 1471 and it is unlikely that the grant would otherwise have been cancelled so promptly.

Given these assumptions about the conditional nature of life grants there was no reason to wait for legal process before redistributing office after the rebellion. The only cause for delay was likely to be uncertainty about what was available. For the crown itself this was not a problem. Royal grants were exhaustively recorded. Each seal which the grant passed would keep a record of the transaction, the exchequer preserved details of authorized payments and so, piecemeal, did the officers responsible for making the payments: receivers, customers and the like. It was relatively straightforward to compile lists of grants for the king's information, and a number, with marginal annotation, survive among Richard's signet archive.[10] How far the king then used such lists to take the initiative in patronage is, however, another matter. The first formal stage in the process of securing a grant was for the would-be recipient to petition the crown, and it

[8] *CPR 1461–7* p. 8; *CPR 1476–85* pp. 68, 549.
[9] PRO, DL 37/47A no. 9.
[10] *Harl. 433* III pp. 191–206, 213–14.

has been argued that the initiative in patronage was therefore coming from below, with the king's role largely limited to saying yes or no.[11] This may often have been the case, as, for instance, when the chancery clerk William Morland petitioned Richard for an annuity of £20 until he could be found a benefice worth £40. Before the petition was handed on to the chancery, these sums were crossed out and £10 and £20 inserted instead, suggesting that Morland had not known what the king was prepared to give before he presented his petition.[12] But there must sometimes have been preliminary discussion, as was certainly the case in the sixteenth century.[13] To take an extreme example, Buckingham surely did not petition for viceregal authority in Wales without some encouragement from the king. The role of petitions in initiating the formal process of making a grant thus does not necessarily preclude an element of royal direction.

How often the king acted on his own initiative to the extent of spontaneously granting a particular piece of patronage can only be speculation. Perhaps an intermediate stage is more plausible, with the king letting it be known that he was prepared to be generous towards an individual, or even that he wanted takers for a particular post. But, however the system worked, it seems unlikely that after a major rebellion, when royal authority was at stake, the king simply sat back and waited for petitioners. The rapid injection of loyal members of the ducal affinity into key offices, such as the appointment of Thomas Tunstall and Richard Huddleston as captains of Conway and Beaumaris early in November, surely owes something to royal needs as well as private enterprise.[14] This possibility gains some support from the existence among Richard's signet warrants of commissions authorizing a named individual to seize a particular office. Such commissions were generally, although not invariably, later translated into a conventional grant. Thus Sir Thomas Wortley was commissioned at the beginning of December to seize Buckingham's stewardship of Scaresdale (Derbs.) and in the following

[11] For the importance of petitioning see Tuck 1971, pp. 4–5.
[12] PRO, C 81/1531/36; *CPR* 1476–85 p. 449.
[13] Ives, *Brereton* pp. 23–4. Although, as Ives suggests, preliminary discussion may have been the norm for courtiers like Brereton, lesser figures may have been more inclined to pin their hopes on a single, written approach.
[14] *Harl. 433* 1 pp. 95–6.

March a formal grant of the office to Wortley passed the signet and subsequent seals. The distinction between grant and commission was sometimes hazier than this. Wortley received four warrants relating to office in Staffordshire and Derbyshire, of which the first (the example quoted) was described as a commission and the other three as grants by commission.[15] In spite of this apparent confusion, the introduction of the rather cumbersome concept of a commission in this context perhaps implies a degree of royal initiative in the selection of Wortley.

For grants which resulted from private enterprise, however, it was up to the individual to discover what was available and how this was done at this period can only be surmised.[16] Presumably there was a flourishing grapevine rooted in the royal service. The centralized lists were no doubt available to those with the right connections. The frequency with which exchequer officials were able to secure lucrative farms demonstrates the advantages of inside knowledge. Other royal officials would be well informed about their own areas. In the aftermath of the rebellion, the men appointed to arrest traitors or seize their land and chattels were particularly well placed in this respect, and a number subsequently secured grants in the counties they had investigated. John Grey of Wilton, for instance, who headed the commission to enquire into treason in Bedfordshire and Buckinghamshire, later received a grant of Wilshamstead (Beds.), forfeited by Roger Tocotes.[17] As one would expect, the grapevine most strongly favoured men who moved in court circles. Local knowledge could be useful, but only with the court connections necessary to translate it into a successful bid for patronage. These various elements come together in a successful petition of the protectorate. John Cottington, a minor member of the Gloucestershire gentry who had links with both Edward IV and Gloucester, petitioned for office within the Forest of Dean which Edward IV had granted to William Slatter. Cottington claimed that Slatter had accompanied Sir Edward Woodville to sea and had thereby forfeited the office. The speed of Cottington's response is impressive. The first public statement that Woodville was deemed a traitor was Gloucester's order for his arrest on 14 May – an order

---

[15] *Ibid.* p. 162, II p. 41; *CPR* 1476–85 p. 436.
[16] Ives, *Brereton* is helpful on Tudor practice.
[17] *CPR* 1476–85 pp. 389, 393.

which did not name Slatter. Within about twelve days Cottington had presented his petition and had it accepted.[18]

Few men were as quick off the mark after the rebellion. It is noticeable that many of the grants of office made in November and December had not been forfeited by the rebels at all, but were already in the king's hands. Some of these may be in response to earlier petitions working their way to the head of the queue, but it may also be that the rebellion had shown who ought to be rewarded before it was known what patronage had become available. The earliest grants of forfeited office tend to be those seized from notorious rebels, such as Buckingham himself. In the case of lesser rebels it evidently took longer for men to discover what was available, and the growing volume of grants in January and February probably owes less to the legalization of the forfeitures by the act of attainder than to the fact that the act provided an accessible check-list of unreconciled rebels.

The redistribution of forfeited land was rather more hedged around with legal restrictions – at least in theory. It is possible that land held as a direct grant from the king was treated as any other royal grant and could be withdrawn at the king's will in response to disloyalty. This is not apparent in a general forfeiture such as followed the 1483 rebellion, but Hastings' widow was allowed custody of her husband's inherited estates after his execution, while land granted to him by Edward IV reverted to the crown.[19] In the case of inherited estates legal process was unnecessary only if the treason were manifest, which seems to have been defined as appearing against the king in arms when the king himself was present with his banner displayed. This also justified complete forfeiture, including land held to the rebel's use or in tail. Otherwise some form of legal process was required and the degree of forfeiture might vary. The common law protected land held to use or in fee tail, whereas the degree of forfeiture imposed by a parliamentary act of attainder could be as severe as the king chose.[20]

Such legal niceties, however, only came into play after the event. For a king faced with rebellion, common sense demanded that he get his hands on the rebels' land first and sort out any problems afterwards. The commissioners appointed in

---

[18] *Harl. 433* I p. 48. Letters patent were issued considerably later: *CPR 1476–85*, p. 457.

[19] *Harl. 433* II pp. 4–5.

[20] Bellamy 1970, pp. 192–5, 201–3.

November and December 1483 were given blanket authority to enter the land of the rebels; discovering the extent of the land and, indeed, the identity of the rebels, was left to them. Under such conditions mistakes would inevitably occur and the subsequent act of attainder included the standard proviso that those wrongly ejected from their land were entitled to traverse the findings in chancery in the usual way. But although a king in a hurry could afford to take short cuts in order to take possession of the land, when it came to regranting that land due legal process became more important. Before the land was regranted two requirements should have been met. The owner of the property should have been identified and his forfeiture given legal sanction. This was primarily to protect the rights of owners who might otherwise find themselves unjustly disseised, but it also gave the recipient confidence in his title. A land grant which immediately embroiled the beneficiary in lawsuits was not a particularly attractive proposition. Both safeguards were ignored by Richard III, who in numerous cases made grants from the forfeited estates before parliament met. It is possible that he regarded the forfeitures as authorized by the local hearings before the commissioners to arrest the rebels: not enough is known of their proceedings to be sure of their legal status. But it is clear that he was prepared to dispense with formal enquiries into land-ownership because the act of attainder admits as much and retrospectively validates any grants made without previous enquiries.[21]

It is not difficult to see why Richard III was willing to ignore the letter of the law. In his attempts to reassert royal authority it was the distribution of land which was crucial. The grant of office gave the recipient some standing in local affairs, even if it was only a degree of influence over the deputy who did the work for him, but it was land which gave the real stake in local politics. In spite of the various non-tenurial manifestations of bastard feudalism, noblemen who dominated a locality in the fifteenth century normally still did so because of their landed interest. The assumption that it was land which conferred status operated among the gentry also, and sheriffs and justices of the peace were usually expected to hold land in the counties they served. It was at this level that Richard most urgently needed to repair the damage done by the rebellion, and the terms of the problem were

---

[21] *Rot. Parl.* VI pp. 249–50; Wolfe 1971, p. 193.

obvious. If he was to rely on outsiders, he had to buy them a stake in local society with land; office alone was not enough. Thus when John Hoton was chosen to spearhead efforts to re-establish royal control in Southampton, he was not only made constable of the castle there but also given the forfeited Berkeley land in the county. He was clearly expected to step into William Berkeley's shoes, and, appropriately, made the Berkeley manor of Bisterne his base for the remainder of the reign. By July 1484 Hoton's position as the dominant local figure is nicely exemplified by his gift of a buck to Southampton's mayor.[22]

The practical advantages of land-ownership are also spelt out in Kent, where three northerners were each given a single manor and then a place on the commission of the peace.[23] The tactic may look crude but it had the desired effect, with at least two of the men (William Harrington and John Savage) subsequently taking an active part in the work of the commission.[24] Such considerations explain Richard's eagerness to begin redistributing land before parliament met, but the eagerness was not, of course, only on his side. Men were anxious to receive a share of the spoils and do not seem to have been much deterred by the possible illegality of the grants. In some cases the difficulty was acknowledged and circumvented by a grant of the right to enter a manor or have its custody, which was then converted into an outright grant after the act of attainder was safely passed.[25] But in other cases the recipient secured an outright grant immediately and as there seems to be no legal difference in the status of the land concerned, the determining factor was presumably the recipient's willingness to gamble on securing a valid title. Where the former owner was a notorious rebel and the recipient a household man assured of royal favour the risk was probably small, and the number of outright grants, after a slow start, rose steadily in December and early January.

As this implies, there were two elements in Richard's distribution of patronage after the rebellion. One was the need to give

---

[22] Southampton RO, SC 5/1/19 fo. 33v; *Harl. 433* I p. 102, II p. 58; *CPR 1476–85* p. 412. The grants to Hoton were made on the same day: December 11. For his designation as 'of Bisterne': Stagg, *New Forest Docs.* p. 3.

[23] *Harl. 433* II pp. 54–5: William Harrington (Calehill), Edward Stanley (Rolvenden) and John Savage (Nettlestead).

[24] PRO, KB 9/951/28, 60.

[25] e.g. the grant of Oakham to lord Grey of Codnor: *Harl. 433* II p. 52; *CPR 1476–85* p. 433.

loyal supporters enough standing in the affected areas to act as effective royal agents. The other was an obligation to reward his supporters by sharing the windfall with them. Forfeitures on this scale were not expected to be used solely for the king's own ends, whether financial or political, but to be spread around. The rebellion, in other words, provided an opportunity to display largesse as well as engage in some political engineering. The two elements are not distinct. Men established in the rebel counties through patronage were being rewarded on an exceptionally lavish scale, and Hoton's grant of Bisterne was phrased as a reward for his good service in the king's taking of the throne and against the rebels.[26] Conversely, generous gifts for past service, by advertising the king's good lordship, helped to make royal service more attractive and thereby had a political function of their own.

The two elements merge in another sense: it can be surprisingly difficult to be sure whether an individual's patronage was or was not intended to give him an active role in the area concerned. Sometimes the answer is obvious. Ralph Banaster, who had betrayed Buckingham, was given the duke's manor of Ealding (Kent), but is unlikely to have been destined for a political role in the county; the grant was a straightforward reward.[27] So, probably, was the grant, late in the reign, of the office of bailiff of the hundreds of East and West Budleigh (Devon) to Richard Lloyd, an Essex yeoman of the crown. Lloyd may have owed the grant to Sir James Tyrell, a fellow East Anglian with interests in the south west. But the grant cannot have been envisaged as more than a source of income, for during this period Lloyd was a member of the garrison at Guisnes.[28] Even without this French commitment, the office looks too insignificant to allow an Essex man to play an active role in Devon. But only a little extra patronage would have made the question less straightforward, as another recipient of patronage in Devon, the Yorkshireman John Keighley, demonstrates. He was made constable and master of the game at Okehampton with an annual fee of £20, later adjusted to the more realistic level of £5 plus an annuity of £15. He also received land valued at £8 some twenty miles away on the other side of Dartmoor.[29] The grants were financially valuable but the

[26] PRO, PSO 1/58/2955.
[27] *Harl. 433* II pp. 58–9.
[28] *Ibid.* I pp. 250, 272, II p. 107; Campbell, *Materials* I p. 503.
[29] *Harl. 433* I pp. 148, 259, II p. 118, III p. 147.

office was relatively minor and the land was made up of small pieces in two parishes, a combination which suggests that the grant was seen as a source of revenue rather than as a means of allowing Keighley to settle in Devon. But although the grants would hardly support an independent local role, it is possible that Keighley had moved south in conjunction with one of the other northerners active in the area, such as Sir Thomas Malyverer at Plymouth or Halneth Malyverer at Launceston, and that the grants therefore endorsed a new regional interest rather than creating it.[30]

At the other extreme there are men whose role was indubitably to replace Edward IV's nexus of local servants and whose grants were made with that in mind. They are characterized by major grants of land and office within a relatively compact area; membership of, and active participation in, the local commission of the peace; and, in some cases, selection as sheriff. A good example is provided by one of Richard's retainers from county Durham, Robert Brackenbury. His closeness to the king was demonstrated by his appointment, early in the reign, to the key office of constable of the Tower of London. In the following March he received a group of grants which show that his horizons were beginning to widen. One, the keepership of the royal lions, merely extended his collection of Tower office, but he was also made receiver of a group of manors in Essex and Kent from which most of the Tower offices were paid, and was granted forfeited lands in Kent valued at just under £140 p.a.[31] On the strength of the land grant he was appointed to the next commission of the peace for the county, issued on 17 July, and seems to have become a fairly regular attender.[32] By this date he had already acquired important influence in the county by virtue of a commission to seize forfeited land. The first formal reference to the commission does not occur until 21 August 1484, when Brackenbury and the yeoman of the crown John Kendale were authorized to enquire into the lands of attainted traitors in Kent, Sussex and Surrey and seize any which had not been granted away. On the same day Brackenbury was issued with a writ of aid noting that he had been made receiver general of the land.[33] The commission was effective, however, at least a month earlier than this. On 22 July the

---

[30] For examples of group movement see below, pp. 195–6.
[31] *CPR 1476–85* pp. 364, 383, 385, 405.
[32] PRO, KB 9/951/28, 60; Canterbury RO, FA 7 fo. 11v.
[33] *CPR 1476–85* p. 485; PRO, C 145/330.

Kent commissioners of the peace, with Brackenbury among them, heard a case arising from Brackenbury's activities. According to the indictment, Brackenbury had been commissioned to seize the manor of Dymchurch for the king, and had vested his authority in John Kendale, who had duly entered the manor with two of Brackenbury's servants. The matter came before the commissioners because Dymchurch was a Fogge manor and, embarrassingly for the king, it was claimed by one of the other royal servants in Kent, Sir Ralph Ashton. Two of Ashton's sons had led an attack on Dymchurch in which Brackenbury's servants were beaten up. After a relatively late start Brackenbury had become a force to be reckoned with in Kent, and in November his position was further strengthened by his appointment as sheriff.[34]

Brackenbury's gains did not stop there. He received further local office in Kent and by the end of the reign had made significant acquisitions in other counties, although most of these were rewards for a trusted royal servant rather than vehicles for the extension of royal authority.[35] His yearly income from royal service must have approached £500, a figure which puts him among the four or five best-rewarded household servants. But if the scale of his reward is unusual, Brackenbury is in other respects typical of the men to whom Richard turned as agents in the southern counties. Most are known to have been members of the royal household, and given the trust reposed in them it is probably safe to assume that they all were. Those for whom household status is recorded were mainly knights and esquires of the body, which is predictable, given the role they were intended to play in local society. Their high standing within the household was not, however, usually matched by their eminence within their native counties. The families from which they were drawn were not, by and large, of the first rank. Moreover, the men concerned were not usually heads of families. Brackenbury was a second son. Other younger sons planted in the south included John Musgrave and Thomas Stafford, both active in Wiltshire. Their colleague there, George Neville, was illegitimate.[36] Marmaduke Constable, employed first in Kent and then in the north midlands, was the heir of the Constables of Flamborough (Yorks.) but, as his father

[34] PRO, KB 9/951/28; *CFR* 1471–85 no. 862.
[35] *CPR* 1476–85 p. 521; *Harl. 433* II pp. 186, 212.
[36] Leadam 1902, pp. 141–5.

was still alive, had not yet taken on the family's responsibilities in the north. There are some exceptions to this pattern, such as Edward Redmane, who inherited his family's estates in Yorkshire and Westmorland in March 1483 and was active in the south west on the king's behalf from the following November. He managed to keep both interests in play, and in January 1484 was probably combining the roles of sheriff of Somerset/Dorset and parliamentary representative of Carlisle.[37] But given the degree of involvement which the king expected of his agents in their new counties, a lack of commitments elsewhere was probably perceived as an advantage, particularly as it also meant that the men concerned could more readily be spared from their home areas. Richard's leading northern retainers, men like Sir John Conyers or Sir James Harrington, showed no sign of moving south.

The matter of which men could best be spared also helps to explain the marked northern emphasis among Richard's plantations. In part this reflects the strength of the king's earlier connections with the region, since the first requirement for the royal servants in the south was personal loyalty to the king. But this is not the whole answer. Richard had also had an East Anglian affinity, for instance, but few of its members were given long-term commitments outside the region. The obvious exception, Sir James Tyrell, had acquired his interests in the south and west before Richard's accession, although they took on an added importance after the 1483 rebellion.[38] Richard presumably felt that his southern retainers were simply too useful where they were to be given new regional interests. The north was important to the king, and he was anxious to keep close personal control over it, but it was also the area where he was most secure. The removal of a few retainers, most of whom left kinsmen active in the north, was not going to undermine his authority, something which was arguably not true elsewhere.

The use of patronage to create a major new power base for a trusted servant was a tactic largely confined to those areas where the king felt least confident of the local gentry. Some of the clearest examples therefore come from Wiltshire, where the king

---

[37] *Test. Ebor.* III p. 280; *CFR* 1471–85 no. 797; Wedgwood 1938, p. 487 (Redmane's identification as the Carlisle member is speculative).

[38] The only other example is Sir Robert Chamberlain, who was made constable of Beaumaris late in the reign: *CPR* 1476–85 pp. 509–10. For his earlier links with Gloucester see above, p. 77.

regarded all the gentry as suspect. Three royal servants were introduced into the county by Richard III. The first was probably the king's esquire Thomas Stafford, the younger brother of Humphrey Stafford of Grafton (Worcs.). Thomas had been feuding with the Woodvilles in the previous reign and was probably an early recruit to Richard's cause.[39] His closeness to the king was signalled by his receipt of patronage in the lean days of July 1483, and after the rebellion he stepped promptly into Roger Tocotes' shoes. He had received the lion's share of Tocotes' land in the county by 29 November and apparently made it his main residence, since later in the reign he could be described simply as 'of Bromham', Tocotes' home.[40] Stafford followed this up with an impressive collection of local office, largely forfeited by Tocotes but with one or two extras from elsewhere, including William Collingbourne's parkership of Ludgarshall.[41] The grants to Stafford's two colleagues cannot be dated, but were probably effective by December 1483 when they joined him on the commission of the peace. This is supported, in the case of John Musgrave, by his selection as parliamentary representative of Salisbury in the following month. Musgrave, a Cumberland esquire of the body, was apparently the city's own choice since they had another candidate in reserve in case he refused to act, and his selection shows that his political role in the county was already recognized.[42] Like Stafford he seems to have removed physically to the county, where he was given land forfeited by Thomas Melbourne, and in March 1485 he headed the witnesses to a transfer of land in Laverstock, one of the manors which he had been granted.[43] The third newcomer, George Neville, was given the land in Wiltshire and elsewhere which John Cheyne had been granted by Edward IV – a reminder that Richard III was not the only king to use patronage to create a new power base for a favoured servant. Neville's grant was not made formally until July 1485 but was probably effective much earlier.[44]

In all three cases it was the land grant which did most to establish the recipient in local society and the size of the grant

---

[39] Carpenter 1986, p. 35.
[40] *CPR* 1476–85 p. 363; *Harl. 433* I pp. 136–7, II p. 37; PRO, KB 29/115 m. 12 dorse.
[41] *Harl. 433* I pp. 140–1, II p. 37.
[42] Wilts. RO, G 23/1/2 fo. 151v.
[43] *Harl. 433* III p. 145; *Tropenell Cart.* I p. 64. Musgrave also received minor office centred on Salisbury: *CPR* 1476–85 pp. 478, 507.
[44] *CPR* 1476–85 pp. 549–50.

reflects this. The land given to Musgrave and Stafford was in each case valued at a little over £100. Neville's grant is unvalued, but carried an annual rent of £15 which, at the usual Ricardian rate of a shilling in the mark, gives a value of £200. In all, about twelve men received land worth more than £100 as a way of moving them into a new area. Although the number may seem modest, it constituted a significant upheaval in the established pattern of influence and land-ownership in the south. Nor was this the limit of Richard's 'plantations'. A smaller endowment could serve the same purpose, and a similar number of men moved into the rebel counties with land worth £50–£100; some may have moved on the strength of still smaller grants.

Southampton provides examples across the whole range. The county had been linked with Wiltshire as the area where Richard was least confident of the local gentry, and numerous incomers were settled there in the course of the reign. Five outsiders gained a place on the commission of the peace as a direct result of royal initiatives. The first was Robert Carre of Alnwick (Northumb.). His home town would suggest a Percy connection, but he cannot be firmly linked with the earl in the 1470s and may have looked instead to Gloucester, particularly as he had been in the service of Warwick in the 1460s.[45] He received forfeited Ovedale land valued at £70. The grant is undated but, as Carre was one of those appointed to seize rebel land in the county in the immediate aftermath of the rebellion, he may have taken effective control of the estates as early as November 1483. The land was improperly seized, which suggests that Carre acted in haste.[46] He was added to the commission of the peace in December 1483 and in the following year was pricked as sheriff for the county.

Another newcomer of comparable standing was John Hoton, whose assumption of William Berkeley's role has already been discussed. He was not added to the bench until October 1484 but was active in the county immediately after the rebellion, when he was made responsible for administering an oath of loyalty sworn by the inhabitants of Southampton.[47] The influence of other newcomers among the JPs rested on a narrower landed base. In

[45] *Test. Ebor.* III p. 338; *Percy Bailiff's Rolls* p. 25. Some Percy connection is suggested by Carre's appointment as Henry VII's constable of Middleham: *CPR* 1485–94 p. 89.

[46] *Harl. 433* II p. 32 ('Carver'), III p. 151; *CPR* 1476–85 p. 523. The land was claimed by the widowed stepmother of the rebel William Ovedale, who had been seised jointly with her husband: Berry 1833, p. 74.

[47] Southampton RO, SC 5/1/19 fo. 31v.

March 1484 Sir John Saville of Thornhill (Yorks.) was added to the commission on the strength of his appointment the previous month as lieutenant of the Isle of Wight. His only landed stake in the county was the reversion of Corhampton.[48] The commission was next revised in October, when, as a consequence of continuing unrest along the south coast, the number of royal servants was increased. Hoton was added then, as was another royal esquire, Richard Hansard of Walworth (co. Durham). Hansard held no land in the county, and his local role rested on his appointment in December 1483 as constable of Odiham, a grant later extended to give him custody of the whole lordship.[49] Also added to the commission was Sir Christopher Ward, a Yorkshire knight of the body from Givendale near Ripon. His interest in the county was negligible, and his addition to the commission was obviously to strengthen it in the face of threatened invasion rather than as a tribute to his local influence. He held minor office within the New Forest, but his main interest in the south was the result of his custody of the land of Jane Lewkenor and of the rebel Thomas Lewkenor. This gave him a significant interest in Sussex (in 1485 he could be described as 'of Trotton', one of the manors he held there), but it also gave him custody of Worldham (Hants).[50]

These men do not account for all the royal grants in the county and probably not for all the plantations. Richard made land grants to seventeen other people, of whom at least seven were northerners, and gave office to numerous others. Among the recipients who probably took an active interest in the county as a result was the royal esquire William Mirfield, a Yorkshireman who was given the strategically important posts of constable of Portsmouth and Porchester on the same day as his kinsman Sir John Saville was put in charge of the Isle of Wight.[51] Even the recipients of more modest grants sometimes seem to have been active in the region. Henry Braythwaite, a northern yeoman of the crown, was given land worth £12 6s 8d forfeited in Southampton itself by William Overey and Roger Kelsale. He was also made customer in place of Kelsale, which suggests, although does not prove, an active presence in the port.[52] Other likely arrivals were the group

---

[48] *CPR 1476–85* p. 410; *Harl. 433* III p. 155.

[49] PRO, C 67/53 m. 7; *CPR 1476–85* pp. 412, 442; *Harl. 433* I p. 257.

[50] *Harl. 433* I pp. 149, 152–3, II p. 108; *CPR 1476–85* p. 531.

[51] *CPR 1476–85* p. 425. William's kinsman and namesake, Sir William Mirfield, later stood surety for Saville: *CCR 1476–85* no. 1417.

[52] *Harl. 433* II p. 83, III p. 142; *CFR 1471–85* nos. 745, 748.

of Durham men given office in the New Forest, whose geographical origins link them with Hoton and Hansard. Robert Veysey and Roland Harper belong to this group, as, probably, do Christopher Welfield and Henry Smith, although the latter's name is too common for certain identification. It is impossible to prove that all these men had physically moved into the area (their local patronage could be explained by Hoton or Hansard remitting some of the spoils of their new influence back home), but some had certainly done so. Veysey and Smith took up residence with Hoton at Bisterne and in the next reign were to be accused of 'poaching' the New Forest deer. Among the men accused with them was at least one other probable northerner, Thomas Lockwood, and the implication is that Hoton had taken a group of kinsmen and acquaintances south with him.[53] Such imported support was essential to give the newcomer credibility in the short term, particularly as his immediate responsibilities (arresting rebels and seizing their land) might involve a degree of force. Another of Richard's plantations who certainly turned to his own circle for backing was Edward Redmane. His seizure of property on the king's behalf in the south west was accomplished with the help of John Redmane, Geoffrey Swale and Henry a Chamber. All three are described as 'of Cotehele', the Edgecombe manor on the Tamar which Edward Redmane himself had seized for the crown, but at least two (and probably all three) were Yorkshiremen. John Redmane was a kinsman of Edward and had been in the service of Edward's elder brother William. Geoffrey Swale probably belonged to the family of Swale Hall in West Grinton (Yorks.) and was a kinsman of the royal servant John Swale, who was himself rewarded with land in Somerset.[54] Elsewhere in the south west Sir James Tyrell had the backing of some of his Welsh associates.[55]

Richard's plantations were thus more broadly based than might appear at first sight. Some of the men whose own patronage looks too slight to have given them a stake in southern affairs may in fact

---

[53] Hampton 1985a, pp. 8–9; Stagg, *New Forest Docs.* pp. 3, 6, 24. A Thomas Lockwood was bailiff of Almondbury in the honour of Pontefract: PRO, DL 29/526/8390.

[54] PRO, KB 9/369/22, 9/1060/33; *Test. Ebor.* III p. 280; Plantagenet-Harrison 1879, p. 236; *Harl. 433* III p. 142. John Redmane may be Gloucester's retainer but is perhaps more likely to be a namesake: PRO, DL 29/648/10485. Edward's brother Richard also moved into Cornwall, where he is recorded acting as a juror: PRO, KB 9/367/4.

[55] A point I owe to an unpublished paper by Nicholas Kingwell, presented at the University of Keele in 1985.

have been supporting more important figures. The men planted in the south were, moreover, accompanied by others who received no royal grants and who are now, as a result, generally invisible. Rather than twenty or thirty individuals planted in the south there were as many enclaves of outsiders, with each individual surrounded by a coterie of associates who backed him in carrying out the king's wishes and were rewarded with a share of the spoils. This gives substance to the Crowland chronicler's complaint that the south suffered a northern invasion.[56]

The plantations were one of the most striking features of Richard's reign, and one which has attracted considerable attention in recent years.[57] The policy shows the normal use of royal patronage being pushed to its logical extreme. Where patronage normally recognized and enhanced local standing it was here being used to create it. This in itself was not new, but it is rare to find the tactic used so systematically to create royal influence in a specific area rather than to benefit a favoured servant. In the immediate context of the reign, there can be little doubt that the newcomers planted in the south spearheaded the king's attempts to restore his authority in the rebel counties. Their importance can be seen in their domination of the shrievalties in 1484. They accounted for one third of the new sheriffs, and the proportion was much higher (over two thirds) in the counties south of the Thames/Severn line.

The plantations must, however, be kept in perspective. The number of primary plantations, although their impact may have been dramatic, was not large. In numerical terms alone it would be nonsense to assume that the newcomers literally governed the south for the king. In any case, that was not how medieval government worked. Most local government was self-government, and the gentry who supplied it had, by and large, weathered the rebellion. The purpose of the plantations was the more limited, and more realistic, one of taking over the local functions of the household nexus which Edward IV had created and which had been so deeply implicated in the rebellion. The men concerned would be expected to play a major role in the administration of the royal lands, carry out the king's orders, and act as a line of communication between the king and the country at large. In the short term, the second duty may have been the more

---

[56] *Crowland* pp. 170–1.
[57] Pollard 1977.

important, embracing as it did such necessary tasks as arresting rebels and seizing their land, but in the longer term the third would be crucial. It was the household which kept the king informed, as Richard's instructions to Thomas Stafford demonstrate.[58] In time, men like Stafford would also have acted as the focus around which a new royal affinity could develop among the local gentry, the essential prerequisite for any return to normality in the king's dealings with the southern counties.

Plantation, in other words, was intended to fill a specific gap rather than bring about a wholesale transfer of power in the south. But even in this limited aim of securing reliable local servants it should be seen as a last resort. The use of outsiders was not an end in itself. The royal servants planted in the south shared with other forms of new men the theoretical advantage that, because their power was the king's creation, they were more amenable to royal control. However, in practice this was outweighed by the fact that, to be an effective royal agent, the individual had to be integrated into the political and social life of the region. Richard's policy of plantation is itself a tacit admission of this basic fact of political life. If Richard had wanted to use outsiders he had only to issue orders to his northern servants. The lavish grants of land and office were, on the contrary, designed to create a new group of *insiders*. In the event, this long-term role had no chance to materialize. Henry VII's accession and the ensuing act of resumption wiped out Richard's plantations within two years of their establishment. But there is no doubt that for Richard the 'outsideness' of the plantations was generally a difficulty rather than an advantage. They were used because, in the particular conditions of 1483, Richard chose to rate loyalty above local contacts. Where the two were combined he showed himself more than willing to exploit existing connections.

From Richard's point of view, the ideal situation was one where a member of his northern affinity had southern interests upon which the king could build. Richard had already shown himself alert to this possibility and in Hertfordshire had been advancing northerners even before the rebellion broke. Elizabeth Woodville's possession of the duchy of Lancaster lands in the county had resulted in a marked Woodville presence there by the end of Edward IV's reign. Justices of the peace had included

---

[58] *Harl. 433* II p. 37; quoted above, pp. 16–17.

Rivers, Sir Thomas Vaughan and John Forster, the queen's treasurer and receiver general. As protector, Gloucester took action against all three: Rivers and Vaughan were executed and Forster imprisoned.[59] It was against this background that Richard undertook a major overhaul of the commission in July 1483. He added one local man, Richard Swanessey, but the other three new justices were all Yorkshiremen with secondary interests in Hertfordshire. Two owed those interests to marriage. Edward Goldsborough, the third baron of the exchequer, had married the widow of Ralph Grey junior. Nicholas Leventhorpe was a member of the Yorkshire stem of one of the major administrative dynasties of the duchy of Lancaster. The duchy connection had led to the establishment of a Hertfordshire branch of the family, which had a tradition of service on the commission of the peace, but Nicholas' claim to inclusion rested on his marriage to the widow of Richard West lord de la Ware, which had led to his establishing a southern household at Hatfield Broad Oak (Essex). The third northerner was Richard Scrope, the brother of the king's associate John lord Scrope of Bolton. The Scropes held the Hertfordshire manor of Sawbridgeworth and, to judge by Richard Scrope's will, he had looked after the family's interests in the county.[60]

In this particular case Richard's use of the Yorkshiremen, beyond putting them on the bench, cannot be documented. Elsewhere such men found themselves intensively employed. In Norfolk and Suffolk it was members of two local families with West Riding connections, the Hoptons and Wentworths, who headed the December commission to enquire into treason.[61] Sir Ralph Ashton, who had arrived in Kent through his marriage with Elizabeth Kyriel, became a force to be reckoned with in his new county. Richard consolidated Ashton's influence with a major grant of forfeited land and used him as one of his main agents in the county. He was an active member of the commission of the peace and was also employed in enquiring into the possessions of rebels, administering the oath of loyalty in the county and

---

[59] Myers, 'Household of Queen Eliz.' p. 213; *Rot. Parl.* VI pp. 332–3.

[60] Swanessey: BL, Harleian ms 1546 fo. 1. Goldesborough: *VCH Herts.* II p. 197. Leventhorpe: PRO, C 67/50 m. 1; Essex RO, D/DB T15/3/(3–4). Scrope: *Test. Ebor.* III no. 122; *VCH Herts.* III p. 337.

[61] *CPR* 1476–85 p. 393.

mustering men.[62] Such timely moves were, inevitably, rare, but Richard could also call upon a few northerners who had moved south under his own aegis in the previous reign. The clearest example is John Huddleston, who had held office in Gloucester's lordship of Sudeley (Glos.). He remained active in the county and was also employed by Richard in the south march, where he was used to muster men and was put in charge of the duchy of Lancaster lordships in the region.[63]

Richard also proved willing to use those former household men of Edward IV who, although based in the south, had a northern background. When the king expressed mistrust of all the gentry and royal servants in Wiltshire, this did not in fact extend to Edward Hardgill of Mere, an usher of the chamber of Edward IV and Edward V. Hardgill remained in Richard's household, and was trusted sufficiently by the king to be given the sensitive and crucial office of sheriff of Wiltshire in the immediate aftermath of the rebellion.[64] The explanation is probably that he was a kinsman of Richard's retainers the Hardgills of Lilling (Yorks.), although no firm identification has been made. Another of Edward's ushers employed by Richard was Halneth Malyverer. He had moved south in the previous reign as a result of his marriage to one of the Carminewe heiresses and had been settled at Ashwater (Devon) since the 1460s.[65] He came originally from Allerton Mauleverer (Yorks.) and although he had not been active in the north during Gloucester's ascendancy other members of his family had come to the duke's attention, probably through the proximity of Allerton to the duchy of Lancaster lordship of Knaresborough. Halneth's uncle William was sufficiently close to the duke to be given the task of seizing forfeited land during the protectorate, and was later employed by Richard in Kent.[66] Halneth's brother Thomas was put in charge of Plymouth as part of the moves to resist Tudor in November 1483 and subsequently acquired further interests in the region. Halneth himself was one

---

[62] PRO, KB 9/366/32, 9/951/60; Canterbury RO, FA 7 fo. 11v; *HMC, 5th Report* p. 527; *Harl. 433* II p. 77; *CPR 1476–85* pp. 392, 445; BL, Add. ms 29616 fos. 250v, 251, 261v, 262.

[63] PRO, DL 42/20 fo. 20; *Harl. 433* I pp. 153, 178.

[64] *CCR 1476–85* no. 10; *CFR 1471–85* no. 797; *CPR 1476–85* pp. 348, 361, 454–5.

[65] Meyrick Cary mss, box 10 (unnumb.) contains a rental of Ashwater made for Malyverer in 4 Edw. IV. For the Carminewe lands see further below, p. 284.

[66] *Harl. 433* II p. 76, III p. 2; *CFR 1471–85* no. 801; *Visit. Yorks.* p. 201.

of the commissioners to arrest rebels in the south west and was also made sheriff of Devon in November 1483.[67]

It would be wrong, however, to think of Richard III as totally reliant on northerners, even in the immediate aftermath of the rebellion. He had had southern associates as duke of Gloucester, a number of whom he now used in their home counties. William Houghton of Birtsmorton (Worcs.), for instance, headed the enquiry into treason in Worcestershire. Richard may also have had contacts in the south west, where he had held the de Vere lands in the previous reign. This could explain the sudden rise to prominence of Piers St Aubin, the only local member of the commission to arrest rebels in Devon and Cornwall.[68] There were also a few other local men, even in the counties most badly affected by the rebellion, whose links with Richard were more tenuous but whom the king was evidently prepared to trust. One of these was John Rogers of Freefolk (Hants) who was given the crucial post of sheriff of his county in place of the traitor William Berkeley in autumn 1483. He was one of only two local men (the other being the mayor of Southampton) among the eight commissioners appointed in 1484 to inspect archers mustered at Southampton before their embarkation for Brittany. Both Rogers and his son-in-law John Brocas were among Richard's commissioners of the peace.[69] In Kent a number of local men were active on the commission investigating treason and administering oaths of loyalty, one of whom, John Bamme, was made sheriff after the rebellion.[70] In time, the numbers of such men would probably have increased and they would have taken on more duties. In the short term, however, they tended to be overshadowed by men who had stronger links with Richard himself.

In seeking to restore royal authority, Richard's response was inevitably shaped by the nature of the rebellion. Since it had been primarily a revolt of the upper household element within the

---

[67] Thomas: *Harl. 433* II pp. 34–5; *CPR 1476–85* p. 531; *CFR 1471–85* no. 890; he succeeded Halneth as sheriff, *CFR 1471–85* no. 860. Halneth: *CFR 1471–85* no. 797; *CPR 1476–85* p. 371.

[68] *CPR 1476–85* p. 371. St Aubin may have been a Tyrell associate; they were granted patronage at the same time and it was St Aubin who seized the disputed Arundel lands and gave them to Tyrell: *Harl. 433* I p. 160, II p. 34.

[69] *CFR 1471–85* no. 797; PRO, C 81/1531/50; *Inqs p. m.* III no. 626.

[70] *CPR 1476–85* p. 392; *Harl. 433* II pp. 75–7; *CFR 1471–85* no. 798. Bamme had probably been known to Richard since the mid 1470s: Reaney and Fitch, *Essex Fines* IV p. 73.

southern shires, measures had to be taken to recreate that household presence. But the king's response may also reflect his own preferences. It seems clear that, by the end of 1483, Richard had become less willing to see individuals exercise regional (as distinct from local) authority. After the experiment with Buckingham, the reign produced no figures comparable with Hastings or Gloucester himself in the 1470s, or Warwick or William Herbert I in the 1460s. This was not for want of resources. The massive forfeitures at Richard's disposal gave him the means to create similar hegemonies had he so wished. On the whole, however, the king preferred to see influence spread among lesser figures. Within the southern counties this can be seen particularly clearly in the south west, which also demonstrates one of the concomitants of the policy: Richard's almost total failure to create a new generation of aristocracy. His reign completed the attrition of magnate influence in the region which had begun under Edward IV. Clarence's downfall in 1478 had brought the earldom of Devon back to the crown. As protector, Gloucester resumed the duchy of Exeter, which had become a vehicle for Woodville influence, and his accession confirmed the eclipse of Dorset, whose position in the region had rested largely on the Bonville lands.

None of these estates was used as the foundation of a new power base. Richard may have toyed with the idea of creating one new peer in the region, but nothing had come of it by the time of his death. Richard Ratcliffe was given the bulk of the earldom of Devon estates – a staggering £666 worth for the younger son of a Cumberland esquire.[71] It is clear, however, that even if Ratcliffe were intended for the peerage, Richard's motive was to reward a friend, not to set up a loyal nobleman as a way of mediating royal authority in a troublesome region. In spite of the land grant Ratcliffe played no recorded part in the south west, although his potential importance was recognized by the bishop of Winchester, who made him his constable of Taunton.[72] Ratcliffe was not even added to the local commissions of the peace. In fact the only southern commission to which he was added was that for Surrey, presumably on the strength of his custody of the manor of Guildford, a choice which strongly implies that any southern role

[71] *CPR* 1476–85 p. 472.
[72] Greatrex, *Reg. St Swithun* p. 141.

envisaged for Ratcliffe was to be within easy reach of Westminster.[73]

Nor did the king show much interest in building up the power of any of the region's lesser nobility. The most obvious candidate for an extended role was John lord Dynham. He had been one of Edward IV's key supporters in the region, something recognized by Richard when, as protector, he made Dynham steward of the duchy of Cornwall. In the course of Richard's reign, however, Dynham's role as the king's local agent dwindled. In part this may be due to Dynham's increased involvement at Calais, where Hastings' removal had left him effectively in control, but it probably also reflects growing royal mistrust. By March 1484 Sir James Tyrell had replaced Dynham as steward of the duchy, after the way had been cleared by the reissue of Dynham's life grant as a grant during good behaviour.[74]

Few of Dynham's fellow barons fared much better, at least within the south west itself. Lords Audley and Stourton were tainted by the treason of kinsmen, and although Richard kept both of them on his commissions of the peace and of array, neither seems to have increased his local influence.[75] John Broke lord Cobham, by contrast, was clearly acceptable to the new king and was given additional land in the south west, but was employed in Kent, where his primary interests lay.[76] The only local baron to gain in stature was lord Zouche, whose links with the inner court circle ensured that he was perceived as an ally by the king almost from the outset. He headed the commission to investigate treason in Dorset and Somerset, where his own land lay, and also showed signs of extending his influence into Devon and Cornwall under the aegis of his father-in-law John lord Scrope of Bolton, with whom he served on a commission of *oyer et terminer* in October 1484.[77] This hardly constitutes a major

---

[73] *Harl. 433* II p. 33.

[74] *Harl. 433* I pp. 20, 125, 130; *CPR 1476–85* pp. 430, 474. Tyrell's grant did not pass the great seal until August, but it is clear from the signet enrolments (which actually reverse the two grants) that it must have been made at the same time as the regrant to Dynham late in February, and that the regrant must therefore have been made to clear the way for Tyrell's assumption of the office. The signet warrants themselves do not survive. For Dynham see further below, pp. 291–3.

[75] Neither received local land or office. Audley was made treasurer: *CPR 1476–85* p. 488.

[76] *Harl. 433* III p. 143. For Cobham's land in the south west see *CP* III p. 346.

[77] *Harl. 433* III p. 148; *CPR 1476–85* pp. 371, 493; Roskell 1959b, pp. 152, 156–7. He was sufficiently well placed to be able to secure land for one of his servants: *Harl. 433* III p. 146.

local role, but the severity of Zouche's treatment after Bosworth may indicate that he had been more closely identified with Richard's regime than is now apparent.

With the possible exception of Zouche, the only baron to play a significant role in the south west was the northerner, John lord Scrope of Bolton, who had already emerged as a reliable ally before the rebellion broke. In its immediate aftermath he was established at Exeter, which was to remain his base for the rest of the reign. He was added to local commissions of the peace, headed the commission to arrest rebels in Devon and Cornwall, was put in charge of the forfeited temporalities of the bishopric of Exeter, and remained, it seems, in overall control of measures against local unrest.[78] He was also given responsibility for the defence of the western coast and it is probably this military role which explains his arrival in the region.[79] High military office was still considered the preserve of the aristocracy and Scrope was, in effect, replacing the marquis of Dorset, who had been responsible for keeping the sea after Edward IV's death.[80] But although, as this demonstrates, Richard found a reliable local nobleman useful, there is no suggestion that Scrope was intended to become an independent force in the region. It is significant that although Scrope was given the duchy of Exeter manor of Bovey Tracey, Richard chose to spread the rest of the duchy land among several recipients rather than taking the opportunity to put Scrope in control of the duchy interest as a whole. Overall, although Scrope's land grant was potentially valuable, it was an extremely scattered collection, of which more than half was granted in reversion.[81]

Two other northern peers, Northumberland and Fitzhugh, were given land in the south west, but neither developed much of a local role. Northumberland was given the Brian lands, formerly held by Clarence, to which he had a claim through his mother Eleanor Poynings.[82] As far as Richard was concerned, the grant offered a way of rewarding the earl without strengthening his

[78] PRO, C 81/1392/14, 16, 17; KB 9/369/22, 9/370/32; Devon RO, Exeter receivers' accounts, 1–2 Ric. III, 2 Ric. III–1 Hen. VII; *CPR 1476–85* p. 371; *Harl. 433* II pp. 47, 124.

[79] PRO, C 76/168 m. 27; C 81/1531/56; E 404/78/3/40.

[80] Horrox, 'Financial memoranda' p. 220.

[81] *CPR 1476–85* p. 501; *Rot. Parl.* VI pp. 242–3. Other beneficiaries included Thomas Broughton, Thomas Everingham and Thomas Burgh: *Harl. 433* I pp. 133, 136, 169–70.

[82] *Harl. 433* I p. 134; Wolffe 1971, p. 193.

position in the north and there is no suggestion that Northumberland was expected to take a major role in southern affairs.[83] The earl was given no part in the measures against the rebels and was not added to local commissions of the peace. Some of his associates may, however, have taken a rather more active role. Philip Thirlwall was given land in Dorset and was one of the commissioners of array there. His colleagues on the commission included one of the Haggerstons of Ellingham (Northumb.).[84] Fitzhugh's links with the region predated the rebellion. He held land in at least one Dorset manor, which explains why he was added to the commission of the peace for the county during Gloucester's protectorship. He was subsequently given more land there and in Somerset, where he was also added to the bench, but there is no evidence that he was active on either commission and there can be little doubt that his interests remained primarily northern.[85]

The southern counties were not the only region where the 1483 rebellion forced Richard to re-examine the crown's position. The defection of Buckingham had reopened the question of how royal authority should be exercised in Wales and the north midlands. In neither area had the duke established himself sufficiently to command a local following and Richard therefore did not have to contend, as in the south, with a disaffected gentry. But Buckingham had been expected to fill the political gaps caused by the removal of the prince of Wales and lord Hastings, and other solutions now had to be found. Wales presented by far the greater problem. No king had entirely solved the question of how to exercise effective control of the principality and the marches.[86] Edward IV's final solution had been to vest royal authority in a council nominally headed by the prince of Wales, which allowed the mediation of royal influence without too much risk that the king's power would be usurped by any individual. Henry VII was later to adopt the same policy, and it clearly also appealed to

---

[83] See further below, pp. 214, 216–18.

[84] Thirlwall: *Harl. 433* III p. 140; he was also made controller of the custom in Poole: *CPR* 1476–85 pp. 403, 421. In 1472 he could be described as of Nafferton (Yorks.), a Percy manor: PRO, C 244/114/96. Haggerstons: Henry was the commissioner, John (presumably a kinsman) was given land in the county: *Harl. 433* III p. 146; Somerville 1953, p. 538.

[85] *Harl. 433* II pp. 119–20; Hutchins 1861–74, I p. 190 (a reference I owe to the kindness of W. E. Hampton); *CFR* 1485–1509 no. 152.

[86] The problems are surveyed in Griffiths 1972b.

Richard III, who used it elsewhere. The difficulty was that Richard had no obvious candidate to head a reconstituted Welsh council. Although the instrument creating Richard's son prince of Wales emphasized his Welsh role, in practice the importance of the north led Richard to use his son as a focus for loyalties there rather than in Wales. When, later in the reign, Richard adopted the same tactic in Calais, his illegitimate son John provided the necessary royal figurehead, but the Calais council was on an altogether smaller scale and it is unlikely that a royal bastard would have been accepted as head of the Welsh council.[87]

One alternative was to put power into the hands of a single dominant magnate, as Edward IV had done with reasonable success in the 1460s when William Herbert I had become 'king Edward's master-lock'.[88] Richard III had reverted to this technique, although on a more spectacular scale, when he gave Buckingham virtually viceregal authority, but the result hardly encouraged further attempts. The range of candidates was, in any case, extremely narrow. Most of the important Welsh lordships had by this date fallen to the crown, and among those still in private hands the Talbot estates were occupied by a minor. It is a comment on the decline of the traditional lordships that the two most obvious candidates for an extended role in 1483, William Stanley and William Herbert II, were relative newcomers whose family fortunes were founded on royal service in the previous generation. The Stanleys' own lands lay primarily in Lancashire and Cheshire and this gave them a natural interest in north Wales which had been developed under Henry VI and further encouraged by Edward IV.[89] The family's refusal to support Buckingham in 1483 had stemmed from their dislike of his expansion into north Wales, and with the failure of his rebellion the way seemed clear for a further extension of Stanley influence. To some extent this expectation was met. Sir William Stanley, the brother most active in Wales in the previous reign, was given a major grant of former Neville and Mowbray land along the march, including Dinas Bran and Holt. Within ten days of Buckingham's death, Stanley had been granted the duke's former office of justiciar of north Wales and was later made constable of Caernar-

---

[87] *Harl. 433* I pp. 81–2. For the north and Calais see below, pp. 215–16, 292.
[88] Griffiths 1972b, p. 159, citing Lewis Glyn Cothi.
[89] Griffiths 1976, pp. 19–21; Lowe 1981, p. 560.

von.[90] A Stanley kinsman, William Griffith of Penryhn, was made chamberlain of north Wales, an office now of more practical significance than the justiciarship.[91] But although, as this suggests, Richard was prepared to see Stanley influence in north Wales increased, there was no question of Sir William taking over the role envisaged for Buckingham. Other key offices in north Wales went to a group of northern associates of the king, perhaps as a deliberate counter-weight to Stanley influence. Richard's patronage of Sir William looks more like the recognition of his obligations to the family than the enthusiastic endorsement of a Stanley hegemony.

The royal attitude to William Herbert II is rather more ambiguous. Herbert's father had been Edward IV's leading agent in south Wales in the 1460s and his death in 1469 had left a vacuum in the area which had been filled in the short term by Gloucester himself. At this stage, Edward IV had apparently anticipated that Herbert's role would be taken in due course by William II, who succeeded to his father's land and office in 1471. But the new earl of Pembroke failed to live up to the king's expectations, or perhaps Edward's own attitude to Wales underwent a change, and the later years of the decade saw the steady erosion of Herbert influence in favour of the circle around the prince of Wales. This change of emphasis was apparent from at least 1473, but was made permanent in 1479, after the death of Herbert's wife, Mary Woodville, had loosened his links with the prince's associates.[92] In March that year William Herbert and his brother bound themselves not to enter Wales for a year, an undertaking which cleared the way for a major territorial reordering by the king. Herbert surrendered the earldom of Pembroke (which was annexed instead to the prince's duchy of Cornwall) and in return received the title of earl of Huntingdon and a less valuable endowment in Somerset and Dorset. According to the later parliamentary act which embodied the change, it was made for the 'reformation of the weal public and restful governance and

---

[90] CPR 1476–85 pp. 368, 516; Harl. 433 I p. 138. This was in place of an earlier grant of Buckingham's lordship of Thornbury. In the first parliament of Henry VII Stanley could therefore claim that the land was an 'exchange' and so managed to keep it at a time when Richard's *grants* were voided: Rot. Parl. VI p. 316. For Berkeley's acquiescence see M. K. Jones 1988, pp. 10–13.

[91] Smith 1966, pp. 159–60; Griffiths 1972a, p. 29.

[92] Lowe 1977; Hicks 1979a, pp. 80–1.

ministration of justice in the said parties of south Wales'.[93] At one level, this meant no more than that the family no longer fitted into Edward's plans for Wales, but it seems that the Herberts had also become identified with local disorder, although there is no way of telling whether this was cause or effect of their loss of favour. The 1470s saw a major dispute between the Herberts and the sons of Roger Vaughan, in which the royal council repeatedly tried to intervene.[94] The financial sanctions imposed on the Herberts in this context may have provided the pressure on William II to submit to the territorial exchange, since the act states that it was also made for 'the contentacion of great sums of money' due to the prince from the earl.

The death of Edward IV did not bring any improvement to Herbert's position. Gloucester's grants to Buckingham confirmed Huntingdon's exclusion from Welsh affairs, and it was only with the duke's rebellion that Huntingdon emerged unequivocally as one of Richard's supporters. The Herberts were duly rewarded for their loyalty. Huntingdon himself was made justiciar of south Wales and steward of the duchy of Lancaster lands there, as well as chamberlain of the prince of Wales. His brother Walter received land in Bedfordshire and Surrey, while their illegitimate brother William, an esquire of the king's body, was given land in Gloucestershire and office in the march. Lesser associates and kinsmen were rewarded with annuities.[95] The family's return to royal favour was crowned by Huntingdon's betrothal to Richard's illegitimate daughter Katherine, an alliance which brought the earl a major new landed endowment. There are problems in deciding its exact value, but at best Huntingdon and his wife received land worth £1,000 p.a. and at worst they probably had an endowment of around £600.[96] But even now that Herbert was his son-in-law, Richard showed no inclination to restore the Herbert hegemony on his behalf. In particular, the king failed to reverse the territorial readjustment imposed by his brother. The earldom of Pembroke was not given back to

---

[93] PRO, C 244/127/16; *Rot. Parl.* VI p. 203.

[94] PRO, C 244/120/3–4, 6–7, 10, 45–8, 244/123/5–6, 22, 22A, 244/127/5. Roger Vaughan was the stepbrother of William Herbert I: Griffiths 1972a, pp. 219–20.

[95] *CPR 1476–85* pp. 367, 470; *CPR 1485–94* p. 141; *Harl. 433* I pp. 94–5, 139, 190, III p. 154.

[96] Royal records contain two separate versions of the grant and it is unclear whether both were operative: PRO, SC 11/827; *Harl. 433* II p. 137, III p. 141. For a similar ambiguity see Horrox 1982, p. 39.

Herbert. Instead, its key estates were placed under the control of a royal household man, Richard Williams, while much of the land given to Herbert lay in the south west, thus endorsing the 1479 settlement.[97]

Richard's unwillingness to create new Welsh hegemonies threw him back on the use of a range of lesser royal servants. Many of these were inherited from Edward IV. Since most of Buckingham's grants were reversions, a significant proportion of Welsh constableships and stewardships was still held by former servants of Edward IV at the time of the rebellion, and the refusal of such men to support Buckingham meant that Richard was prepared to keep them in office. Sir John Donne, for instance, continued to hold office at Kidwelly, and probably also at Carmarthen, on the strength of his original grants from Edward IV.[98] In a few cases Richard was prepared to reinstate officials dislodged by Buckingham. Richard Mynours of Treago (Herefs.) thus resumed his office of chamberlain of south Wales and entered the king's household.[99] But such restoration could not be taken for granted, as John Mortimer found at Monmouth, and there was no question of restoring the Woodvilles and their associates. The aftermath of the rebellion did accordingly see some changes in the pattern of office holding, with the main beneficiaries being former associates of the new king. A group of strategically important offices in north Wales went to members of Richard's northern connection. Thomas Tunstall was made constable of Conway, while Richard Huddleston became captain and sheriff of Anglesey and constable of Beaumaris. Other Huddlestons shared the pickings. Richard's youngest brother Henry was made *rhaglaw* of Anglesey and Caernarvonshire and another kinsman, James, was given the ferry between Anglesey and the mainland.[100] It is difficult to be sure how strong this northern presence was designed to be. Certainly the two minor grants entailed no local activity: the office of *rhaglaw* was notoriously a form of reward for royal servants with no intention of taking an interest in Wales, and James did not, of course, organize the running of the ferry.[101] But, as in the south of England, relatively insignificant grants

97 *Harl. 433* I p. 109; *CPR 1476–85* p. 414; *Rot. Parl.* VI p. 203.
98 PRO, DL 29/584/9254: Griffiths 1972a, p. 203.
99 Griffiths 1972a pp. 160–1, 189; Mynors 1953, p. 112.
100 *Harl. 433* I p. 167; *CPR 1476–85* pp. 368, 369, 372, 431.
101 Griffiths 1974, pp. 71–2.

of this kind were an appropriate reward for men who had moved into an area in attendance on more influential figures and it is possible that there was a real Huddleston presence in Wales.

Richard's servants were certainly active elsewhere in Wales. They dominated the commission appointed to seize the Stafford lands and reassert control over the crown lands in Wales and the march.[102] This was nominally headed by Huntingdon, but there is little doubt that the other commissioners did all the work. Two are known ducal retainers with existing Welsh interests. Sir James Tyrell had been Gloucester's leading agent in Glamorgan, while Morgan Kidwelly (the duke's attorney) was the son of Edward IV's receiver of Kidwelly.[103] The other commissioners were Richard Croft, Richard Williams, Nicholas Southworth and John Edwards. Croft was the younger of two namesakes in the service of the Yorkist kings. In the previous reign his elder brother Sir Richard Croft of Croft (Herefs.) had been a member of the prince's council and a dominant figure in the region. Under Richard III, however, Sir Richard's interests seem to have shifted towards the court, where he replaced William Hopton as treasurer of the household after Hopton's death in February 1484.[104] Richard junior, an esquire of the body, already had interests along the march, where he had been receiver of the Talbot estates during the minority of the earl of Shrewsbury and of the earldom of March lands in Shropshire.[105] The background of Richard Williams is unclear, but he received patronage in the Forest of Dean during the protectorate and was in the royal household by August 1483, which makes it likely that he had been in the service of Gloucester or his brother, probably the former in view of his sudden rise to prominence.[106] Nicholas Southworth was clerk of the kitchen, one of the key administrative posts within the household, and came originally from Cheshire. John Edwards' background is unknown. He was made escheator of Herefordshire in November 1483 and was one of those appointed to enquire into treason there in the following month, and this

[102] *Harl. 433* II p. 32.
[103] *Ibid.* III p. 205; PRO, Prob 11/7 fos. 68v–69.
[104] Lowe 1977, p. 278; *BB* pp. 288–9.
[105] PRO, C 67/51 m. 17; *Harl. 433* II pp. 83–4; Lowe 1981, p. 559.
[106] *Harl. 433* I pp. 26–7; *CPR 1476–85* p. 405. He may have been escheator of Herefordshire under Edward IV: *CFR 1471–85* no. 135.

sudden arrival in local affairs may again imply an earlier connection with Gloucester.[107]

The commission was the main force in royal efforts in Wales. Although it is not explicitly stated in the extant note of the commissioners' appointment, one of their responsibilities was to find the staff needed to manage the crown lands. It was they who chose Richard Owen of Carmarthen as receiver of Kidwelly, although the appointment was not regarded as final until ratified by the king.[108] It is likely that they also had effective control of the Stafford lands in Wales, few of which were regranted by the king. It is therefore significant that the most active members of the commission were Richard's own men. Contemporary references to the work of the commission normally mention Tyrell and Kidwelly, while Tyrell and Williams were the two commissioners with the strongest interests in Wales. Tyrell's role in Wales was important enough for the king to express anxiety about what might happen there when he was moved to Calais later in the reign.[109] Richard Williams dominated Pembrokeshire for the king. He not only received office but a major land grant there, a combination which makes him the nearest Welsh equivalent to Richard's southern plantations. He was also unique among Welsh constables in being required to exercise the office of constable of Pembroke in person.[110] The requirement probably arose from the strategic importance of the region, and explains why Williams is not mentioned as active outside the county.

Although Richard preferred, as in England, to give sensitive tasks to men with a background of service to himself, the degree of change should not be exaggerated. Many of Edward IV's men remained in post under Richard III and, indeed, went on to serve the Tudors. William Mistlebrook, for instance, whom Richard used to seize forfeited chattels in 1483, had been one of Edward IV's auditors in Wales, later became Richard's auditor of the duchy of Lancaster lands there, and finally died at Denbigh in

---

[107] *CFR* 1471–85 no. 801; *CPR* 1476–85 p. 392. It is unclear whether he should be identified with the namesake who joined Tudor in Brittany and was rewarded with office in the earldom of March: *CPR* 1485–94 p. 10.

[108] PRO, DL 29/584/9254; DL 42/20 fo. 46v. Morgan Kidwelly was Owen's surety for carrying out the office, which implies that Owen was his own choice: DL 41/34/1 fo. 117; and see Griffiths 1972a, pp. 189–90.

[109] *Harl. 433* II p. 197.

[110] *Ibid.* I pp. 109, 143, 246; *CPR* 1476–85 pp. 414, 501.

1492 while travelling in the service of Henry VII.[111] Behind such examples lies a more general continuity. After his experiment with Buckingham, Richard's solution to the problem of exercising authority in Wales was basically that adopted by his brother in the 1470s in that it relied on royal household men and administrators. Richard's men, however, had no regional focus for their efforts such as had been provided by the council at Ludlow and as a result their efforts inevitably lacked the status and coherence of the 1470s. The 1483 commission to seize land may have provided a framework of a sort, but its limitations are obvious. In the short term it is understandable that Richard should have taken the approach he did, but the resulting power structure may well have been too loose to be entirely effective.[112]

The other area affected by Buckingham's rebellion, the north midlands, posed quite different problems. The main vehicle of royal authority in this area was the duchy of Lancaster land centred on the honour of Tutbury (Staffs.). The officials of the duchy lordships, drawn from the local gentry families, formed a ready-made affinity which looked to whoever had control of the honour. For the first part of Edward IV's reign this had been the duke of Clarence, who had been given the estates themselves by his brother. In 1473, as part of Edward's attempts to limit his brother's power, the estates were resumed, and effective control of them passed to William lord Hastings, who was given the major offices in the honour. The Tutbury affinity was accordingly absorbed into Hastings' retinue, a development reflected in the surge of indentures made by Hastings in 1474.[113] But the affinity's loyalty to Hastings remained contingent on his control of the duchy estates, and when he was executed the duchy servants looked naturally to Buckingham, the new controlling interest within the honour. Again, however, loyalty to the duchy overrode loyalty to the individual lord, and the duchy connection did not follow Buckingham into rebellion. Richard's position in November 1483 was thus straightforward: the affinity was still intact, all that was needed was a new leader. The king, however,

---

[111] *Harl. 433* I p. 184, II p. 31; Smith 1966, p. 162; Weever 1631, pp. 538–9.

[112] It is interesting to speculate whether, in the longer term, Huntingdon might have been an appropriate figure-head for a reconstituted council. His status as royal son-in-law, together with his traditional standing in Wales, might have made him an acceptable candidate, and his much reduced landed interest should have limited the risk of such a council becoming the tool of a renewed Herbert hegemony.

[113] Dunham 1955, pp. 119–20.

took no action until he was at Nottingham late in March 1484. The delay may have been because the north midlands was among the least of Richard's problems, but it may also suggest that he was having difficulty settling on a suitable candidate. That possibility gains some support from his final choice. Sir Marmaduke Constable, who was made constable and steward of Tutbury, Castle Donington (Leics.) and the High Peak (Derbs.), was a Yorkshire knight of the body and the eldest son of Sir Robert Constable of Flamborough. He looks an eminently suitable choice, except that to use him in the midlands Richard had to withdraw him from Kent where, in the previous December, he had been given the rule of the forfeited Stafford estates.[114] His place in the county was in effect taken by Brackenbury, who was becoming a force in Kent at around this time, and the reshuffle was not damaging to Richard's interests. But the fact that it was necessary is an early sign that Richard had little room for manoeuvre, and this was to become increasingly obvious.

Although Richard's policy in the north midlands seems at first sight to continue that of his brother, Constable did not, in fact, step into Hastings' shoes. Richard made no attempt to create a power base for his servant apart from that provided by the offices themselves. Although Richard had substantial Stafford forfeitures at his disposal in the region, none of them came Constable's way. Instead, he was given land at the very periphery of the duchy interest, in Leicestershire.[115] In this, it is true, his position was not much different from that of Hastings, whose own land had been largely outside the sphere of duchy influence, but Hastings' interests further north had been strengthened by his control of the Talbot wardship. More significant was the different relationship of the two men to the duchy connection itself. Where Hastings had been encouraged to absorb it into his own retinue, Constable was specifically forbidden to do so. In autumn 1484 he was issued with instructions for the administration of the honour of Tutbury which began by directing him to take an oath from all the inhabitants that they would be loyal liegemen of the king and would be retained by no other person.[116] This may have been aimed primarily at Gilbert Talbot, whose family was influential in

---

[114] PRO, DL 42/20 fo. 24v; *Harl. 433* II pp. 60, 81. For his activity in Kent see also: *Harl. 433* II p. 76; PRO, KB 9/950/18.

[115] *CPR 1476–85* p. 471.

[116] *Harl. 433* III pp. 116–18.

the region and who was perceived as an opponent by Richard III, but the ban also applied to Constable. It emphasizes the extent to which he was intended to be a royal agent rather than an independent force in the region – a role confirmed by the general tenor of his other instructions. There was thus no longer to be a local intermediary between the king and the duchy connection, and the new relationship was demonstrated by Richard's grant of fees to numerous local men. Many were made while he was in the region in the spring of 1484, and another round followed on his next visit to Nottingham in the autumn.[117] Removing the local focus of the affinity could have caused problems, but in the event did not do so, almost certainly because the north midlands was one of the very few areas where Richard stayed for extended periods during his brief reign and where he could therefore begin to build the sort of immediate relationship between himself and local men which he had achieved in the north. The result can be seen at Bosworth, where the north midlanders were the one major addition to his support compared with 1483. No method of asserting royal control was as effective as the presence of the king himself.

The other region where the royal presence was greater than usual in this reign was the north east.[118] This was the heartland of Richard's power, and the king's increasing reliance on his northern servants in the aftermath of the 1483 rebellion made it essential that he retain his hold on the loyalties of the region. Specifically this meant that he could not afford to see the supremacy which he had held under Edward IV pass into other hands. In the case of the north there is no doubt that Richard's avoidance of a strong independent presence was a matter of policy rather than pragmatism. There was a ready-made replacement for Richard himself, had the king chosen to use him. The earl of Northumberland had loyally seconded Richard in the previous reign and had given practical support to his usurpation. In backing Gloucester in 1483 the earl may already have been hoping to step into Richard's place in the north once the duke was established at Westminster, but if so he was to be disappointed. The new king did indeed keep the existing power structure intact, but with himself still at the head of it. In effect, Richard sought to continue as lord of the north while also king of England. The ducal

[117] PRO, DL 42/20 fos. 25–6v, 36v–37v.
[118] Edwards 1983.

household in the north remained in existence as a focus for the loyalties of the retinue, while immediate control lay with the former ducal council. Both were now formally headed by Richard's son, and, as with the Ludlow council in the previous reign, the identification of the council with the prince gave status and authority to the efforts of men who were often relatively insignificant royal servants. It was an ideal solution to the particular problems raised by the north and it is not surprising that Richard chose to use his son there rather than in Wales.

In April 1484, however, the prince died and the king was forced to reconsider his policy. His revised solution is embodied in articles drawn up probably while he was in the north in the summer of that year.[119] These re-established both the council and its associated household and, although the formality of the ordinances rather disguises the fact, it is clear that Richard wanted to keep change to a minimum. Inevitably there was some difference of emphasis. The previous council and household had been nominally the prince's, albeit in reality the king's. Now that ambiguity was removed. The council in the north was to be a royal council, whose warrants were to be endorsed *per consilium Regis*.[120] One manifestation of this change was the choice of Sandal as the base for the royal household in the north and as the main residence of the head of the council, although the council itself was to meet in various centres. Sandal was part of the duchy of York and its use, rather than one of the Neville castles, was probably intended to spell out that Richard's servants were taking responsibility for the whole region and not just for the king's personal estates. Richard may also have taken the opportunity to overhaul the titular membership of the council to produce a social spectrum more appropriate to a royal (as distinct from a private) council. His young nephew the earl of Warwick is known to have been nominally associated with the council after its re-establishment, but in the absence of any other record of membership the extent of the changes can only be a matter of speculation.[121] In any

---

[119] *Harl. 433* III pp. 107–8, 114–15. Both are undated, but the household was deemed to have been set up on 24 July (the day Richard left Yorkshire) and in the articles establishing the council Richard undertook to name the lords of the council 'afore his departing'.

[120] *Ibid.* p. 108. Communications from the Ludlow council had apparently been sent under the prince's signet: *Coventry Leet Book* pp. 428–9, 432–3, 434–5, 441–2 *etc.*

[121] Raine, *York Records* I p. 116. For speculation as to membership before the prince's death: Reid 1921, pp. 59–61; Arnold 1984, p. 128.

case, it is likely that much of the council's routine work lay in the hands of men previously associated with the ducal administration, such as John Dawney of Cowick (Yorks.), who had been treasurer of Richard's son at the beginning of the reign and then became treasurer of the household in the north.[122]

The most significant change lay in the headship of the council. Richard's choice spells out his policy towards the north. He appointed none of the leading regional magnates, but instead turned to an almost complete outsider, his nephew John de la Pole, earl of Lincoln. The de la Poles had come originally from Yorkshire, and still maintained interests in Hull, but their northern links were by this date subordinate to their later acquisitions in East Anglia and the Thames valley. The choice of Lincoln may have been dictated partly by the fact that hitherto such regional councils had been headed by a close member of the royal family, since the earl was not only Richard's eldest nephew but arguably his heir presumptive. His lack of independent standing in the north is likely, however, to have been at least as important; certainly it was something which Richard made no attempt to remedy. Lincoln had already received a major land grant for his good service against the rebels, but only one of those manors lay in the north and no further grants of northern land or office came his way.[123] It seems clear that Lincoln, like Constable at Tutbury, was to act for the king, not as an independent force, and for this his 'outsideness' was a positive advantage. His role is emphasized by the fact that, as head of the council, he was to live in the Sandal household. Although the council was given some say in the running of the household it was explicitly the *royal* household in the north, intended to give an institutional identity to Richard's northern servants, and Lincoln's residence within it spelt out that he, too, was one of those servants.

This degree of subordination to the royal interests could not have been achieved had Northumberland been appointed to head the council. This was not just a matter of his independent standing in the north. In the previous reign Northumberland's affinity had in effect merged with Gloucester's, a blurring which had been further encouraged by Richard's accession. Several Percy associates had entered Richard's household, where they accounted for

[122] *Harl. 433* II p. 153, III p. 115; Horrox 1986b, pp. 87, 97.
[123] *CPR* 1476–85 pp. 388–9.

around an eighth of his known knights, for instance.[124] As this implies, the blending of the two affinities worked to Richard's advantage as long as he was the dominant partner, but it would have been correspondingly easy for the balance to tilt the other way. Had Northumberland been recognized as the main royal representative in the north, local members of Richard's own connection could have begun to look first to him for lordship, just as Edward IV's local servants had been drawn into Gloucester's orbit in the 1470s. This was a risk Richard could not afford to run, and his patronage of the earl treads a cautious line between the need to reward Northumberland generously for his help and Richard's fears of yielding authority in the north. Northumberland thus received a major land grant, probably the most valuable of the reign, but one which did not seriously challenge Richard's position in the north. A third of the land (by value) lay in the south west, although this was not an entirely cynical move on the king's part since much of it was land to which Northumberland had a claim and which he presumably valued. The remainder consisted of the forfeited Stafford lordship of Holderness, which complemented existing Percy interests in the East Riding.[125] This was one of the few areas of Percy involvement in the north where Richard did not have much of a stake and where he could therefore afford to be open-handed, although the fact that Holderness was entailed to one of the earl's younger sons may imply royal unwillingness to see so important a lordship annexed permanently to the patrimony of the main line.[126] This apart, the earl's northern gains were minimal. He was made warden general of the Scottish march, but this was merely a titular promotion, which left him in control of only the east and middle marches, not of Gloucester's former west march, where Richard's deputy (first lord Dacre, then Richard Ratcliffe) remained in command.[127] On balance, Northumberland may even have been losing ground in the north. Richard avoided any appearance of a direct attack on the earl's position, but the king's more attractive lordship may

---

[124] Marmaduke Constable, John Everingham, William Evers, William Gascoigne, Hugh Hastings, John Pickering, Christopher Ward. One of the knights inherited from Edward IV, Thomas Burgh, also had Percy connections.

[125] *Harl. 433* III pp. 152–3; Wolffe 1971, p. 193.

[126] Compare Hicks 1984, p. 27, who argues that the earl himself wished to endow his younger son.

[127] PRO, C 81/1531/9, 66; Hicks 1978, pp. 90–1; compare Reid 1921, pp. 60–1. Ratcliffe's appointment is undated but was presumably after Dacre's death in May 1485.

have continued the erosion of the earl's independence which had begun in the previous reign.[128]

Northumberland was the obvious casualty of Richard's plans for the north east, but he was not the only one. Even more ruthless was the king's treatment of Ralph Neville, who inherited the earldom of Westmorland in November 1484.[129] Like Northumberland, Neville had co-operated in Richard's seizure of power and against the rebels and was rewarded with land in the south, in Somerset and Berkshire, although a significant proportion of this was in reversion.[130] He, too, was denied an extended role in the north which, in his case, was tantamount to denying him his due place in northern society. The second earl, Neville's uncle, had been an elderly nonentity during the period of Gloucester's ascendancy, and Richard was evidently unwilling to see the balance of power altered after his death. By the time Ralph Neville inherited the title, the lordship of Raby (the centre-piece of the earldom) was in the king's hands, as, perhaps, was the custody of Ralph's own young heir. The background to this development is unclear, but it was presumably a consequence of the second earl's enfeoffment of part of his Durham land, including Raby, in the late 1470s to his great nephew and a group of trustees who were predominantly Gloucester's men. The resulting eclipse of the Neville interest foreshadowed Tudor policy in the north, although the underlying assumptions were probably rather different. Richard III was not primarily concerned with bringing an outlying region under royal control. In a sense, that had already been achieved by his accession. His more immediate problem was to maintain his personal role in the north once the balance of his own interests had shifted decisively southwards. Whether, in the long term, he could have translated his personal influence into crown authority without resorting to the use of noble intermediaries is another question.[131]

Richard's anxiety to keep the north under his immediate control inevitably makes it something of a special case, but the limited role assigned to the northern earls can nevertheless be paralleled elsewhere. Another area where Richard had held land

---

[128] Horrox 1986b, pp. 96–9.
[129] For what follows see Pollard 1986, pp. 122–3. I am grateful to Dr Pollard for discussing the matter further with me.
[130] *CPR* 1476–85 p. 427.
[131] Horrox 1986a, pp. 7–8.

himself was East Anglia. Here, however, unlike the north, the first signs were that Richard was prepared to yield power after his accession. One of his earliest actions as king was to create John Howard duke of Norfolk, with control of the former royal connection in the region. This had had various components, all of which now passed to the Howards. The new duke was given the available Mowbray land, previously annexed to the court interest through its nominal control by the young duke of York. This was augmented by the local estates of the executed earl Rivers and by the de Vere land which had previously been held by Gloucester himself. Howard was also made chief steward of the duchy of Lancaster in the south, while his son took over from Rivers as steward of the duchy in Norfolk.[132]

The scene was set for the new duke, an efficient and loyal supporter of the new regime, to develop a regional hegemony along now familiar lines. But in practice this does not seem to have happened. Instead, the region saw considerable activity by men who were primarily Richard's own servants, rather than members of the Mowbray/Howard connection, and it seems unlikely that this can be explained simply as Howard taking over the former Gloucester circle. Both the sheriffs chosen for Norfolk/Suffolk during the reign were esquires of the body and relative newcomers to the region. Richard Pole had been Gloucester's receiver there and had come originally from Wiltshire, while Ralph Willoughby, his predecessor as sheriff, was a north midlander.[133] It was also largely to his own men that Richard turned to reinforce the local commissions of the peace after the 1483 rebellion. In Essex the two new justices in December were both members of Richard's ducal affinity. Thomas Lynom had been a ducal man of business, acting as Gloucester's receiver and probably as his solicitor, since he became solicitor general after the duke's accession. After the rebellion he was made escheator of Essex and Hertfordshire, which gave him responsibility for the forfeited land there.[134] His fellow newcomer to the Essex bench was Robert Percy of Knaresborough, Richard's controller of the household. In the course of the reign Percy received substantial land from the crown, including some of the de Vere land in

[132] *Harl. 433* I pp. 72, 75, 80–1; *CPR 1476–85* pp. 359, 365.
[133] See above, pp. 79, 85–6.
[134] BL, Cotton Julius BXII fo. 224; PRO, C 81/1640/39–42; *CFR 1471–85* no. 801; *CPR 1476–85* pp. 166, 460, 523–4, 559–60.

Norfolk which Richard had put into the hands of feoffees while duke of Gloucester. None of the recorded grants includes Essex land and it is possible that Percy's connection with the county was the result of activity there in the 1470s as a ducal retainer.[135] In Suffolk Ralph Willoughby was added to the commission, and in Norfolk there were three newcomers, Pole, Hugh Hastings and John Everingham. Hastings and Everingham were both northern knights of the body whose links with Richard coexisted with membership of the Northumberland connection. Hastings had his own landed interests in Norfolk, where he held the manor of Elsing, although he does not seem to have played much part in local affairs until Richard chose to exploit his connection with the county. The reasons for Everingham's arrival on the scene are obscure. He was the head of the Everinghams of Birkin in the West Riding, a family whose duchy of Lancaster connections had probably brought them to Gloucester's attention. As far as is known, Everingham had no East Anglian land, but his gift of venison to John Howard in July 1483 hints at some connection either with the region or its new lord.[136]

Richard's apparent *volte-face* in the matter of leaving East Anglia to Howard is explained by the extent of local involvement in Buckingham's rebellion. A number of former Mowbray retainers were implicated, including the Brandons, and their complicity revealed Howard's inability to control the Norfolk connection.[137] As in the other areas affected by the rebellion, Richard's response was to turn to men outside the former court connection, whose loyalty he could rely on. This was not necessarily intended to be a final rejection of a regional role for Howard. Effective affinities took time to develop and the new duke had only been in charge for a matter of weeks.

It would also be unwise to see Richard's change of heart as indicative of a fundamental opposition to all regional hegemonies following Buckingham's defection. It seems clear, for instance, that Richard was prepared to consider creating a power base for his friend and chamberlain Francis viscount Lovell. The Lovell family lands were scattered throughout England but included

[135] *CPR* 1476–85 pp. 434, 436; *CCR* 1476–85 no. 1168.
[136] Hastings: see above, p. 63 and Campling 1937, pp. 317–8 (this corrects *Test. Ebor.* III p. 273n. which conflates the two branches of the family). Everingham: *Inqs p.m.* II no. 574; *Test. Ebor.* IV p. 171; Collier, *Household Books* p. 417; Hicks 1978, p. 106.
[137] Richmond 1986, pp. 175–6.

a significant interest in the Thames valley, upon which Richard immediately began to build. Lovell was made constable and steward of Wallingford in August 1483, having been given effective control as early as May.[138] After Buckingham's rebellion had revealed Richard's weakness in the region Lovell's local position was further strengthened. He was given the lion's share of the forfeited land in Oxfordshire and Berkshire, together with much of the forfeited office.[139] This was a type of patronage characteristic of the plantations and the aim is likely to have been the same, except that in Lovell's case the influence conferred was on a regional rather than a local scale.

The tactic, however, appears to have failed and there is no suggestion that Lovell was able to establish a regional dominance. In part this may again be due to lack of time. In spite of Lovell's inherited interests in the area he was starting more or less from scratch in 1483. He had not gained control of his inheritance until 1477 and by then his own interests seem to have shifted decisively northwards. In autumn 1483 he was simply out of touch with Oxfordshire, as revealed not only by the disaffection among his local associates, but also by his lack of awareness that their loyalty was even suspect. As late as 11 October Lovell thought that his kinsman William Stonor could be trusted to lead men to join the royal army.[140] The Lovell affinity in the region had evidently been allowed to disintegrate, and by the end of the reign there is still no sign that Lovell had begun to pick up the pieces. Stonor remained in opposition and was involved in another rising in 1484. The Norreys family, allied to Lovell by marriage, did secure pardons for their part in the rebellion but advanced no further towards royal favour.[141] Nor is there any evidence of Lovell drawing other local families into his orbit. On the contrary, the two Lovell associates who can be identified in local affairs were both outsiders. Edward Franke of Knighton in Richmondshire was made sheriff in autumn 1484, while Richard Rugge of Shropshire was added to the Berkshire commissions of array.[142] As with his

---

[138] *CPR* 1476–85 p. 365; *Harl.* 433 III p. 3.
[139] *CPR* 1476–85 p. 508; *Harl.* 433 I pp. 251, 282, III pp. 148–9.
[140] *Stonor Letters* II p. 163.
[141] John Norreys was pardoned in time to escape attainder, but his brother William's pardon failed to pass the great seal: *CPR* 1476–85 pp. 371, 458; *Harl.* 433 I p. 181, II p. 91. Lovell's sister Frideswide was the wife of Edward, the son of William Norreys.
[142] Franke: *CFR* 1471–85 no. 861; Horrox 1986b, p. 85. Rugge: PRO, C 67/53 m. 2; *CPR* 1476–85 p. 400; see above, p. 144.

royal master, Lovell's reaction to insecurity in the south seems to have been to look elsewhere for support.

In time Lovell might have been able to reanimate his family's links with the area, but it remains unclear how far he was really interested in doing so. There is little evidence that he was actively involved in the region. Instead his interests seem to have focussed on the royal court. He was recognized by contemporaries as an effective line of contact with the king and as such was a regular recipient of gifts from those anxious for royal favour, including Selby abbey and the corporation of Salisbury.[143] In this respect his position is similar to that of Richard Ratcliffe or William Catesby, and the three men are linked in William Collingbourne's famous jibe, 'The Cat, the Rat and Lovell our Dog rule all England under the Hog'.[144] All three did outstandingly well from royal patronage but none seems to have been particularly active in local affairs as a result. Unless Collingbourne simply chose the three names which best fitted his animal imagery, the verse must refer to the influence wielded by the three men at the centre. Another contemporary observer agreed. The Crowland chronicler identified Ratcliffe and Catesby as two of the men upon whom Richard particularly relied.[145] It looks as though Lovell is an example of the type of nobleman who becomes more visible, and perhaps genuinely more common, in the next century: a man whose local role was subordinate to his position at court, and whose importance derived less from a regional power base than from having the ear of the king.

If Lovell chose to concentrate his energies on the court, the decision was presumably his own. There is little doubt that the king was prepared to see him dominate the Thames valley, and the career of Lovell's predecessor as chamberlain, William lord Hastings, had demonstrated that it was possible to combine the office with the active prosecution of royal interests beyond the court. Lovell's apparent preference for one rather than the other is a reminder that a lord's failure to take on an active local role might owe more to his own inclination (or ability) than to royal policy.

Richard's willingness to build up Lovell's regional power

[143] Wilts. RO, G 23/1/44/6; *Cat. Anc. Deeds* v, A 11064.
[144] Roskell 1959b, pp. 162–4.
[145] *Crowland* pp. 174–5.

suggests that his attitude was essentially pragmatic, as his brother's had been. Both kings were more concerned to make the best of the situation in which they found themselves than to pursue abstract principles. If a nobleman offered the most reliable way of getting something done, then he would be used. Richard thus had no hesitation in making use of the earl of Arundel's influence in the Cinque Ports when it came to taking measures against invasion.[146] His reign did, however, bring a change of emphasis. After Buckingham's defection Richard was less ready than his brother had been to countenance major new power blocs, and this is symptomatic of a real change in the position of the king. After 1471 Edward IV was secure on his throne, as can be seen in his unchallenged manipulation of property descents. Richard III, by contrast, was markedly insecure. The 1483 rebellions not only revealed the collapse of the royal affinity in much of the south, they also established a rival claimant to the throne, something guaranteed to put political loyalties under exceptional pressure. A more insidious result was to force Richard onto the defensive in the north, where the maintenance of control over his retinue became crucial to his ability to rule the south.

From autumn 1483, therefore, the attainment of security was central to Richard's policies.[147] The shock of the rebellion, and particularly of Buckingham's involvement, may have predisposed the king to mistrust noble hegemonies. A more potent consequence, however, was Richard's tendency to equate security with the use of his own associates. It was this, more than any abstract desire for accountability, which lay behind the king's almost total reliance on household men to restore royal influence. His retinue included noblemen whom he was prepared to trust, but on the whole they were powerful in the wrong places, and even had the king chosen to use them it would have taken time to develop major regional hegemonies in the south. For immediate results it was more effective to turn to lesser men active within a more limited area. As this implies, it would be wrong to see Richard's response to the rebellion as the embodiment of his considered views on royal authority. It was, rather, a series of expedients, which would probably have been modified given time and a degree of stability. There is no reason to suppose, for example,

---

[146] PRO, C 81/1531/3; Southampton RO, SC 5/1/19 fo. 4; *HMC, 2nd Report* p. 91.
[147] A point strongly made in Ross 1981.

that the king was assuming a permanent reduction in the contribution of the nobility. He might have looked to create new
noblemen in the Hastings mould. By the end of the reign some of
his associates had received enough land to justify ennoblement.
Existing peers might have developed a stronger regional role. The
Howards are the obvious candidates, but Richard also appears to
have been on good terms with a group of younger noblemen,
whose accession to major estates could have changed the political
landscape within a decade. The king was evidently willing to trust
his eldest nephew, John de la Pole earl of Lincoln, the son of the
duke of Suffolk.[148] The young earl of Shrewsbury reputedly
fought for Richard at Bosworth, in spite of his uncle Gilbert's
hostility, and could in time have acted for the king in the north
midlands and the Welsh march.[149] Arundel's heir, Thomas lord
Maltravers, seems to have been particularly close to the king,
who made him a councillor and chose him as his deputy at the
Garter feast of 1485 because of his 'nobleness, prowess and
circumspection'.[150]

Richard's response to the rebellion thus did not commit him
permanently to a particular form of rule. But it did go some way
towards committing him to a particular personnel. His policy of
establishing a new group of royal servants in the south by
distributing forfeited land and office among his own retainers had
created an influential body of men with a vested interest in the
continuing exclusion of the 1483 rebels. For the king himself, by
contrast, it was to become increasingly important to win back his
opponents. Their alienation provided Tudor with a ready-made
faction, and one which could still command some local loyalties
in those areas where Richard himself was weakest. The king thus
proved consistently willing to receive those rebels prepared to
make approaches to his regime. In the short term this was
uncontroversial, with the king's renewed favour adequately
expressed by a pardon and perhaps the grant of a pension from
their forfeited estates. But if the reconciliation were to be made
permanent it would sooner or later demand the restoration of at
least some of the land itself, and this could only be achieved at the
expense of Richard's closest supporters. This conflict of interest

[148] See above, p. 216.
[149] Bennett 1985, p. 157.
[150] PRO, C 81/1530/49; *Harl. 433* II pp. 215–6.

had become a political issue within a year of the act of attainder being passed, and, in the short term at least, Richard had little option but to respect the wishes of his proved allies. The rebellion, and his own reaction to it, had committed him to reliance on a dangerously self-limiting power base.

Chapter 5

THE KING'S HOUSEHOLD

Richard III's efforts to restore authority in the aftermath of the 1483 rebellion were directed primarily at securing service. He needed to re-establish a network of men who would act at his command and, in particular, he needed to ensure a reliable household presence at a local level. Both Yorkist kings regarded the household as the cutting edge of royal authority. Household men did not have a monopoly of service, but they did tend to take on all its most important elements, and the resulting equation of household office with a major local role is characteristic of the Yorkist period. It was not, however, invariably the case in medieval England. The royal household was only one element in a spectrum of service. Its primary purpose was to provide the king with the personal attendance, both honourable and menial, which his status demanded. For duties beyond the court the king could call on a wider circle of support: on his subjects, and on acknowledged servants whose performance of specialized or sensitive tasks set them apart from ordinary subjects. The latter can be regarded as the king's retinue. They were perceived as standing in a special relationship to the crown without being members of the domestic household.

None of these elements was self-contained. The line between servants and subjects was inevitably fluid given the subject's obligation to act on the king's behalf if required. The body servants of the honourable household were men of standing who took on local responsibilities both as a duty and as a reward. Similarly the retinue was perceived as an extension of the household, and the dividing line is not always obvious. The terms king's knight or king's esquire, usually taken to denote royal servants without a specific domestic role, were on occasion used as generic terms for men within the household. Edward IV's serjeant porter and serjeant of the chandlery could both be described as king's esquires.[1] Such imprecision was characteristic of a society which regarded service as open-ended and personal. It is, significantly, grants (rather than royal warrants) which are most explicit about household status, since grants are based on petitions from men anxious to stress their claim to royal favour. In his own warrants the king seems to have been happy with looser, more ambiguous phrases, such as 'our servant N' or 'our wellbeloved squire N'. For most purposes the king evidently thought in terms of subjects or servants, with the latter apparently including anybody who performed an identifiable service for the crown, whatever their status *vis à vis* the household.[2]

Such ambiguities make it difficult to discuss the relative roles of household and retinue with any precision. What is more, the terminology of household office itself was not static. New terms were introduced, existing ones shifted their meaning. To the Yorkist compiler of the *Black Book* esquires of the body were among the elite of the king's personal attendants: 'noble of condition ... their business is many secrets'.[3] To the Lancastrian kings, by contrast, they appear to have been seen mainly as a bodyguard, which explains why 230 of them marched in Henry IV's coronation procession.[4] Despite the difficulty of comparing assumptions about the household in different periods, it does seem as if under the Yorkists the spectrum of service was tending to polarize. Most of the leading roles away from court were performed by household men – or it may be more realistic to say that the kings sought to formalize their relations with their most important local servants by giving them a place within the household. In effect, the household was absorbing the retinue.

This can be illustrated by a straightforward numerical comparison. Under Henry IV, over the reign as a whole, there were thirteen chamber knights and 142 king's knights, a ratio of 1:11.[5] By the end of the Yorkist period the balance had been reversed. Richard III had fifty known knights of the body (the equivalent of

---

[1] *CCR* 1461–8 pp. 213, 351; *CCR* 1468–85 no. 206.
[2] e.g. *Harl. 433* II p. 182.
[3] *BB* p. 111.
[4] Griffiths 1981a, p. 55; Sutton and Hammond, *Coronation* p. 94. They were apparently the descendants of the fourteenth-century esquires of the household: Given-Wilson 1986, p. 22.
[5] Given-Wilson 1986, appendix VI.

the chamber knights) and just four king's knights.[6] The total of king's knights is certainly too low, but the shift in emphasis remains striking.

The roots of the change, as of much else in the Yorkist household, lie in the proliferation of household office under Henry VI.[7] Much of this growth may have been accidental, the consequence of Henry's inability to say no. It was much criticized in its day and became a major target of York's reforming zeal. In spite of this, it established assumptions about the identification of royal service with the household which were to remain part of the intellectual luggage of the political community throughout the Yorkist period. Edward began his reign by cutting back the royal establishment, partly no doubt as a financial expedient but perhaps also in conscious tribute to his father's political manifesto. In the 1460s he had ten knights of the body, a figure comparable to Henry IV's complement.[8] In the 1470s, however, the figure began to grow, and it did so in part through the regrading of members of the retinue. King's knights became carvers or knights of the body, for example.[9] By 1483 Edward had at least thirty knights of the body, with a similar growth among the esquires of the body.

The *Black Book* of Edward IV's household (compiled c.1471–2) appears to reflect the transitional stage in this development and, in spite of its conscious air of conservatism, may have been partly intended to formalize the change. It does not include the king's knights and esquires, since these were not specific household posts, but it does contain another category: the knights and esquires of the household. These are almost unique in the *Black Book* in that their local standing is stressed before their household function. The knights were to be the 'most valiant men of that order of every country'; the esquires 'to be chosen men of their possession, worship and wisdom, also to be of sundry shires by whom it may be known the disposition of the countries'.[10] This is surely an

---

[6] Lists of the Yorkist household exist only for a few years in the 1460s. Unless otherwise stated, all the figures quoted are based on my own lists, compiled from a variety of other sources. They must always be regarded as minima. For the knights of the body, compare the cryptic reference to *xlx* (40, 60?) knights attending Richard at his coronation: Sutton and Hammond, *Coronation* pp. 32, 214.

[7] Griffiths 1981a, pp. 296–7; and see further below.

[8] PRO, E 101/412/2.

[9] *BB* p. 240 (n. 97); Morgan 1973, pp. 13–14.

[10] *BB* pp. 108, 127–8.

attempt to define a household role for the king's knights and esquires which was midway between the knights and esquires of the body and the royal servants outside the household. However, the idea does not seem to have caught on. The title 'knight of the household' is virtually unknown in this period outside the *Black Book*. Esquires of the household can be found under both Yorkist kings, but the term was evidently being used as a catch-all for those esquires within the household who were not esquires of the body, rather than as a distinct category. Thus Edward IV's gentleman usher William Middleton could be described as an esquire of the household, as were some of Richard III's serjeants at arms.[11] Even so, the numbers were much below those envisaged by the *Black Book*, which suggests a minimum of forty, twenty of whom were to be on duty at any one time. Some thirteen are known under Edward IV and fifteen under Richard III. The failure of knight and esquire of the household to survive as specific categories may have been due to the practical difficulties of maintaining a distinction between them and the knights and esquires of the body. Whatever the reason it is clear that the growth in household numbers at this level took the form of an expansion of the ranks of knights and esquires of the body rather than of the technically inferior category.

The expansion of the household to embrace men who would once have been part of the retinue meant that the household's own character changed. The traditional picture of the household as a close circle around the king no longer held good. When a king had fifty knights of the body it was impossible for them all to be on intimate terms with him. The household had become instead a pool of servants, from which some men were picked as the king's confidants while others, the majority, were not. Presumably all the household men were acceptable to the king, but this need not imply a very close bond. It is significant that such fragments of evidence as survive suggest that entry to the household had become an expression of royal favour to the applicant's sponsors as much as a mark of confidence in the individual candidate.[12]

This fundamental shift of attitude caused a series of changes. One was certainly an increased continuity in household member-

---

[11] Middleton: *CPR* 1476–85 pp. 157, 242; *Archaeol.* 1 p. 353. Serjeants (Thomas Otter, Richard Beeston): *CPR* 1476–85 pp. 369, 528; *Harl. 433* II p. 64; *Cat. Anc. Deeds* VI C4115.

[12] e.g. *PL* I p. 617. See also the large number of noble retainers in the Yorkist household.

ship between reigns, since only a handful of men were so closely identified with the king that a change of reign brought their departure from the household altogether.[13] Many of the men close to one king might find it possible to survive in office under his successor, but at a further remove from the centre of things. This was what happened to Edward IV's knight of the body Ralph Hastings. After Richard's accession he remained in the household, but inevitably lost the influence which had accrued to him as brother of Edward IV's best friend. He also saw much of his patronage granted elsewhere, in spite of its nominal confirmation by the new king.[14] The fate of Richard's northern knights of the body in 1485 was similar. Most had made the transition to Henry VII's household within months of Bosworth, but with diminished authority. Sir John Conyers, for instance, lost his preeminence within the honour of Middleham.[15]

The growth of the household must also have had an effect on the amount of personal attendance expected from its members. For the honourable household, attendance at court had always been part-time, although evidence of exactly how this was organized is rare. A fragmentary rota from 1471 gives the tour of duty as eight weeks and implies that five or six knights of the body were on duty at any one time.[16] If there were then around fifteen knights this would mean roughly two months on duty to four months off: a ratio which ensured reasonable continuity of service while allowing the knights adequate time to pursue their private interests. But if the same system still prevailed when there were fifty knights the element of personal service would have become attenuated. This was presumably acceptable to the Yorkist kings, both of whom expected some household men to take on responsibilities which would in any case have kept them away from court for most, if not all, of the year. Richard Williams, for instance, was ordered by Richard III to perform the duties of constable of Pembroke in person.[17]

---

[13] Compare the low continuity rates cited for the fourteenth century by Given-Wilson 1986, pp. 56, 195. Continuity always increased lower down the household, however, *ibid.* p. 213.

[14] *CPR* 1461–7 pp. 13, 14; *CPR* 1476–85 pp. 385, 460, 462; *Harl. 433* 1 pp. 83–4, 163; PRO, C 81/1392/2.

[15] Coles 1961, p. 135.

[16] *BB* pp. 199–200. Compare Turner, *Manners and Expenses* p. 276, which seems to imply a three week spell of duty by John Howard in 1464.

[17] *CPR* 1476–85 p. 414.

The rota was perhaps seen as no more than a way of guaranteeing a minimum attendance upon the king, and was augmented by longer, voluntary attendance by those closest to him. In 1479 John Paston III could refer casually to the men 'who wait most upon the king', as if there were acknowledged gradations of attendance.[18] If so, it implies the sort of double standard suggested above in the matter of closeness to the king. The household now embraced two elements: men whose main interests lay away from court but whose links with the king were formalized by household membership; and men supplying the traditional requirement of close personal attendance. Without the Yorkist checker rolls to reveal who came into court when, this remains speculation, but it would explain the difference between, say, Richard Ratcliffe and William Ingilby, two northern knights of the body of Richard III of vastly different standing. Ratcliffe was the trusted and lavishly rewarded courtier, whose opinions the king hardly ever opposed; Ingilby the unremarked local supporter with an annuity of £20.[19]

As this implies, the Yorkist changes in the structure of service may have been more apparent than real. The degree of personal contact between the king and many of his household men must have been fairly limited. But the change in emphasis was important. It meant that the household was acknowledged to be the king's foremost agent in local affairs, in the sense that the king's most active and influential local servants were almost invariably household men. This is not to say that the retinue had completely lost its role in local affairs. Both Yorkist kings retained significant numbers of the gentry. Richard, indeed, had deliberate recruiting campaigns in Wales and the north midlands, and also took many of his former ducal affinity into his retinue.[20] Some leading local administrators appear to have remained outside the household, such as John Agard of Foston (Derbs.), who was receiver of Tutbury and of part of the Clarence lands, and who was made escheator of Staffordshire in 1483.[21] Richard's handful of king's knights also included figures of the stature of John Ferrers of

[18] *PL* I p. 617.
[19] Ratcliffe: *Crowland* pp. 174–5; and see above, pp. 202–3. Ingilby: PRO, DL 42/20 fo. 41.
[20] *Harl. 433* I pp. 94–5; PRO, DL 42/20 fos. 26–9, 38v–39v; for the northern retinue see further below, pp. 267–8.
[21] *Harl. 433* I pp. 193, 256, II pp. 65, 142–3, 168, 170; *CFR* 1471–85 no. 801; PRO, DL 5/2 fo. 7; Sutton 1986b, p. 130.

Tamworth or William Harrington.[22] But it is fair to say that the typical member of the retinue was now a minor figure, in terms both of his background and of the duties he was called upon to perform. Among them, for example, was Walter Amadas of Dartmouth. In December 1483 he was one of two royal servants responsible for taking possession of captured Breton ships. He is not recorded as receiving any fee from the crown, but was well-enough connected to be able to secure the repayment of £70 which he was owed by Edward IV.[23]

By the 1480s the Yorkist household is likely to have overtaken the retinue in local affairs, not only in the relative importance of the work its members undertook but in absolute numerical terms as well. An examination of the enrolled signet warrants and patent rolls of Richard III yields some 250 'king's servants' other than known household men. This is likely to be only a selection of the total, and an overall figure of around 400 seems a reasonable estimate. At the same time the household, excluding menial servants of only domestic significance, probably stood at something over 600. In the mid 1460s Edward IV's household had included 120 grooms, around 325 yeomen, 77 esquires and 10 knights.[24] There are no comparable figures for Richard's reign, and relying on casual references means that the upper levels are far better documented than the yeomen and below.[25] Richard III's known household men include 50 knights of the body, 48 esquires of the body, 60 esquires of the household (including gentlemen ushers, marshals and serjeants at arms) and 138 yeomen of the crown.[26] Given that the upper levels had certainly expanded by 1483, the lower ones are unlikely to have shrunk, and a total of 600 may therefore even be on the low side. Of course, not all these men performed a major role beyond the court, but even the humblest of them are likely to have been at least as active as the lower levels of the retinue.

The reasons behind this proliferation of men who combined a local role with household membership are complex. To some

[22] Ferrers: PRO, C 81/1392/20; *Harl. 433* I p. 131, II p. 185. Harrington: *Harl. 433* II pp. 54–5.

[23] *Harl. 433* I p. 159, II p. 61; *CPR 1476–85* p. 327. He was perhaps the father of one of Henry VIII's serjeants at arms, which implies a fairly modest status: Vivian 1895, p. 12.

[24] PRO, E 101/412/2.

[25] The household status even of some leading knights of the body is known only from a single reference, e.g. Sir Charles Pilkington: PRO, C 56/1 m. 15.

[26] For the categories adopted here see below, pp. 243–9.

extent the pressure for change may have come from the king. It had always been recognized that household men stood in a particularly close relationship to their master and that this made them effective royal servants beyond the court as well as within it, although ironically the growth at the upper levels of the household must have diminished this closeness. After his exile in 1470–1 Edward was also eager to increase the magnificence of his household on the Burgundian model, and one obvious way of doing that was to take into the household men who were already acknowledged as standing in a special relationship to the crown.[27]

But changes in household size and even, to some extent, in structure cannot be presented only as an exercise in royal will. Both depended ultimately on the readiness of men to enter the household, and the Yorkist kings may have been responding to demand as much as creating it. Their household had a near monopoly of the most attractive forms of royal patronage, a situation which was probably another legacy from the previous reign. Henry VI had not only presided over an increase in the size of the household: at the same time his generosity to the men around him had ensured that most royal patronage was granted within the household.[28] This made membership of the household the ultimate goal of would-be recipients of royal favour, an attitude which persisted under Edward IV.

Henry's reign not only taught the gentry the usefulness of household connections. It also demonstrated the advantages to the king of a strong household presence in the shires. Although the creation of that presence probably owed little to conscious policy, at least on the part of Henry himself, once it was there it was exploited effectively. It was household men who attempted to block York's landing in 1450, and queen Margaret subsequently made good use of the household connection in the west midlands.[29] It was not surprising that the Yorkists, on the receiving end of such tactics, learnt the lesson. York's criticism of the household was as much a compliment to it as his son's refinement of the same techniques.

Henry VI's regime may have made one further contribution to the development of the Yorkist household. In peacetime the household was the single heaviest item of royal expenditure.

[27] *BB* pp. 3–4.
[28] Griffiths 1981a, chaps. 13–14.
[29] *Ibid.* pp. 776–86, 801–2; Griffiths 1976.

Under Henry VI it had run very seriously into debt and in the early years of Edward IV costs continued to outstrip income. The *Black Book* was an attempt to remedy this state of affairs by enforcing rigorous accounting techniques, particularly with respect to the payment of daily wages. The stables were to keep a checker roll of comings and goings so that those household servants paid by the day should not receive more than their due.[30] There was, however, another way of limiting wages, which had been adopted in 1445 in an attempt to reduce the cost of Henry VI's household. It was then ordered that household servants in receipt of a significant income from royal patronage should receive no daily wages while in court. For priests and squires patronage of £40 called the order into play, for yeomen the limit was 20m.[31]

The only explicit reference to this practice in the *Black Book* concerns household chaplains, who were to receive no wages if they held a benefice worth £40.[32] The same principle was, however, almost certainly applied to other servants as well. Its adoption was encouraged by the fact that several categories of Yorkist servant were in any case not paid by the day, but were granted an annual fee by letters patent. The serjeants at arms are the clearest example, and the only one admitted by the *Black Book*. They received £18 5s p.a., generally from town or county revenues.[33] Many yeomen of the crown also received fees by letters patent, in their case £9 2s 6d p.a.[34] Individual members of other household categories might also be paid in this way. Some of Richard's esquires of the body were granted 50m p.a., specifically as a fee of the crown.[35] The concept of a flat fee was thus well established, and it was only a short step from this to regarding a salaried local office, or other patronage, as a fee in lieu of daily wages. That this step was indeed taken is shown by the yeomen of the crown, some of whom received a fee but no further grants, while others received salaried local office but no

[30] *BB* pp. 5–13, 21–6.
[31] *BB* p. 66.
[32] *BB* p. 111.
[33] *BB* p. 131. This meant that they, and others like them, need not be included on the checker roll, but only on the great roll of the household, kept probably by the controller: *BB* p. 101.
[34] e.g. *Rot. Parl.* VI p. 87; *Harl. 433* III pp. 193–8.
[35] e.g. *CPR* 1476–85 pp. 379, 380, 448; *Harl. 433* I pp. 92, 127. Carvers generally received £40, e.g. *Harl. 433* III p. 193.

recorded fee. A few received neither and may have been paid daily as the *Black Book* envisaged.[36]

This substitution benefited both sides. For the household man, an office was a more attractive option than a wage or fee. They were lump sums; an office, by contrast, would confer influence and might also bring other perks. Parkerships, for instance, which were often used as rewards for yeomen, might carry the right to windfalls or to free pasture.[37] It was thus not uncommon for a yeoman to be feed by an office of lower face value than the fee of the crown, which was 6*d* per day. Among Richard III's yeomen, Robert Bukstede was made keeper of the manor and park of Ditton (Bucks.) at 3*d* p.d. and Richard Dickonson was forester of Galtres (Yorks.) at 4*d* p.d.[38] Where the discrepancy was very great the office might be augmented by an annuity. John Twisleton of Darrington near Pontefract was parker of nearby Cridling at a fee of £3 0*s* 8*d* and received an annuity of £6.[39] Even when an annuity was included the crown was still saving money on the deal. The office would have had to be filled anyway and giving it to a household man was saving a second wage.

The practice helps to explain the close links between local office and household status which clearly prevailed under the Yorkists, with men losing local patronage when they left the household. It also explains why the compiler of the 1478 household ordinance felt it necessary to specify that he had not included holders of local office in his calculation of household size.[40] Local office had probably always served as a method of feeing members of the retinue, and the fact that it was now largely used to support the household can be seen as a further manifestation of the household's tendency to absorb the retinue.

The accretion of local office and influence around the household is a counter-weight to the more familiar process whereby administrative functions arose within the household and then went out of court. For many areas of government this was past history by the Yorkist period. The staff of the chancery and the exchequer were no longer considered part of the household, for instance, although in many respects household and bureaucracy,

---

[36] *BB* p. 116. Under Edward IV the yeoman Piers Curtis was given land specifically in lieu of a fee: PRO, DL 42/20 fo. 48.

[37] *Harl. 433* I pp. 114, 177; Fortescue, *Governance* p. 151.

[38] Bukstede: *CPR 1476–85* p. 406. Dickonson: *CPR 1476–85* p. 412.

[39] PRO, DL 29/526/8390; DL 42/20 fos. 82v–83; *Harl. 433* I p. 225; *Test. Ebor.* IV p. 49n.

[40] Longleat ms 65 fo. 10v.

particularly at their upper levels, remained a single community.[41] This blurring was accentuated by the fact that the household was still home to some administrative agencies. The king's secretary and his four clerks were treated as members of the household by the compiler of the *Black Book*.[42] This is given a more personal dimension by the will of one of Edward IV's secretaries, William Hatcliff, who died in 1480.[43] The only colleague he mentions, apart from his clerks, is the dean of the chapel royal, whom the 1478 ordinances regarded as the secretary's equal within the household; an equality which probably led to their eating together in hall, for instance.[44] The supervisor of his will was a courtier, Richard Fiennes lord Dacre, the chamberlain of queen Elizabeth, with whom Hatcliff had gone on embassy to Burgundy in 1475.[45]

The most interesting example of this continuing overlap between domestic and administrative service is the flowering of the Yorkist chamber as a major financial department.[46] In household terms, the chamber was the king's private apartment, as distinct from the hall where he made his public appearances. Its executive officers were the ushers of the chamber, who ensured its smooth running and may have played some part in regulating access to the king. Below them were the yeomen of the chamber, whose main function was to guard the king and his possessions, and the grooms, who performed the necessary menial tasks – or at least ensured that others did so.[47] The chamber was also the home of other officers whose functions touched the king most closely, such as his chaplains and esquires of the body.[48] It had always had a financial dimension, with the king's private hoard of jewels and cash kept there, and it was this aspect of its responsibilities which was elaborated under the Yorkists. By the end of Edward IV's reign, the revenues of most crown estates and prerogative wind-falls were being paid into the chamber and the relevant accounts

---

[41] See, for instance, the meshing of household, administrative and urban connections in the will of Richard Fowler, chancellor of the duchy of Lancaster (d. 1477): PRO, Prob 11/6 fos. 248v–250. See also above, pp. 24–5.

[42] *BB* pp. 110–11. Compare the description of Gloucester's secretary, John Kendale, as 'gentleman of the household of the duke of Gloucester': *CCR* 1476–85 no. 950.

[43] PRO, Prob 11/7 fos. 8v–9; Otway-Ruthven 1939, pp. 66, 155.

[44] *BB* p. 224.

[45] Ross 1974, pp. 102, 224.

[46] The definitive account is Wolffe 1971, chap. VI.

[47] *BB* pp. 114–15, 117, 120–1.

[48] *BB* pp. 111–12.

audited there.[49] The death of Edward IV brought a temporary setback, but Richard revived the chamber system of finance and ran it effectively.

One manifestation of the chamber's dual role was the household status of many Yorkist receivers. Of the twenty receivers whom Richard ordered to pay their money into the chamber in January 1484, nearly half are known to have been in his household or that of his brother.[50] This sample does not include all the household receivers. A further five men who held major receiverships were among Richard's esquires of the body: Robert Brackenbury, Geoffrey Franke, Richard Pole, John Sapcote and Ralph Willoughby.[51] Other receivers are to be found elsewhere among the chamber staff. John Green, for instance, was a yeoman of the chamber and receiver of the Isle of Wight.[52]

This merging of financial and domestic functions did not depend on the development of chamber finance. Indeed, the reverse is more likely to be true. Household men had acted as receivers earlier in the century, and their numbers increased significantly under Henry VI as part of the household's engrossment of the available patronage. The existence of such men may have been a *sine qua non* of chamber finance, since they were probably more willing than their financial colleagues to pay their revenues directly to the king and to act on instructions given verbally or under the king's personal seal. The emergence of chamber finance was thus not a discrete administrative development, but a further example of the household's tendency to absorb local office. Royal receivers had never been just accountants. Their responsibility for the king's estates spilled over into a wide range of local functions. Richard Welby, the receiver of the honour of Richmond in Lincolnshire, was appointed to investigate rights of common in Sutton fen.[53] John Hayes, receiver of the Clarence lands in the south west, was put on a committee to raise money for repairs to the bridge and sluice at Highbridge (Som.).[54]

---

[49] Chamber revenues are listed in Horrox, 'Financial memoranda' p. 230.

[50] *Harl. 433* II pp. 70–1. John Penley, Thomas Fowler, John Isham, Robert Coorte, John Harcourt, Nicholas Spicer, Martin Haute, David Middleton, Richard Croft. John Luthington is described as a king's esquire.

[51] *CPR 1476–85* pp. 364, 385, 485, 535; *Harl. 433* I pp. 155, 233, II pp. 24–5, 29, 113, 117.

[52] *Harl. 433* II p. 33.

[53] PRO, C 67/53 m. 4; DL 42/20 fo. 55v.

[54] *Harl. 433* II p. 206.

The local power that such men wielded made the office of receiver both an appropriate responsibility and a satisfactory reward for household men. Even after chamber finance had begun to emerge, it seems to have been usual for household men to be made receivers rather than vice versa.[55] Robert Coorte, for instance, is recorded as a groom of the chamber in 1466. In the 1470s he became active in the service of the prince of Wales as auditor of the duchy of Cornwall. He held the same post under Richard III and Henry VII, and at his death in 1509 sought burial within the priory church at Wallingford, one of the duchy honours. He was also made receiver of the duchy of Lancaster in the south parts after acting as Elizabeth Woodville's receiver in her duchy lands.[56] That this was the usual sequence is suggested by the fact that neither Yorkist king thought it essential to give household office to receivers inherited from the service of other lords, and even important receivers such as John Hayes appear to have remained outside the household as a result.[57]

The Yorkist household was Janus-faced. All but its humblest members looked inwards, to meet the king's domestic needs, and outwards to the provinces, where they not only had interests of their own but acted as agents of the king's wishes. This division of the household into men with or without a local role is crucial to any discussion of its political functions, but it does not correspond to the Yorkists' own formal division of the household into the *domus magnificencie* and the *domus providencie*, a division which corresponds roughly to the later distinction between the household above and below stairs. The *domus magnificencie* included the men who came into direct contact with the king and his guests and who thus constituted the public face of the household. The *domus providencie* provided the administrative and menial underpinning of this public activity, buying and roasting the meat which members of the *domus magnificencie* carried to the king's table, carved and served, for instance.[58]

The implied subordination of the *domus providencie* is, how-

[55] Receiverships were, however, rarely granted under the great seal, which makes dating difficult: *ibid.* 1 p. xxvii.

[56] PRO, E 101/412/2 fo. 34v; SC 6/1302/1 m. 5 dorse; Prob 11/16 fo. 111; *Harl.* 433 1 pp. 73, 196, 11 pp. 36, 70, 88; Ives 1968, p. 227n.; Somerville 1953, p. 623; Ashmole 1719, 1 p. 51.

[57] Hicks 1980, p. 48; Wolffe 1971, pp. 166–7.

[58] *BB passim*; Morgan 1987, pp. 31–4.

ever, misleading. The officers who headed this arm of the household were men of standing with a significant role beyond the court. At their head was the steward of the household, an honorific post held in Richard's reign first by the earl of Surrey and then by lord Stanley.[59] Next in importance came the treasurer (Sir William Hopton, followed by Sir Richard Croft) and the controller, Sir Robert Percy.[60] These last three, who were among Richard's closest allies, were important locally as well as at the centre. Percy, for instance, was made sheriff of Hertfordshire and Essex in 1484 and had to cope with disaffection there in the following winter.[61] Below them in the hierarchy was the clerk of the kitchen, Nicholas Southworth, whom Richard used to reassert royal authority in Wales in the aftermath of Buckingham's rebellion.[62] Southworth's second in command, Richard Gough, was also active beyond the court. He not only found himself victualling the fleet and seeing to supplies for Dunbar, jobs which could be regarded as an extension of his household role, but was also charged with the administration of some forfeited land in London.[63] Men who held office within the individual departments of the *domus providencie* might also have a concurrent local role. Richard's serjeant porter, Thomas Mering, was a man of standing in Nottinghamshire, where he was active on the commission of the peace.[64] On the other hand, the waits and minstrels of the *domus magnificencie* had no independent local standing, although their summer tours through the countryside may have given them an intelligence-gathering role.

As these examples imply, the Yorkist division of the household also fails to match the distinction between honourable and menial service. The gentry members of the *domus magnificencie*, who came into court for part of the year to attend upon the person of the king, were undoubtedly providing honourable service, but so were many of the *domus providencie*. The office of clerk of the kitchen was a recognized stepping-stone to a high-grade administrative career, whether held within the royal household or an aristocratic one. John Paston III, talent-spotting for lord Hastings,

59 PRO, C 67/51 m. 18; M. K. Jones 1986a, p. 49 (n. 85).
60 *BB* pp. 288–90 (who conflates Robert Percy father and son; the controller died at Bosworth).
61 See below, pp. 278–9.
62 See above, pp. 210–11.
63 *CPR* 1476–85 p. 455; *Harl. 433* II pp. 108–9, 134, 151.
64 *Test. Ebor.* IV pp. 179–82; *Harl. 433* III p. 141; PRO, KB 9/366/3.

239

thought that Richard Stratton would make a suitable clerk of the kitchen. Stratton had begun his career as purveyor with Adrian Whetehill, the controller of Calais, before moving into the service of Whetehill's brother-in-law John Ratcliffe, lord Fitzwalter. In Paston's words: 'This man is mean of stature, young enough, well witted, well mannered, a goodly young man on horse and foot. He is well spoken in English, meetly well in French and very perfect in Flemish. He can write and read.'[65] It is the portrait of a young, upwardly mobile professional. Stratton's final position is not known, but one of the Yorkist clerks of the kitchen, John Elrington, ended up as treasurer of the household.[66]

The departments of the *domus providencie* were also headed by men whose service was undoubtedly honourable rather than menial. Richard III's serjeant of the pantry, John Ratcliffe, was one of the Ratcliffes of Derwentwater, the brother of the king's close friend Richard Ratcliffe, and husband of the Fenwick co-heiress.[67] For that reason it is difficult to believe that Ratcliffe literally collected the day's bread from the bakehouse or the carving knives from the jewel house, as the *Black Book* stipulated.[68] Similarly there was surely no question of Thomas Mering turning out in person to spar the gates. Their service was honourable, in other words, because they did not actually perform it, and this sets them apart both from the staff of the chamber, whose service was honourable because it was tendered to the king, and from the administrators, whose service was honourable because it was a proper career for a gentleman.

Once the possibility of honourable non-performance has been admitted, it becomes impossible to be sure at what level the servants of the *domus providencie* actually carried out the duties assigned to them, and hence at what level service became menial. The typical department of the *domus providencie* had five grades of officer: the serjeant at its head, a clerk (the department's administrator), the yeomen, grooms and pages. There is little doubt that to the level of yeoman, and probably to that of groom, these offices were honourable in the sense that their holders were considered gentlemen. Edward IV's yeoman of the scullery, William Parker, could be described as a gentleman of the

[65] *PL* I p. 600; see also Ives 1983, pp. 12–13.
[66] *BB* pp. 288, 290; PRO, DL 29/263/4125; Prob 11/7 fo. 59.
[67] *Harl. 433* I p. 105; Hampson 1940, p. 218.
[68] *BB* pp. 169–70.

household and was one of the royal servants deputed to attend on the duchess of Burgundy during her state visit to England.[69] Even if such men performed some duties within their department, it is clear that there would be further levels of servants below them to do most of the unpleasant or heavy work under their supervision.

Some, at least, of these offices were also honourable in the more restricted sense that they were considered appropriate rewards for members of the minor gentry whose main areas of activity lay outside the court. Many of the serjeantries were probably in this category. Richard III's serjeant of the cellar was John Poleyn of Scotton Hall in the forest of Knaresborough, an associate of Sir Robert Percy.[70] One of his colleagues, the yeoman of the cellar John Brown, was also based in the forest of Knaresborough, where he made his home in the manor house within the royal park of Hay.[71] Another Yorkist yeoman, Richard Forster, who held office in the butlery, was active in the east midlands.[72] Even the office of groom might be held by men of standing. Edward IV's groom of the ewery was John Ward esquire, the brother of Sir Christopher Ward of Givendale, one of Richard III's knights of the body.[73]

This wide range of status among the officers of the *domus providencie* made this branch of the household a good starting point for a career in the royal service. It was probably relatively easy to rise within the *domus providencie* itself. William Ratcliffe, who was a yeoman of the cellar in 1485, was serjeant by the time he came to make his will in 1500.[74] It was also possible to move across into the *domus magnificencie*. Administrators perhaps found it easiest. Richard Lawrence, who held the responsible post of yeoman of the jewel house from the 1470s, had previously been clerk of the scullery.[75] But other moves were possible. John Gough of Bristol began as a groom of the privy larder in 1462, advanced to yeoman of the larder by 1464 and became a messenger of the chamber by 1471, while retaining his office in the larder. From messenger it was an obvious step to serjeant at arms,

[69] *CPR* 1467–77 p. 374; *CCR* 1476–85 no. 213; Nicolas, *Wardrobe Accounts* p. 164.
[70] Pullein 1915, pp. 45–8; PRO, DL 42/20 fos. 17, 46v; DL 5/1 fos. 96v, 113.
[71] PRO, DL 29/482/7777–9; *Rot. Parl.* VI p. 96; *Harl.* 433 I pp. 128, 202; *Reg. Thomas Rotherham* I p. 192.
[72] *CPR* 1461–7 p. 433; *CFR* 1471–85 no. 808; PRO, DL 42/20 fos. 13Av–14.
[73] *Plumpton Corresp.* p. 25; *Test. Ebor.* IV p. 274; *CPR* 1476–85 p. 423.
[74] *Rot. Parl.* VI p. 352; PRO, Prob 11/14 fo. 179.
[75] *CPR* 1467–77 pp. 84, 496; *CPR* 1476–85 pp. 122, 417; *BB* pp. 122–3.

a post he held by the end of Edward's reign.[76] William Collingbourne, serjeant of the pantry in 1464, rose to become a gentleman usher.[77]

It is accordingly unsatisfactory to treat the two arms of the Yorkist household as separate entities. It is true that the two hierarchies do not entirely match, with the officers of the *domus magnificencie* tending, because of their closeness to the king, to be of higher status than their nominal counterparts in the departments below stairs. These inconsistencies, however, are no more extreme than those within the *domus magnificencie* itself. Because of the personal dimension of service, an individual's place within the hierarchy did not necessarily define his importance, and an influential esquire of the body like William Catesby could clearly carry more weight than many of the knights of the body. Despite the difficulties of definition, the two wings of the household had far more in common than is usually admitted and can be discussed as a single entity.

The departments of the *domus providencie* provide a convenient starting point, with their clearly defined hierarchy of serjeant, yeoman, groom, page. Nominally the grooms and pages correspond to the grooms and pages of the chamber within the *domus magnificencie*, and the type of duty ascribed to them in the *Black Book* is broadly similar, consisting largely of fetching and carrying. There is no doubt, however, that the chamber staff's closeness to the king did give them the higher status, although the Yorkist grooms cannot rival the standing and influence of the Tudor grooms of the privy chamber. Many are no more than names, which suggests a modest background, although some were drawn from gentry families. One of Richard's grooms of the chamber, Henry Norreys, was the seventh son of William Norreys of Speke (Lancs.).[78] John Trefry, one of Edward's grooms, was more eminent. He was the head of the Trefrys of Trefry (Corn.) and was sheriff of his county in 1483.[79] Another of Edward's grooms was the Plymouth merchant Thomas Grayson, who went on to become a yeoman of the crown and to carve out a career for

[76] *CPR* 1461–7 p. 272; *CPR* 1467–77 p. 109; *CPR* 1476–85 p. 309; *CCR* 1468–76 no. 707; *Rot. Parl.* v p. 539.
[77] *CPR* 1461–7 p. 293; *Archaeol.* 1 p. 353.
[78] *CPR* 1476–85 p. 460; Ormerod 1850, pedigree facing p. 160.
[79] PRO, E 405/70 m. 4; Vivian 1887, p. 459; Som. RO, DD/Wo 37/8/unnumb. He was described as an esquire in 1483 and knighted by Tudor on landing: *Rot. Parl.* vi p. 246; Gairdner 1898, p. 364 ('Treury').

himself as the king's expert on maritime matters in the south west.[80]

With the yeomen, the relationship of the two arms of the household becomes clearer. Within the *domus providencie* the status of the yeomen was probably partly determined by the importance of their department. Yorkist yeomen of the wafery are entirely invisible and are unlikely to have been men of much standing, whereas Richard Forster in the butlery was clearly the equal of the yeomen of the crown in the *domus magnificencie*. The *Black Book* specifies that some of the yeomen of the crown had special domestic duties within the *domus magnificencie*, acting as yeoman of the robes or the bed, for instance, and this may have helped to blur the line between them and their colleagues below stairs. The ceremonial distinction, however, remained important, and yeomen within the *domus providencie* were never described as yeoman of the crown. The household accounts of the 1460s appear to list the two groups separately, although without making the distinction entirely explicit.[81]

Within the *domus magnificencie* itself all the yeomen were on an equal footing and were technically yeomen of the crown. A yeoman of the chamber was a yeoman of the crown who had been assigned to duties in the chamber, and the two terms are thus regularly used of the same man, with no suggestion that promotion was involved. When Richard III's yeoman Thomas ap John was made porter of Newport in February 1484 he was described as a yeoman of the chamber; when payment was ordered in the following January he was identified as a yeoman of the crown.[82] His colleague Richard Lloyd was described as a yeoman of the crown in the signet copy of a grant and as a yeoman of the chamber in the corresponding letters patent.[83] The *Black Book*, while treating yeoman of crown and chamber separately, reveals that the difference in their responsibilities was negligible.[84] Similarly the yeomen ushers of the chamber were nominated as necessary from the yeoman of the crown.[85] Edward IV could write to 'our servant Roger Kelsale, one of the

---

[80] *CPR 1467–77* p. 595; *Harl. 433* II pp. 163–4; Horrox, 'Financial memoranda' pp. 219, 227, 236; PRO, E 405/71 m. 2.

[81] PRO, E 101/412/2 fos. 37–8.

[82] *CPR 1476–85* pp. 405, 410; *Harl. 433* II p. 197.

[83] *Harl. 433* I p. 272; *CPR 1476–85* p. 471.

[84] *BB* pp. 116–7.

[85] *BB* p. 116.

yeomen of our crown and usher of our chamber'.[86] Richard's servant William Bolton was described as a yeoman usher in August 1483, a yeoman of the crown in December 1483 and in March 1484, and as an usher again in the following October.[87]

Within the household hierarchy the yeomen definitely outranked the grooms, but there was probably little to choose between them in terms of their social background, something emphasized by the regularity of promotion from one to the other. In the *domus magnificencie* the yeomen of the crown reveal the same wide social range as the grooms of the chamber. Some were drawn from the gentry. Richard's yeoman Roger Hopton was the head of a family seated at Ackworth, within the honour of Pontefract. The family was of limited importance, but was related by marriage to some of the leading men of the region. Roger himself married a daughter of Sir John Saville of Thornhill, an important member of the duchy of York connection.[88] Another yeoman with a gentry background, although a less impressive one, was Richard Revell of Morton (Derbs.), the fourth son of Thomas Revell, a serjeant at law who had settled at Higham (Derbs.).[89] Other yeomen had a mercantile background. John Davy of Fowey, yeoman of the crown of both Yorkist kings and of Henry VII, was captain of the royal ship the *Carvel of Eu*. He was employed to guard the fishing fleet and, under Richard III, was active in the attack on Breton shipping, something which seems to have shaded into piracy on his own account.[90] His independent standing is unclear but, to judge by his better documented colleague John Taillour, is unlikely to have been particularly exalted. Taillour, a yeoman of the chamber, held the influential post of surveyor of the customs in the west parts under both Yorkist kings. After 1485 he was involved in opposition to Henry VII and one result is a number of references to him which reflect his private status rather than royal office holding. A pardon of 1489 begins by describing him as a merchant of Exeter, but then continues, less impressively, to identify him as a tailor of Zeal and a hosier of Kingsbridge (Devon). His land in Kingsbridge was later said to be worth 5s p.a. which, even allowing for under-valuation,

[86] Southampton RO, SC 2/9/1/unnumb.
[87] PRO, C 81/1392/19; *CPR 1476–85* p. 429; *Harl. 433* II pp. 13, 44.
[88] Wedgwood 1936, pp. 467–8; Hampton 1979, no. 349.
[89] PRO, DL 42/20 fo. 21; Williams 1971, p. 141.
[90] *CPR 1476–85* pp. 118, 258, 317, 355, 466; Horrox, 'Financial memoranda' p. 219; *Cely Letters* nos. 115, 205; Oppenheim, *Naval Accounts* pp. 28–9; Richmond 1967, pp. 9–10.

puts into context Richard III's grant to him of land valued at
£18.[91]

The yeomen of the crown had originally been the king's
bodyguard, and the *Black Book* bears witness to this role in its
emphasis on their physical prowess rather than social standing.
They were to be 'cleanly and strongest archers, honest of conditions and behaviour, bold men ... chosen men of manhood,
shooting and specially of virtuous conditions'.[92] But they had
also taken on responsibilities beyond the court. They ran many of
the king's errands, which not only involved them in carrying
messages but in taking direct action. In 1468, after the arrest of the
earl of Oxford, it was reported that 'the yeomen of the crown be
ridden into divers counties to arrest men that be appeached'.[93]
When they were acting on the king's behalf they wore a badge in
the shape of a crown in silver gilt on one shoulder. In 1443 an
account of disturbances in Norwich described men riding 'with a
crown upon their arms and with bows and arrows as yeomen of
the crown of the lord king'.[94] In this case rioters were only
feigning to be yeomen of the crown, but real yeomen could also
be tempted to use their insignia improperly for their own ends. In
the dispute over Gregories, the duke of Gloucester roundly
criticized the yeoman of the crown William Ascham for wearing
his insignia when he accompanied Thomas Wethiale in entering
the disputed property: 'not doubting if the king's good grace had
knowledge thereof, you would be shent [disgraced]'.[95] Dispos-
ing of these potent emblems of royal authority exercised several
yeomen. John Smethurst gave his to Norwich cathedral and
Thurstan Hatfield bequeathed his for the repair of the church of
Our Lady at Glossop, while John Twisleton gave his to the image
of Christ in the Carmelite friary at Doncaster.[96]

This expansion of the yeomen's role beyond the king's person
perhaps explains why Henry VII chose to initiate a new specialist

---

[91] *Harl. 433* I p. 156, II pp. 157–8, III p. 194; *Rot. Parl.* VI p. 504; *CPR* 1485–94 p. 258; *Inqs p.m.* III no. 718.
[92] *BB* p. 116.
[93] *Plumpton Corresp.* p. 20.
[94] *Records of Norwich* I p. 340.
[95] Essex RO, D/DQ/14/124/3/40.
[96] Blomefield 1739–75, II pp. 508–9; PRO, Prob 11/9 fo. 231v; *Test. Ebor.* IV p. 49n.
Comparable insignia remained in use until early modern times and the badge of one of
George I's messengers was sold at Phillips, 4 July 1986 (item 102). I am grateful to Anne
Sutton for drawing my attention to the catalogue entry.

bodyguard: the yeomen of the guard. But the Yorkist yeomen had not entirely lost their protective function. They remained responsible for guarding the king overnight, when they were to be 'girded with their swords or with other weapons ready'.[97] This, together with the potentially violent nature of some of their other duties, meant that martial skills were still valued. Richard Scopham, yeoman of the crown from the 1470s until his death in 1502 and a citizen and brewer of London, proudly bequeathed to his sons 'a goblet of silver the which I won at shooting' and 'a piece of silver the which I won at wrestling'.[98]

Above the yeomen in the household hierarchy came the esquires. The serjeants who headed the departments of the *domus providencie* ranked as esquires.[99] So, on the other side of the household, did the marshals of the hall.[100] The marshals, also known as ushers of the hall, do not have their own entry in the *Black Book* but are regularly mentioned in passing. They performed the same duties in the hall as the gentlemen ushers in the chamber; that is, the general ordering of business and supervision of other staff.[101] The two offices, marshal and gentleman usher, were treated as equal in the 1478 ordinances and the two offices were apparently held together on occasion. William Griffith of Penrhyn, marshal of both Yorkist kings, was also described as a gentleman usher of the chamber in Edward IV's reign.[102] It seems likely, however, that in practice the gentlemen ushers, in frequent personal contact with the king, outranked the marshals, and to some extent this is supported by a comparison of their social backgrounds and of the rewards they received.

Among Richard's marshals of the hall, Roger Dyneley was a younger son of a family which had moved from Lancashire to Yorkshire in his father's day. He is unlikely to have inherited any land of his own, but acquired land in Manston in the West Riding by marriage. Royal service brought him an annuity of 20m from Pontefract and a minor office within the honour which had been held by his father. He also secured the farm of a corn-mill and

[97] *BB* p. 117.
[98] *CPR* 1476–85 pp. 90, 379; PRO, Prob 11/13 fo. 91.
[99] See above, note 1.
[100] e.g. *CPR* 1461–7 p. 293.
[101] *BB* pp. 91, 112, 114–15.
[102] *BB* p. 225; *CPR* 1476–85 p. 18; *CCR* 1476–85 no. 1098; *Rot. Parl.* VI p. 200; PRO, DL 42/20 fos. 20Av–21.

fishery at Castleford.[103] His colleague, Richard Forthey of
Faversham, was a victualler and purveyor who had been in
Gloucester's service in the previous reign, when he had also been
one of the victuallers of Calais. In Richard's reign he continued to
be purveyor for Calais and also for the royal fleet.[104] Of the
ushers, Humphrey Littlebury held Kirton in Holland (Lincs.)
which he had inherited from his father Sir Robert and which was
worth some £25 p.a. He also held Stainsby, in the same county,
in his wife's right. From royal service he acquired an annuity of
20m and the influential post of customer in the port of Boston. He
also, unlike either of the marshals, served on a major local
commission, that of array for the parts of Holland.[105] Robert
Eyre was head of a family seated at Padley (Derbs.) and at his
death in 1498 held land valued at £26. He had links with the
Talbots, Lovells and lord Hastings, whose deputy he had been as
steward of High Peak. Under Richard III he received an annuity
of 10m and the farm of the money paid for lead-mining rights in
the Peak. He was a commissioner of the peace and of array in
Derbyshire.[106]

Nominally the equal of the marshals and gentlemen ushers, but
socially their inferiors, were the serjeants at arms, who were also
rated as esquires of the household. This earned them the designation 'esquire' in pardons and the like, but their personal status was
lower than this. Few Yorkist serjeants are more than names,
which in itself suggests an origin in the lower gentry at best. Those
who can be identified, and who are therefore likely to represent
the upper end of the social range, are closer to the yeomen of the
crown than to other esquires in their background, and one of
Edward's serjeants, Alexander Cely, was simultaneously a yeoman of the chamber.[107] John Waynflete was in the household by
1464 and is described explicitly as a serjeant at arms in 1471. He
was a merchant and shipowner of Southwold (Suff.), which made
him a natural choice to accompany John lord Howard to sea

[103] PRO, DL 29/526/8390–1; DL 42/20 fo. 77v; *Harl. 433* I pp. 121, 129; Foster 1874, I *sub* Dyneley.
[104] *HMC, 11th Report*, part III p. 102; PRO, C 1/64/907; *Harl. 433* II pp. 92–3, 146–7.
[105] *CPR 1476–85* p. 454; Horrox, 'Financial memoranda' p. 228; *Lincs. Pedigrees* II p. 599; *Inqs p.m.* I no. 324.
[106] Meredith 1964, pp. 1–3; *Inqs p.m.* III no. 819; PRO, DL 42/19 fo. 74v; DL 42/20 fos. 25v, 82–v.
[107] *CCR 1476–85* no. 1280.

against the Scots in 1481. Unusually among the serjeants, he proved unable to weather the dynastic revolution of 1485 and ended up in the Tower.[108] His colleague Geoffrey Wharton is also first mentioned in royal service in 1464 and explicitly as a serjeant in 1471. He was one of the Whartons of Westmorland, but descended from a younger son and apparently without significant interests in the region.[109]

Tudor serjeants were equally minor figures, as the willingness of one of them, John Poulson, to devil for William Brereton of Malpas suggests.[110] This discrepancy between public and private status is probably explained by the nature of the serjeants' work. Like the yeomen, they guarded the king and executed his commands, although in the serjeants' case the obligation may have been almost full-time.[111] This was hardly the sort of work that leading members of the gentry would have much interest in, at least not on a regular basis, but it required authority on the part of the executant. Hence the relatively high status attached to the office but the low status of its holders. Unlike the yeomen, serjeants do not appear to have been issued with a special badge of office, but as esquires of the household they were entitled to wear the king's livery, which, in the 1440s at least, was characterized by a crown embroidered on each sleeve.[112]

Outranking these various categories of esquire were the esquires of the body, whose superiority also carried over into the wider world of court ceremonial, where they took precedence over all esquires but the eldest sons of knights.[113] However, their household status does not invariably reflect the background of the men concerned. Some esquires of the body were indeed the heads of important gentry families, like Richard's esquire Edward Redmane, the head of the Redmanes of Harewood (Yorks.) and Levens (Westm.). Others had less exalted backgrounds. Nicholas Spicer was described in 1471 as a gentleman of Bristol. He was in Gloucester's service in Wales in the 1470s and entered his

---

[108] *CCR* 1461–8 p. 405; *CPR* 1461–7 p. 327; *CPR* 1467–77 p. 263; *CPR* 1476–85 p. 381; PRO, C 67/53 m. 3; Campbell, *Materials* 1 p. 208.
[109] *Rot. Parl.* v p. 536; *CCR* 1468–76 no. 684; Plantagenet-Harrison 1879, p. 256.
[110] Ives, *Brereton* pp. 71–2, 79, 80.
[111] *BB* p. 131 (and notes); compare also Given-Wilson 1986, pp. 54–5.
[112] PRO, E 101/409/12 fo. 92, a reference I owe to the kindness of Anne Sutton. The crowns were made of silver spangles, sewn on with silk.
[113] *BB* p. 225; Pegge 1791, pp. 30–1.

household in 1483 as a gentleman usher. He was promoted to esquire of the body, a common move, within a matter of months, perhaps in tribute to his administrative acumen, since his household post was coupled with a major collection of Welsh receiverships.[114] Expertise of a different kind advanced another of Richard's esquires, the converted Portuguese Jew Edward Brampton. His household career, based on military aid to the king, was then powered by lending money to the crown, which carried him in quick succession from gentleman usher to esquire of the body and finally to knight of the body.[115] The knights outranked the esquires of the body, but their social background was very similar and promotion from one to the other was not uncommon. Royal servants of this standing might have their closeness to the king marked by the gift of a royal livery collar, although these were not confined to the household. Under both Yorkists the chain was of linked suns and roses, with a pendant lion (of March) for Edward IV and a boar for Richard III. Sir Thomas Charleton possessed one of Edward's livery collars; made of gold with the roses and lion enamelled white, it weighed 8 oz. and was valued at £8.[116]

At the head of the *domus magnificencie* stood the chamberlain, corresponding in terms of status to the steward of the *domus providencie* but distinguished by his far greater closeness to the king. Both Yorkist chamberlains, Hastings and Lovell, were the close friends of their royal masters, and their appointment to head that section of the household most intimately concerned with the king's personal comfort and well-being both reflected and enhanced their importance at court. Hastings could be described as the man who could 'do with the king and with all the lords of England ... most of any man alive'.[117] There is, however, nothing to suggest that the composition of the chamber was the chamberlain's creation, let alone that the officers owed obedience to him rather than to the king. The household was an expression of the king's will, and although Hastings was influential and well

---

[114] *CFR 1471–85* no. 18; *CPR 1476–85* p. 437; *Harl. 433* I p. 185, II pp. 8, 37, 38, 160; WAM 4110 m. 1.
[115] *CPR 1467–77* pp. 340, 357; *CPR 1476–85* pp. 416, 479, 481; Collier, *Household Books* p. 4; Roth 1920.
[116] WAM 6646; it was sold after his death, WAM 6625. See also PRO, Prob 11/7 fo. 34v; Tudor-Craig 1973, pp. 24–5; *Harl. 433* III pp. 109, 111.
[117] *PL* I p. 581.

regarded Richard clearly expected the household to survive his
fall in 1483.[118]

Hastings' importance is a reminder of the personal dimension of
the Yorkist household. Men could be advanced, as he was,
because the king liked them, as well as because their local standing
made it politically expedient. Equally, power could be manifest at
the centre as well as, or even instead of, in the shires. For the
Yorkist period the external functions of the household, its role as
the king's local agent, are far better documented than its internal
functions, such as controlling who should be allowed access to the
king and hence influencing what information came to the king's
ears. It is only occasionally, as in Collingbourne's disgruntled
couplet about Richard's advisors, that one can glimpse how
crucial influence at the centre could be in setting the tone of an
entire regime.

It is correspondingly easy to evaluate the Yorkist household,
and the careers of its individual members, solely in terms of local
involvement. This is not unreasonable: most forms of power in
the Middle Ages sooner or later acquired a local dimension. When
Morgan Kidwelly was described as being 'of great might and
favoured' in Dorset, it was recognized that his local influence was
a direct consequence of the power which he wielded at the centre,
as attorney general of Richard III.[119] But local power can be an
unreliable measuring stick. Viscount Lovell's undoubted influence
at court was not matched by his local stature, except in so far as
the sheer volume of his patronage betrays his closeness to the king.
In Edward IV's reign the importance of Thomas Grey, marquis
Dorset, lay in his acknowledged success as an intermediary at
court rather than in his position as a landowner in the south
west.[120] Contemporaries kept a close eye on shifts of influence at
the centre. John Paston III, offered the backing of Anthony
Woodville at a time when Woodville was in the king's bad books,
commented gloomily, 'whereof I am nothing proud, for he may
do least with the great master'.[121] Such assessments rarely survive,
however, and influence within the Yorkist court can be discussed
only in the most general terms, something which may have led

---

[118] Compare Richmond 1986, pp. 182–3.
[119] *Rot. Parl.* VI p. 321.
[120] *Stonor Letters* II p. 146; Lyell and Watney, *Acts of Court* pp. 123, 125.
[121] *PL* I p. 566.

Tudor historians to exaggerate the novelty of the court-centred politics of Henry VIII's reign.[122]

As the examples of Dorset and Anthony Woodville suggest, there was more to court than the household. Noblemen, councillors, visiting dignitaries, government officials and members of the retinue all contributed to its composition, and it is inevitable that in a personal monarchy any attempt to define the court turns into a definition of government. The result is an endlessly shifting and complex society. Household men too came and went, their movements partly regulated by rota but also by less formal considerations. They were probably under some obligation to come into court if it visited their part of the country or on festal occasions. They could also, presumably, choose to come at other times to pursue a particular request or just to keep in touch. Contemporaries found it baffling. The compiler of the 1478 household ordinance confessed rather helplessly that the size of the household fluctuated 'because of the increase and decrease and variations of officers'.[123] Obviously Walter Map's *cri de coeur* of the 1180s would still have struck a chord 300 years later:

As Augustine lived in time and spoke of time, yet could not comprehend it, so I live in court, and speak of it, yet can say with the same puzzlement that I cannot comprehend the court... I leave it, knowing the whole court. I return and recognize no one. I feel a stranger. Yet it is only the members who have changed. The court itself stays the same, triumphantly the same.[124]

As Map admitted, the court, however kaleidoscopic, retained its own identity. In the Yorkist period it was probably the household which did most to set the prevailing tone. This was partly a consequence of its size, far greater than in Map's own day. But it was also the household, however fluid its own membership, which provided the formal and constant ritual with which the king was surrounded and which gave visual expression to his dignity. The Yorkist kings were well aware of the value of the orchestrated public image. In 1480 the royal yeomen and their servants who attended the king's sister Margaret duchess of Burgundy during her state visit to England, one hundred men in

---

[122] e.g. Starkey 1981, p. 276.
[123] Longleat ms 65 fo. 10.
[124] Quoted by Murray 1978, p. 85.

all, were dressed in blue and murrey cloth, the Yorkist colours. In addition, two knights of the body were dressed in purple and blue velvet and four esquires of the body in purple and blue satin. The colour scheme was continued in the livery of the king's bargemen and in a pillion for the duchess' use, covered with blue and purple cloth of gold fringed with blue and purple silk.[125] The whole was a dramatic statement of the strength and unity of the household, and hence of the king's power.

The household also set the tone of the court in another sense. For most people it was the main line of approach to the king. John Paston III, drawing up a list of men who might gain him access to the king, began at the top, with his own master lord Hastings, but was also aware of the value of other household contacts: 'I think that Sir George Brown, Sir James Radcliffe and other of my acquaintance which wait most upon the king and lie nightly in his chamber will put to their good wills.'[126] Similarly, the mayor of Bristol, accused of treason in 1479, approached several leading courtiers for help, but his first move was to get hold of a local household man (Thomas Ash, a yeoman of the chamber who was controller of the port of Bristol) and hurry with him to court.[127] Often the household contact itself was sufficient. In 1469 Thomas Wingfield undertook to show the king the damage done by the Pastons' opponents to their lodge at Hellesdon (Norf.) and tell him what had happened.[128]

The impression conveyed by such examples is that access to the king was relatively straightforward in the late fifteenth century, with the household acting as a channel rather than a barrier. Most men, certainly those of any standing, knew someone in the household or could scrape acquaintance, and even quite humble household servants could get word to the king and his family. In 1500 a Nottingham yeoman of the crown boasted of his success:

When that the said John Hewyk was come home from the king and queen he came home by the said town of Howes and when he was come thither, folks of the said town asked the said John Hewyk how he had done, and he said that he had done reasonably well and that he had

---

[125] Nicolas, *Wardrobe Accounts* pp. 163–6.
[126] *PL* I p. 617.
[127] Veale, *Red Book of Bristol* text, part 4, p. 61; Ross 1974, p. 102.
[128] *PL* I pp. 544–5. Edward, unimpressed, was heard to remark that it might have fallen down by itself.

spoken with the queen's grace and should have spoken more with her said grace, had [it] not been for that strong whore the king's mother.[129]

Access by itself, however, was not enough, and perhaps the very openness of the late medieval court was testimony to the kings' skill in fending off unwelcome suitors. When Sir William Brandon tried to enlist the support of Edward IV for his master the duke of Norfolk, the king said, 'Brandon, though thou can beguile the duke of Norfolk and bring him about the thumb as thou list, I let thee wit thou shalt not do me so, for I understand thy false dealing well enough.'[130] Brandon, according to an eyewitness, 'departed from the king'. Withdrawal was also the only option open to the royal esquire Thomas Norton when he fell foul of Edward IV. Norton was responsible for the attack on the mayor of Bristol in 1479, but then delayed in coming to court to present his version of events. 'And when the said Thomas Norton came into the king's presence the king estranged his look from him, and he perceived that and departed from the court... And all the court hath him in such loathness that no creature accompanied nor made him any cheer.'[131]

It is clear that Edward IV, however approachable and affable he could be, was not to be trifled with. His brother's brand of personal monarchy, although less well documented, was probably very similar. As duke of Gloucester, Richard had had an equally short way with offending servants. Two of his men involved in the dispute over Gregories felt the rough edge of his tongue. Thomas Avery, a Southwark scrivener, was told, 'Ye be the doer of all this matter, and it were more meet for you to keep your shop than go about such matters.' Thomas Wethiale fared no better.

[The duke] said to Wethiale that he did wrong to enter with a yeoman of the crown any gentleman's livelihood without the king's writ, and also to noise such matters in the name and to the disslander of the said noble prince, saying that he knew him well enough, and how he had laboured to have been in service with the earl of Arundel, with lord Dacre, with the lord Cobham and other.[132]

---

[129] *Records of Nottingham* III p. 301. Hewyk's comments about Margaret Beaufort were construed as treasonable language.
[130] *PL* I p. 544.
[131] Veale, *Red Book of Bristol* text, part 4, p. 71.
[132] Essex RO, D/DQ/14/124/3/40.

It is no accident that these examples show both men insisting that they knew 'well enough' the history of their servants. A good lord needed to keep informed in order to evaluate his servants' demands and their usefulness to him.[133] At his death, Edward IV was famous for his grasp of such detail, although even he made mistakes occasionally. In 1460 it was brought to his attention that Richard Gwynneth, later his serjeant porter and almost certainly already in his service, was claiming to be his servant. Edward denied it: 'of [him], as far as we can remember, we have no knowledge'.[134] Such lapses were probably inevitable when for the Yorkist kings to keep track of their servants meant remembering several hundred household men, apart from a wide circle of retainers and contacts. Even at best it is likely that many of the men around the king were no more than names with a few details attached; the king, in other words, knew about them without necessarily knowing them well personally.

That may have been enough for the king's purposes, but for ambitious courtiers it was only second best. It was the king's interest and friendship which unlocked the greatest rewards, and acceptance into his service was thus not an end in itself. The next, and more important, stage was to insinuate oneself into the king's favour. For men setting out on a household career, court must have seemed a discouragingly crowded place. In 1461 Clement Paston reported on his nephew's first introduction to court:

I feel by W. Pecok that my nephew is not yet verily acquainted in the king's house, nor with the officers of the king's house. He is not taken as none of that house, for the cooks be not charged to serve him nor the sewer to give him no dish, for the sewer will take no man no dishes until they be commanded by the controller. Also he is not acquainted with no body but with Wekys, and Wekys had told him that he would bring him to the king, but he hath not yet done so. Wherefore it were best for him to take his leave and come home, until you have spoken with somebody to help him forth, for he is not bold enough to put forth himself.[135]

---

[133] See, for instance, BL, Cotton Caligula BVI fos. 518–9, a 1522 list of royal annuitants in Northumberland, with details of their wealth and a thumbnail character sketch of each.
[134] *Tropenell Cart.* II p. 65; *CPR* 1461–7 p. 148.
[135] *PL* I pp. 199–200. 'Wekys' was John Wykes, an usher of the king's chamber. A Gloucestershire man by birth, he was known to the Pastons through office holding in East Anglia: *CPR* 1461–7 pp. 23, 123, 124, 179; *CFR* 1471–85 no. 199; *CCR* 1476–85 no. 1244.

John Paston, however, persevered, spurred on, like the rest of his colleagues, by the rewards to be gained from royal service. Some of these were in any case virtually independent of royal favour. The mere fact of being in the household could enhance an individual's standing. A particularly blatant attempt to exploit household office was made in 1481 by William Brandon, the son of the Mowbray retainer who had had such short shrift from Edward IV some years previously. In a case in King's Bench, Brandon took it upon himself to remind the chief justice, William Huse, of the household connections of one of the defendants. Huse ordered him out of court, 'or verily you will be where he is', but may have taken the point. The case was deemed 'subtle' and never decided.[136] It is not surprising, in the light of such examples, that a fifteenth-century coiner of collective nouns opted for a 'threat of courtiers'.[137]

Household men also stood to benefit from the desire of others to gain access to the king.[138] Such rewards were in proportion to the individual's closeness to the king, but even quite humble men could make a comfortable income. In 1469 Hull gave a yeoman of the crown 13s 4d, almost a month's wages, for carrying a message from the king.[139] At the other extreme, men able to 'do with the king' could make their fortune. William lord Hastings, who spent over twenty years in that happy position, initiated two major building programmes on the proceeds.[140] Those Tudor courtiers who ornamented their homes with royal emblems may not only have been demonstrating loyalty but making due recognition of the source of their wealth, just as lord treasurer Cromwell decorated his castle of Tattershall with purses in the 1440s.[141]

The incidental rewards of service no doubt sweetened the lot of the household man and did something to offset the cost of life at court. But the major gains, as everyone knew, came directly from the king. Putting an accurate monetary value on royal generosity is virtually impossible. Edward IV, for instance, intervened on behalf of his servant John Trevelyan, who was having difficulty making good a claim to his wife's inheritance against the vested

---

[136] Ives 1983, p. 238.
[137] Morgan 1987, p. 68.
[138] *Ibid.* p. 61.
[139] Hull RO, BRF 2/378.
[140] *PL* I p. 581. Hastings undertook building at Ashby de la Zouch and Kirby Muxloe; he may also have had plans for Bagworth, nearby: Jones 1975.
[141] Starkey 1981, pp. 272–3.

interests of the de la Poles. Edward ordered his brother-in-law Suffolk to admit Trevelyan's claims and the duke yielded. The king had thereby secured his servant an estate later valued at over £8 p.a., probably an underestimate. To buy a comparable property could have cost in the region of £300.[142] The land was also the centre-piece of Trevelyan's holdings, giving the family a stake in local society whose value was, to them, incalculable.

Even where royal grants were made with a price attached, the face value is an imperfect guide to their true worth. In Richard's reign, royal land grants seem on the whole to have been valued realistically. When Thomas Wortley was granted the manor of Madeley (Staffs.) it was valued at £42 p.a.; the Stafford receiver had accounted for £41. Similarly, when Alexander Quadring received Greys in Sible Hedingham (Essex) it was valued at 20m p.a.; in Gloucester's hands it and two other manors had jointly yielded £33 14s.[143] But land also conferred power, which cannot be priced in simple cash terms. Office, too, gave influence, including, in many cases, the right to appoint subordinates. As steward of the duchy of Lancaster honour of Bolingbroke, Sir Thomas Burgh had the offices of constable and bailiff of Lincoln in his gift.[144] The exercise of office also brought financial rewards over and above the nominal salary, particularly when the holder had dealings with the public and could charge for his services. The value of these hidden extras could be considerable. In the reign of Edward IV, Anthony earl Rivers made Thomas Molyneux his deputy in the office of captain and constable of the town and castle of Beaumaris. Molyneux paid £100 outright and undertook to pay the earl a further 100m p.a., so clearly expected to earn more than that.[145] The holder's salary is not recorded, but is likely to have been between £20 and £40 (the fees at Conway and Caernarvon respectively) so that the holder was probably earning twice as much again from other sources.[146] The only royal grants which can be taken at anything like their face value were annuities. These may even have been worth slightly less than their nominal value since recipients might have had to make gifts to the

---

[142] Som. RO, DD/Wo 29/4 fos. 12v, 18v; *Inqs p.m.* III no. 581. For the cost of land see note 149 below.
[143] *CPR 1476–85* pp. 388, 415; *Harl. 433* III p. 232; PRO, DL 29/637/10360A.
[144] PRO, Prob 11/10 fo. 241v.
[145] Lancs. RO, DDM 3/4. Another example of subcontracting an office (that of coroner of the household) is recorded in WAM 5925, but no values are given.
[146] *Harl. 433* III p. 251.

appropriate accounting official to secure payment. Hull, for instance, gave the port's customer 12*s* and two pike to have his goodwill over an annuity granted to the town by Edward IV.[147]

The monetary value of an individual's patronage, for all its imperfections, does at least give some idea of relative rewards within the royal service. The fees of the crown represent the standard return. Thus yeomen could expect around £9, esquires £30 and knights £40. Such sums were worth having, particularly for the humbler royal servants, but at best they probably allowed a consolidation of status rather than actual social advancement. William Knight of Stockbridge (Hants) can stand as an example. He was a yeoman of the chamber of Edward IV, who made him ranger in the forest of Bere (Hants) at £3 p.a., apparently in lieu of a fee of the crown. Knight transferred to Richard's household, but then supported the 1483 rebellion and was attainted. This was a passport to Tudor favour, and Knight was reinstated as a yeoman of the crown by Henry VII, this time with a formal fee of the crown, 'for service done in England and beyond the seas'. He also regained his rangership, which left him better rewarded than under Edward IV. But when he came to make his will at Westminster late in 1495 he had to ask his executor to pay for his burial, 'as at this time I have but little money left to bring me in earth', and to repay a debt of 2*s* which Knight had incurred. The worst of Knight's financial difficulties may have been only temporary – the result of a serious illness away from home – but his general circumstances, as implied by the will, were clearly modest. His executor was to be reimbursed with forty sheep and a bull at pasture at Longstock, just north of Knight's home. It was a royal property, and Knight's grazing rights may have been one of the perks of his household office. The only other bequest was to the servant who had accompanied Knight to London, who was given one of his master's gowns and 13*s* 4*d*.[148]

Some men apparently received less than the standard rate. These are the servants for whom no grants are recorded, leaving them, presumably, with just a daily wage when they were in court plus any informal benefits which came their way. It is likely that many of the lesser servants of the crown were in this position – since royal grants are one of the main sources of evidence about

[147] Hull RO, BRF 2/377.
[148] *CPR* 1476–85 p. 159; *CPR* 1485–94 pp. 78, 156; *CPR* 1494–1507 p. 85; *Harl. 433* I p. 255; *Rot. Parl.* VI p. 246; PRO, Prob 11/12 fos. 148v–9.

household membership, unrewarded servants easily escape mention. But there are also cases at the upper levels of the household, such as William Benstead of Bennington (Herts.), one of Richard's esquires. He was childless and had evidently decided to cash in his land rather than letting it pass to his heir general, his father's sister Ellen. He sold a major block of land to Edward IV for £500 and followed this up by selling a further manor to Robert Stillington for £300 in 1485. With gains of this order, royal patronage may not have been particularly enticing. Household service did, however, provide Benstead with contacts which he may have valued. When he was involved in a case in King's Bench in Richard's reign he was able to field an impressive collection of sureties.[149] Among Richard's knights of the body, John Babington of Chilwell is not known to have received royal grants, although in 1483 he was made sheriff, which he may have considered an acceptable reward.[150]

This modest return was not, of course, what men dreamed of when they entered the king's service. Grants with a face value of two or three times the standard fee of the crown were not uncommon. Two of Richard's yeomen were given constableships carrying fees of £20: Nicholas Rigby at Bodiam and Roger Bikley at Llandovery (Carms.).[151] Smaller grants could also mount up. The yeoman John Abell of Buntingford (Herts.) was porter and gaoler of Hertford castle, keeper of the park of Rochford (Essex) and receiver of the temporalities of the diocese of Ely. He was also given a Cambridgeshire manor valued at £7 p.a.[152] Much of the collection is unvalued, but in fees alone he probably received £10 or so and the real value would be higher. Among the esquires grants totalling £100 were well within the bounds of possibility. In Richard's reign the figures were inflated by the massive grants of forfeited land which followed Buckingham's rebellion, but high totals could be reached even without that. John Huddleston's collection of office in Gloucestershire and the south march carried fees of over £50, topped up with an annuity of 100m from Monmouth.[153] Knights were in a similar position. In the particular circumstances of Richard's reign, land

---

[149] *CCR* 1476–85 nos. 1369, 1372, 1389; *CPR* 1485–94 p. 87; *Inqs p.m.* III nos. 42, 609, 649; PRO, KB 29/115 m. 12 dorse.
[150] PRO, E 404/78/2/10; *CFR* 1471–85 no. 797.
[151] *CPR* 1476–85 pp. 521, 535.
[152] *Ibid.* pp. 247, 411, 452; *Harl. 433* I pp. 233, 263.
[153] *CPR* 1476–85 pp. 379, 448; *Harl. 433* I pp. 153, 178.

grants meant that many received patronage valued at £200 or £300, but other grants could yield £100 or so. Thomas Burgh of Gainsborough (Lincs.) received an annuity and office together worth around £100, coupled with land worth £200.[154] Sir James Tyrell collected stewardships and other local office in south Wales and the south west. Even before Richard's accession he was receiving fees of £110 from office within the duke's own Welsh land, and the office he added within the crown lands after 1483 probably doubled this.[155]

Rewards of this magnitude, although always in the minority, were at least within the reach of the average household man. Within each generation, however, there were also a few close associates of the king whose rewards were quite exceptional. Tyrell was one of them, and the offices mentioned above were only part of his gains. He accumulated three wardships, two before Gloucester's accession valued at over £229 p.a. and a third, the wardship of Robert Arundel of Trerice (Corn.), in 1484. He was also a chamberlain of the exchequer and, from early in 1485, lieutenant of Guisnes. His closeness to Richard brought him grants from men and institutions anxious to have his lord's goodwill. His income from all these sources was probably of the order of £1,000 p.a. In 1488 he assessed his losses in Wales, as a result of Richard's defeat at Bosworth, as £3,000.[156] Among his fellow knights of the body, Richard Ratcliffe received land valued at £666 p.a. and a collection of office which may have taken his income, too, to around £1,000 in real terms, although most of the grants are unvalued. He replaced Sir John Saville as steward of Wakefield late in 1484. He also became one of Richard's main agents in the north west, succeeding Dacre as the king's deputy on the west march and being made permanent sheriff of Westmorland.[157] Among the lesser rewards which came his way were the parkership of Guildford with the custody of the manor there and a forfeited Breton ship.[158]

William Catesby's haul may have been in the same league. He received a major land grant valued at £273 p.a. He was given the wardship of Anthony Acton, and was one of a group of royal

[154] *CPR* 1476–85 pp. 385, 424; *Harl. 433* I p. 165, III pp. 203–4; Somerville 1953, pp. 576, 583.
[155] Pugh 1971, p. 201; *CPR* 1476–85 p. 474; *Harl. 433* I pp. 190, 208–9, 286, III p. 204.
[156] Pugh 1971, pp. 201–2; *CPR* 1476–85 p. 430; PRO, C 76/169 m. 25; Steel 1954, p. 4.
[157] *CPR* 1476–85 pp. 472, 512; *Harl. 433* I p. 233; PRO, C 81/1531/66.
[158] *Harl. 433* I p. 282, II pp. 33, 53.

associates who paid £1,000 for the custody and marriage of the young earl of Wiltshire. Together with the chief justice William Huse, the dean of the chapel William Beverley and the treasurer of the chamber Edmund Chaderton, he was granted a significant block of Stafford estates for seven years with which to settle the debts of the executed duke of Buckingham, a responsibility which no doubt gave scope for considerable profit, particularly as they were not required to render account. Catesby seems to have been the driving force in the consortium, and it was to him that the occupiers of the land were ordered to pay their revenues. Among his offices he was chancellor and chamberlain of the exchequer, and chancellor of the earldom of March, the latter with a fee of £40. He was deputy butler throughout the south west. Local offices included the stewardship of the duchy of Lancaster lands in Northamptonshire, with a fee of £10, and (jointly with Lovell) the constableship and stewardship of Rockingham with its members. The latter was granted during Catesby's life, suggesting that he was the prime mover, and he, rather than Lovell, was usually regarded as the holder. He was also granted the North-amptonshire hundred of Guilsborough.[159] This was not the limit of his gains. He did well from those anxious to secure royal favour, among them the abbeys of Selby and St Albans and the archbishop of Canterbury. He also exploited his closeness to the crown in more dubious ways. In 1484 he purchased, illegally, the manor of Kirby Bellars (Leics.), presumably trusting to his influence at court to rescue him from any awkwardness.[160]

But if life at the top was lucrative, it was also hazardous. The average household man was usually able to weather a change of ruler, keeping his place in the royal service and sometimes even his royal grants. The handful of men closest to the king, however, found themselves vulnerable at a change of reign. One of Edward IV's best rewarded household men, John Cheyne, was one of the few men penalized by Richard III almost from the outset.[161] Few of Richard's own favourites survived Bosworth, and none did so with their gains intact. Brackenbury and Ratcliffe died in the battle. Catesby was executed afterwards, a distinction he shared with the most generously rewarded of Richard's yeomen,

---

[159] *Ibid.* I pp. 91–2, 137, 183, 241, 285, II pp. 95, 135, 138, 175, 180, 202, III pp. 149–50; *CPR* 1476–85 pp. 360–1, 419, 465, 497–8.
[160] Roskell 1959b, pp. 161–4; *Reg. Thome Bourgchier* p. 65; Ives 1983, p. 109.
[161] *CPR* 1467–77 pp. 533–4; Ross 1974, p. 234; Sutton and Hammond, *Coronation* p. 321.

William Bracher.[162] Under Edward IV Bracher's rewards had been unexceptional: a fee of the crown and minor office in Dorset. He transferred smoothly to Richard's service and was close enough to the new king to receive early patronage. In August 1483 he was made parker of Okehampton and in December added the posts of bailiff and parker of Barrington (Som.), the three offices together bringing fees of over £10. At the same time he was given an annuity of £40 until land became available. It materialized in the following March: three Somerset manors valued at £40 10s. He was also made farmer of the subsidy and ulnage in Devon and Cornwall and granted the custody of Fordington (Dorset) for twenty years at £70 p.a.[163] His reward was at a level more appropriate to an esquire, or even a knight, but Bracher remains a shadowy figure and the reasons behind his unusual gains and the brutality of his treatment after Bosworth are unknown. Of Richard's other close associates, Lovell remained in opposition until his death. Tyrell, conveniently in France when Bosworth was fought, managed to transfer to Henry VII's service, albeit with much reduced influence, but he was executed for treason in 1502. The fate of Richard's inner circle is an exemplum of lord Mountjoy's advice to his sons: 'nor desire to be great about princes, for it is dangerous'.[164]

If only the great among the household men faced death or disgrace as the wages of their service, all household servants shared the general problem of how to give some permanence to their gains. Annuities and office were at best held for life, more commonly until a change of king or the recipient's departure from the household. Given the relatively modest background of many household men, the loss of such grants could be a major financial blow. The former Yorkist serjeant at arms Roland Symondes was said in 1491 to be 'too poor to have the means of sustenance'.[165] The only type of grant which was at all likely to be made to the recipient and his heirs was land, the rarest form of patronage. This did not, in any case, guarantee long-term possession. Most of the land available for redistribution in this period had been forfeited, and forfeitures might be reversed. The less tangible benefits which flowed from proximity to the king were by their very nature even

[162] *Crowland* pp. 182–3.
[163] *CPR* 1476–85 pp. 366, 373, 390; *CFR* 1471–85 no. 752; PRO, C 81/1641/143.
[164] Morgan 1973, p. 23.
[165] *Reg. Thomas Rotherham* 1 p. 234.

more precarious: 'Winter's weather and woman's thought / And lord's love changeth oft.'[166]

Royal servants needed to find some way of transmuting their gains into a form which would outlast royal favour. In the Middle Ages this generally meant investing wealth and influence in land, which could then be transmitted to the next generation, and the most effective way of doing this was through marriage. Heirs and heiresses were part of the armoury of royal patronage. Edward IV sold the wardship of the Fitzwarin heir to his knight of the body Giles Daubeney, who married the boy to his daughter Cecily.[167] But royal favour could also help in less tangible ways, giving the seeker after heiresses the edge in any competition. A likely example of a marriage helped by household membership was that of John Sapcote, an esquire of the body, to Elizabeth, the widow of Fulk Bourgchier lord Fitzwarin and the sister of John lord Dynham. Sapcote was originally from Huntingdonshire and was active in estate management for the king and others. In 1477 Fitzwarin made Sapcote his steward. After Bourgchier's death Edward IV made Sapcote receiver general of the Fitzwarin lands and within a month he had married the widow.[168] Another Yorkist servant whose household status may have helped him to a good marriage was Edward's yeoman usher of the chamber John Ferriby, an East Riding man of modest means. He entered the king's household in 1461 and two years later was granted forfeited land in Beverley, which he made his home. A few months later he married Margaret, the widow of Thomas Roos esquire of Routh in Holderness, who brought him further land in the East Riding.[169]

As well as trying to convert the benefits of service into a heritable form, it also made sense for families to produce a succession of royal servants so that the benefits did not dry up with the death or retirement of an individual. The ideal, from the servant's point of view, was for the king to be persuaded to transfer patronage from one generation to another, but this was extremely rare. The Yorkist kings liked to keep their freedom of action and were careful to avoid anything which would imply a hereditary title to a particular grant. Even grants in survivorship to

[166] Davies, *Medieval Lyrics* no. 65.
[167] *CPR* 1476–85 p. 177; Wedgwood 1936, pp. 259–60.
[168] *CPR* 1476–85 pp. 218, 228; *CCR* 1476–85 no. 264.
[169] *CCR* 1461–8 p. 102; *CPR* 1461–7 pp. 57, 189, 208; *Test. Ebor.* III pp. 178–81.

father and son were uncommon.[170] One family which achieved a
partial transfer under Edward IV were the Wingfields. Sir Robert
was a knight of the body and later controller of the household,
and in the course of his career received a number of grants in East
Anglia. He died without children in 1481, by which time his
nephew John was in the household as an esquire of the body. John
secured one of his uncle's grants: the custody of an estate during
the idiocy of its owner. Edward also allowed him part of another.
Where Sir Robert had been steward of the honour of Richmond
in Norfolk and Suffolk, John was given the office in Norfolk
alone, a clear statement that the transfer was not automatic.[171]

Although direct continuity of this kind was the exception, there
remained advantages in establishing a household dynasty to
maintain access to the king. The Fiennes family succeeded triumphantly. Sir Roger had been a knight of Henry V and went on
to become treasurer of Henry VI's household. His younger
brother James was an esquire of the body and later chamberlain of
Henry VI, achieving the barony of Saye and Sele. James' closeness
to the king brought his downfall, and he was murdered in Cade's
rebellion of 1450, but the family's identification with the crown
continued. By the time of James' death his son William was in the
household as a knight of the body. Roger also died in 1450,
leaving two sons, Richard and Robert, of whom the latter was
already established in the king's service. Richard subsequently
supported the Yorkists and in 1462, when he had become lord
Dacre of the south, he was said to be, with Hastings, 'now greatest
about the king's person'. Dacre later became chamberlain of
queen Elizabeth, whose possession of the duchy of Lancaster
lordship and rape of Pevensey chimed in well with the family's
Sussex interests. Dacre's heir, John, was one of Edward's knights
in the 1460s, and in the late 1470s the mantle passed to Thomas
Fiennes (probably John's brother), an esquire of the body. This
successful connection ended abruptly in 1483. Dacre, predeceased
narrowly by John, died in that year, leaving an under-age
grandson as heir.[172] Thomas Fiennes backed Buckingham's re-

[170] Richard III made eight such grants, and three to mothers/sons. There is little evidence of
the Yorkist kings formally granting reversions (Richard's grant of Guisnes to Ralph
Hastings is a rare example), but the frequency of less formal promises cannot be assessed.
For a Lancastrian example see Morgan 1987, pp. 39–40.

[171] *CPR* 1476–85 pp. 132, 211, 285.

[172] Griffiths 1981a, pp. 330, 339–40, 877; Ross 1974, p. 69; Myers, 'Household of Queen
Eliz.' p. 222; *BB* p. 200; *CPR* 1476–85 pp. 180, 261, 378.

bellion, a choice which led to his own attainder and brought all his Sussex kinsmen under suspicion.[173] But the family was not left unrepresented in the household. Dacre's brother Robert had settled in Suffolk, where he had built up some links with Gloucester in the 1470s. Certainly by April 1484, and probably in the previous January, he had entered Richard's household as a knight of the body, a move which on Fiennes' part was probably intended as a first step towards retrieving the family fortunes. Robert may have been behind the pardon which Thomas secured in July, although there are no signs that Thomas, or Robert on his behalf, was able to regain his forfeited land.[174]

The Fiennes family was unusual in producing royal favourites in successive reigns, but their enjoyment of household office over three generations can be paralleled. The Darcies of Maldon (Essex) managed it. Sir Robert Darcy was an associate first of the duke of Bedford and then of York. He is not recorded in the household after Edward IV's victory, but his wife Elizabeth was lady mistress of the royal nursery. Their son Thomas was one of Edward IV's esquires of the body, and his son held the same office under Henry VII.[175] The Wingfields did even better. The two Yorkist generations already mentioned were preceded by Sir Robert of Letheringham (d. 1452), a courtier of Henry VI. The family's involvement in opposition to Richard III endeared them to the Tudors, and Wingfields held office in the households of both Henry VII and VIII.[176]

As these examples suggest, the reign of Richard III brought some disruption to the established patterns of household service. Thomas Fiennes and John Wingfield both left the household then, as did Thomas Darcy, although in his case it is just possible that ill health was the cause (he died in 1485).[177] This had not been Richard's intention. On the contrary, he began his reign expecting almost complete continuity in the household, and even after Buckingham's rebellion his brother's men formed a significant component of his household. Of fifty knights of the body, sixteen are known to have been in Edward's household, although this includes four who had combined service to Edward IV with

---

[173] PRO, C 244/134/29, 244/136/28; *Rot. Parl.* VI p. 245.

[174] PRO, C 244/114/118; *CPR* 1476–85 pp. 391, 478, 573–4.

[175] Griffiths 1981a, pp. 99, 672; Weever 1631, p. 609; *CPR* 1476–85 p. 241. The Tudor lord Darcy belonged to a different family.

[176] Griffiths 1981a, pp. 309, 587; Wingfield 1925, pp. 33, 40–1, 44, etc.

[177] Darcy had Haute connections: King 1869, p. 5.

membership of Gloucester's retinue. Among the esquires of the
body the proportion is higher: nineteen out of forty-eight. Lower
down the household the patchiness of surviving evidence makes
this sort of numerical analysis suspect, but continuity is likely to
have been greater again. Among the serjeants at arms, whose fees
were granted by patent and who are therefore well recorded,
three-quarters (twenty-one out of twenty-eight) of Richard's
men are known to have served his brother. This office was
politically uncontroversial, and high levels of continuity had been
established by the end of the fourteenth century.[178]

The losses in the household were largely made good by
recruitment from Richard's own connection or from subsidiary
retinues such as those of Northumberland and Lovell. This was
taken for granted. However highly a new king valued continuity,
he was also under an obligation to reward the men associated with
him before his accession. This was true of all kings, not only
usurpers – unless, like Henry VI, the king had literally come to the
throne as a babe in arms. Legitimate heirs, indeed, might even
have valued continuity less highly than usurpers. But the former
retainers whom Richard took into his household did distort its
normal balance. There may have been a degree of social distortion. Some of Richard's recruits were from very modest backgrounds. Ratcliffe and Brackenbury, for instance, were second
sons of middling gentry families. A few of the esquires, such as
Richard Williams, came from families so obscure that they
cannot be identified. This was not in itself unusual. One of the
attractions of household service was the opportunity of advancement which it gave to men in relatively modest circumstances,
and it would be difficult to argue that the number of such men in
Richard's household was significantly higher than usual. Many of
the newcomers to his household were the heads (or heirs) of
leading gentry families, such as the Constables of Flamborough or
the Bigods of Settrington, whose local standing was later exploited
by the Tudors. What was unusual about Richard's reign was the
number of household men from humble backgrounds who
became disproportionately influential. This can be explained by
Richard's preference for men from his own retinue and, in
particular, the fact that men planted in the south were often
chosen just because they had no major interests elsewhere.

[178] Brown 1972, p. 21.

Richard was, to a far greater extent than usual, creating the local standing and influence which he wished to exploit.

This was a reflection of a more marked distortion within the household: a geographical imbalance in favour of the north. After Buckingham's rebellion, twenty-eight out of Richard's fifty knights of the body came from north of the Humber/Mersey. Among Edward's knights, over the reign as a whole, about six did so (ten if king's knights are included). The bias is less marked among Richard's esquires of the body, fifteen out of forty-eight, and probably diminished still further at the lower levels of the household. Viewed from a strictly utilitarian standpoint, this northern emphasis was a waste of royal resources. Ideally, household men should have been drawn evenly from the whole country, and although Richard achieved this artificially by his plantations the north was still distinctly over represented.

The northern element in the household was wasteful in another sense. The usual pattern of household membership was for one representative of a particular family to enter the household. This suited the king, allowing him to spread his favours more widely. It also suited his servants. The advantages of household membership had a price attached. Life at court was expensive. A contemporary poet thought there was no point in seeking advancement there unless 'thou have the penny ready', and John Paston II soon found himself short of money, in spite of spending his allowance 'not riotously, but wisely and discreetly'.[179] Service was also time-consuming, at least for anyone who wished to make his mark. The sensible solution was to keep a single member of the family there, who could mediate royal favour to his kinsmen. It is no coincidence that John Paston III began to contemplate entering the king's service only after the death of his brother John II. Some exceptions can be found, particularly when a single family had very far-flung territorial interests, but Richard's reign is unusual both in the number of examples and in the density of family representation. Two Musgrave brothers, Richard and John, were simultaneously esquires of the body.[180] The Gowers of Stittenham also produced two household men: Thomas, the head of the family, was a knight of the body and his uncle Edward an usher of the chamber.[181] Sir John Huddleston was a knight of the body and

[179] Davies, *Medieval Lyrics* no. 126; *PL* I p. 200.
[180] PRO, DL 42/20 fo. 38v; *CPR* 1476–85 p. 478; Hutchinson 1794, I pp. 273–4.
[181] *CPR* 1476–85 pp. 381, 424; Horrox 1986b, p. 83.

his sons Richard and John knight and esquire of the body respectively.[182] The brothers James and Robert Harrington were both knights of the body and James' son John an esquire of the household.[183] The Tunstalls produced one knight and two esquires of the body.[184] If relations by marriage are included even higher totals can be reached. One son and four sons-in-law of Sir Robert Constable of Flamborough were knights or esquires of the body: Marmaduke Constable, William Evers, Gervase Clifton, Ralph Bigod and William Tirwhit.[185]

The pressure towards this development was presumably coming from both sides. For the king's northern retinue, the great gains to be made from household membership were apparently outweighing any consideration of cost. Richard, meanwhile, must at least have acquiesced in, and perhaps even encouraged, their entry into his household. He badly needed reliable servants and the northern retinue was an obvious source. But such bunching squandered resources, in that it contributed to the geographical weighting of the household in favour of the area where Richard was most secure.

The density of northern representation within the household was also both cause and effect of the pronounced northern grasp on Richard's patronage. The three Huddlestons account for one receivership, one master forestership, two parkerships, three stewardships, four constableships and annuities totalling 170m.[186] The Tunstalls' haul was two constableships (including Calais), a Welsh shrievalty, land worth £150 and a fee of 50m.[187] This concentration of influence becomes even more marked if men described as 'king's servants' are included. Two more Musgrave brothers were retained by Richard III, as was another Huddleston and another Harrington.[188] Only two of the Conyers clan were in the household, Sir John and his son Richard, but another was described as a king's servant and three more received royal grants.[189] The Metcalfes of Nappa produced no known household

[182] *CPR* 1476–85 pp. 369, 379; PRO, E 404/78/3/37.

[183] PRO, DL 42/20 fos. 32v, 46v; *Harl. 433* II p. 16.

[184] *CPR* 1476–85 pp. 368, 376; PRO, C 76/168 m. 34.

[185] Foster 1874, II *sub* Constable of Flamborough.

[186] *CPR* 1476–85 pp. 363, 369, 372, 379, 448; *Harl. 433* I pp. 153, 178, 201, 222.

[187] *CPR* 1476–85 pp. 368, 376, 479; *Harl. 433* I pp. 127, 138, II p. 91, III p. 147.

[188] Nicholas and William Musgrave: *Harl. 433* II p. 162. James Huddleston: *CPR* 1476–85 p. 431. William Harrington: *CPR* 1476–85 p. 484.

[189] *CPR* 1476–85 pp. 391, 439, 450; *Harl. 433* II p. 23, III p. 151; PRO, SC 11/827.

men but no fewer than ten were described as king's servants or received patronage.[190] Blanket patronage of this sort was quite exceptional and, in terms of the political return, quite unnecessary. It is hardly surprising that the north was later to regard Richard's reign as a sort of golden age – or that the south took a more jaundiced view.[191]

The influx of northerners into Richard's household emphasizes the attractiveness of royal service. It is also, less obviously, evidence of the central role which the household had assumed in the effective exercise of royal authority at a local level. Edward IV's household, following a trend initiated in the previous reign, met most of the king's needs in this respect and, as a result, a substantial household had become essential. This is not to say that the household was the only vehicle of local influence. Most authority at a county level or below was exercised, as it had always been, by men who were prepared to act on the king's orders when required but who were not identified with the crown. The household had, however, become the king's preferred way of formalizing links with his acknowledged servants, and in consequence had become the main agent of direct royal intervention, absorbing many of the local functions of the retinue.

The Yorkist household was thus the heir of the Lancastrian connection, and a more effective one than is now usually allowed. To castigate Edward IV's affinity as 'strongly court-centred' misses the point.[192] The court dimension was not an alternative to local loyalties and local influence. The household provided a focus, and a source of strength, for men whose primary function was still to act for the crown at a local level. In his use of the household, Edward IV was paying tribute to the power of regionalism in contemporary society, but was doing so in a way which did not fragment his own authority. By taking local gentry into the household, and by further enhancing their power, Edward was harnessing regionalism to his own ends. The political nexus which resulted was Edward's answer to that perennial problem of medieval monarchy: what constituted the proper

---

[190] *CPR* 1476–85 pp. 363, 455–6, 517, 539; *Harl. 433* I pp. 68, 71, II p. 28. This excludes men whose only patronage from Richard dates from before his accession.
[191] Palliser 1986, p. 73; Pollard 1977, pp. 161–3.
[192] Ross 1974, p. 330.

balance of central and local forces. It was a question to which there was no single correct answer, but Edward's solution was better than most.

Under Edward IV the king's affinity was more broadly based, and inherently more stable, than recent critics have been prepared to admit. In so far as it was a royal creation it was vulnerable to the changes following the king's death – and would have been equally vulnerable had Edward simply lost his grip. But this weakness was a corollary of personal monarchy. As long as power was a matter of personal relationships no political structure could be permanent; and had Edward lived, the details of his polity might have changed as radically as they did after his death. The mutability of royal power structures was increased by the fact that the king was concerned with the whole country. Royal power rested on a basis wider, and consequently more fluid, than the territorial hegemonies which have been credited with producing the most durable affinities. Indeed, where a king's power did rest primarily on a territorial connection, he soon ran into trouble. Henry IV's much-admired Lancastrian connection allowed him to seize the throne, but it was an inadequate basis for a national monarchy and his tendency to rely on it as king prompted criticism.[193]

This was Richard III's problem. In essence he adopted Edward's practice of turning to household servants for local action, but the impact of the policy was seriously distorted by the regional bias which became apparent at the upper levels of the household after 1483. In much of England Richard's reliance on household servants was regarded as an autocratic imposition, rather than the act of co-operation between the centre and locality which it should have been. This was not the king's intention, and there is no suggestion that Richard was using the household as a deliberate counter-weight to local independence. Like Henry VI before him, Richard discovered that although a strong, local, household presence could be a valuable bond between king and country, if mishandled it could become equally divisive. The household had always been a sensitive subject politically, simply because it was so closely identified with the king. Any increase in its involvement in local affairs was accordingly creating a larger

---

[193] Brown 1972, pp. 14–20; Given-Wilson 1986, pp. 198–99.

area of potential conflict, and although Edward IV avoided the danger by recruiting a household which was integrated into the wider local community, Richard's much narrower connection left him vulnerable.

The Yorkist expansion of the household inevitably led to the dilution of the relationship between the king and his servants. The sheer scale of the household meant that for many men the relationship with the king could only be an impersonal one, and although some household men did become the close friends of their master, there are signs that for the average household servant loyalty was becoming a matter of obligation rather than commitment. Men recognized that the benefits of royal favour demanded some return. Richard III, ordering his esquire of the body Henry Vernon to join his army before Bosworth, threatened him with 'forfeiture to us of all that you may forfeit and lose'.[194] This was putting membership of the household on the same sort of footing as any other form of service, and the household's control of so much local office may have further blurred the distinction. When Edward IV was raising troops in 1470 he appealed not to his household men as such, but to the holders of life office from himself or his queen.[195]

This could have been a weakness. Loyalty based on obligation was in the last resort less secure than loyalty rooted in a personal relationship. The earl of Northumberland's retainers deserted him in 1489 in spite of being in receipt of fees, much to the poet Skelton's disgust.[196] To some extent, however, this loss of the special relationship implied by household service was counterbalanced by a growing belief that service to the king was special in a different sense. Late fifteenth-century kings were setting themselves apart from the rest of the political community, so that service to them became something special simply because it was performed for the king.[197] Household servants of the king were thus bound by obligations which derived not just from reward, but from the fact that their master was the king – which imposed a different standard of loyalty.

---

[194] *HMC, Rutland* I pp. 7–8.
[195] *Coventry Leet Book* p. 353.
[196] Skelton, 'Upon the doulours dethe ... of the ... erle of Northumberlande' stanzas 5–6, 13–14.
[197] Starkey 1987b, p. 3.

What these trends amounted to in practice was the institutional-ization of household service, with loyalty increasingly owed to the king rather than the individual. This did not make the household any less reliable in its role as a royal agent. At most it may have made the household as a body less prepared to back the king in actions considered extreme or unacceptable, but given that medieval kings had always depended on the uncommitted for the bulk of their support this was hardly a novel restriction.[198] The major change is likely to have been in the atmosphere of the household itself. It was becoming what the administration and the court had become long ago, a collection of the useful as well as the committed. But this was a reflection of royal strength rather than weakness, since it derived from the willingness of men to serve the king just because he was the king. Institutional loyalty of this kind helps to explain why Richard III was able to keep such leading members of his brother's connection as Thomas Burgh, Thomas Montgomery or Richard Croft within his household. Such continuity was invaluable as a way of evening out any imbalances resulting from a king's personal inclinations and following, although in Richard's case the king's reservations about the reliability of his brother's men meant that he made relatively little use of the servants he had inherited.

One aspect of the Yorkist expansion of the household brought an inevitable reaction. The Tudor kings' retreat into their privy chamber restored the explicit distinction between the men closest to the king and those whose value to him lay largely beyond the court, a distinction which had been fudged under the Yorkists.[199] It is doubtful, however, whether this return to older assumptions made much practical difference. It may have made it easier to limit access to the king, but accessibility was in the last resort a matter of the king's will rather than of the structure of his household. The reassertion of a household elite, whose power derived largely from their physical proximity to the king, may also have been partly intended to give substance to claims that it was the court, rather than the localities, which was the real source

[198] There is a possible parallel here with the suggestion that the gentry of this period were becoming less willing to offer unquestioning obedience to their lords, e.g. Richmond 1970, pp. 690–2. The parallel cannot, however, be taken too far, since the crown was more likely to be the beneficiary than the victim of gentry independence. Given-Wilson 1986, pp. 264–6 surveys the field.
[199] Starkey 1987c.

of power. This view of things, however, derived from what the king wanted to believe at least as much as it reflected practical realities. In essence the household remained what it had always been: the line of contact between the king and the wider political community.

Chapter 6

THE COLLAPSE OF THE REGIME

In retrospect, the 1483 rebellion was the turning point of Richard's reign, embroiling him in problems from which he was never entirely to escape. In the short term, however, the rebels' complete collapse brought him a few months of unchallenged authority. The parliament which met in January 1484 was notably obedient, endorsing Richard's title to the throne and acquiescing in an exceptionally long list of attainders.[1] Another measure of the king's apparent security was the number of rebels who made their peace with the crown in the early months of 1484. The spate of royal pardons in this period has sometimes been seen as evidence only of Richard's desperation to win back support, but this is misleading.[2] Pardons, like other forms of royal patronage, generally called for some initiative on the part of the recipients and reflect their wishes as well as those of the crown. It was very rare for the crown to make an unsolicited grant of pardon under the great seal, although the king might encourage former rebels to seek pardon by allowing it to be known that their petitions would be accepted. While he was at Nottingham in the spring of 1484, Richard drew up a list of rebels whom he was prepared to pardon.[3] It is possible that the men on the list were notified by signet letter, and an extant signet list of eight pardons may represent the Nottingham list.[4] But inclusion in the list was not in itself sufficient warrant for the issue of a formal pardon. Any 'sorrowful and repentant subject' still had to petition the

---

[1] Ross 1981, pp. 184–7; Roskell 1965, p. 297.
[2] Ramsay 1892, II p. 527: 'In vain he scattered offers of pardon and restitution ... not a man would stoop to pick one of them up.'
[3] PRO, C 81/1531/48; partially printed by Richmond 1986, p. 198.
[4] *Harl. 433* I p. 181. If this interpretation is correct it follows that pardons recorded *only* in the signet register cannot safely be taken as evidence of a rebel's intentions. None of the rebels listed, however, can be proved not to have accepted the pardon. John Harcourt is sometimes said to have died in exile in June 1484 (e.g. Hillier 1986, p. 122), which would make his acceptance of the pardon unlikely, but this appears to rest on a misunderstanding of his i.p.m.: *Inqs p.m.* I no. 329.

crown, which almost certainly entailed waiting upon the king in person together with sponsors prepared to vouch for the rebel's obedience.[5] Many, perhaps all, rebels then had to find financial sureties for their future good behaviour and, in some cases, for their observance of additional restrictions. Sir Thomas Lewkenore agreed to live with his brother-in-law Sir John Wood, the treasurer of England, and William Berkeley similarly bound himself to live in a place appointed by the king.[6] Only when these preliminaries had been completed was a formal pardon granted.

Some fourteen attainted rebels took steps to secure a pardon in the five months after parliament rose. Such men had nothing to lose and much to gain by suing for pardon. Although it did not cancel their attainder or restore forfeited land, it lifted the death penalty and brought the individual back within the law, so that his family and friends could 'receive or cherish him with victuals and other things necessary to his sustenance' without incurring the king's displeasure.[7] The decision to seek pardon thus implied some recognition of the regime in power but not necessarily real commitment to it, and several of the men pardoned in 1484 did later renege as Tudor's cause gained credibility. There was little the king could do to prevent such second thoughts, since the various sticks and carrots at his disposal were, in the last resort, of only limited value. The rebel William Berkeley of Beverstone had been pardoned in March 1484 after his uncle Edward and brother-in-law John lord Stourton had put up 1,000m for his good behaviour. By the end of the year Berkeley had defaulted, leaving his kinsmen to foot the bill.[8]

Loyal service could earn pardoned rebels the restoration of their estates, but at best this was a slow business and might never be completed if the beneficiary of the forfeiture were someone close to the crown.[9] By the end of Richard's reign only six out of twenty-eight pardoned rebels had received a royal grant, and in most cases this fell short of an outright grant of land. William Ovedale, for instance, was allowed to farm one of his manors.[10] The Gaynesfords were granted the revenues of one of theirs,

5   See the reference to Sir William Norreys' 1471 pardon: *Stonor Letters* I p. 118.
6   *CCR 1476–85* no. 1242; PRO, C 244/134/31.
7   *Harl. 433* II pp. 206–7.
8   PRO, C 81/1530/27; C 244/134/31; *CCR 1476–85* no. 1393.
9   Hicks 1984, pp. 19–21.
10 *CFR 1471–85* no. 885.

although they may have enjoyed effective control of the manor itself if, as has been suggested, the John Molle given its custody by Richard III was a Gaynesford associate.[11] A few other rebels perhaps benefited similarly from grants to kinsmen. Land forfeited by Nicholas Latimer, for example, was given to Latimer's son-in-law John Mordaunt.[12] By contrast to this laborious rebuilding of an inheritance, a successful rebellion held out the prospect of a complete reversal of the attainder. Walter Hungerford was one of the very few rebels to regain some of his land from Richard III, but this did not prevent him rejoining Henry Tudor.[13] The only certain method by which the king could hold the loyalty of such men was to achieve a position strong enough to make renewed opposition seem unattractive.

This Richard proved unable to do. He had a breathing space of barely six months before he was once again facing disaffection, and although former rebels continued to make their peace with the crown it is clear that on balance Richard was losing ground. The first sign of continuing opposition came from the south west. Most of the leading rebels there had joined Tudor in Brittany, and only one attainted rebel from the Exeter sector sought pardon in the course of the reign,[14] compared with almost all the rebels assigned to the Newbury sector and half those from the south east. This may reflect a stronger degree of commitment to Tudor's cause in this traditionally Lancastrian region, and it probably also owes something to the military geography of the rebellion, as the south west was one of the few areas to face the royal army.[15]

On 6 July 1484 the king ordered the setting up of a commission under John lord Scrope of Bolton, the leading royal agent in the south west, to try James Newenham and others who had lately confessed great treasons. Newenham had obtained a pardon in the previous May and had perhaps been implicated in the 1483 rebellion, but no more is known of this later treason.[16] Later in the same month Richard appointed a strengthened commission, again headed by Scrope, to investigate the treason of Richard Edgecombe of Cotehele; John Lenne of Launceston, mercer; John

[11] *Harl. 433* II pp. 126, 213; Conway 1925, pp. 117–18, although these references postdate Richard's reign.
[12] *CPR 1476–85* p. 527; *CCR 1476–85* nos. 1243, 1379; Ives 1983, pp. 468–9.
[13] *Harl. 433* I pp. 259–60; Vergil p. 561.
[14] John Trevelyan: *CPR 1476–85* p. 504.
[15] *Crowland* pp. 164–5.
[16] PRO, C 67/51 m. 27; C 81/1392/14; *CPR 1476–85* pp. 492–3.

Belbury of Liskeard, mercer; and John Toser of Exiland, dyer. The men had conspired to send money to two of the exiled rebels of 1483, Robert Willoughby and Piers Courtenay, the bishop of Exeter.[17] The driving force was Edgecombe, a neighbour of Willoughby, who had been indicted for his part in the 1483 rising but had obtained a pardon in time to escape attainder.[18] He had planned to send Lenne to Brittany with cash under cover of trading in tin and wool. Toser's contribution, and probably that of Belbury, was to supply the goods shipped to Brittany, and the two men were subsequently pardoned their involvement. Edgecombe's land and goods were seized but he managed to escape to Brittany.[19] In itself the conspiracy was not particularly threatening. Although the indictment accuses Edgecombe and Lenne of aiding the rebels 'to the destruction of the crown', the sums involved were modest, totalling a little over £52, and there is no suggestion that they were intended for anything other than the rebels' subsistence.

More threatening, at least in theory, was the summer's other manifestation of unrest. On 10 July, in London's Portsoken ward, William Collingbourne and others conspired to send Thomas Yate to the rebels in Brittany to incite Tudor to invade England on St Luke's day (18 October). Eight days later, on 18 July, Collingbourne committed one of the most famous treasons of the Middle Ages by preparing bills and writings in rhyme and ballads of seditious language and pinning them to the doors of St Paul's. Although the conspirators chose London in which to publicize their opposition to the regime, the heart of the conspiracy was again in the west country. Collingbourne himself was a Wiltshire man, a former servant of Edward IV, who had lost his place in local affairs in the aftermath of the 1483 rebellion. His plan was for Tudor to land in Poole, his arrival to coincide with a rising in his favour organized by Collingbourne and his ally John Turberville of Friarmayne (Dorset), a kinsman of bishop John Morton of Ely.[20] How much came of this is unclear. The commission of *oyer et terminer* to investigate Collingbourne's treason was not issued until 29 November, after the date of the projected invasion, but

[17] PRO, C 81/1392/16; KB 9/369/19; *CPR* 1476–85 p. 493.
[18] Holinshed, *Chronicles* III p. 421; *CPR* 1476–85 p. 456.
[19] *Harl.* 433 I p. 245; PRO, KB 9/369/22; *Crowland* pp. 180–1.
[20] PRO, KB 9/952/3, 9 (the salient points are printed in Holinshed, *Chronicles* III pp. 422–3, from a 'register book of indictments'); C 81/1531/58; *CPR* 1476–85 pp. 519–20. Morton's mother was a Turberville: Hutchins 1861–74, II p. 594.

there is no sign that Tudor acted on the conspirators' suggestion. The early autumn was, however, marked by continuing unrest in England. On 29 September Richard ordered one of his yeoman of the crown, Thomas Grayson, to arrest certain persons in the west parts of the realm who had been detected in actions 'against their natural duty and liegeance'.[21] No further details are given, but as Grayson was a Plymouth man the trouble may have been in that area. A few days later, on 4 October, Robert Holand was given a writ of aid for the arrest of certain traitors, again unspecified.[22]

The difficulty of linking these stray references into a coherent pattern demonstrates the nature of the threat which they posed to Richard III. Individually the outbreaks do not seem to have amounted to much, but they entailed a persistent nibbling at royal security which Richard probably found more difficult to counter than concerted opposition. He did what he could to deter his opponents by making an example of those arrested. In ordering the trial of three west-country merchants in October he added that their punishment was to be 'in fearful example of other', and Collingbourne suffered the full penalty of hanging, castration and disembowelling, in contrast to earlier rebels who had apparently been hanged.[23] Recognizing that the major threat lay in the conjunction of rebels at home with the circle around Tudor, Richard attempted to police shipping in the Channel. In March 1484 the earl of Arundel's son John and John lord Scrope were both at sea for the defence of the realm.[24] In August fears of treason, as much as of piracy, were probably behind the king's orders to Arundel that no one was to fit out a ship without giving security that it would not be used against the king's subjects, friends or confederates.[25]

These measures, however, only scratched the surface of the problem. The king needed to deal with Tudor himself, whose court in Brittany gave a focus to the disaffected. Throughout the spring and summer of 1484 Richard attempted to put military and diplomatic pressure on duke Francis of Brittany to hand over Tudor, or at least withhold support from him.[26] By September the plan was very close to success, helped by the temporary

[21] *Harl. 433* II p. 164.
[22] *Ibid.* p. 165.
[23] PRO, C 81/1392/17; *Great Chron.* pp. 235–6.
[24] Southampton RO, SC 5/1/19 fo. 4; PRO, C 76/168 m. 27.
[25] *HMC, 2nd Report* p. 91.
[26] Ross 1981, pp. 196–9.

incapacity of duke Francis which left effective power in the hands of his treasurer Pierre Landais. In that month William Catesby arrived in Brittany, presumably in the expectation of being able to escort Tudor back to England.[27] But news of the agreement betwen Landais and Richard came to the ears of John Morton, then based in Flanders, and he was able to warn Tudor in time. Henry fled across the border into France, where he was later joined by the rest of his followers. Richard's scheme thus rebounded against him. Tudor in Brittany had been a considerable nuisance; Tudor in France was potentially a far more serious threat. Relations between France and England had been strained since before Edward IV's death, and Tudor made an admirable weapon against Richard III. By mid October Tudor had made his way to the French court and in the following month Charles VIII agreed to underwrite the costs of an invasion of England.[28]

The first fruits of Tudor's enhanced importance may have been the outbreaks of opposition in Calais and East Anglia at the end of October. Unlike the amorphous unrest earlier in the year, these seem to have been the prelude to a coherent plot which drew on new support. In England the trouble began in Essex, with an armed rising in Colchester led by the Brandons: Sir William and his sons Thomas and William. The rebels then seized a boat at East Mersea on 2 November and escaped to join Tudor in France.[29] The episode itself was brief, but Richard evidently believed that it heralded further trouble in the region and late in December was ordering preparations to resist the rebels should they arrive in Harwich.[30] By this date the unrest seems to have spread to other countries, and the commissioners of array in Surrey, Middlesex and Hertfordshire were warned to be ready at half a day's notice to resist 'any sudden arrival' of the king's rebels and traitors.[31]

The conspiracy appears to have had most support in Hertfordshire. Ralph Penne of Aldenham suffered forfeiture for his part in the unrest. He had probably been drawn in by the Brandons, with whom he had had connections in the previous reign.[32] Also

---

[27] Griffiths and Thomas 1985, p. 111.
[28] *Ibid.* pp. 118–20; Ross 1981, pp. 199–200; Davies 1987, pp. 6–7; Antonovics 1986, pp. 172–3.
[29] PRO, KB 9/953/2, 15, 17–18. Sir William Brandon remained in sanctuary at Colchester: *Rot. Parl.* VI pp. 291–2 ('Gloucester', but Colchester is clearly meant).
[30] *Harl. 433* II p. 183. The town was still being defended in late March, p. 223.
[31] *Ibid.* p. 182.
[32] *Ibid.* p. 184; BL, Harl. ms 1546 fo. 2; PRO, C 244/129/144A.

involved was Robert Clifford, who had interests in the county through his marriage with the widow of Sir Ralph Josselin. He was pardoned in April 1485, after earlier promising to inform the royal council of anything which came to his ears affecting the king.[33] At a lower social level, the group of Hertfordshire yeomen indicted in King's Bench in 2 Richard III were probably also implicated. The process against them was halted in May 1486 on the grounds that it had been begun 'by the sinister labour and malice of [Henry VII's] adversaries'.[34] They include a group from Ware, a royal manor where John Sturgeon was steward, and Sturgeon appears to have fallen under some disfavour at around this time. He was not restored to the commission of the peace at the end of his term as sheriff of Essex and Hertfordshire in November 1484, and in December surrendered the stewardship of Ware to Robert Brackenbury. Sturgeon was promised repayment of his outstanding wages, which suggests that he had not been personally implicated in the unrest, but Richard perhaps blamed him for failing to keep the area loyal.[35] His replacement as sheriff was the king's close associate Sir Robert Percy, implying that Richard also thought that the remaining local gentry were in some degree suspect.

This unrest in England has received less discussion than the concurrent disaffection within Calais, which caught the attention of Tudor writers. At the end of October word reached the king of a plan to rescue the Lancastrian earl of Oxford, John de Vere, who had been a prisoner in Hammes, one of the Calais forts, since his abortive rebellion in 1473. On 28 October Richard ordered his yeoman William Bolton, a member of the Calais garrison and perhaps the source of the original warning, to ship the earl back to England. Robert Brackenbury was sent to Dover early in November to meet the earl and, presumably, conduct him to the Tower.[36] But Richard was too late. At the beginning of

---

[33] PRO, C 244/136/92; *CPR* 1476–85 p. 533. Robert's brother Roger was also in trouble at around this time. Exeter records mention him passing through the city as a prisoner: Devon RO, Exeter receiver's account 2 Ric.III – 1 Hen.VII. Compare London accounts of his capture at Southampton and execution on Tower Hill: Fabyan, *Chronicles* p. 671; *Great Chron.* p. 236.

[34] Campbell, *Materials* I p. 428.

[35] *Harl. 433* II p. 186; *CPR* 1476–85 p. 561; *CFR* 1471–85 no. 797. Henry VII restored Sturgeon to the bench.

[36] PRO, C 81/1392/19; C 67/53 m. 6; Canterbury RO, FA 7 fo. 26.

November the lieutenant of Hammes, James Blount, freed de Vere and went with him to join Tudor in France, accompanied by John Fortescue, the porter of Calais.[37] The Hammes garrison remained loyal to Blount and in the following month the castle was besieged by the commander of Calais, John lord Dynham. Oxford returned with a relieving force in January 1485, raised the siege and, apparently, led the garrison off to swell Tudor's forces.[38]

The two outbreaks of opposition were certainly connected. They can be linked, for instance, by the involvement of John Fortescue, the porter of Calais, who was of Ponsbourne (Herts.) and probably had a hand in the unrest there. His home lay in the area known to have been involved: other rebels were drawn from Cheshunt, Ware and Watton at Stone.[39] The Brandons also spanned the two outbreaks. Their Essex rising, according to the indictment, was to aid the earl of Oxford as well as Tudor and others, and Thomas Brandon accompanied Oxford back to Hammes in 1485.[40] The most interesting link, however, is formed by Oxford himself. The de Vere estates, now largely in the hands of John Howard, lay predominantly in Essex and it is possible that the Brandons hoped to call on residual loyalties to the de Veres. One of their leading supporters was John Risley, who held office in the former de Vere lordship of Lavenham. Among the smaller fry involved were John Starling of Castle Hedingham and Thomas Taillour of Stansted Mountfitchet, both de Vere properties.[41] The plan may have been for Oxford to invade in Tudor's name. Richard's preparations at Harwich suggest that he feared something of the sort. But the initial scheme can hardly have been Oxford's own. A more likely instigator is John Morton, bishop of Ely, who had connections with the Brandons and Fortescue.[42] Richard seems to have been aware of Morton in the background. The efforts the king made to win over those involved make this unrest unique in Richard's reign. On 16 November he offered a pardon under the signet to James Blount, whose defection must by then have been known, and on 30 November followed this up with a confirmation (again under the

[37] Ross 1981, p. 202 (and refs. there given); Davies 1987, p. 7.
[38] Davies 1987, pp. 7–8 and notes.
[39] *Ibid*. p. 9; Campbell, *Materials* 1 p. 428.
[40] PRO, KB 9/953/15; Davies 1987, p. 7.
[41] Virgoe 1982, p. 142; PRO, KB 9/953/17; Campbell, *Materials* 1 p. 428.
[42] Davies 1987, pp. 5, 9.

signet only) of all the offices granted to Blount by Edward IV.[43] Morton received an unsolicited pardon less than a fortnight later and is unique in receiving it under the great seal.[44] On Christmas Eve, two days after the order to defend Harwich, the king held out another olive branch by making one of Morton's former servants, William Timperley, receiver general of the Ely estates, with authority to remove all the officers appointed since the see came into the king's hands and to replace them with men 'such as he will answer for to the king'.[45]

The unrest in England and Calais had apparently petered out by the end of January. This owed nothing to Richard's overtures, which were ignored, and was probably because Tudor was not yet ready to act. Like Collingbourne, the Brandons appear to have been thinking in terms of an English rising as a prelude to Tudor's invasion, and without that second element the English efforts had no real focus. But although Richard had thus again weathered disaffection without difficulty, the latest episode had some ominous implications. It demonstrated the enhanced credibility of Henry Tudor who, from being a last-minute expedient in 1483, had become a persuasive alternative candidate. In part this was due to Tudor's promise, made at Christmas 1483, that he would marry Elizabeth of York if he became king. It was largely, however, due to his endorsement by France, which made overt resistance to Richard III a more feasible option. It is probably not a coincidence that some formerly pardoned rebels defaulted at just this time. As well as William Brandon, who had been pardoned in March 1484, William Berkeley fled to France in October.[46] Polydore Vergil, who was well informed about this stage of Tudor's career, notes that once Henry was based in France he was joined by other fugitives from England.[47]

The conspiracies of autumn 1484 also drew attention to weaknesses in Richard's own power structure. The involvement of James Blount called into question the reliability of several other Calais officials who, like him, dated from the Hastings era. Calais was an obvious springboard for an invasion of England and

[43] *Harl. 433* I p. 230.

[44] *CPR 1476–85* p. 535; see also *Great Chron.* p. 237.

[45] *Harl. 433* II p. 183; *Foedera* XI p. 846. A month after his appointment Timperley was described as a servant of Thomas Thwaites, the controller of Calais, and issued with letters of protection: PRO, C 76/169 m. 16.

[46] PRO, C 81/1392/17; *CPR 1476–85* p. 423.

[47] Vergil p. 556.

tensions had been heightened by rumours of a French attack in the previous August. Richard immediately began an overhaul of the office holders there.[48] The trouble in East Anglia, meanwhile, underlined what the 1483 rebellion had already suggested, that the new duke of Norfolk could not keep the region loyal to the king. The duke was in theory the political heir of the Mowbrays and de Veres, but the 1484 unrest found former Mowbray retainers, the Brandons, exploiting the de Vere interest in Tudor's favour. Howard's relative isolation meant that men from his own circle were prepared to contemplate rebellion. Among the Colchester rebels was John Scraton, whose father and namesake had been in Howard's service. Scraton senior was evidently also implicated. When he was arrested in Colchester in the following year, John Howard wrote to the town's bailiffs in his own hand ordering them to keep him fast, 'for I am sure I have grounds to prove him as false as his son'.[49]

Scraton was a very small fish, but his involvement was symptomatic of what must have been the most alarming aspect of the rebellion: the extent to which it drew on men hitherto loyal to Richard III. At the core of the Essex rising were men who had been involved in 1483, the Brandons, Sir William Stonor and Thomas Nandyke. But their ally John Risley was an esquire of Richard's body, who had been rewarded with land in Hampshire forfeited by some of the 1483 rebels.[50] At Calais, Blount and Fortescue were also esquires of the body.[51] A possible associate in Hertfordshire was a fourth esquire of the body, William Benstead. A yeoman from his manor of Bennington was involved, and in April 1485 the royal servant Edward Skelton was given custody of the manor, one of those sold by Benstead to Edward IV in reversion.[52] Other royal servants were subsequently to follow this lead. The esquire of the body John Mortimer, who was to fight for Tudor at Bosworth, may have moved into overt opposition by February 1485, when John Huddleston replaced him as steward of the duchy of Lancaster land in Gloucester-

[48] See below, pp. 290–4.
[49] PRO, C 244/136/8; Turner; *Manners and Expenses* pp. 273, 288. Scraton junior was in the service of John Reynsford, and it was Humphrey Reynsford who stood surety for Scraton senior after his arrest: Collier, *Household Books* p. 197.
[50] Virgoe 1982, pp. 142–3 and notes; PRO, C 237/53/36.
[51] PRO, C 67/51 m. 18; *CPR 1476–85* p. 379.
[52] Campbell, *Materials* I p. 428; *Harl. 433* II p. 214; *Inqs p.m.* III no. 649.

shire.[53] Piers Curtis, Richard's keeper of the great wardrobe, had forfeited his land and office by mid May 1485 and taken refuge in Westminster sanctuary.[54]

Richard's inability as king to retain the loyalties even of his own servants is a damning indictment of his regime. All the men mentioned above were former servants of Edward IV and their reservations about Richard may thus have been rooted in the events of June 1483. But the fact that they apparently avoided involvement in the rebellion of October 1483, only to move into opposition a year or more later, suggests that any initial doubts had been compounded by Richard's policies as king. The aftermath of the 1483 rebellion saw a gap opening up between the king's immediate circle, largely made up of the former ducal connection, and the rest of the political community. The plantations are the most obvious manifestation of this tendency, and the Crowland chronicler's condemnation of the policy captures a genuine sense of outrage.[55] The individuals planted in the south, and the friends and relations who accompanied them, were perceived as an unjust imposition on local society, and this view can only have been reinforced by the fact that many of them formed a recognizable geographical clique. Three years after Richard's death, an enquiry into New Forest game found that 500 deer had been killed in Richard's reign by a group identified simply as 'the northern men'.[56]

This local resentment is not to be explained simply as a dislike of 'foreigners'. Medieval gentry, when it suited them, did evince a strong sense of local solidarity, particularly in their belief that local government should be in the hands of men with a stake in the region concerned.[57] But this regionalism was essentially pragmatic. The gentry of a given area never constituted a closed society. Families died out and were replaced, often from outside the region. Noble retinues which spanned several counties were frequently a means of injecting 'outsiders' into an area. The royal affinity performed a similar role, with the king's servants regularly given responsibilities outside their home area. All of this was taken for granted and was generally acceptable to contemporary

[53] Somerville 1953, pp. 636, 648.
[54] *Harl. 433* I p. 287; Sutton and Hammond, *Coronation* p. 328. For earlier disaffection in the wardrobe see Sutton 1981a, p. 4.
[55] *Crowland* pp. 170–1.
[56] Stagg, *New Forest Docs.* p. 24.
[57] Virgoe 1981, pp. 81–3.

opinion. What made Richard's plantations different was that the men concerned, rather than finding a niche for themselves within the existing framework of local society, were being forced in as a deliberate substitute for sections of that society. Their position depended on the removal, and continuing exclusion, of an influential and well-connected group of local gentry.

Alongside the general resentment which this generated, some members of local society had more specific grievances. The most obvious category were the dispossessed themselves. The use of their land to endow Richard's allies gave them relatively little chance of regaining it without a dynastic revolution. Some found that property disputes in which they had been engaged were decided against them by royal *fiat* as part of the penalty for rebellion. The Arundel lands claimed by Tyrell were transferred to him within days of the king becoming aware of Thomas Arundel's treason.[58] John Heveningham regained a moiety of the Bruin inheritance, of which he had been disseised by the rebel William Brandon the younger. The enquiry into Heveningham's claims was held in September 1484 and anticipation of its outcome may have contributed to Brandon's renewed opposition of the following month.[59] Thomas Heveningham, John's son by his first marriage, had reputedly been a great favourite of Richard as duke of Gloucester, and the enquiry was held before Richard's solicitor Thomas Lynom so the Heveninghams' victory can never have been seriously in doubt.[60] Halneth Malyverer gained an increased share of the Carminewe inheritance, which he had been disputing in the 1470s with Edward Courtenay.[61] In this case, however, Malyverer received the land by royal grant, not of right, and some of the remaining land was dispersed among other royal associates.[62]

The attainted rebels were not the only ones to suffer loss. At least two of the 1483 rebels parted with some of their land to escape attainder. William Knyvet and John Wingfield are listed in

[58] *Harl. 433* II p. 34; for the dispute see above, p. 174.

[59] *Harl. 433* I pp. 281, 288; *CPR 1476–85* pp. 523–4; Richmond 1981a, pp. 238–9 (n. 316). Heveningham and Brandon had married the Bruin coheiresses.

[60] Blomefield 1739–75, III p. 61. Thomas' mother was a Saville of Thornhill (Yorks.), which helps to explain Gloucester's interest in him: Sutton and Hammond, *Coronation* p. 357.

[61] PRO, C 1/51/121. In 1476 the matter had been settled by arbitration: Meyrick Cary papers, box 10/unnumb. Halneth's wife Jane Carminewe was the sister of Courtenay's mother Margaret.

[62] *CPR 1476–85* p. 502; *Harl. 433* III p. 141.

the act of attainder as involved in the rebellion but are not included in the list of those attainted. Knyvet later claimed that he paid 700m to the king and 100m to the queen, and that he made over four manors to the king, including his castle of New Buckenham (Norf.), and a manor and other land to Sir James Tyrell. Richard was to have paid £300 for the land but, according to Knyvet, did not do so.[63] Wingfield paid for his escape from attainder by releasing his claims to the Mowbray inheritance, including the dower lands of Margaret, widow of Edmund Lenthall, for the benefit of John Howard and William Stanley.[64] Like Knyvet, he sought redress from Henry VII's first parliament.[65] Similarly, pressure was put on John Forster to surrender land in return for a pardon, with Robert Brackenbury the beneficiary.[66] Other unattainted rebels suffered forfeiture. Richard Edgecombe's land and goods were seized by Edward Redmane, and Sir Gilbert Debenham removed £100 in cash from Sir William Brandon's house in Southwark in the week after the Essex unrest of autumn 1484.[67] Lesser figures also suffered confiscation. Redmane seized ten oxen, fourteen cows and 200 sheep from John Bartelete at Newton (Corn.) in September 1484, and a group of Hailsham men who captured the rebel John Redeness were rewarded with thirty cows belonging to John and his father.[68]

Such forfeitures represented a major upheaval in southern society. Confiscations on this scale were always unpopular with landed society at large, and in this case the resulting uneasiness is likely to have been intensified by the questionable legality of some of the king's actions.[69] Richard's need to gain control of the

---

[63] *Rot. Parl.* VI p. 298.

[64] *Harl. 433* II p. 110; *CCR 1476–85* nos. 1184, 1380. Edmund Lenthall was the nephew of Elizabeth Fitzalan. By her husband Thomas Mowbray Elizabeth was the ancestress of the Mowbrays, Berkeleys and Howards. She subsequently married Robert Goushill, by whom she had two daughters: Joan, who married Thomas first lord Stanley, and Elizabeth, who married Sir Robert Wingfield (John's grandfather). I am grateful to Mr W. E. Hampton for his help in unravelling this descent.

[65] *Red Paper Book* p. 62. Wingfield's rights were protected in parliament's confirmation of the land grant to William Stanley: *Rot. Parl.* VI p. 316.

[66] *Rot. Parl.* VI pp. 332–3; *Harl. 433* III p. 145. For Forster see above, p. 199.

[67] PRO, KB 9/369/5, 22.

[68] PRO, KB 9/1060/33; *Harl. 433* II p. 35. For other confiscations of livestock and crops, *Harl. 433* II pp. 68–9.

[69] Wolffe 1971, pp. 193, 197. The penalties imposed on the Yorkists in 1459 had evidently caused anxiety, prompting an elaborate justification: Gilson, 'A defence of the proscription'.

rebels' land had led him to cut corners and mistakes were undoubtedly made. Although the act of attainder specifically protected dower rights and land held by a rebel in his wife's right, land in these categories was seized. The grant of Branston (Leics.) to Marmaduke Constable was sanctioned by the attainder of William Norreys, but the manor was held in dower by William's wife Anne (née Horne), the widow of William Harcourt.[70] There even seems to have been initial confusion over who had rebelled. The yeoman of the crown Richard Lloyd was apparently the victim of one such muddle. In March 1484 the king ordered his officers not to seize any of Lloyd's possessions and to return what had already been taken.[71]

Local resentment was probably aggravated by the frequent use of 'outsiders' to seize land, which, as well as being unpopular in itself, may have increased the risk of mistakes being made. Redmane's activity in the south west has already been mentioned. The northerner John Cutte was active in Dorset and Somerset, and was later made responsible for seizing Collingbourne's land.[72] In Kent, Richard employed Roland Machelle of Appleby (Westm.).[73] All three were seizing land for the king, but the practice of giving the beneficiaries of the forfeitures *carte blanche* to identify and seize the land and goods concerned was also common, and must sometimes have led to abuse.

The general confusion allowed some royal servants to indulge in straightforward land-grabbing. In Kent, William Malyverer seized the land of the late William Langley, which had been granted together with the custody of Langley's heir to the rebel Richard Guildford. Malyverer was no doubt acting in his capacity as the county's escheator, but he then hung onto the land and the heir in spite of a royal grant of their custody to Langley's widow and Thomas Quadring.[74] It was in Kent also that Sir Ralph Ashton's sons resorted to force to seize land, while in Dorset Morgan Kidwelly was accused of some sharp practice over his

[70] *Rot. Parl.* VI p. 248; *CPR* 1476–85 p. 471; *VCH Leics.* IV p. 429.
[71] *Harl. 433* II p. 107.
[72] *Ibid.* pp. 31–2, 69, 184, 195. Richard's servant can probably be identified with the Tudor under-treasurer, who died in 1521, although it is possible that they were father and son. By the time of his death, the under-treasurer was established in Essex, but the family's origins, although shadowy, seem to have been in the north: PRO, Prob 11/20, fos. 87–88v; Leland, *Itin.* II p. 30.
[73] *Harl. 433* II pp. 83, 87; Brown 1926, p. 162 and pedigree facing p. 160.
[74] *Inqs p.m.* I nos. 362, 447, 448, 450; *CFR* 1471–85 no. 801; *CPR* 1476–85 p. 541; *Harl. 433* II pp. 18–19.

wife's inheritance.[75] In January 1485 the knight of the body Gilbert Debenham attacked the possessions of Thomas Fastolf. Debenham was accompanied by some of the men who had earlier helped him to enter the Brandon mansion for the king, but this time it seems to have been a matter of private enterprise.[76]

Such cases can be found in any reign, and it is notoriously difficult to produce comparative judgements on medieval lawlessness. But it seems probable that the political uncertainties of Richard III's reign, like the upheavals of 1469–71, did offer increased scope for the pursuit of self-interest. The 1483 rebellion itself conforms to this pattern in some respects, with rebels like Hungerford and Lutterell fighting for inheritances which had seemed beyond reach in the 1470s. The flood of confiscations which followed can only have increased the sense that it was worth dusting down claims and ambitions which would not have been pursued in more stable circumstances. In the nature of things, the main beneficiaries of this process were likely to be the king's men, and this gave further cause for resentment among the wider political community.

The king's own attitude was ambivalent. There is no doubt that Richard was strongly committed to the rule of law.[77] He was, for instance, aware of the dangers inherent in the seizure of forfeited land and tried to limit them, insisting that he was 'utterly determined all his true subjects shall live in rest and quiet, and peaceably enjoy their lands, livelihoods and goods according to the laws of this his land, which they be naturally born to inherit'.[78] The king and his council were also active in the arbitration of land disputes, intending, as one surviving settlement expresses it, 'rest and peace and quiet among all our liege people'.[79] But, like any lord, Richard was also under an obligation to uphold the interests of his servants, upon whom his power rested, and this could mean ignoring, or even endorsing, actions of doubtful legality. The ducal servant Richard Pole had married as his second wife the widow of John Stradling, by whom she had had a son, Edward. The child's wardship had been granted by Edward IV to Richard Fowler, whose widow, with the king's

---

[75] See above, pp. 86–7; *Rot. Parl.* VI pp. 321–4.
[76] PRO, KB 9/369/5, 24–5. During the Brandon episode, Debenham was accompanied by the serjeant at arms John Waynflete, who took no part in the attack on Fastolf.
[77] Sutton 1976; Ross 1981, pp. 173–5.
[78] *Harl. 433* II p. 49.
[79] *Ibid.* III p. 133.

consent, passed it on to Henry Danvers. Pole, as the boy's step-father, evidently wanted the wardship for himself and in April 1483 seized the boy by force in London. Danvers appealed to the chancellor for redress, and the hearing was scheduled for 14 June. The outcome is not known, but in July 1484 Richard III simply granted the wardship to Pole in consideration of his 'true and thankful service'.[80] Such cases cannot have endeared the king's allies to the rest of political society, and, in the south at least, may have meant that the tenurial nervousness caused by Richard's forfeitures developed into an active dislike of the new regime. In 1485 a London attorney, William Crouch of Wetherden (Suff.), was accused of seditious language after he had publicly attacked the quality of the king's justice.[81]

Alongside these general doubts about the propriety of Richard's regime, the king's southern servants had more particular grounds for disenchantment. Under both Yorkist kings the household enjoyed a near monopoly of the most lucrative forms of patronage, and Richard's generosity to the outsiders whom he planted in the south was thus not at the expense of the rank and file local gentry, who were hardly in the running for such rewards. But it was arguably at the expense of those local servants who had remained loyal through the 1483 rebellion. The Courtenays of Powderham (Devon) are a good example. Two of the brothers were in Richard's household. Philip was a knight of the body and received an annuity of £40, payable from the duchy of Cornwall. His home was at Molland, some sixteen miles from Barnstaple, which was the centre-piece of land given by Richard to another of his knights of the body, the Yorkshireman Thomas Ever-ingham of Stainborough. In all, Everingham's land grant in the south west was valued at £200. Philip Courtenay's brother John, of Exminster and Kenn, was an esquire of the body and received an annuity of 40m. His fellow esquire, Halneth Malyverer, who had northern connections, received land valued at £66 and the office of constable of Launceston.[82]

Under normal conditions the Courtenays would have had few grounds for complaint. Their rewards were average for royal servants of their standing, and several comparable household men

---

[80] PRO, C 1/67/36; *Harl. 433* II p. 146. For Pole see above, pp. 85–6. The boy and his mother are said to have been subsequently murdered: Wedgwood 1936, p. 690.
[81] PRO, KB 9/953/45–6.
[82] *CPR 1476–85* pp. 428, 429, 502, 503.

did worse, including some northerners who remained based in the north (where new sources of patronage were limited) rather than moving south. The point was that the Courtenays were living in an area where the patronage at the king's disposal was immense and yet were signally failing to benefit on anything like the scale of the incomers. Richard gave away land in Devon valued at around £1,400, excluding the Brian lands given to the earl of Northumberland.[83] Of the nineteen men who shared this windfall just four were local and their joint gains were of the order of £180.[84] The other south-western counties give a similar picture.

In part, the imbalance reflects the needs of Richard's policy of plantation. The local men were already established in the south; the newcomers needed to have a power base created artificially and that entailed lavish patronage. But this is not the whole story. Of the examples cited above, Malyverer was already established at Ashwater. Everingham, on the other hand, seems to have had little intention of moving south and was added to none of the local commissions. His main interests lay in Calais, where he had been active under Edward IV. Richard made him lieutenant of Ruysbank and employed him as a naval commander.[85] His patronage in the south west was thus not a building block of royal authority but a reward pure and simple. Of course, in any reign some men were well rewarded while others were not – royal favour was never particularly egalitarian – but when Richard so badly needed support in the south it was undiplomatic, to say the least, to use his resources there so largely for the benefit of outsiders.

By the end of 1484 the king was in a vicious circle. The 1483 rebellion had forced him into reliance on his ducal connection, who were outstandingly favoured both in terms of power and reward. This contributed to the further alienation of the south, and with the unrest of autumn 1484 the cycle began again. The disaffection had at its core former rebels like Stonor and was to that extent predictable (just as Woodville opposition had been in

[83] The figure is only approximate, since some grants are unvalued.
[84] Lord Dynham (whose grant was in reversion), his brother Charles, John Taillour of Kingsbridge, Richard Taillour of Topsham: *CPR 1476–85* pp. 480–1, 541–2; *Harl. 433* I pp. 156, 176–7. John Sapcote, who had moved to the county in the previous reign (see above, p. 262), received land worth £80 there: *CPR 1476–85* pp. 431–2.
[85] Hunter 1828–31, II p. 265; *CPR 1476–85* pp. 299, 460; *Cely Letters* pp. 104, 272; *Crowland* pp. 172–3. He is not (*pace* Ross 1981, p. 52) the servant and soldier of Henry VI, who was dead by this date: *Cal. Inq. post mortem sive Escaetarum* IV p. 367.

1483), but it again drew in men whom Richard had trusted: Fortescue and Blount. The result was to make the king even more obsessively mistrustful of men outside his immediate circle.[86] In particular, as in 1483, it made him disinclined to trust former associates of his brother on the periphery of the unrest. The case of John Sturgeon has already been mentioned. A more eminent casualty may have been the Essex knight of the body Thomas Montgomery of Faulkbourne. Montgomery was an elder states-man of the Yorkist household, and Richard was probably delighted to have his backing in 1483. Certainly he rewarded Montgomery with one of the most lavish land grants of the reign: land in Essex valued at £412. At the same time, February 1484, Montgomery was made master forester throughout the county and steward of all the royal land there.[87] Their relationship may have begun to cool as early as August 1484 when Montgomery, who in the previous reign had been the regular recipient of *douceurs* from men who wanted Edward IV's favour, himself made such a gift to Richard's close ally Robert Brackenbury.[88] The real turning point, however, was the unrest in Calais and Essex, both areas where Montgomery had interests. He had been deputizing as lieutenant of Guisnes during lord Mountjoy's illness, and Richard's failure to keep him in post implies that the king considered him partly to blame for what had happened.[89] Later, probably in March 1485, a significant part of the Essex land which Montgomery had been granted was included in the endowment of Richard's projected royal chapel of St Mary in the London church of All Hallows, Barking, with no suggestion that it was only the reversion which was being given.[90]

Richard was being pushed into a corner by his diminishing confidence in all but his own men, and this is clearly shown in his

[86] The tone of Richard's personal devotions betrays the extent to which he saw himself as surrounded by enemies: Tudor-Craig 1973, pp. 96–7. Compare also the later tradition in the Wyatt family that Richard, cross-questioning Henry Wyatt (sent by Tudor to Scotland), lamented that his own servants showed no such fidelity: Loades, *Papers of George Wyatt* p. 5; Muir 1963, pp. 1, 40. I owe the Wyatt tradition to Dr Helen Baron.

[87] Morgan 1973, pp. 15, 20; Morgan 1987, pp. 58–9; *Harl. 433* I p. 133, II pp. 102–3, III p. 145. The grant did not pass the great seal until April: *CPR 1476–85* p. 430.

[88] *CPR 1476–85* p. 542. It was perhaps motivated by Montgomery's inability to secure payment for some of his Essex offices: PRO, DL 29/41/799, 29/59/1128.

[89] PRO, C 81/1531/2. Montgomery subsequently married Mountjoy's widow: *Inqs p.m.* I no. 1040.

[90] *Harl. 433* III pp. 144–5; Horrox 1982. There are problems over which of the two extant endowments was meant to be effective, but both include some of the land granted to Montgomery.

handling of Calais after the defection of Blount and Fortescue. This had also called into question the loyalty of Blount's elder brother lord Mountjoy, the lieutenant of Guisnes. Mountjoy was already seriously ill (he died in October 1485) and his responsibilities were being carried by Montgomery, while Ralph Hastings had been promised the reversion after Mountjoy's death.[91] Richard was not prepared to trust either Montgomery or Hastings with so sensitive a post, and on 22 January made James Tyrell lieutenant of Guisnes, still nominally during Mountjoy's illness.[92] The choice of Tyrell is an indication of the gravity with which Richard viewed the situation, but it solved the problem of royal authority in one area at the expense of another. Tyrell had played a leading role in the restoration of royal influence in Wales and was now simply taken off that job and sent to reside in Guisnes. Richard recognized that this left a gap in Wales and tried to plug it by ordering the officials in Glamorgan and Morgannok, the heart of Tyrell's power base, 'to accept [him] as their governor and leader as he hath been heretofore, notwithstanding that the king sendeth him to Guisnes'.[93] But this was very much second best and Richard must have known it. The contracting circle of men whom Richard was prepared to trust with major responsibilities was evidently beginning to cause problems. Richard's difficulties are also suggested by the long delay before he chose a replacement for James Blount at Hammes. Not until mid May did he appoint Thomas Wortley, a Yorkshire knight of the body previously active in the forfeited Stafford estates in the north midlands.[94]

The appointment of Tyrell and Wortley completed the process of bringing the three subsidiary Calais fortresses under the control of reliable royal servants. Ruysbank, where the lieutenant had been Hastings' brother-in-law John Donne, had been given to Thomas Everingham in February 1484, when Donne was suspected of complicity in the 1483 rebellion.[95] But this still left Calais itself. The governor there was John lord Dynham who, like James Blount, had been inherited from the Hastings regime. Dynham had got off on the wrong foot with his query about the validity of oaths to Edward V, and any reservations about his

[91] *CPR 1476–85* p. 385.
[92] PRO, C 76/169 m. 25; *Harl. 433* I p. 255.
[93] *Harl. 433* II p. 197 (sent two days after his appointment).
[94] *Ibid.* I p. 282; the appointment was for seven years.
[95] *Ibid.* II p. 32, III p. 31; *CPR 1476–85* p. 460.

reliability which Richard harboured as a result were revived by Blount's defection. It was Dynham who besieged Hammes, paying out money of his own on the enterprise; but as subsequent events were to show, this was not enough to regain Richard's confidence.[96] Perhaps the king blamed Dynham for the failure of the siege. Richard did not, however, remove Dynham altogether, probably fearing recriminations from the garrison, which may still have dated largely from the Hastings era.[97] Instead he inserted a level of command above him. On 11 March Richard made his illegitimate son John captain of Calais and its three fortresses. John went to Calais in person, escorted by Brackenbury, but was to wield only limited authority there until he was twenty-one.[98] Instead, although this is not stated, effective power probably rested with some form of council, on the analogy of the Ludlow council or the council of the north. The raw material of such a council already existed, with several of the leading men of Calais enjoying the status of royal councillor and, presumably, being called upon to advise on French matters. Richard may have added to their number, since the Calais contingent among his known councillors was larger than in his brother's day, but there is no formal statement of the king's intentions such as survives for the council in the north.[99]

The elevation of John of Gloucester was a massive snub to Dynham, even if it made relatively little difference to the balance of power in the short term, and Richard evidently felt that he should sugar the pill. Dynham himself was granted £600 by way of reward shortly before John's appointment. His brother Charles was confirmed in his custody of the Dernford lands and pardoned his annual payment of £160 for them. It is perhaps also significant that a land grant made under the signet to Charles in March 1484 finally passed the great seal on 13 March 1485, two days after the appointment of John of Gloucester.[100] The tactic succeeded, in so far as Dynham stuck loyally to his post for the rest of Richard's reign, but he cannot have been happy with the situation, particu-

---

[96] Davies 1987, p. 8n.

[97] See the north midlands contingent in the Guisnes garrison of 1486: Campbell, *Materials* I pp. 503–5.

[98] PRO, C 76/169 m. 26; Canterbury RO, FA 7 fo. 26; *Foedera* XII pp. 265–6; *Harl. 433* I p. 271.

[99] Lander 1976, p. 319; compare *Cely Letters* p. 272. Most of the Calais councillors were appointed to treat with France in 1483: *Foedera* XII pp. 195–6.

[100] *CPR 1476–85* pp. 471, 541–2; *Harl. 433* I pp. 143, 265, 267, 270.

larly as he had already surrendered major duchy of Cornwall office to Tyrell.[101]

Events at Calais demonstrate both Richard's growing sense of insecurity and its consequences. Whether or not the king was justified in his suspicions is, as in the aftermath of the 1483 rebellion, beside the point. The number of men whom he was prepared to trust with significant power had fallen to the point where effective royal authority was beginning to be eroded. The same trend can be seen, although on a broader scale, in the patronage of this period, with few grants of substance made to men who had not previously benefited from royal favour. It is impossible to be sure whether this contraction was entirely of Richard's own choosing or whether, as Collingbourne's couplet would suggest, it was also due in part to the king's favourites controlling access to him. But whatever its cause, it can only have enhanced Tudor's new attractiveness. The king himself was aware of this, and the winter of 1484/5 saw a concerted effort by Richard to undermine his rival's support. His unsolicited pardons to Morton and Blount were one manifestation of this policy. Another, more successful, was his overtures to the Woodvilles, whose hostility had been one of the starting points of the 1483 rebellion. Richard publicly signalled his goodwill to his erstwhile opponents at his Christmas court of 1484, where the attention which he paid to the princess Elizabeth scandalized the Crowland chronicler.[102] The first results of this policy became apparent on 12 January, when Richard Woodville and John Fogge bound themselves in the sum of 1,000m to bear themselves well and faithfully. Fogge's pardon, together with a grant of part of his forfeited land, followed in February. Woodville's pardon was issued in March, as was that of his kinsman and fellow rebel Richard Haute of Ightham.[103] The king also managed to win over Elizabeth Woodville, who at some point in this period persuaded her son Thomas marquis Dorset to leave Tudor's company and return to England. Dorset's attempt failed – he was pursued by Humphrey Cheyne and escorted back to Tudor – but Richard

---

[101] See above, p. 203. For a rosier view of Dynham's relations with Richard see Ross 1981, p. 161. His career flourished under Henry VII: Chrimes 1972, pp. 107–8; Davies 1987, p. 27n.

[102] *Crowland* pp. 174–5. Richard's propaganda was inclined to be heavy-handed: Ross 1981, pp. 208–9.

[103] PRO, C 244/136/130, 132; *CPR* 1476–85 pp. 511, 543.

continued to regard him as a recruit and he is not included in subsequent proclamations against the rebels.[104]

Cheyne's action demonstrates that, for many rebels, Tudor was now a valid claimant in his own right, regardless of his endorsement by the Woodville circle. But some of the 1483 rebels may have been influenced by the Woodvilles' change of heart. Their kinsman Reginald Pympe was pardoned in March 1485.[105] Other attainted rebels pardoned in the first five months of 1485 included Roger Tocotes, Amyas Paulet and William Ovedale.[106] The king's policy of *rapprochement* was, however, at odds with his growing tendency to retreat into the security of his own connection. The king was anxious to undermine Tudor by detaching his supporters from him, and, as the threat from Tudor grew stronger, Richard became more willing to encourage the process by giving former rebels modest grants from their confiscated estates. The handful of such grants dates mainly from February to May 1485. But Richard was not prepared to see real power pass into the hands of former rebels. None of them was restored to local commissions, for instance.[107] The king's reservations were not surprising, but they meant that he reaped no direct benefit from the rebels' return to the fold. At the same time, the men concerned were being given no opportunity to develop a commitment to his regime, so that their loyalty was likely to remain distinctly provisional. Even more damaging in this respect was the attitude of the king's followers. They had benefited extensively from the rebels' forfeitures, in some cases literally making their fortune, and now did not want to see their gains threatened by even a partial restoration of the confiscated land.

This conflict of interest surfaced dramatically in spring 1485, over the possibility of Richard's marriage to his niece Elizabeth. This would have sealed his new alliance with the Woodvilles. It would also have diminished Tudor's appeal to Yorkist sentiment. After the *débâcle* of autumn 1483, Tudor had rallied Yorkist support by swearing to marry Elizabeth of York should his claim to the throne prove successful. Until this, Richard had been

---

[104] Vergil p. 559; Ross 1981, p. 208n. Edward Woodville remained unreconciled, as did Rivers' son-in-law Robert Poyntz: Gairdner 1898, p. 365.

[105] *Harl. 433* 1 p. 268; Conway 1925, p. 120.

[106] *CPR 1476–85* pp. 504, 507, 534.

[107] The John Gaynesford on Surrey commissions is not the rebel but his cousin and namesake of Crowhurst (Surrey): Greenfield 1863, pp. 212ff. Wedgwood 1936, pp. 367–8 conflates the two men.

content for his nieces to stay in sanctuary with their mother, with a guard in the precinct to avert any rescue attempts. But Tudor's action revealed the unwisdom of allowing the girls to remain in political limbo. On 1 March 1484 Richard came to an agreement with Elizabeth Woodville, who handed her daughters into his care on condition that they would be well treated. Among the detailed clauses of the agreement, Richard promised to 'marry such of them as now be marriageable to gentlemen born'.[108] This, indeed, was probably the object of the whole exercise rather than just one more carrot to tempt the girls out of sanctuary, but it was more easily promised than performed. The princesses' dynastic significance, as well as their status, made the choice of husband difficult, and it was probably not until early in 1485 that Richard found a husband for the second daughter, Cecily. She was married to Ralph Scrope of Upsall, brother of the king's ally Thomas lord Scrope and a member of the royal household.[109]

It is significant that it was the second daughter who was married first. Elizabeth's marriage was politically the more urgent, to pre-empt Tudor's plans, but it also raised more problems. Her dynastic importance meant that it was crucial for her husband to be the king's man, to minimize the danger of setting up one more claimant to the throne. It is therefore not surprising that after the death of Richard's wife, Anne Neville, on 16 March 1485, Elizabeth should have been one of the candidates under consideration for the king's second wife.[110] By marrying her himself, Richard would have undermined Tudor's position without the risk of replacing one rival with another.

Tudor's reaction when he heard of the plan reveals how much weight was attached to his undertaking to marry Elizabeth. The version of events which reached France was that Richard had already married his niece, as well as finding a husband for Cecily, and in Vergil's graphic phrase the news 'pinched [Henry] by the very stomach' because he feared that it would make his followers forsake him. Tudor and his advisors accordingly cast around for another bride and settled on a sister of William Herbert earl of Huntingdon. Tudor knew the family, having been a ward of

---

[108] *Harl. 433* III p. 190.
[109] The marriage was dissolved in 1486 to allow Cecily's marriage to Henry VII's half-uncle, John lord Welles: Helmholz 1974, p. 160 (n. 89); Chrimes 1972, p. 36n.
[110] Another was Joanna of Portugal: Williams 1983 summarizes Portuguese references to the negotiations.

William Herbert I in the 1460s, and such a match would have offered useful political connections. Most obviously it might have given Tudor the backing of the Herberts themselves, although it was to be Huntingdon's brother Walter who was to be approached rather than the earl himself – either because Huntingdon, as Richard's son-in-law, was thought to be incorruptible, or because Walter was considered the effective head of the connection. The marriage would also have linked Tudor with the earl of Northumberland and John lord Grey of Powys, who had married Herbert sisters, and both men are known to have been approached by Tudor.[111] In spite of these contacts, a Herbert marriage would have been very much second best, not only. because it lacked the dynastic appeal of the other, but because it would have identified Tudor with the interests of a narrow section of the nobility.

The scurry to find a replacement bride for Henry proved premature. Richard did not marry Elizabeth. It is impossible to be sure how seriously the match had been intended. The personal predilections of the couple are unknown, although Elizabeth at least has been credited with wanting the marriage.[112] On a political level the marriage would have offered few real advantages apart from the blow to Tudor, and any assessment of how strongly Richard pursued the idea thus depends largely on how far the desire to undermine his rival is thought to dominate his policies.[113] It does seem clear that the possibility was mooted, at least, and that it ran into outright opposition from Richard's advisors. According to the Crowland chronicler, whose facts need not be doubted even if his glosses are suspect, the strongest opposition came from Catesby and Ratcliffe, who told the king to his face that if he persisted in his plan his northern followers would rebel against him. The fact that Richard did indeed back down, to the extent of denying that he had ever entertained the idea, is proof enough that the threat was taken seriously.

The council apparently claimed that they were afraid of the damaging effect which the marriage would have on the king's public image, but the chronicler is clear that the real motive of the

[111] Vergil p. 559; Chrimes 1972, pp. 16–17, 38–9; Horrox 1983.

[112] Buck, *Richard the Third* pp. 190–1. Compare the violent refutation in Vergil's manuscript history: Vergil (ed. Hay), *Anglica Historia* pp. 2–3 (toned down in Vergil p. 565). The contrast is noted by Hanham 1975, p. 19 (n. 4).

[113] *Crowland* pp. 174–5 takes this view: '[Richard] saw no other way of confirming his crown and dispelling the hopes of his rival.'

plan's opponents was fear of a Woodville revival.[114] He interprets this as anxiety among the circle closest to the king lest the Woodvilles should seek revenge for the deaths of Rivers and Grey; but a more plausible, and more broadly-based, motive is an unwillingness to see the forfeitures of the Woodvilles and their allies reversed. Richard's associates had tasted exceptional wealth and influence as a result of the king's alienation from much of his brother's establishment. They could not be expected to welcome an end to that state of affairs, and their opposition to the marriage in effect offered Richard a choice between the continuing loyalty of his existing supporters and possible new alliances with former opponents won over by the match. Put like that it was no choice, and it is hardly surprising that Richard, whatever the strength of his own commitment to the marriage, yielded. His public re-nunciation, made before 'the substance of all our household', was an implicit assurance that he still regarded the interests of his servants as paramount.[115]

By spring 1485, therefore, the king's power base was not only narrow but self-limiting. His reliance on his own connection in the aftermath of the 1483 rebellion had created a group of powerful servants with a vested interest in the continuation of the status quo. In the short term the king's own inclinations were pushing him in the same direction. The obvious insecurity of his regime made him ever less willing to gamble on the loyalty of men outside his immediate circle. But this was not a policy which could be maintained indefinitely. Quite apart from its unpopu-larity beyond the charmed circle, it was ultimately counter-productive. The overhaul of the power structure at Calais left Tyrell over-extended and the ubiquitous Brackenbury may also have been feeling the pressure. As early as July 1484 he had been delegating responsibilities because of 'other arduous business touching the king's right'.[116] Sooner or later the king would have to extend his power base, and Richard's readiness to pardon rebels and make overtures to the Woodvilles shows that he knew it. But if he was to widen his support significantly he needed to be secure on the throne. Only then would it be worthwhile for the disaffected to make a real commitment to his regime, and only

---

[114] *Ibid.* pp. 174–7.
[115] Halliwell, *Letters* I p. 159.
[116] PRO, KB 9/951/28.

then would Richard have the political elbow-room to risk experimenting with loyalties.

In the long term, time was probably on Richard's side. In 1485 Tudor was winning support at the expense of the king, but much of Henry's credibility derived from French backing. If French policy changed, or even if there were undue delays before Henry invaded, that momentum would have been lost.[117] That, however, was not much comfort to Richard III in the immediate circumstances. The seepage of loyalty continued, with men and supplies finding their way across the Channel to Tudor.[118] Within England there were more conspiracies and rumours of conspiracies. One, involving two fellows of Peterhouse (Cambridge), may have originated with Morton.[119] Another apparently involved a group of Sussex gentry, including Thomas and Roger Fiennes and John Devenish, and may have centred on Winchelsea.[120] In April Edward Gower was ordered to seize the land of the 'king's rebel' John Peke.[121] Richard did what he could to contain this growing resistance. His orders against seditious speech were widely publicized.[122] He also seems to have engaged in counter-espionage, although it is impossible to gauge its success.[123] What he wanted above all, however, was a decisive victory against Tudor. Since there was no obvious alternative claimant, Tudor's removal would give Richard the security he needed to establish his regime on a sounder basis.[124] A military victory would also validate Richard's title to the throne, a spiritual endorsement which he badly needed.[125]

Not all the king's problems were susceptible of a military solution. One such was the question of the Yorkist succession. Richard's only legitimate son Edward had died in April 1484. The child's death was not only a personal blow to the king but left him

---

[117] Ross 1981, pp. 200–1; Chrimes 1972, pp. 36–7.

[118] Condon 1986, pp. 210–11; PRO, E 404/79/1/102 (a reference I owe to the kindness of Miss Condon).

[119] Davies 1987, pp. 9–10.

[120] PRO, C 244/136/27, 28, 30; E 405/74; *CCR 1476–85* no. 1456.

[121] *Harl. 433* II p. 215. Peke had been bound to appear before the royal council in Oct. 1483: PRO, C 244/134/119.

[122] Halliwell, *Letters* I pp. 158–60 (copy to York); Southampton RO, SC 2/9/1/20. An earlier letter had gone to Windsor: BL, Add. ms 12520 pp. 1–2.

[123] Davies 1987, p. 10.

[124] *Crowland* p. 176. When he heard of Tudor's landing the king rejoiced; after his victory he would 'comfort his subjects with the blessings of unchallenged peace' (my translation).

[125] Armstrong 1948a, p. 69.

dynastically vulnerable.[126] It was this which gave a veneer of credibility to rumours that Richard had murdered his wife in order to marry again, and which also explains why, after Anne's death, the king so rapidly opened negotiations for a second marriage. But at best Richard would not have an adult heir of his body for approaching twenty years and he may have thought it advisable to indicate an heir presumptive. The only source for this is the Warwickshire antiquary John Rous. He claimed that Clarence's son, Edward earl of Warwick, was given precedence at court after the prince's death, but that Richard then had second thoughts and looked instead to another nephew, John de la Pole earl of Lincoln, the son of the king's sister Elizabeth.[127] The account is plausible, as long as it is interpreted as implying informal recognition rather than a formal designation as heir. Warwick was the obvious heir − *too* obvious indeed. He was barred from the throne by his father's attainder, but that was a flimsy barrier and without it his title was better than Richard's own.[128] If Richard were prepared to acknowledge Warwick as heir there was no logical reason why the boy should not already be king. To set against this, Warwick was a minor in the royal household and hence an unlikely figurehead for opposition. Richard's control of the person of the earl may explain why Warwick's title was never canvassed by the rebels.[129] On balance, however, Lincoln was undoubtedly the safer candidate from Richard's point of view, simply because his title was indisputably weaker than the king's. His proximity to the throne was acknowledged by his appointment as lieutenant of Ireland and head of the council in the north.[130]

Richard III's other major problem was financial. Most early writers on the reign recognized this, although their treatment of the subject is generally unsympathetic. The assumption is that Richard caused his own problems by squandering the wealth at his disposal. In the view of the Crowland chronicler, Edward IV had amassed a great treasure which Richard spent on staging an elaborate celebration of his accession (tantamount to a second

---

[126] *Crowland* pp. 170–1.
[127] Rous, *Hist. Regum Angliae* pp. 217–18.
[128] Levine 1959, p. 392n. Warwick's possible Lancastrian claim (his father had been recognized as heir to Lancaster in 1471) is discussed by Levine 1973, pp. 33–4.
[129] Warwick's claims shot to prominence after Bosworth: Davies 1987, p. 27; Bennett 1985, p. 130; Goodman and MacKay 1973, p. 93.
[130] *CPR 1476–85* p. 477; *Harl. 433* III p. 114.

coronation) in the north, so that by the time he returned to London in November none of the money was left.[131] Elements in this picture are accurate as far as they go; Richard's triumphal visit to York clearly was a lavish occasion, for instance.[132] But the contrast between Edward's providence and Richard's prodigality is unjust. Edward IV had indeed been a skilful financial manager, restoring the crown to solvency after the disastrous years of Henry VI. But his gains had been eroded by the military activity of the last years of his reign, and by the time Richard took the throne there were no cash reserves.[133] Richard thus had to meet the cost of his coronation and a politically crucial progress out of regular income alone, which was itself running at a lower level than in his brother's reign. Three days after the investiture of the prince of Wales at York, Richard borrowed £100 in ready money from the abbot of Furness and smaller loans from royal associates followed.[134] News of Buckingham's rebellion thus found the king badly placed to meet extraordinary expenditure. Some money was gathered in. On 16 October the sheriff of Lincoln paid 50m, to be allowed against his account, for the great costs which the king would have to bear.[135] In the short term, however, most of the costs of the expedition were probably met by the participants. In the south west Thomas Grayson found 100m to equip an Exmouth ship sent against the rebels and £40 to reward the men of war detailed to capture Tudor. William Gaske of Saltash paid £86 of his own money 'for the resistance of our rebels and traitors'.[136] Richard ordered Grayson and Gaske to be reimbursed, but most men were probably repaid, if at all, in less direct ways. On 10 December Sir William Parker was granted Pentlow Hall (Suff.) for his service 'in especial in this our journey for repressing of our enemies and rebels at his proper costs and charge'.[137]

When Richard returned to London towards the end of November he almost immediately approached leading citizens for

[131] *Crowland* pp. 160–3, 168–9.
[132] *Harl. 433* II p. 42; Sutton and Hammond, *Coronation* pp. 80–1, 173–4, 178–9.
[133] For the financial position see above, pp. 108–9. There is a question mark over the fate of Edward's plate and jewels, sequestrated by the archbishop of Canterbury: *Reg. Thome Bourgchier* pp. 52, 54. *Crowland* pp. 160–3 implies that Richard seized them, which is possible.
[134] *Harl. 433* II pp. 13, 25–6, 27.
[135] PRO, E 404/78/2/4.
[136] PRO, E 404/78/3/25; PSO 1/57/2903.
[137] PRO, PSO 1/57/2902; *Harl. 433* I p. 101.

financial help.[138] He then set about restoring his regular income to the levels which had been reached under his brother. One step towards this was achieved when parliament granted him tonnage and poundage for life.[139] Richard also revived the chamber's financial role, which had been shaken by the death of Edward IV and the uncertainties of Richard's own early months. In January 1484 a number of leading royal receivers were ordered to pay their issues to the king, in other words into the chamber.[140] At around the same time the internal organization of the chamber was overhauled. Edward's treasurer of the chamber, Sir Thomas Vaughan, had been one of the victims of Richard's coup and was not immediately replaced. In the early months of his reign Richard may, in effect, have acted as his own treasurer, with most of the recorded payments made directly to him. From late December, however, as chamber activity picked up again, payments began to be made regularly to master Edmund Chaderton, one of the king's chaplains.[141] Chaderton had also been one of Edward IV's chaplains and had moved easily across into Richard's service, perhaps commended by his Bothe and Neville connections.[142] He was granted a benefice within Richard's own manor of Calverton in July, only the third presentation of the reign.[143] On 22 November he was made clerk of the hanaper by word of mouth and on 26 April was formally appointed treasurer and receiver of the king's chamber, a post he was to hold for the rest of the reign.[144] Unlike Vaughan, who had had interests away from the king and must often have acted by deputy, Chaderton's service was probably full-time.

With the chamber running smoothly, the king turned his attention to increasing its income. A surviving run of signet memoranda dating from October 1484 preserves two detailed attempts to tighten up financial administration, particularly as it related to the crown lands.[145] The more wide-ranging is headed,

---

[138] *Great Chron.* pp. 235–6; *Harl. 433* II pp. 66–7.

[139] *Rot. Parl.* VI pp. 238–40.

[140] *Harl. 433* II pp. 70–1.

[141] *Ibid. passim* (see index under chamber). For Chaderton, see also n. 138 above.

[142] PRO, E 405/68 m. 1 dorse; *CCR 1468–76* no. 1442; *Test. Ebor.* IV pp. 67–8; Emden 1957–9, I pp. 382–3.

[143] *CPR 1476–85* p. 362. The two earlier presentations were of William Baynton and Thomas Barowe, pp. 361, 366.

[144] *Ibid.* pp. 375, 449. Unusually, Chaderton remembered Richard in his will, if, as seems likely, *Ricardus secundus* is an error for *tertius*: PRO, Prob 11/11 fo. 305.

[145] *Harl. 433* III pp. 116–20; Wolffe 1971, pp. 186–8.

'A remembrance made as well for hasty levy of the king's revenues growing of all his possessions and hereditaments as for the profitable estate and governance of the same possessions.' It begins with measures to improve the exchequer's debt collection and make its records more readily accessible to the crown. It then considers the land revenues handled by the chamber and makes various suggestions for improving their yield, including the appointment of stewards with legal training, 'for many causes concerning the king's profit and the weal of his tenants'. It also urged that wardships and temporalities should be kept in the king's hands rather than farmed – a policy which Richard adopted with the estates of the three attainted bishops. Again, an important secondary aim was to keep the king well informed. Auditors and receivers were to make a yearly report on the condition of the lordships in their charge, 'by the which the king's grace should know all the lordships that pertaineth to his crown'.

The king's personal involvement is demonstrated in the other document, a list of instructions to the steward of Tutbury, Sir Marmaduke Constable, which translates the general precepts of the *Remembrance* into a guide for local action. Royal direction here extended into the minutiae of estate management. For example, Constable was to see that only suitable wood was felled for fencing. The same attention to detail can be seen elsewhere. In November 1484 William Catesby was authorized to sell wood in a particular coppice to raise money for fencing More End park. The coppice was to be opened for the purpose, but then fenced again to protect the new growth there.[146] The warrant exemplifies both the royal concern for the profitable exploitation of resources and the detailed local knowledge necessary to make it feasible.

In this respect, Richard was following in his brother's footsteps, and the continuity of approach can be seen most clearly in the duchy of Lancaster. Edward's duchy council kept up a steady pressure on the local officials, and some of their specific commands foreshadow the general principles enunciated by the *Remembrance*. In Tutbury, the council ordered a stop to the tradition of bailiffs farming their office for a lump sum. At Snaith the deputy steward was to be a 'sad, learned man', to the benefit of the tenants and the crown. Such measures presupposed local knowledge and the council undertook two major progresses, one

---

[146] *Harl. 433* II p. 175.

in Yorkshire and one in the north west, in order to investigate the estates for themselves.[147] The minutes of Richard's duchy council, although less full, reveal the same preoccupations. In spring 1484 the council turned its attention to the lordships of Bolingbroke and Pontefract and drew up lists of ideas for improving their yield. It noted, for instance, that the receiver of Bolingbroke should be asked about the level of profit from the court held in Lincoln castle, 'for the profits thereof be so little considering so many suitors that owe suit to the said court'.[148]

The crown estate to which Richard III devoted so much thought was a very large one. Excluding forfeitures and other temporary acquisitions, it may have yielded a disposable income of the order of £22,000 − £25,000 p.a.[149] Richard held more land than his brother. His own accession had brought a moiety of the Warwick inheritance to the crown. He also repossessed the southern duchy lands with which Edward had endowed his queen, and did not make any specific provision for his own wife. These gains more than covered the permanent alienations which Richard made from the crown lands as they had stood at his brother's death. He granted away much of the land in the south west which had been held by Clarence and which had come back to the crown on the duke's attainder. He also acknowledged the claims of the heirs general to the Mowbray inheritance with which Edward had endowed his second son, although in the event this proved only a partial loss to the crown. John Howard, duke of Norfolk, received his share of the available inheritance, including the Mowbrays' principal residence of Framlingham. William Berkeley, who had waived his claims to a share in Edward's reign, confirmed his surrender. In March 1484 he bound himself to make an estate of the Mowbray land to the king when requested. He also undertook to grant Richard the reversion of those Mowbray lands in Yorkshire which his wife Joan had been granted for life by Katherine Neville, one of the two surviving Mowbray dowagers. Berkeley duly made the grant to the crown in October and although the Yorkshire lands are then described as being in reversion, it is clear from other evidence that Richard

---

[147] PRO, DL 5/1 fos. 24, 106v. The Yorkshire progress is fos. 89vff; the Lancashire progress (fos. 136ff) has been printed: Myers, 'Official progress'.
[148] PRO, DL 5/2 fo. 4.
[149] Wolffe 1971, pp. 188–91. The partial list of Edward's landed revenues in Horrox, 'Financial memoranda' pp. 221–2, gives a *clear* income of around £10,732.

had bought out the countess' interest with an annuity of £134 to her husband during her lifetime. The reversionary lands were indeed assigned to the expenses of Richard's northern household before the date of the formal agreement with Berkeley.[150] The king thus kept a significant part of the land enjoyed by Edward IV. He seems also to have secured the land held by the senior dowager, Katherine Neville, at her death in 1483.[151] Berkeley's only gains were the title of earl and an annuity of 400m during the lifetime of the remaining dowager – the payment of which he found difficulty in securing.[152] He was rescued from the bargain by Richard's death without heirs of his body at Bosworth, by which, under the terms of their agreement, the land reverted to Berkeley.

Richard's land holdings were inflated by massive forfeitures. Much, perhaps most, of the confiscated land was granted away almost at once, but Richard, unlike his predecessors, usually reserved an annual rent from the land and took steps to ensure that it was paid, even by his closest allies.[153] The going rate was one shilling in the mark, which yielded around £700 p.a., excluding grants in reversion from which the rent had not yet materialized. The value of the land which remained in the king's hands is unknown. The major acquisition to do so was the Stafford inheritance. Richard granted away some of the land, notably the lordship of Holderness, and assigned part of the remainder to the settlement of the duke's debts, but the core of the estate remained with the crown and may have yielded around £1,000 p.a.[154] The lesser properties which the king kept in his own hands cannot be valued but perhaps brought in as much again. In the west country the forfeited estates were put into the receivership of John Hayes and were expected to yield at least £300 p.a., which was assigned to the royal household.[155] In addition to this recurrent income, the forfeitures produced an enormous, once-for-all windfall of confiscated goods which it is

[150] *Harl. 433* III pp. 115–16, 120–1; *CPR 1476–85* p. 487; *CCR 1476–85* nos. 1225, 1353; Crawford 1985, pp. 83–5. I am also grateful to the late Professor Ross for discussing the subject with me.

[151] *Harl. 433* II pp. 23, 67–8.

[152] *Ibid.* I p. 151; PRO, E 404/78/3/68.

[153] PRO, SC 11/827; E 401/954; E 402/56. Coward 1983, p. 18 (n. 46) observes that Richard's policy anticipated the practice of Henry VIII.

[154] Rawcliffe 1978, pp. 125–9. Thornbury alone was thought to yield at least £200 p.a.: *Harl. 433* III p. 158.

[155] *Harl. 433* III p. 158.

now impossible to value. In July 1484 the king's attention was drawn to possessions of the duke of Buckingham valued at 1,000m in the custody of a London tailor, including two great carpets (each £40), three sets of bed hangings (£120) and four pieces of arras (£40).[156] Edward Redmane's seizure of the Edgecombe manor of Cotehele and its contents netted plate and household goods valued at around £325, as well as stock and produce.[157] The parcels of plate which Richard received from Henry Horne may also be part of the spoils, the price perhaps which Gervase Horne paid for his freedom after involvement in the rebellion. They consisted of a silver gilt altar set: a chalice, a pax, two candlesticks, a holy water vessel and a crucifix with figures of Mary and John at its foot.[158] Much of the haul was probably given away by the king, or never came into his hands at all. Margaret Beaufort, for instance, complained in the next reign of the loss of silver and gilt cups which came into Brackenbury's possession.[159] But even so the yield must have been spectacular.

In spite of these gains Richard continued to face financial difficulties and early in 1485 resorted to a nationwide attempt to raise loans.[160] The move was bound to be unpopular, and the fact that Richard made it at all (let alone in a period when he badly needed support) suggests that he was in serious trouble. Edward IV's financial demands in the last months of his reign had been resented, and in the parliament of 1484 Richard had gone out of his way to disassociate himself from them. He had avoided asking for any direct taxation and had eschewed any future resort to benevolences, the forced gifts which had been Edward's most unpopular financial expedient.[161] As has frequently been pointed out, Richard was within his rights in asking for loans. They carried a promise of repayment, unlike benevolences, and were justified by the king's plea of necessity.[162] But it was tactless, to say the least, for Richard to approach his subjects for money barely a year after his repudiation of his brother's demands. There may

---

[156] PRO, E 207/21/18/7.
[157] PRO, KB 9/369/22.
[158] *Harl. 433* I p. 1, II p. 74.
[159] Campbell, *Materials* I p. 233.
[160] All the material relating to the loans, unless otherwise stated, is from *Harl. 433* III pp. 128–33. For Richard's earlier resort to loans see above, pp. 300–1; Horrox 1984, pp. 327–8; Sutton 1985, pp. 292–3.
[161] Ross 1974, p. 386; Ross 1981, pp. 178, 188–9; Sutton 1985, p. 292.
[162] The definitive discussion of the distinction is Harriss 1963.

also have been doubts about Richard's ability to repay the loans, and, had he defaulted, the loans would indeed have been, as the Crowland chronicler insisted, benevolences by any other name.[163]

The loan was organized with great care. Pairs of royal servants were assigned a group of counties and issued with individual letters for the loans required. Most of the letters detailed only the sum sought, not the recipient, and it was left to the commissioners to place these at their discretion. Some were directed to named individuals. Thus Richard Croft and Thomas Fowler, active in Oxfordshire, Berkshire and Buckinghamshire, were given thirteen blanks, for various sums, and five already addressed. The commissioners were also supplied with a form of words with which to exhort potential lenders. They were to point out that the money was needed for the defence of the realm, an aim which 'every true Englishman' ought to support. Rather like modern mail-order companies, the commissioners were instructed to flatter those they approached by assuring them that the king 'writeth to you before other, for the great love, confidence and substance that his grace hath and knoweth in you'.

The first batch of letters was issued on 21 February and had a face value of over £9,000. Some are unvalued, including those to London, and the target was perhaps £10,000. More letters were issued in the course of the following month. On 9 March the king's remembrancer John Fitzherbert was made responsible for approaching bishops and religious houses for a total of £4,390. Additional letters sent to regional collectors represent a further £15,000. How much of this was actually raised is unknown. Only a small proportion can be traced in the exchequer records, although more may have escaped record by being paid directly into the chamber. The Easter receipt roll includes loans of £4,400, of which perhaps half was the result of the commissioners' efforts.[164] Of the loans which were made in response to the king's letters the sum paid was, in almost every case which can be checked, smaller than the amount requested. Roger Harecourt, asked for £200, paid 200m, while Roger Townsend, Edmund Bedingfield and William Calthorpe, approached for £100, each

[163] *Crowland* pp. 172–5. The first instalment of repayment was promised at Martinmas (11 Nov.) and with the prospect of Tudor's invasion in the summer it is difficult to see how repayment could have been made.

[164] PRO, E 401/952; Steel 1954, p. 320. The remaining loans were from the usual mixture of customs officials, foreign merchants and the like.

lent 100m. This, however, was usual, and does not in itself imply
that Richard was meeting undue resistance.[165] More worrying
were the numbers who apparently lent nothing. Even allowing
for the possibility that some had paid into the chamber, the return
was only a fraction of the anticipated yield. The implication
appears to be that Richard's reign had lost credibility and that
men were avoiding payment either because they did not expect to
be repaid or because they thought that they could get away with
not paying. The latter attitude may well have been encouraged by
the status of Richard's commissioners. All were reliable royal
servants with connections in the counties concerned, but they
were not leading local figures. Yorkshire, Nottinghamshire and
Derbyshire were the responsibility of Stephen Hatfield of Skef-
fling in Holderness and Edmund Talbot of East Retford.[166]
Worcestershire, Warwickshire and Leicestershire were committed to the serjeant at arms Thomas Otter, a former Neville servant
based at Berkeswell (War.), and to Walter Grant, a yeoman of the
queen's chamber who had been given the custody of Maxstoke
castle after its forfeiture by Buckingham.[167] Richard had servants
of higher standing in most of the areas concerned, so his selection
of men such as Grant was presumably deliberate. Perhaps he
thought that they would be more efficient loan collectors than
leading members of the local gentry, who were more likely to be
the friends and kinsmen of the men approached for money. If so,
results do not seem to have borne out the theory, in spite of the
Crowland chronicler's attack on 'selected men ... who extorted
great sums of money from the coffers of persons of almost every
rank'.[168]

The chronicler also seems to imply that the king was experimenting with other methods of raising money, although these are
left unspecified for fear of putting ideas into other heads. He
probably had in mind Richard's efforts to tighten up the exploitation of his feudal rights, a policy which the king was attempting to
formalize at just this time. In March 1485 the king appointed
commissioners to enquire into concealed royal rights in Cornwall
and Devon, and a revised commission was issued for the two

[165] Harriss 1963, p. 15.
[166] Horrox 1986b, pp. 87, 94.
[167] Otter: *CPR* 1476–85 p. 369; *Cat. Anc. Deeds* VI no. C4115. Grant: *CPR* 1476–85 p. 417.
[168] *Crowland* pp. 172–3.

counties jointly in May.[169] The commissioners, who were mainly local men of middling status, were to enquire into all lordships, manors, lands, advowsons, wards, marriages, reliefs, escheats, escapes of felons and all alienations of land without licence. Such a policy was the logical concomitant of the Yorkists' concern to increase their land revenue, and Edward IV had already made a start, although, since the proceeds went into the chamber, his success cannot be assessed.[170] The gains could clearly be considerable. In Richard's reign Sir William Say was fined £1,000 for not preventing the marriage of Isabel Cheyne before the chancellor had given licence.[171] The king's eagerness to extend the policy is therefore explicable on financial grounds alone. But, as Tudor developments were to demonstrate, an investigation into concealed royal rights offered other advantages. It enlarged the field within which royal patronage could operate. It also gave scope for putting pressure on individuals whom the king wished to punish or whose power he wished to limit, and the fact that Richard began his enquiries in the disaffected south west suggests that he was alert to this possibility.

Richard's financial difficulties arose largely from his military commitments. From his brother he inherited not only an empty treasury but the policies which had emptied it: a war with Scotland and the makings of a war with France. Under other conditions Richard would probably have pursued both with enthusiasm. He had apparently not supported his brother's treaty with France in 1475, and the campaign against Scotland was clearly a cause to which he felt considerable personal commitment.[172] Financial exigency, however, demanded a more conciliatory approach and Richard gradually (and, in the case of Scotland, grudgingly) drew back from Edward's aggressive position. His withdrawal was made the more urgent by the growing disaffection within England itself, which imposed a whole new series of military demands. Most obviously, it committed the king

---

[169] *CPR* 1476–85 pp. 543, 546. The commissions' significance was noted by Cam 1963, p. 215. For Henry VII's development of the policy see Chrimes 1972, pp. 208–12.

[170] *Crowland* pp. 138–9; Horrox, 'Financial memoranda' p. 230. Among the few surviving examples is a fine of double the value of his marriage imposed by the duchy council on Thomas Boteler in 1482: PRO, DL 5/1 fo. 56.

[171] PRO, E 401/951. The money was transferred to the chamber by Chaderton.

[172] Ross 1981, pp. 34–5, 193–4; Macdougall 1986, p. 166; Tudor-Craig 1973, pp. 67, 71. Compare also Richard's interest in the association of St Mary's chapel in All Hallows, Barking, with the Scottish victories of Edward I: Horrox 1982, p. 38.

to defensive measures at home, but it also had consequences in the field of foreign policy. Richard's efforts to extract Tudor from Brittany were backed up by an attack on Breton shipping, and in the first half of 1484 he was maintaining fleets in both the Channel and the North Sea. Another facet of the same policy was the king's undertaking to provide Brittany with 1,000 archers, the unstated *quid pro quo* being the surrender of Tudor. The archers were duly mustered, but Tudor escaped and the money was wasted.

The episode is symptomatic of the way in which the threat from Tudor placed Richard under the double disadvantage of carrying a heavy financial burden and having nothing to show for it. The collapse of the 1483 rebellion meant that Richard was unable to vindicate himself with a military victory but was instead committed to continuing measures against men whose opposition generally melted away before it could be tackled. From the point of view of the king's public image, of which Richard showed himself extremely conscious, activity directed against internal opponents was in any case always unsatisfactory, arousing none of the popular enthusiasm which could be generated by a campaign against another state. Richard's own propaganda recognizes as much in its emphasis on the foreign backing accorded to Tudor and in its consequent appeal to xenophobia.[173] What the king wanted, and was never able to achieve, was to unite the country behind him in opposition to an external threat. In August 1484, when a French attack on Calais was rumoured, he ordered Arundel to prepare the inhabitants of the Cinque Ports for resistance:

letting them wit that the king is that prince which for the defence of this realm and all the possessions of the crown of England is disposed to employ his own royal person as far as ever any king hath done in years past to the encouraging of his faithful subjects and confusion of all his enemies.[174]

Richard's military involvement, even without a full-scale foreign campaign, is enough to explain his lack of money. No medieval king could hope to meet major defence costs out of his regular income. But none of the reign's early chroniclers was

---

[173] *Harl. 433* II p. 230, III pp. 124–5. For Richard's self-image see further below, pp. 330–1.
[174] PRO, C 81/1531/3. Richard's view of foreign war as a domestic glue is shared by Richmond 1986, pp. 186–90.

prepared to leave the story there. As far as they were concerned, the king's problems were rooted in his over-lavish generosity. Even the Crowland chronicler, who shows the greatest awareness of the military pressures on the king, sets the tone for his discussion of the royal finances with an acerbic account of the prodigality of Richard's visit to York in autumn 1483. His description strikes a note echoed by all the later Tudor writers: '[the king] arranged splendid and highly expensive feasts and entertainments to attract to himself the affection of many people'.[175] Vergil ascribed the king's poverty by the time parliament met to the lavish rewards he had given 'to clear himself and gain the thanks of the commons'.[176] The suggestion reached its apogee with More, who, in a famous passage, gave it a further twist by characterizing Richard's patronage as not only financially misjudged but politically inept as well: 'Free was he called of dispense and somewhat above his power liberal, with large gifts he got him unsteadfast friendship, for which he was fain to pillage and spoil in other places and got him steadfast hatred.'[177]

Most subsequent writers have echoed this judgement. There is no doubt that Richard was extremely generous with his grants. The forfeitures of his reign gave him the opportunity of being open-handed at no apparent cost to the crown; but the sheer volume of forfeitures also had the less desirable effect of pushing up the level of other grants by raising the expectations of potential recipients. This inflationary effect can be seen particularly clearly in the case of land grants. They had always been the rarest form of royal patronage, and in Edward IV's later years had been largely confined to the royal family. Under Richard III land became a regular reward for members of the nobility and the upper levels of the household, with well over 150 men receiving land grants in the course of the reign. The value of individual grants was also unusually high. About seventy men were given grants worth more than £50, and half of them received land valued at £100 or more. In most cases the land in question had been forfeited, but Richard's generosity spilled over into the crown lands. Ratcliffe's 1,000m worth was part of the earldom of Devon. The duchy of Exeter, which Edward had used to endow his stepsons and their families, was now parcelled out among Richard's servants. The

---

[175] *Crowland* pp. 160–1.
[176] Vergil p. 554.
[177] More, *Richard III* p. 8.

high average value of these grants also set the pace in other types of patronage. Some of Richard's servants who did not move south were consoled with large annuities from the northern crown lands. John Conyers was given an annuity of 200m and Thomas Gower a little under £100.[178] Both were important royal servants, central figures in the Middleham and Sheriff Hutton connections respectively, but it is difficult to believe that they would have been feed at this level had not their colleagues been receiving forfeited land worth £100 or more.

Annuities in general provide the best index of royal generosity. Unless a king was prepared to make major inroads into his demesne, which Richard on the whole was not, his land grants were largely dictated by the availability of forfeitures and escheats. Office also provided relatively little scope for manoeuvre, since medieval kings had not acquired the habit of multiplying office to meet demand and were not fond of granting reversions. Most estates (the main source of office) thus had a more or less fixed complement of officials. Annuities by comparison were almost infinitely flexible. They could be granted in any number up to, and in some cases beyond, the limit of the revenue concerned. They could also be of any value, allowing them to be tailored to the king's needs, although there are signs that some recipients saw them as transferable units of patronage.[179] They were usually regarded as the least attractive form of royal grant, offering no scope for extra profit or the exercise of power, and were regularly used as a stopgap until land or office became available. But, as this implies, they were certainly better than nothing, and for both king and recipient they offered a relatively easy form of reward.

In Richard's reign the burden of annuities increased on virtually every estate for which figures survive. It is most marked in the northern duchy of Lancaster lordships, which provided much of the reward for those of Richard's ducal connection who remained based in the north. Excluding fees for office, the honour of Pontefract carried annuities worth £122 13s 4d at Edward IV's death. Richard allowed £36 13s 4d of this to lapse, but granted an additional £107 10s 5d in the course of his reign. In the Lincolnshire honour of Bolingbroke the increase was £72 13s 4d,

[178] *CPR* 1476–85 pp. 424, 482; *Harl. 433* I p. 253.
[179] e.g. Walter Hungerford's petition for the annuity forfeited by Edmund Haute: *Harl. 433* I p. 48.

almost doubling the £83 6s 8d granted by Edward IV.[180] The king's personal estates were treated in the same way, and may have been charged with fees beyond the limit of their revenues, something which also seems to have been the case in the duchy lands.[181] On the whole these increases represent more, as well as larger, annuities. From Bolingbroke, Richard was rewarding three new annuitants, including the recorder of London, Thomas Fitzwilliam of Mablethorpe, and paying an additional annuity to the Lincolnshire knight of the body Thomas Burgh. But Richard did also grant a few very large annuities, which might take up a disproportionate share of a particular source of revenue. Thomas Howard earl of Surrey was given £1,100 during the lifetime of his father, the duke of Norfolk. The grant, in lieu of landed endowment, was charged upon the duchy of Cornwall and probably absorbed around half the clear revenue of the duchy as it had stood at Edward's death.[182]

The chroniclers' assumption that Richard's generosity was the consequence of his insecurity as king was to some extent true. This is not to say that he used his grants to buy support in the literal sense of a modern employer headhunting with a cheque book, but like any of his contemporaries he would have taken it for granted that generosity to existing servants encouraged others. Some of his grants also had the practical aim of creating a new power base for their recipients, a policy which derived directly from the king's weakness in the south. In a wider sense, too, Richard's generosity was a reflex of his own acute sense of the uncertainties of his position: the lavish grants were prompted by gratitude for the loyalty of his associates as much of his anticipated support crumbled around him. The fulsome thanks for services rendered which are a feature of some of Richard's grants may owe more to the composer of the petition than to the king, but were presumably considered to strike the right note.

It is unlikely, however, that the king's open-handedness derived solely from the situation in which he found himself after autumn 1483. Even before his reign began, Richard revealed a fondness for the grand gesture, regardless of consequences. Its earliest manifes-

[180] PRO, DL 29/526/8390–2, 29/263/4125–6.
[181] Pollard 1986, p. 113. In the duchy lands not all the grants recorded in PRO, DL 42/20 appear in the receivers' accounts.
[182] *Harl. 433* 1 p. 213 (revising the earlier grant on p. 206); *CPR*1476–85 p. 479. The clear yield of *all* the estates of the prince of Wales in 1483 was of the order of £5,000: Horrox, 'Financial memoranda' p. 221.

tation was his grant of viceregal power in Wales to Buckingham, followed by the promise of the Bohun inheritance. The grant to Ratcliffe, although modest by comparison, can be regarded in the same light. All three can be interpreted as a reward for past support, but the grants go far beyond any rational assessment of the value of that support. A more intriguing example, for which there was still less justification, was Richard's promise of Southwark to the city of London.[183] The offer was made at a royal banquet on Twelfth Night 1484 and was noted in the city's *Journal* a week later. Richard apparently offered not only to bring Southwark within the liberty of the city, but to give £10,000 towards walling the new acquisition. London was important to the king as a money market and Richard was doubtless anxious to preserve the close relationship which his brother had built up with the city. But although such considerations provide a context for the king's offer, they do not really explain it. The gift was almost certainly beyond Richard's power to make. Southwark was a mass of conflicting jurisdictions and it is doubtful whether authority there could have been transferred to the city by royal *fiat* alone. In the short term, finding a spare £10,000 was also beyond the king's reach, although the grant could have been spread over a period of years. It is not surprising that the king thought better of the offer, and there is no echo of the scheme in any royal sources. The city, too, probably realized that the grant lay outside the realms of possibility and there is no evidence that they tried to take the matter further.[184] It was in the nature of personal monarchy for kings to make the occasional rash promise from which they then needed to retreat, and the elaborate mechanism for securing a formal grant was in part designed to cope with such eventualities. But the offer to London does have affinities with grants which were made. Richard's remission of York's fee farm, although feasible in itself, was evidently promised before the practical consequences had been thought through.[185] Richard clearly liked to be seen to be generous, and this presumably shaped his routine patronage as well as producing the occasional exceptional gift.

[183] Sutton 1985.
[184] Given the context in which the grant was made, it is tempting to believe that the king was drunk at the time and that both sides knew it.
[185] Attreed 1981, pp. 30–6. Compare also Richard's grandiose plans for a chantry of 100 priests in York minster: Palliser 1986, p. 60.

Generosity, largesse, was part of the chivalric ideal to which Richard subscribed.[186] But largesse was not only the opposite of avarice, it was also the denial of prodigality. The popular mirror for princes, the *Secretum Secretorum*, urged kings to give 'after thy power, and that with measure', since a king who gave more than his kingdom could afford would destroy himself:

For the cause of the destruction of realms is superfluity of expenses above the revenues and rents of cities. And so failing the king's expenses, he stretcheth his hands in the goods and rents of his subjects. And they cry unto the most highest and glorious God. And He suffreth emissions of bad angels to scourge them, so that the people riseth against their governors.[187]

This traditional view of the prodigal ruler clearly influenced More's criticism. But it is far from obvious whether Richard was indeed spending more than he could afford on his grants. All royal grants involved enriching the recipient at the expense of the crown. A land grant diminished the royal demesne, an annuity reduced the king's income, offices and farms presupposed that the holder would be making some profit on the deal. Therefore the less the king gave, the more wealth would remain at his disposal. Had Richard made only half his land grants, the saving would have met the annual cost of the Calais garrison, for instance.[188] The sheer cost of patronage had always been recognized. When royal finances were causing particular anxiety, as in Henry VI's reign, restraint in the matter of patronage was urged. Conversely, critics of royal patronage on political grounds had always found an attack on its cost their readiest weapon.[189] But this simple equation of patronage with lost revenue ignores what the king stood to gain from his grants. They were, in a very immediate sense, what made effective government possible, and for medieval kings virtually any price, short of actual bankruptcy, was justified if their patronage had the desired political effect.

This attitude explains why so many late medieval suggestions

---

[186] Keen 1984, pp. 216–18; Sutton 1986a, pp. 60, 70–1.

[187] *Secretum Secretorum* I pp. 32–5 (quotation from p. 33).

[188] The land grants listed in *Harl. 433* III pp. 140–55 (not a complete list) are valued at over £12,000: Wolffe 1971, p. 192. The Calais garrison cost £630 a month after Edward IV's death, when it had been increased to counter the French threat: Horrox, 'Financial memoranda' p. 224.

[189] This tendency for patronage to be most visible at times of political conflict has led some historians to see all patronage as a squandering of resources better put to other uses, e.g. Wilkinson 1964, p. 258.

for increasing the royal revenue remained a dead letter. Sir John Fortescue addressed himself to the proper balance of income and patronage in his *Governance of England*, and the result exemplifies the problems. As a politician himself, he appreciated the necessity of kings being able to reward their supporters, and saw this as a compelling reason for the crown to amass wealth. But as soon as the increase of revenue is presented as the central royal goal it begins to limit the scope for that very generosity which the wealth was meant to facilitate. For Fortescue, the criterion for the proper distribution of office was the effective commission of its duties. It followed that a man should only be allowed to hold a single office, although Fortescue makes an exception for brothers of the king, who might be permitted two.[190] This concession, offered in all seriousness, betrays how far Fortescue has been led from practical realities by the logic of his argument. No royal duke was likely to be satisfied with two offices, and neither would lesser mortals be happy with the limit of one. Much of the attraction of royal service lay in the possibility, however remote, of major gains, and Fortescue's suggestion would have ruled that out completely.

In practice, the crown's accumulation of wealth could never be an end in itself.[191] Its value only became apparent when it was spent, just as, in a broader context, royal power could not be manifest without delegation. Some degree of compromise was always necessary, as the Yorkist kings were well aware. Their own plans for enhancing royal revenue did occasionally clash with the claims of patronage. Richard's instructions to Constable, for instance, with their insistence that unsuitable deputy parkers should be sacked and new ones found, struck at the cherished right of officials to appoint their own deputies. Generally, however, the Yorkist kings managed to strike a reasonable balance between the conflicting demands of income and patronage. Where there was an outright clash, good lordship came first, but elsewhere they pursued their financial interests aggressively. The same approach was adopted by their brother Clarence, who turned a blind eye to deer poaching by his retainers but took other offenders to court.[192]

---

[190] Fortescue, *Governance* pp. 119, 150–3.
[191] In this context it is significant that although chroniclers admire the treasures thought to have been amassed by Edward IV and Henry VII, in the next breath they accuse the kings of avarice.
[192] Hicks 1974, pp. 352–3.

The absolute cost of patronage was thus less important than its efficacy and cannot be judged in isolation from it. If Richard's land grants gave him security at home, then it was worth having to scrape together money from elsewhere to pay the Calais garrison – although, if the troops mutinied, priorities would have to be reassessed. The application of resources could not be immutable. Measuring the efficacy of royal patronage is necessarily subjective, but it can be regarded as successful if it contributed to stable and effective government; or, to put it in explicitly royalist terms, if it allowed the king to rule as he wished without alienating too much support. If it failed in these aims then any patronage, however affordable, was arguably prodigal.

On these terms Richard III's use of patronage can be judged as, at best, only a partial success. It had an immediate value, allowing him to create a body of loyal servants in areas where his authority had been challenged. But this was essentially a holding operation which needed to be supplemented by measures to win the support of the local political community, and there is little evidence that Richard's patronage was contributing to the creation of a new following. Inevitably it would take time to build bridges between the incomers and local opinion, and Richard's policy had less than two years within which to justify itself. But the king's immense resources ought at least to have let him hold his own, and this he failed to do. By the end of 1484 he was losing ground, and part of the reason must be that his patronage was proving counterproductive. The king's growing tendency to trust and reward only a limited circle of men meant that anyone outside the circle was unlikely to be persuaded that royal service was worthwhile. The fact that Richard was prepared to be extremely generous to his allies was irrelevant if access to that generosity did not seem possible.

This stands More's criticism on its head. Richard's problem was not that he wasted his resources by giving major grants to men who then proved disloyal. Although his errors in that line were spectacular they were also rare. The problem was rather that Richard's generosity to his committed supporters seemed to close the door against others instead of opening it. Of course no king could be expected to reward his admitted enemies, at least not on a regular basis; but Richard's reaction to opposition was to turn against the uncommitted as well as the outright opponents. It was an attitude which could only increase his political isolation, and although it is easy to be wise after the event, some of the patronage showered on his northern connection might more usefully have been employed elsewhere. There were plenty of men in the south prepared to acquiesce in Richard's regime, whom the king employed on commissions and the like, but most were given little reason to translate tolerance into enthusiasm.

By spring 1485 a decisive victory over Tudor offered Richard the best, if not the only, hope of extricating himself from the problems of the last two years. Tudor's death would have left opponents and waverers alike with little alternative but an accommodation with Richard, and the resulting security would have given the king greater freedom of action – although whether he would actually have had the will to break himself of his dependence on Tyrell, Brackenbury and the rest is another question. That victory, however, was not forthcoming. On 22 August 1485 it was Tudor who defeated Richard III and could claim the justification of a trial by battle.[193]

But the moral of Bosworth is ambiguous. Although the course of the battle is notoriously controversial, it is clear that Richard came very close to victory. Even admitting his defeat, the line-up on the morning of 22 August could be interpreted as a vindication of Richard III. His army was by far the larger, if one leaves the problematical Stanley contingent out of the calculation. Moreover, Tudor's army included a substantial foreign contingent, whose presence says nothing about Richard's acceptability or otherwise to his subjects. Relatively few Englishmen, or Welshmen, were so opposed to Richard III that they were prepared to do battle against him.

Although the result of Bosworth should not be taken as a considered verdict on Richard III, it cannot be dismissed as an unfortunate mistake. The battle did expose the extent to which Richard had failed to establish himself. As far as one can judge, the men who supported the king in August 1485 were largely those who had backed his coup in June 1483, with the addition of some of the duchy of Lancaster connection from the north midlands.[194] Richard's apparent failure to widen his power base beyond this

---

[193] *Rot. Parl.* VI p. 267.

[194] One of the men attainted by Henry, Richard Revell, was a royal official at Tutbury: Horrox 1986b, p. 99. Other north midlanders probably fought for Tudor under Sir Gilbert Talbot. Various traditions, although implausible in detail, testify to this local division: Bennett 1985, pp. 112–14.

contrasts with the situation at the battle of Stoke in 1487, where the spread of Henry VII's support was significantly wider than it had been at Bosworth. Among the men knighted or made banneret by Henry at Stoke were several former servants of Richard III or their close kinsmen, including Thomas Tyrell, George Hopton, John Sapcote, William Tirwhit and George Neville.[195] In the first two years of his reign Henry was little more secure, if at all, than Richard had been, and his royal title was weaker, but he had succeeded in making his service attractive enough to win new backing. He had done so, moreover, with considerably fewer resources at his disposal, and his success suggests what forces Richard, as king, ought to have been able to mobilize in 1485.[196]

In military terms Richard's limited power base may not have mattered very much; he still had the bigger army. But it was symptomatic of a lack of enthusiasm for his cause which may have had more immediate consequences. Most early accounts of the battle imply that the king's troops were unwilling to engage.[197] This cannot be taken entirely at face value. Richard's army did lose and common sense would suggest to the survivors the wisdom of pleading coercion.[198] But morale in the army must have been undermined by fears of treachery. By the time battle was joined it was probably already obvious that, as in 1483, Richard's measures against the rebels had been sapped by disaffection within his own camp. At least one of the royal commissioners of array in Somerset, John Biconnell, took his forces to Tudor.[199] Another royal associate in the south west, the former Lancastrian Thomas Ormonde whom Richard had knighted and added to the commission of the peace for Devon, was probably

---

[195] Bennett 1987, p. 129. George Hopton was the son of Richard's treasurer of the household. The James Harrington knighted on this occasion was of Brixworth (Northants), not one of the Ricardian family.

[196] The extent of Richard's support is controversial. The ballad *Bosworth ffeilde* suggests that twenty-three noblemen turned out for Richard: *Bishop Percy's Folio Ms* III pp. 233ff. Ross 1981, appendix II is inclined to accept it as a source; Richmond 1986 is not. It is at least clear that if twenty-three noblemen did turn up at Bosworth, many must have kept out of the battle, otherwise the result is inexplicable.

[197] Bennett 1985, appendix, collects the evidence.

[198] e.g. *Rot. Parl.* VI p. 328. For a more enthusiastic view of Richard from just before the battle: Hunter 1828–31, I p. 75.

[199] Hampton 1979, no. 265. This was in spite of Biconnell's links with Zouche, who turned out for Richard: *Inqs p.m.* I no. 536.

intriguing for Tudor.[200] Even if such defections were not yet public knowledge, it would be surprising, given the betrayals which had characterized all previous opposition to Richard III, if the king and his men had *not* been expecting treachery. The anonymous bill-writer who assured Norfolk that the king was 'bought and sold' probably did no more than confirm what was generally assumed.[201] The last charge by Richard and his knights can be seen as the military equivalent of the king's political reliance on a small circle of trusted men in response to treachery.

By the time of the charge it must have been obvious that Richard had again been let down by his presumed supporters. The irony of the battle is that the immediate cause of Richard's defeat came not from the disenchanted south but from the north. Of the nobility attainted for their part in the battle only Lovell, apart from Richard himself, has any claim to be considered a northerner, and there is no doubt that his support of Richard derived from personal rather than regional loyalties. Norfolk and his son Surrey were both attainted. Norfolk died in the battle, fighting for the king in spite of the warning to abstain and in spite of Richard's tendency to interfere in East Anglia. The other noble casualty was Walter Devereux, lord Ferrers of Chartley, who may have been present as the representative of Richard's son-in-law the earl of Huntingdon.[202] Also attainted was John lord Zouche, whose commitment probably owed something to his family links with Catesby.[203] By contrast, the earl of Northumberland led his forces to the battle but then stood aloof, perhaps honouring an earlier undertaking to Tudor.[204] The earl had presumably decided that an inexperienced king, with no connections in the north east apart from Percy himself, would allow him

---

[200] *CP* x pp. 131–3; Sutton and Hammond, *Coronation* p. 379; Devon RO, Exeter receiver's account 2 Ric. III – 1 Hen. VII; Exeter, Dean and Chapter Library, ms 3779 fo. 63v.

[201] Bennett 1985, p. 114.

[202] *Rot. Parl.* VI p. 276. Even *Bosworth ffeilde* does not suggest that Huntingdon was present.

[203] Roskell 1959b, pp. 152, 156–7. Another member of the Catesby circle to be attainted was Roger Wake, Catesby's brother-in-law: Barron 1906, pp. 321–2. For Zouche's climb back to partial favour: Lander 1976, p. 274.

[204] Bennett 1985, p. 161; Hicks 1978, pp. 89–90, 97. Ross 1981, pp. 221–2 is alone in suggesting that the earl failed to engage because his position made it impossible. How far Northumberland had already conspired on Henry's behalf is debatable. It has been suggested that his apparent failure to raise troops from York was deliberate: Bennett 1985, p. 90; Kendall 1955, pp. 347–8; Palliser 1986, p. 72. The presence of two Carres and a Pigot in Henry's army might be a Percy link, although none of them can be firmly identified: *CPR* 1485–94 pp. 4, 6, 17.

the regional hegemony which Richard had denied. His refusal to engage may have meant that many of the king's own northern supporters, as well as the Percy retinue, were kept out of the battle if, as seems likely, the earl had been responsible for raising the north east while the king was based at Nottingham.[205]

Northumberland's attitude is explicable. What is less clear is how widely it was shared within the north. The earl of Westmorland also had grounds for dissatisfaction and, if he was present at the battle at all, probably adopted Northumberland's tactics and stayed on the sidelines. Behind their private grievances may have been a general uneasiness at the north's new relationship with the crown. In the 1470s much of Richard's regional power had derived from his role as the king's agent in the north, but it was still possible to view him as a local magnate mediating royal influence to the benefit of himself and his fellow peers. In 1483 this situation changed dramatically. Richard intended to remain lord of the north and in consequence royal power would be exercised directly, challenging the influence of local magnates. The tensions and resentments associated with this policy as practised by the Tudors are likely to have been stirring by 1485. Indeed, Richard's adoption of the policy may have seemed a greater threat than the later Tudor efforts, simply because he had the local knowledge and contacts to push it through effectively. There is no evidence, however, that this uneasiness extended to the gentry. In time their relationship with Richard would inevitably have lost much of its immediacy, with a corresponding increase in the attraction of local magnates, but in 1485 the ties of personal loyalty and gratitude were still strong enough to minimize the effects of Richard's departure from the north.[206]

The defection of Northumberland set the scene for Richard's defeat, but the *coup de grâce* was delivered by the Stanleys. Richard's relations with the family had been chequered. Their interests had clashed as early as 1470, when Edward's endowment of his brother had been partly at the Stanleys' expense, and subsequent royal hesitation over the proper balance of power in the north west cannot have helped matters. In the end, Edward endorsed Stanley influence, and there are hints that Gloucester resented his exclusion.[207] Certainly Richard treated lord Stanley

---

[205] Richmond 1986, p. 178 notes the small number of northerners among those attainted.
[206] Horrox 1986a, p. 7.
[207] See above, pp. 67–70.

as a potential enemy in June 1483, and although Stanley's imprisonment proved brief his release may have owed less to Richard's conviction of his loyalty than to fears of Stanley reprisals.[208] On their side, the Stanleys must have feared that Richard's accession would be followed by readjustments to the balance of power in the north west. The new king had numerous Lancashire followers whose influence could be enhanced at the Stanleys' expense, notably the Harringtons of Hornby, who had their own feud with the Stanleys. Richard's summons, in August 1483, to all the leading gentry of Lancashire to attend upon him at his entry into Yorkshire may have been seen as a prelude to a more direct relationship between them and the crown, bypassing the Stanleys.[209]

By September 1483 the scene may well have been set for a confrontation between the Stanleys and the new king. Fears for their regional position, coupled with the influence of lord Stanley's wife, Margaret Beaufort, made the brothers obvious recruits for a rebellion against Richard III. In the event they backed the king, almost certainly because of Buckingham's decision to join the rebels. Richard's gratitude for their unexpected support manifested itself in lavish patronage. William Stanley received land along the Welsh march with a clear value of around £600; his brother lord Thomas was given more scattered land valued at nearly £700.[210] This was not the limit of the family's gains. William, who was in Richard's household as a knight of the body within days of the rebellion's collapse, was made chief justice of north Wales and constable of Caernarvon. Thomas succeeded Buckingham as constable of England and as knight of the garter. He later became steward of the household and, with his son George lord Strange, was a member of the royal council.[211] Another of Thomas' sons, Edward, was given a role in Kent, while a third, James, received ecclesiastical preferment.[212]

In spite of all this, the Stanleys may have been dissatisfied. It is possible that William had had hopes of a rather larger share of Buckingham's massive collection of Welsh office. His grants simply left him one among many royal associates in the region,

---

[208] M. K. Jones 1986a, p. 33.
[209] *Harl. 433* II pp. 10–11.
[210] *Ibid.* I p. 242, III p. 144. William's grant is valued in Longleat ms 682.
[211] *CPR 1476–85* pp. 367, 368; *Harl. 433* I p. 138; Anstis 1724, II pp. 220–1; M. K. Jones 1986a, p. 49 (n. 85); Lander 1976, pp. 318–19.
[212] *Harl. 433* I p. 272, II pp. 55, 76.

albeit an influential one. Lord Thomas, meanwhile, may have expected the enhancement of his position in Lancashire and this too was not forthcoming. Richard's policy in the county merely confirmed the status quo. The king carefully rewarded his own Lancashire followers elsewhere, to avoid any appearance of undermining Stanley authority.[213] At the same time, he endorsed the Stanley connection by granting thirty of its members annuities on the same day as lord Thomas received an annuity of £100.[214] But he did nothing to extend Stanley's influence in the county. In particular, Richard kept in his own hands the offices which he had held in the region before his accession. Lord Stanley probably coveted the chief stewardship of the duchy of Lancaster in the north, which he secured almost immediately from Henry VII.[215] That was too important to Richard's own northern influence to be regranted, but the king also showed no inclination to part with his other offices, such as the stewardship of Penwortham, which could have served as a useful gesture of goodwill to lord Stanley while making little difference to the king's position.[216]

By the early months of 1485 the relationship of king and Stanleys appears to have been cooling. It is impossible to be sure whether the king had ever entirely trusted the brothers, even in the winter of 1483–4, but it is in any case likely that as Tudor gained in strength the king became increasingly mistrustful of the Stanleys' Beaufort links. In February 1485 Richard made James Harrington chief forester of Bowland. Harrington had previously held the office as Richard's deputy, so his appointment made little practical difference, but given the rivalry between the Harringtons and Stanleys the grant may have been intended, and was almost certainly seen, as a snub to lord Thomas.[217]

Far more threatening to the Stanleys' position was Richard's apparent intention of reopening the question of the Harrington inheritance – by implication, with the aim of readjusting the settlement in the Harringtons' favour.[218] This must have repre-

---

[213] e.g. Ralph Ashton in Kent and Robert Harrington in Leics.

[214] *Harl. 433* I pp. 100, 104; dated by PRO, DL 42/20 fo. 11–v. The identification of the annuitants with the Stanley connection is suggested by the fact that in almost every case their annuities were honoured after Bosworth by lord Stanley, the relevant receiver. Richard's allies, by contrast, were only paid the Easter 1485 instalment: PRO, DL 29/90/1654–5.

[215] Somerville 1953, p. 422 (granted 10 Oct. 1485).

[216] PRO, DL 29/90/1653–5.

[217] PRO, DL 42/20 fo. 46v; DL 29/90/1653.

[218] Whitaker 1878, p. 476.

sented the point of no return. Richard would hardly have raised the matter were he not so profoundly mistrustful of the Stanleys that he no longer cared about alienating them, while for lord Stanley in particular it must have spelt out that the family's regional influence would be safer under Henry Tudor. Unfortunately, Richard's plan cannot be dated, but his mistrust of the Stanleys had become overt by the end of July 1485, when he ordered lord Strange to court as surety for his father's good behaviour.[219] This move had some effect, in that it almost certainly kept lord Stanley himself out of the battle in the following month.[220] William Stanley, too, found it necessary to be circumspect. He brought his troops to the field but at first did not commit himself to either side. Since the Stanleys had surely by now burnt their boats as far as Richard was concerned, the fact that William still hesitated may imply that the king looked much the stronger side. Only when Richard was embroiled in his personal onslaught on the troops around Tudor did Stanley move, throwing in his forces on Tudor's side. His intervention was decisive. Richard's companions were overwhelmed and the king himself hacked to death.

[219] M. K. Jones 1986a, p. 34. Griffiths and Thomas 1985, p. 143 would set it much earlier, by the beginning of May, when a John Savage was arrested at Pembroke – something which they interpret as evidence of a Stanley/Tudor intrigue. However, the context in which the arrest is mentioned (*Harl. 433* III pp. 172–3) does not seem to support the identification of Savage with one of the two namesakes in the Stanley circle. The implication seems to be that this Savage was a humbler figure.

[220] Hanham 1975, pp. 21, 134.

CONCLUSION

Bosworth was the battle which should have been fought in October 1483. Richard, backed largely by the men who had brought him to power, faced an army whose English contingent consisted of former servants of Edward IV, including the Stanley and Talbot connections.[1] There had, of course, been changes. Buckingham was dead, and the rebels had a new noble commander in the person of John de Vere, earl of Oxford. Tudor had acquired foreign backing, without which the issue might well not have come to battle at all. Richard had mobilized at least part of the duchy of Lancaster connection in the north midlands. On balance the greater gains were Tudor's, and the battle line exposes the king's failure to master the situation in which he had found himself. Once the rebellion of 1483 had revealed the hollowness of Richard's claims to embody the continuity of the Yorkist polity, he never really regained the initiative. His apparent triumph over the rebels did not, in the event, establish him securely on the throne, perhaps in part because it was so obviously a victory by default. None of the rebels who subsequently made their peace with the crown was prepared to support Richard in battle. Several had already rejoined Tudor. Edgecombe, Berkeley and the Brandons had reconsidered their allegiance within months of receiving a pardon. Robert Skerne of Kingston on Thames, pardoned early in December 1483, also joined Tudor in exile and fought for him at Bosworth.[2] Walter Hungerford and Thomas Bourgchier of Barnes were summoned to arms by the king and set off in Brackenbury's company, but managed to give him the slip and join Tudor.[3]

[1] Gilbert Talbot had been one of Edward IV's esquires of the body: Wedgwood 1936, p. 838.

[2] *CPR* 1476–85 p. 375; *CPR* 1485–94 pp. 36–7. Rewarded with an office, he lived to enjoy it for only a week: *CPR* 1485–94 p. 154.

[3] Vergil p. 561. Compare *Great Chron.* p. 237, which implies that Brackenbury acquiesced in their departure.

Richard had also failed to tap significant new support to make good the defections. Part of the explanation is certainly that he had insufficient time. Trust could not be established overnight, and it is possible that he began building bridges with men who, by the end of the reign, had still not advanced sufficiently in royal favour to be either useful to the king or visible to the historian. His willingness to make advances to the Woodvilles and their circle shows that he acknowledged the need for a deliberate broadening of his power base, such as Edward IV had achieved in the early days of his reign. In the short term, however, Richard's inclination was clearly to take refuge in the security of his own retinue. This was partly an automatic reaction to the shock of his betrayal by so many of his brother's men. The policy of plantation also offered an obvious way out of his immediate difficulties.

Richard evidently favoured solutions which demanded quick decisive action – his coup of 1483 rests on a whole series of them – but he seems not always to have thought through the consequences. His dependence on his own retinue evoked the very threat of factionalization which his usurpation had claimed to avert, and therefore heightened rather than relieved the political anxieties which had triggered the 1483 rebellion. It also played into Tudor's hands. Richard's redistribution of the forfeited land gave Tudor a ready-made following whose chance of restoration now seemed remote. This, together with the king's attack on his brother's men in the parliament of 1484, had the effect of endorsing Tudor's claim to be the real upholder of Yorkist traditions. The result can be seen in the line-up at Bosworth, where Tudor's army was at least as 'Yorkist' as Richard's. Tudor even had Edward IV's standard bearer, John Cheyne, on his side, although he was not used in that capacity.[4]

The break in the continuity of service caused by the 1483 rebellion, although dramatic, was far from complete. It is most marked, as one would expect, in the circle closest to the king. It is possible to identify a small group of men, perhaps no more than six or seven, whose advice Richard took and whom he used on particularly sensitive assignments. Of the five undisputed members, Ratcliffe, Lovell, Catesby, Tyrell and Brackenbury, none was a former servant of Edward IV and only one, Catesby,

---

[4] PRO, E 404/77/2/32. At Bosworth the role was apparently filled by William Brandon: Bennett 1985, p. 166.

was not a member of Richard's ducal retinue but had earned his inclusion solely by supporting Richard's seizure of power. Such men dominate discussion of the reign and, if Collingbourne is to be believed, dominated the reign itself. Beyond them was the wider circle of former ducal retainers and their associates who enjoyed a major share of the available power and reward. But even they represent only a proportion of the men who were prepared to put their influence at the king's disposal. A significant number of Edward IV's men remained in Richard's household, the central administration survived largely unchanged, and local gentry continued to act on the king's behalf.

Few of these men appear to have been particularly close to the king. Some may, as a result, have come to resent the dominance of the king's own connection, and a few were sufficiently alienated to withdraw their support altogether. Most, however, remained obedient. In part they are likely to have been motivated by self-interest: the belief that it was 'better to govern than be governed'.[5] But there was also a fundamental sense that the king ought to be obeyed. Although service was at heart a personal relationship, it had an impersonal dimension in that the king evoked respect not only by his own efforts and his own personality (by his good lordship, in short) but also as the embodiment of order. The men who sat on commissions, heard complaints and investigated problems were providing local government as well as (perhaps even rather than) demonstrating their loyalty to the king. The central administration had developed a professional ethos which amounted to loyalty to the office rather than the man, a view which seems on the whole to have strengthened, rather than weakened, obedience to the *de facto* ruler. The household was moving in the same direction – at least to the extent that a close relationship with the king was not a prerequisite of membership. The household, even the *domus magnificencie*, was now simply too big for that to be feasible.

Abstract obedience to the crown was not, of course, a substitute for personal loyalty. Effective royal initiatives still relied heavily on the bonds between king and trusted royal servants, as Richard's own reign shows. But the duty of obedience, reinforced by its manifest advantages, was a source of considerable strength for the individual ruler, allowing even the worst of kings surpris-

---

[5] *Stonor Letters* II pp. 134–5.

ing room for manoeuvre before his incompetence began to catch up with him. However one interprets Henry VI's reign, for instance, it illustrates what could be called the king's right to fail. Henry VII was ill advised to date his reign from the day before Bosworth. It gave practical expression to his claim to be king *de iure* and Richard a mere usurper, but it also penalized men for supporting an acknowledged ruler, which was a dangerous precedent.[6]

Although Richard III's increasing reliance on his own affinity generated tensions, and caused problems for the king himself when his allies were over-extended, the residual authority of kingship meant that his reign never actually ceased to be viable. Had he defeated Tudor at Bosworth there is no reason why he should not have gone on, as Henry himself was to do after Stoke, to die in his bed, respected if not much loved. The administrative framework was intact, and a few years of security would have given Richard the chance to reconsider his power base, had he been prepared to take it. In a sense, therefore, any judgement on Richard's reign has to be seen as provisional. The critic of the reign only has to consider how the Tudors would now be regarded if Henry VII had lost at Stoke, to realize the dangers of too many easy assumptions about the intractability of Richard's problems. But it would be equally unrealistic to ignore Richard's unpopularity altogether. The fact that he generated opposition among men with little material reason for dissent, and that the disaffection then continued to spread among his own associates, says something about what contemporaries regarded as the acceptable parameters of political behaviour.

There is no doubt that Richard's deposition of his nephew was profoundly shocking. To anyone who did not accept the pre-contract story, which was probably the majority of observers, the usurpation was an act of disloyalty. Gloucester, both as uncle and protector, was bound to uphold his nephew's interests and his failure to do so was dishonourable. Of all the medieval depositions it was the one which, with whatever justification, could most easily be seen as an act of naked self-aggrandizement. It was also the first pre-emptive deposition in English history. Its underlying justification was not that Edward V had failed, but the likelihood that he might fail. Richard claimed to be acting to avert

---

[6] Chrimes 1972, p. 50; Horrox 1983, p. 156.

the threat that the young king's choice of advisors would destroy the balance of power established by Edward IV. This raised enormous problems. Deposition was always a last resort, even when it could be justified by the manifest failings of a corrupt or ineffective regime. How could one sanction its use as a first resort, to remove a king who had not only not done anything wrong but had not yet done anything at all?

Richard's answer was to side-step the issue altogether by declaring his nephews illegitimate and so barred from the succession. It is doubtful, however, whether this really satisfied many contemporaries. Even if there was an element of truth in the pre-contract story it was obvious that it was not the first cause of Richard's decision to take the throne, particularly as publication of the story had apparently been preceded by claims that Edward IV himself was illegitimate. Although it was the princes' bastardy which validated Richard's title to the throne, he did not announce it until after the crucial decisions had been made. It was Richard's belief that the political establishment would support him for the sake of stability, whether out of cowardice or conviction, which allowed him to think of making himself king.

That belief was to prove the major misjudgement of Richard's career, but it was, perhaps, understandable. His appeal to the preservation of Edward IV's power structure had already allowed him to make himself protector and dismantle the power of the Woodvilles without difficulty, which is eloquent testimony to the political community's commitment to the status quo. But in the event their apparent desire for peace at any price stopped short of endorsing usurpation, although Richard himself seems not to have been aware of this until it was too late. It was the duke himself who destroyed his brother's polity in the name of preserving it.

This was certainly not his intention. Even if his usurpation is ascribed solely to ambition, he was manifestly committed to the survival of his brother's power base, as a source of strength for himself if for no other reason. It is likely that Richard also had a genuine respect for his brother's achievements – in which, after all, he had played an outstanding role – and wanted to see them preserved. This was an area where Gloucester's private interests and those of the realm could seem to coincide, for if the Woodvilles' closeness to the young king were to upset the political balance then it would almost inevitably be to the detriment of the duke's position. Gloucester may thus very easily have persuaded himself that he was indeed the appointed saviour of the Yorkist regime. His discovery that his seizure of power had not had the support of a significant number of his brother's men was probably a considerable personal blow as well as a political disaster.

The rebellion of 1483 left Richard with two major problems. The defection of many of the court circle in the south forced him to find alternative methods of exercising authority, which exacerbated his unpopularity in those areas most badly affected. The rebellion also produced an acknowledged rival for the throne. This was guaranteed to put any king under exceptional pressure, simply because it made rebellion a viable and, to some extent, respectable form of political criticism. The result was to limit the king's freedom to make mistakes. Edward IV's reign demonstrates this very clearly. His policies in the 1470s were not much different from those of the 1460s, but the assurance and success with which they were put into practice were appreciably greater after the removal of the Lancastrian claimant to the throne. Richard's two problems were thus linked. Only the decisive defeat of Tudor would give him the necessary elbow-room to re-establish himself in the south, either by buying him time to build up a new local affinity or by making an overt attack on his northern connection less likely. But the king could not afford to wait for the final judgement of battle. In the short term he had to find other methods of strengthening his position.

For Tudor commentators, who have been echoed by most subsequent writers, Richard's main weapon in his search for security was the patronage at his disposal – by which is usually meant the battery of material benefits in his gift: land, office, money, marriage. This, however, was of only limited utility. Richard did indeed disburse his resources with a lavish hand to reward his allies and to build up influence for them which he could then exploit. But such grants could not be used to buy new support unless the king were prepared to gamble on loyalty by rewarding the uncommitted or the actively hostile. Patronage of declared opponents would be rare in any reign, and after the 1483 rebellion Richard also seems to have been unwilling to endorse the influence of the merely acquiescent, at least in the south. On the whole, therefore, his grants only confirmed the status quo by rewarding the committed. In theory the grants should still have played a part in recruiting new support. The possibility of reward was of crucial importance in drawing men into royal service, and

Richard's liberality should have encouraged the waverers. In practice it seems not to have done so, and may even have had the opposite effect. Collingbourne's couplet testifies to a belief that the king's favours were restricted to a clique and, whether the judgement was valid or not, this view of the court can only have diminished the force of Richard's generosity. Lavish patronage was no inducement to service if the circle of beneficiaries seemed to be closed.

Richard's own answer to the question of security, apart from his efforts to winkle his rival out of Brittany, appears to have been an ideological one. In his public pronouncements he hammered home the doctrine that a king's ultimate justification lay in the quality of his rule, and presented himself as the ruler whom England needed if the realm was to enjoy peace and prosperity. In particular, Richard, like his father and brother before him, identified himself with the 'common wealth' of the kingdom.[7] This concept had various dimensions. At its most literal it implied material well-being. In a letter concerned with the regulation of the cloth trade, Richard could describe himself as, 'a Christian prince above all things earthly intending the common wealth of this his realm, the increase [of] wealth and prosperity of his subjects'.[8] The common wealth of England also derived from the proper exercise of justice, a subject close to Richard's heart. One of his proclamations begins: 'The king's grace willeth that for the love that he hath for the ministration and execution of justice for the common wealth of this realm, the which he most tendereth...'[9] Running through these various expressions of royal concern for the common wealth is Richard's self-identification with order and stability. Just as he had claimed to represent 'surety and firmness here in this world' against the Woodvilles' attempts at subversion, so he promised 'the most comfort, weal and surety' of his subjects instead of the 'murders, slaughters, robberies and disinheritings' intended by Tudor.[10]

The king's assumption of the moral high ground was clearly expedient, but it should not therefore be dismissed as insincere. His public statements reveal an informed perception of what the

---

[7] Starkey 1986, pp. 14–26 charts the early use of the term.
[8] PRO, C 81/1531/64.
[9] *Harl. 433* III p. 124. Compare Bacon, *Henry VII* pp. 38–9.
[10] Nichols, *Grants from the Crown* p. xl; *Harl. 433* III p. 125.

ideal king should be,[11] and it is not inconsistent with his manifest ambition and liking for power to suggest that he had cast himself in that role when, in 1483, he had decided that he would be the best candidate for king. As his security crumbled around him, his attempts to live up to this ideal intensified. Partly, no doubt, this was aimed at winning over his critics, but Richard may also have been driven by a desire for personal redemption. In his private devotions he addressed himself to St Julian, who had achieved salvation through a lifetime of service after unwittingly murdering his parents.[12] It seems plausible that Richard, whose coup had left him with blood on his hands, saw the quality of his kingship as a means of obtaining spiritual, as well as political, security. In this context it is significant that he placed considerable emphasis on his obligations as a Christian prince, including his duty to reform morality.[13] On a more personal note he seems to have dreamt of leading a crusade, one of the ultimate expiations of sin. His reported outburst to Nicholas von Poppelau, 'with my own people alone and without the help of other princes I should like to drive away not only the Turks but all my foes', has an authentic ring.[14]

Even if Richard himself were sincere, his appeal to good rule was profoundly flawed. Some of its contradictions had been apparent from the very outset, when Richard's emphasis was still on the continuance of his brother's regime. His argument that continuity could be achieved through something as radical and divisive as a deposition was both morally and logically suspect. More specifically, Richard's claim to represent continuity sat uneasily beside his immediate attack on elements of his brother's power structure. Suspicion of the Woodvilles' intentions may have meant, as Richard hoped, that their removal was accepted as a necessary sacrifice for the preservation of the rest of the political framework. But the execution of Hastings was another matter, and although Richard used the same arguments in justification they are unlikely to have commanded much belief.[15] The

---

[11] Sutton 1986a offers a sympathetic survey.
[12] Tudor-Craig 1973, p. 96. Julian seems not to have been one of Richard's preferred saints before 1483 (Sutton 1986a, pp. 65–6), which suggests that the king may have been attracted by the parallel between the saint's legend and his own accession, specifically, perhaps, his treatment of the princes.
[13] *Harl. 433* III p. 139.
[14] Ross 1981, p. 142. Compare Henry IV's wish to visit Jerusalem: McNiven 1985, p. 764.
[15] Mancini pp. 90–1.

dramatic insertion of Buckingham into Wales could have toppled the regime as early as October 1483, had not the duke himself switched sides.

The 1483 rebellion spelt out these weaknesses in Richard's position. In response, the king tacitly admitted the contradiction. Although in practice Richard's policies remained those of his brother, he ceased to emphasize that continuity as the underlying justification of his rule. Instead he presented Edward IV as a man led astray by evil counsel, and himself, by implication, as the purifier of a corrupt regime. There are, however, indications that Richard did not want to cut himself off entirely from his Yorkist roots. He apparently began to see himself as the heir to a tradition of government represented by his father. In a revealing communication to the earl of Desmond in September 1484, Richard chose to portray himself primarily as the son of the duke of York rather than the brother of Edward IV, and hinted strongly at his alienation from his brother's court.[16]

Although the rebellion forced Richard to come to terms with some of the inherent contradictions in his position, it opened up further gaps between the image which the king wished to present to the world and political reality. His emphasis on law and order was undermined by the illegalities associated with the seizure of confiscated estates and by the actions of some of his supporters. His claim to act for the common wealth of the whole realm was challenged by his identification with a sharply defined clique. Most damaging of all was Richard's manifest inability to deliver the promised political stability. His appeal to order had been his strongest card. The political establishment, and the wider community of the realm, had experienced the dramatic collapse of order in 1469–71. Many would also have remembered the tensions of the late 1450s. Such breakdowns of stability were gravely threatening to the interests of the landowning classes, and Richard showed himself a shrewd judge of the political temper when he chose to make the peace and quiet of his subjects a central issue in his propaganda.[17] As a result he was condemned out of his own mouth. His reign saw a series of risings and conspiracies. More serious, for his subjects, were the resulting readjustments of landholding and influence at a local level. Not only were they unsettling in themselves but they triggered a new round of self-

---

[16] *Harl. 433* III pp. 108, 111.
[17] e.g. *ibid.* II p. 49, III pp. 31–2, 124–5, 133.

help and score-settling. It is not surprising that after Richard's death he was branded a hypocrite in the popular imagination.[18]

Had he managed to survive Bosworth, Richard's arguments would probably have been vindicated. It was a commonplace of medieval government that the end did justify the means. Much was forgiven a king if his authority encouraged stability and order. It was only when royal influence was used in an arbitrary manner for the gratification of personal whims that it was likely to become contentious. Richard had already demonstrated that he could run a region justly and effectively, and there was no real reason why he could not have repeated his success on a national scale. In this respect precedent was on his side. Previous usurpers, once they had weathered initial disaffection, had all managed to live down the circumstances in which they had attained power and had died secure in office. Henry VII was to conform to the same pattern. Richard III was the only failed English usurper of the Middle Ages.

Various factors contributed to his failure. Richard seized the throne from what was soon revealed as a dangerously limited power base and, unlike Edward IV and Henry VII who were in the same position, he lacked the sanction of a decisive military victory. This was a practical deficiency, but it was also an ideological one. All other medieval depositions took place against a background of widespread dissatisfaction with the previous regime. This did not necessarily make the act of deposition any less traumatic, but it gave the new ruler some additional claim on the support of his subjects. Richard III lacked even this degree of consensus. The cure which he was offering seemed to many worse than the disease, and his seizure of power fatally divided the Yorkist establishment. In dynastic terms his usurpation was a disaster: Richard destroyed the house of York. He also destroyed himself; and Halle, the most perceptive of the later Tudor writers, is surely right to see his reign as a tragedy.[19] In political terms, however, Richard's intervention had less dramatic consequences. His alienation of so many of his brother's leading associates helped to ensure that in terms of both personnel and policies Henry VII reigned as the heir of York rather than of Lancaster.

---

[18] Palliser 1986, p. 69.
[19] Halle, *Union* (Richard III) fo. 1. This develops an idea already present in Vergil. It was taken up by Shakespeare whose *Richard III* is entitled a tragedy, although the treatment of the king does not justify it.

BIBLIOGRAPHY

MANUSCRIPTS CITED

BRITISH LIBRARY
Additional charter 16564
Additional mss 12520, 29616
Additional roll 16559
Cottonian mss: Caligula BVI
     Julius BXII
     Vespasian FIII
Harleian charter 58.F.49
Harleian mss 793, 1546

PUBLIC RECORD OFFICE, CHANCERY LANE

C	1	Early chancery proceedings
	4	Chancery answers
	56	Confirmation rolls
	66	Patent rolls
	67	Pardon rolls
	76	Treaty rolls
	81	Chancery warrants, series I
	82	Chancery warrants, series II
	145	Miscellaneous inquisitions
	237	Bails on special pardons
	244	Corpus cum causa
	263	Legal miscellanea
DL	5	Duchy of Lancaster, council minutes
	29	ministers' accounts
	37	chancery rolls
	41	miscellanea
	42	miscellaneous books
E	101	Exchequer, K. R., accounts various
	207	bille
	208	brevia baronibus
	401	Exchequer of receipt, receipt rolls
	402	tellers' bills
	404	warrants for issues

E 405	tellers' rolls
KB 9	King's Bench, ancient indictments
29	controlment rolls
Prob 2	Inventories, pre-1661
11	Prerogative Court of Canterbury wills
PSO 1	Privy seal warrants, series 1
SC 6	Special collections, ministers' accounts
8	ancient petitions
11	rentals and surveys

CANTERBURY RECORD OFFICE
FA   City accounts

ROYAL INSTITUTION OF CORNWALL, TRURO
BV 1   Borlase memoranda

CUMBRIA RECORD OFFICE, CARLISLE
D/AYI   Aglionby mss
D/Cu   Curwen mss
D/Hud   Huddleston mss
D/Lec   Egremont mss
D/Lons   Lonsdale mss
D/Mus   Musgrave mss

DEVON RECORD OFFICE, EXETER
ECA Book 51   Hooker's commonplace book
Exeter mayor's court roll, 22 Edw. IV – 1 Ric. III
Exeter receivers' accounts

ESSEX COUNTY RECORD OFFICE, CHELMSFORD
D/DB   Archer-Houblon mss (Hallingbury Place Estate)
D/DCe   Theydon Garnon estate papers
D/DQ   Theydon Garnon estate papers

EXETER, DEAN AND CHAPTER LIBRARY
ms 3779   Ordinary solutions, 1485–1567

HUMBERSIDE COUNTY RECORD OFFICE, BEVERLEY
DDCC   Chichester Constable mss
DDCL   Clark mss

KINGSTON UPON HULL RECORD OFFICE
Bench Book 3A
BRF 2/377–8   Chamberlains' accounts, 1468–70

Bibliography

CORPORATION OF LONDON RECORD OFFICE
Journal of the Court of Common Council 9

LANCASHIRE RECORD OFFICE, PRESTON
DDFz   Brockholes mss
DDHe   Hesketh mss
DDK   Stanley, earls of Derby mss
DDM   Molyneux of Sefton mss
DDTo   Townley mss
DDX   Miscellaneous collections

LONGLEAT HOUSE, WARMINSTER, WILTS
ms 65   regulations for the king's household – seventeenth-century
              copy of 1478 ordinance
ms 516   land added to Windsor by Richard III
ms 563   receiver's account of Penrith, 12 Hen. VII
ms 682   valor of Bromfield and Yale

MEYRICK-CARY PAPERS, in the custody of Messrs Kitsons, Torquay
material relating to Ashwater, unnumbered

SOMERSET RECORD OFFICE, TAUNTON
DD/Wo   Trevelyan mss

SOUTHAMPTON CITY RECORD OFFICE
SC 2/9/1   Royal letters
   5/1   Stewards' books
   7/1   Town court books

WESTMINSTER ABBEY
mss 4110, 5925, 6625, 6646, 16063

WILTSHIRE RECORD OFFICE, TROWBRIDGE
490/1471   Radnor mss, title of Master Hungerford
G 23/1/2   Salisbury, ledger B
G 23/1/44   compotus rolls

YORK, BORTHWICK INSTITUTE OF HISTORICAL RESEARCH
Probate Registers

PRINTED PRIMARY SOURCES

'An extract relating to the burial of K. Edward IV', *Archaeologia* 1 (1770),
    348–55.
Anderson, R. C., ed., *Letters of the Fifteenth and Sixteenth Centuries*, Southampton
    Record Society 22, 1921.

Bibliography

Bacon, Francis, *The History of the Reign of King Henry the Seventh*, ed. R. Lockyer, London, 1971.

Basin, Thomas, *Histoire de Louis XI*, ed. C. Samaran and M.-C. Garand, 3 vols., Paris, 1963–72.

Bentley, S., *Excerpta Historica, or, Illustrations of English History*, London, 1833.

Bishop Percy's Folio Manuscript, ed. J. W. Hales and F. J. Furnivall, 3 vols., London, 1868.

Blair, C. H. Hunter, 'Two letters patent from Hutton John near Penrith, Cumberland', *Archaeologia Aeliana*, fourth series 39 (1961), 367–70.

Boyle, J. R., ed., *Charters and Letters Patent granted to Kingston upon Hull*, Hull, 1905.

British Library, Harleian MS 433, ed. R. E. Horrox and P. W. Hammond, 4 vols., London, 1979–83.

Buck, Sir George, *The History of King Richard the Third*, ed. A. N. Kincaid, Gloucester, 1979.

Calendarium Inquisitionum post mortem sive Escaetarum, 4 vols., London, 1806–28.

Calendar of Close Rolls, 1461–85, 3 vols., HMSO, 1949–54.

Calendar of Fine Rolls, 1461–1509, 3 vols., HMSO, 1949–62.

Calendar of Inquisitions post mortem, Henry VII, 3 vols., HMSO, 1898–1955.

Calendar of Papal Registers XIII part II, HMSO, 1955.

Calendar of Patent Rolls, 1441–1509, 8 vols., HMSO, 1908–16.

Campbell, W., ed., *Materials for a History of the Reign of Henry VII*, 2 vols., Rolls Series, 1873–7.

Cartae et alia munimenta quae ad Dominium de Glamorgancia pertinent, 6 vols., Cardiff, 1910.

The Cely Letters 1472–1488, ed. A. Hanham, EETS 273, 1975.

Christ Church Letters, ed. J. B. Sheppard, Camden Society, new series 19, 1877.

Chronica Monasterii S. Albani: registra quorundam abbatum monasterii S. Albani, qui saeculo xv^mo floruere II *Registra Johannis Whethamstede, Willelmi Albon et Willelmi Walingforde*, ed. H. T. Riley, Rolls Series, 1873.

Collier, J. P., ed., *Household Books of John duke of Norfolk and Thomas earl of Surrey, 1481–1490*, Roxburghe Club, 1844.

The Coventry Leet Book, ed. M. D. Harris, EETS 134–5, 138 and 146, 1907–13.

The Crowland Chronicle Continuations, 1459–1486, ed. N. Pronay and J. Cox, London, 1986.

Davies, R. T., ed., *Medieval English Lyrics: a critical anthology*, London, 1963.

Deputy Keeper of the Public Records, 35th Annual Report, HMSO, 1874.

A Descriptive Catalogue of Ancient Deeds in the Public Record Office, 6 vols., HMSO, 1890–1915.

Dobson, R. B., ed., *York City Chamberlains' Account Rolls, 1396–1500*, Surtees Society 192, 1980 for 1978–9.

Fabyan, Robert, *The New Chronicles of England and France*, ed. H. Ellis, London, 1811.

Foedera, Conventiones, Literae, et cujuscunque generis acta publica, inter Reges Angliae, ed. Thomas Rymer, 20 vols., London, 1704–35.

Fortescue, John, *The Governance of England*, ed. C. Plummer, Oxford, 1885.

Bibliography

Furnivall, F. J., ed., *The Babees Book*, EETS 32, 1868.

Gilson, J. P., 'A defence of the proscription of the Yorkists in 1459', *EHR*, 26 (1911), 512–25.

The Great Chronicle of London, ed. A. H. Thomas and I. D. Thornley, London, 1938.

Greatrex, J., ed., *The Register of the Common Seal of the Priory of St Swithun, Winchester, 1345–1497*, Hampshire Record Series 2, 1978.

Green, R. Firth, 'Historical notes of a London citizen, 1483–1488', *EHR*, 96 (1981), 585–90.

Halle, Edward, *The Union of the two Noble and Illustrious Families of Lancaster and York*, London, 1550; reprinted in facsimile, Menston, 1970.

Halliwell, J. O., ed., *Letters of the Kings of England* I, London, 1848.

Hardyng, John, *The Chronicle of John Hardyng, with the Continuation by Richard Grafton*, ed. H. Ellis, London, 1812.

Hicks, M. A., 'The last days of Elizabeth countess of Oxford', *EHR*, 103 (1988), 76–95.

Historical Manuscripts Commission:
  Second Report, 1874.
  Fifth Report, 1876.
  Sixth Report, 1877.
  Ninth Report, 1883.
  Eleventh Report, part III, 1887.
  Report on the Hastings manuscripts I, 1928.
  Report on the Manuscripts of Lord Middleton, 1911.
  Report on the Manuscripts of the Duke of Rutland I, 1888.

Historie of the Arrivall of Edward IV in England, ed. J. Bruce, Camden Society, original series 1, 1838.

Holinshed, Raphael, *Chronicles of England, Scotland and Ireland*, 6 vols., London, 1807–8.

Horrox, R. E., ed., 'Financial memoranda of the reign of Edward V: Longleat miscellaneous manuscript book II', *Camden Miscellany 29*, Camden Society, fourth series 34, 1987, pp. 199–244.

Ives, E. W., ed., *Letters and Accounts of William Brereton of Malpas*, The Record Society of Lancashire and Cheshire 116, 1976.

Leathes, S. M., ed., *Grace Book A*, Cambridge Antiquarian Society, 1897.

Leland, John, *Leland's Itinerary in England and Wales*, ed. L. Toulmin Smith, 5 vols., London, 1907–10.

Lincolnshire Pedigrees, ed. A. R. Maddison, 4 vols., Harleian Society 50–2 and 55, 1902–6.

Loades, D. M., ed., *The Papers of George Wyatt Esq.*, Camden Society, fourth series 5, 1968.

Lyell, L. and Watney, F. D., eds., *Acts of Court of the Mercers' Company, 1453–1527*, Cambridge, 1936.

McGregor, M., ed., *Bedfordshire Wills proved in the PCC, 1383–1548*, Bedfordshire Historical Record Society 58, 1979.

Mancini, Dominic, *Usurpation of Richard III*, ed. C. A. J. Armstrong, 2nd edn,

Oxford, 1969.

More, Thomas, *The History of King Richard III*, ed. R. S. Sylvester, Yale, 1963.

Myers, A. R., ed., 'An official progress through Lancashire and Cheshire in 1476', *Transactions of the Historical Society of Lancashire and Cheshire*, 115 (1963), 1–29.

The Household of Edward IV, the Black Book and the Ordinances of 1478, Manchester, 1959.

'The Household of Queen Elizabeth Woodville, 1466–7', *Bulletin of the John Rylands Library*, 50 (1967–8), 207–35, 443–81.

Nichols, J. G., ed., *Grants etc from the Crown during the Reign of Edward the Fifth*, Camden Society, original series 60, 1854.

Nicolas, N. H., ed., *Privy Purse Expenses of Elizabeth of York: Wardrobe Accounts of Edward the Fourth*, London, 1830; reprinted in facsimile, London, 1972.

Oppenheim, M., ed., *Naval Accounts and Inventories of the Reign of Henry VII*, Naval Records Society 8, 1896.

Paston Letters and Papers of the Fifteenth Century, ed. N. Davis, 2 vols., Oxford, 1971–6.

'Pedigrees showing the relationship between many of the nobility and gentry, and the blood royal; compiled about the year 1505', ed. N. H. N., *Collectanea Topographica et Genealogica* 1 (1834), 295–319.

Percy Bailiff's Rolls of the Fifteenth Century, ed. J. C. Hodgson, Surtees Society 134, 1921.

Plumpton Correspondence, ed. T. Stapleton, Camden Society, original series 4, 1839.

Putnam, B., ed., *Proceedings before the Justices of the Peace in the Fourteenth and Fifteenth Centuries*, Ames Foundation, 1938.

Raine, A., ed., *York Civic Records* 1, Yorkshire Archaeological Society, record series 98, 1938.

Reaney, P. H. and Fitch, M., eds., *Feet of Fines for Essex* IV, Essex Archaeological Society, 1964.

Records of the Borough of Nottingham, 9 vols., London and Nottingham, 1882–1956.

The Records of the City of Norwich, ed. W. Hudson and J. C. Tingey, 2 vols., Norwich, 1906.

The Red Paper Book of Colchester, ed. W. G. Benham, Colchester, 1902.

'Register of the sepulchral inscriptions ... in the church of the Grey Friars, London', ed. J. G. N., *Collectanea Topographica et Genealogica*, 5 (1838), 274–90, 385–98.

The Register of Thomas Rotherham, Archbishop of York 1480–1500 1, ed. E. Barker, Canterbury and York Society 69, 1976.

Registrum Thome Bourgchier, Cantuariensis Archiepiscopi A.D. 1454–86, ed. F. R. H. du Boulay, Canterbury and York Society 54, 1957.

Rotuli Parliamentorum, ed. J. Strachey *et al.*, 6 vols., London, 1767–77.

Rous, John, *Historia Regum Angliae*, Oxford, 1745.

Secretum Secretorum, nine English Versions, part 1, texts, ed. M. A. Manzalaoui, EETS 276, 1977.

Bibliography

Skelton, John, *Pithy, Pleasant and Profitable Works*, London, 1568; reprinted in facsimile, Menston, 1970.

Stagg, D. J., ed., *A Calendar of New Forest Documents: the fifteenth to the seventeenth centuries*, Hampshire Record Series 5, 1983.

Stephens, G., ed., 'Extracts in prose and verse from an old English medical manuscript', *Archaeologia* 30 (1844), 349–418.

The Stonor Letters and Papers, 1290–1483, ed. C. L. Kingsford, 2 vols., Camden Society, third series 29–30, 1919.

Stow, John, *The Annales of England*, London, 1592.

Sutton, A. F. and Hammond, P. W., eds., *The Coronation of Richard III: the extant documents*, Gloucester, 1983.

Testamenta Eboracensia III, Surtees Society 45, 1865 for 1864.

Testamenta Eboracensia IV, Surtees Society 53, 1869 for 1868.

Trevelyan Papers prior to A.D. 1558, ed. J. Payne Collier, Camden Society, original series 67, 1857.

The Tropenell Cartulary, ed. J. S. Davies, 2 vols., Devizes, 1908.

Turner, T. H., ed., *Manners and Household Expenses of England in the Thirteenth and Fifteenth Centuries*, Roxburghe Club, 1841.

Veale, E. W. W., ed., *The Great Red Book of Bristol*, Bristol Record Society, 5 vols., 1931–53.

Vergil, Polydore, *Angliae Historiae libri vigintiseptem*, Basel, 1555; reprinted in facsimile, Menston, 1972.

    The Anglica Historia of Polydore Vergil, ed. D. Hay, Camden Society, third series 74, 1950.

The Visitation of Cambridge, ed. J. W. Clay, Harleian Society 42, 1897.

The Visitation of the County of Buckingham, ed. W. H. Rylands, Harleian Society 58, 1909.

Visitation of Yorkshire, ed. C. B. Norcliffe, Harleian Society 16, 1881.

W. W. E. W., 'Grant from Richard, duke of Gloucester to Reginald Vaghan – 10 Edw. IV', *Archaeologia Cambrensis*, third series 9 (1863), 55.

Warkworth, John, *A Chronicle of the First Thirteen Years of the Reign of King Edward IV*, ed. J. O. Halliwell, Camden Society, original series 10, 1839.

Wrottesley, G., 'Extracts from the plea rolls', *Collections for a History of Staffordshire*, William Salt Archaeological Society, new series 6 part 1, 1903, pp. 91–164.

Yorkshire Deeds III, ed. W. Brown, Yorkshire Archaeological Society, record series 63, 1922.

SECONDARY WORKS

Anglo, S., 1969, *Spectacle, Pageantry and Early Tudor Policy*, Oxford.

Anstis, J., 1724, *The Register of the Most Noble Order of the Garter*, 2 vols., London.

Antonovics, A. V., 1986, 'Henry VII, king of England, "by the grace of Charles VII of France"', in Griffiths and Sherborne, chap. 9, 169–84.

Armstrong, C. A. J., 1948a, 'The inauguration ceremonies of the Yorkist kings and their title to the throne', *TRHS*, fourth series 30, 51–73.

1948b, 'Some examples of the distribution and speed of news in England at the time of the Wars of the Roses' in Hunt, Pantin and Southern, chap. 25, pp. 429–54.

Arnold, C., 1984, 'The commission of the peace for the West Riding of Yorkshire, 1437–1509' in Pollard 1984, chap. 6, pp. 116–38.

Ashmole, E., 1719, *The Antiquities of Berkshire*, 3 vols., London.

Attreed, L. C., 1981, 'The king's interest: York's fee farm and the central government, 1482–92', *Northern History*, 17, 24–43.

1983, 'An indenture between Richard duke of Gloucester and the Scrope family of Masham and Upsall', *Speculum*, 58, 1018–25.

Axon, E., 1938, 'The family of Bothe (Booth) and the church in the 15th and 16th centuries', *Transactions of the Lancashire and Cheshire Antiquarian Society*, 53, 32–82.

Axon, W. E. A., 1870, *The Black Knight of Ashton*, Manchester.

Baines, E., 1888–93, *The History of the County Palatine and Duchy of Lancaster*, new edn by James Croston, 5 vols., London.

Ball, W. E., 1909, 'The stained-glass windows of Nettlestead church', *Archaeologia Cantiana*, 28, 157–247.

Barron, O., 1906, *Northamptonshire Families*, London.

Bellamy, J. G., 1970, *The Law of Treason in England in the Later Middle Ages*, Cambridge.

Bellasis, E., 1889, 'Strickland of Sizergh', *Transactions of the Cumberland and Westmorland Antiquarian and Archaeological Society*, 10, 75–94.

Bennett, M., 1985, *The Battle of Bosworth*, Gloucester.

1987, *Lambert Simnel and the Battle of Stoke*, Gloucester.

Berry, W., 1833, *County Genealogies: pedigrees of the families in the county of Hants.*, London.

1840, *County Genealogies: pedigrees of Essex families*, London.

Blair, C. H. Hunter, 1937, 'Members of Parliament for Newcastle upon Tyne (June 1377 – January 1558); for Berwick upon Tweed (1529–1558) and Morpeth (1553–1558)', *Archaeologia Aeliana*, fourth series 14, 22–66.

Blomefield, F., 1739–75, *An Essay towards a Topographical History of the County of Norfolk*, continued by C. Parkin, 5 vols., London.

Bolton, S., 1980, 'Sir John Fogge of Ashford', *The Ricardian* no. 69, 202–9.

Borlase, W. C., 1888, *The Descent, Name and Arms of Borlase of Borlase in the County of Cornwall*, London and Exeter.

Briggs, K. M., 1971, *A Dictionary of British Folk Tales*, 4 vols., London.

Brown, A. L., 1972, 'The reign of Henry IV: the establishment of the Lancastrian regime', in Chrimes, Ross and Griffiths, chap. 1, pp. 1–28.

Brown, R. P., 1926, 'Thomas Langton and his tradition of learning', *Transactions of the Cumberland and Westmorland Antiquarian and Archaeological Society*, new series 26, 150–246.

Cam, H. M., 1963, *Liberties and Communities in Medieval England: collected studies in local administration and topography*, London; first printed Cambridge, 1944.

Cameron, A., 1974, 'The giving of livery and retaining in Henry VII's reign',

Bibliography

Renaissance and Modern Studies, 18, 17–35.

Campling, A., 1937, 'Browne of Elsing, co. Norfolk', *Miscellanea Genealogica et Heraldica*, fifth series 9 (1935–7), 317–21.

Carpenter, M. C., 1976, 'Political society in Warwickshire, c. 1401–72', unpublished Ph.D. thesis, Cambridge University.

  1986, 'The duke of Clarence and the midlands: a study in the interplay of local and national politics', *Midland History*, 11, 23–48.

Chippindall, W. H., 1928, 'Tunstall of Thurland castle', *Transactions of the Cumberland and Westmorland Antiquarian and Archaeological Society*, new series 28, 292–313.

Chope, R. Pearse, 1918, 'The last of the Dynhams', *Report and Transactions of the Devonshire Association*, 50, 431–92.

Chrimes, S. B., 1972, *Henry VII*, London.

Chrimes, S. B., Ross, C. D. and Griffiths, R. A., 1972, eds., *Fifteenth-Century England 1399–1509: studies in politics and society*, Manchester.

Clough, C. H., 1982, ed., *Profession, Vocation and Culture in Later Medieval England: essays dedicated to the memory of A. R. Myers*, Liverpool.

Clutterbuck, R., 1815–27, *The History and Antiquities of the County of Hertford*, 3 vols., London.

Coleman, C. and Starkey, D., 1986, eds., *Revolution Reassessed: revisions in the history of Tudor government and administration*, Oxford.

Coles, G. M., 1961, 'The Lordship of Middleham, especially in Yorkist and early Tudor times', unpublished MA thesis, Liverpool University.

Colvin, H. M., Brown, R. A. and Taylor, A. J., 1963, *The History of the King's Works: the middle ages*, 2 vols., HMSO.

The Complete Peerage, G. E. C(okayne), revised by V. Gibbs, H. A. Doubleday and others, 14 vols., London, 1910–59.

Condon, M., 1986, 'The kaleidoscope of treason: fragments from the Bosworth story', *The Ricardian*, no. 92, 208–12.

Conway, A. E., 1925, 'The Maidstone sector of Buckingham's rebellion', *Archaeologia Cantiana*, 37, 97–120.

Coward, B., 1983, *The Stanleys, Lords Stanley and Earls of Derby, 1385–1672*, Chetham Society, third series 30.

Cox, J. C., 1875–9, *Notes on the Churches of Derbyshire*, 4 vols., London.

Crawford, A., 1985, 'The Mowbray inheritance', in Petre, pp. 79–85.

  1986, 'The private life of John Howard', in Hammond 1986, pp. 6–24.

Crowder, C. M. D., 1967, ed., *English Society and Government in the Fifteenth Century*, Edinburgh and London.

Davies, C. S. L., 1987, 'Bishop John Morton, the Holy See, and the accession of Henry VII', *EHR* 102, 2–30.

Davies, W. G., 1955, *The Ancestry of Mary Isaac*, Portland, Maine.

Dobson, R. B., 1965, 'Richard Bell, prior of Durham (1464–78) and bishop of Carlisle (1478–95)', *Transactions of the Cumberland and Westmorland Antiquarian and Archaeological Society*, new series 65, 182–221.

  1984, ed., *The Church, Politics and Patronage in the Fifteenth Century*, Gloucester.

Bibliography

✠1986, 'Richard III and the church of York', in Griffiths and Sherborne, chap. 7, pp. 130–54.

du Boulay, F. R. H. and Barron, C. M., 1971, eds., *The Reign of Richard II*, London.

Duckett, G. F., 1869, *Duchetiana*, London.

Dunham, W. H., 1955, 'Lord Hastings' indentured retainers, 1461–83', *Transactions of the Connecticut Academy of Arts and Sciences*, 39, reprinted Hamden, Connecticut, 1970.

Dunham, W. H. and Wood, C. T., 1976, 'The right to rule in England: depositions and the kingdom's authority, 1327–1485', *American Historical Review*, 81, 738–61.

Dunlop, J. R., 1927, 'Pedigree of the family of Crioll, or Kyriell, of co. Kent', *Miscellanea Genealogica et Heraldica*, fifth series 6 (1926–8), 254–61.

Edwards, R., 1983, *The Itinerary of King Richard III, 1483–1485*, London.

Elliot, H. L., 1898, 'Fitz Lewes, of West Horndon, and the brasses at Ingrave', *Transactions of the Essex Archaeological Society*, new series 6, 28–59.

Emden, A. B., 1957–9, *A Biographical Register of the University of Oxford to A.D. 1500*, 3 vols., Oxford.

1963, *A Biographical Register of the University of Cambridge to 1500*, Cambridge.

Evans, H. T., 1915, *Wales and the Wars of the Roses*, Cambridge.

Foster, J., 1874, *Pedigrees of the County Families of Yorkshire*, 2 vols., London.

Gairdner, J., 1898, *History of the Life and Reign of Richard the Third*, Cambridge, new edn.

Gillingham, J., 1981, *The Wars of the Roses: peace and conflict in fifteenth-century England*, London.

Given-Wilson, C., 1986, *The Royal Household and the King's Affinity: service, politics and finance in England 1360–1413*, Yale.

Goodman, A., 1981, *The Wars of the Roses: military activity and English society, 1452–97*, London.

Goodman, A. and MacKay, A., 1973, 'A Castilian report on English affairs, 1486', *EHR*, 88, 92–9.

Greenfield, B. W., 1863, 'The descent of the manor and advowson of Hampton-Poyle', *The Herald and Genealogist* 1, 209–24.

Griffiths, R. A., 1972a, *The Principality of Wales in the Later Middle Ages 1: South Wales, 1277–1536*, Cardiff.

1972b, 'Wales and the Marches', in Chrimes, Ross and Griffiths, chap. 7, pp. 145–72.

1974, 'Patronage, politics and the principality of Wales, 1413–1461', in Hearder and Loyn, pp. 69–86.

1976, 'Richard, duke of York and the royal household in Wales, 1449–50', *Welsh History Review*, 8, 14–25.

1980, 'Public and private bureaucracies in England and Wales in the fifteenth century', *TRHS*, fifth series 30, 109–30.

1981a, *The Reign of Henry VI: the exercise of royal authority, 1422–1461*, London.

1981b, ed., *Patronage, the Crown and the Provinces in Later Medieval England*, Gloucester.

Bibliography

1983, 'Richard III – king or anti-king?', in Paton, chap. 2, pp. 29–39.

✳Griffiths, R. A. and Sherborne, J., 1986, eds., *Kings and Nobles in the Later Middle Ages: a tribute to Charles Ross*, Gloucester.

Griffiths, R. A. and Thomas, R. S., 1985, *The Making of the Tudor Dynasty*, Gloucester.

Guth, D. J., 1986, 'Richard III, Henry VII and the city: London politics and the "dun cowe" ', in Griffiths and Sherborne, chap. 10, pp. 185–204.

Hairsine, R., 1985, 'Oxford University and the life and legend of Richard III', in Petre, pp. 307–32.

✳Hammond, P. W., 1974, 'An early account of the reign of Richard III', *The Ricardian*, no. 44, 16–18.

1986, ed., *Richard III: loyalty, lordship and law*, London.

Hampson, C. P., 1940, *The Book of the Radclyffes*, Edinburgh.

Hampton, W. E., 1979, *Memorials of the Wars of the Roses: a biographical guide*, Upminster.

1985a, 'John Hoton of Hunwick and Tudhoe, county Durham, esquire for the body to Richard III', *The Ricardian*, no. 88, 2–17.

1985b, 'Sir Robert Percy and Joyce his wife', in Petre, pp. 184–94.

Hanham, A., 1972, 'Richard III, lord Hastings and the historians', *EHR*, 87, 233–48.

1975, *Richard III and his Early Historians 1483–1535*, Oxford.

Harriss, G. L., 1963, 'Aids, loans and benevolences', *Historical Journal*, 6, 1–19.

1981, 'Introduction', in McFarlane 1981, pp. ix–xxvii.

Hearder, H. and Loyn, H. R., 1974, eds., *British Government and Administration: studies presented to S. B. Chrimes*, Cardiff.

Helmholz, R. H., 1974, *Marriage Litigation in Medieval England*, Cambridge.

1986, 'The sons of Edward IV: a canonical assessment of the claim that they were illegitimate', in Hammond 1986, pp. 91–103.

Hicks, M. A., 1971, 'The career of Henry Percy, fourth earl of Northumberland, c. 1448–89, with special reference to his retinue', unpublished MA thesis, Southampton University.

1974, 'The career of George Plantagenet, duke of Clarence, 1449–78', unpublished D.Phil. thesis, Oxford University.

1978, 'Dynastic change and northern society: the career of the fourth earl of Northumberland, 1470–89', *Northern History*, 14, 78–107.

1979a, 'The changing role of the Wydevilles in Yorkist politics to 1483', in Ross 1979, chap. 3, pp. 60–86.

1979b, 'Descent, partition and extinction: the Warwick inheritance', *BIHR*, 52, 116–28.

1980, *False, Fleeting, Perjur'd Clarence*, Gloucester.

1984, 'Attainder, resumption and coercion 1461–1529', *Parliamentary History*, 3, 15–31.

1986a, 'Richard, duke of Gloucester and the north', in Horrox 1986a, pp. 11–26.

1986b, *Richard III as Duke of Gloucester: a study in character*, Borthwick paper 70, York.

Bibliography

Highfield, J. R. L. and Jeffs, R., 1981, eds., *The Crown and Local Communities in England and France in the Fifteenth Century*, Gloucester.

Hillier, K., 1986, 'John Harcourt', in Petre, pp. 122–7.

Hollaender, A. E. J. and Kellaway, W., 1969, eds., *Studies in London History presented to Philip Edmund Jones*, London.

Holt, J. C., 1982, *Robin Hood*, London.

Horrox, R. E., 1981, 'Urban patronage and patrons in the fifteenth century', in Griffiths 1981b, chap. 7, pp. 145–66.

1982, 'Richard III and Allhallows Barking by the Tower', *The Ricardian* no. 77, 38–40.

1983, 'Henry Tudor's letters to England during Richard III's reign', *The Ricardian* no. 80, 155–8.

1984, 'Richard III and London', *The Ricardian* no. 85, 322–9.

1986a, ed., *Richard III and the North*, Hull University.

1986b, 'Richard III and the East Riding', in Horrox 1986a, pp. 82–107.

Hunt, R. W., Pantin, W. A. and Southern, R. W., 1948, eds., *Studies in Medieval History presented to Frederick Maurice Powicke*, Oxford.

Hunter, J., 1828–31, *South Yorkshire: the history and topography of the deanery of Doncaster*, 2 vols., London.

Hutchins, J., 1861–74, *The History and Antiquities of the County of Dorset*, 4 vols., London.

Hutchinson, W., 1794, *The History of the County of Cumberland*, 2 vols., Carlisle.

Imray, J. M., 1969, 'Les bones gentes de la mercerye de Londres', in Hollaender and Kellaway, pp. 155–78.

Ives, E. W., 1968, 'Andrew Dymmock and the papers of Antony, earl Rivers, 1482–3', *BIHR*, 41, 216–29.

1983, *The Common Lawyers of Pre-Reformation England: Thomas Kebell, a case study*, Cambridge.

Jeffs, R., 1961, 'The Poynings-Percy dispute: an example of the interplay of open strife and legal action in the fifteenth century', *BIHR*, 34, 148–64.

Jones, M., 1986, ed., *Gentry and Lesser Nobility in Late Medieval Europe*, Gloucester.

Jones, M. K., 1986a, 'Richard III and the Stanleys', in Horrox 1986a, pp. 27–50.

1986b, 'Richard III and lady Margaret Beaufort: a re-assessment', in Hammond 1986, pp. 25–37.

1988, 'Sir William Stanley of Holt: politics and family allegiance in the late fifteenth century', *Welsh History Review*, 14, 1–22.

Jones, T. L., 1975, *Ashby de la Zouch Castle*, HMSO for D. of E., 12th impression.

Keen, M. H., 1965, *The Laws of War in the Late Middle Ages*, London.

1973, *England in the Later Middle Ages*, London.

1984, *Chivalry*, Yale.

Kendall, P. M., 1955, *Richard the Third*, London.

Kerr, P. W., 1935. 'The Leventhorpes of Sawbridgeworth', *Transactions of the East Herts Archaeological Society*, 9 (1934–6), 129–51.

Kilburne, R., 1659, *A Topographie or Survey of the County of Kent*, London.

Bibliography

King, H. W., 1864, '*Ancient wills (3)*', *Transactions of the Essex Archaeological Society*, 3 (1863–4), 75–94.

    1869, 'Ancient wills (5)', *Transactions of the Essex Archaeological Society*, 4, 1–24.

Kirby, J. L., 1957, 'The rise of the under-treasurer of the exchequer', *EHR*, 72, 666–77.

Kittredge, G. L., 1929, *Witchcraft in Old and New England*, Harvard.

Knecht, R. J., 1958, 'The episcopate and the Wars of the Roses', *University of Birmingham Historical Journal*, 6 (1957–8), 108–31.

Lambert, J. J., 1933, *Records of the Skinners of London*, London.

Lander, J. R., 1976, *Crown and Nobility 1450–1509*, London.

    1980, *Government and Community, England 1450–1509*, London.

Leadam, I. S., 1902, 'An unknown conspiracy against king Henry VII', *TRHS*, new series 16, 133–58.

Levine, M., 1959, 'Richard III – usurper or lawful king?', *Speculum*, 34, 391–401.

    1973, *Tudor Dynastic Problems 1460–1571*, London.

Loades, D. M., 1974, *Politics and the Nation, 1450–1660: obedience, resistance and public order*, Brighton.

    1986, *The Tudor Court*, London.

Lowe, D. E., 1977, 'The council of the prince of Wales and the decline of the Herbert family during the second reign of Edward IV (1471–83)', *Bulletin of the Board of Celtic Studies*, 27 (1976–8), 278–97.

    1981, 'Patronage and politics: Edward IV, the Wydevills and the council of the prince of Wales, 1471–83', *Bulletin of the Board of Celtic Studies*, 29 (1980–2), 545–73.

Lyte, H. C. Maxwell, 1882, *Dunster and its Lords, 1066–1881*, London.

Macdougall, N., 1986, 'Richard III and James III, contemporary monarchs, parallel mythologies', in Hammond 1986, p. 148–171.

McFarlane, K. B., 1971, *Hans Memling*, Oxford.

    1973, *The Nobility of Later Medieval England*, Oxford.

    1981, *England in the Fifteenth Century: collected essays*, London.

McHardy, A. K., 1984, 'Clerical taxation in fifteenth-century England: the clergy as agents of the crown', in Dobson 1984, chap. 8, pp. 168–92.

Maclean, J., 1887, 'Manor of Tockington, co. Gloucester', *Transactions of the Bristol and Gloucestershire Archaeological Society*, 12 (1887–8), 123–55.

McNiven, P., 1985, 'The problem of Henry IV's health, 1405–1413', *EHR*, 100, 747–72.

Medcalf, S., 1981, ed., *The Later Middle Ages*, London.

Meredith, R., 1964, 'The Eyres of Hassop, 1470–1640', *Derbyshire Archaeological Journal*, 84, 1–51.

Metcalfe, W. C., 1885, *A Book of Knights*, London.

Morgan, D. A. L., 1973, 'The king's affinity in the polity of Yorkist England', *TRHS*, fifth series 23, 1–25.

    1986, 'The individual style of the English gentleman', in M. Jones, pp. 15–35.

    1987, 'The house of policy: the political role of the late Plantagenet household, 1422–1485', in Starkey 1987a, chap. 2, pp. 25–70.

Bibliography

Muir, K., 1963, *Life and Letters of Sir Thomas Wyatt*, Liverpool.

Murray, A., 1978, *Reason and Society in the Middle Ages*, Oxford.

Myers, A. R., 1967, 'The character of Richard III', in Crowder, chap. 6, pp. 112–33.

Mynors, H. C. B., 1953, 'Sir Roger Mynors of Duffield', *Journal of the Derbyshire Archaeological and Natural History Society*, 73, 112–13.

Orme, N., 1984, 'The education of Edward V', *BIHR*, 57, 119–30.

Ormerod, G., 1850, 'A memoir on the Lancashire house of le Noreis or Norres', *Transactions of the Historic Society of Lancashire and Cheshire*, 2 (1849–50), 138–82.

Otway-Ruthven, J., 1939, *The King's Secretary and the Signet Office in the XV century*, Cambridge.

Owen, H. and Blakeway, J. B., 1825, *A History of Shrewsbury* I, London.

Palliser, D. M., 1986, 'Richard III and York', in Horrox 1986a, pp. 51–81.

Paton, D. M., 1983, ed., *The 1483 Gloucester Charter in History*, Gloucester.

Pegge, S., 1791, *Curialia: or an historical account of some branches of the royal household*, London.

Petre, J., 1985, ed., *Richard III, Crown and People*, London.

Pilkington, J., 1893, 'The early history of the Lancashire family of Pilkington, and its branches, from 1066 to 1600', *Transactions of the Historic Society of Lancashire and Cheshire*, new series 9, 159–214.

Plantagenet-Harrison, G. H. de S. N., 1879, *The History of Yorkshire* I *Wapentake of Gilling West*, London.

Pollard, A. J., 1968, 'The family of Talbot, lords Talbot and earls of Shrewsbury in the fifteenth century', unpublished Ph.D. thesis, Bristol University.

1975, 'The northern retainers of Richard Nevill, earl of Salisbury', *Northern History*, 11, 52–69.

1977, 'The tyranny of Richard III', *Journal of Medieval History*, 3, 147–65.

1978, 'Richard Clervaux of Croft: a North Riding squire in the fifteenth century', *Yorkshire Archaeological Journal*, 50, 151–69.

1979, 'The Richmondshire community of gentry during the Wars of the Roses', in Ross 1979, chap. 2, pp. 37–59.

1983, *The Middleham Connection: Richard III and Richmondshire 1471–1485*, Middleham.

1984, ed., *Property and Politics: essays in later medieval English history*, Gloucester.

1986, 'St Cuthbert and the hog: Richard III and the county palatine of Durham, 1471–85', in Griffiths and Sherborne, chap. 6, pp. 109–29.

Potter, J., 1983, *Good King Richard? an account of Richard III and his reputation 1483–1983*, London.

Prideaux, W. S., 1898–7, *Memorials of the Goldsmiths' Company*, 2 vols., London.

Pugh, T. B., 1963, *The Marcher Lordships of South Wales 1415–1536*, Cardiff.

1971, ed., *Glamorgan County History* III *The Middle Ages*, Cardiff.

1972, 'The magnates, knights and gentry', in Chrimes, Ross and Griffiths, chap. 5, pp. 86–128.

Pullein, C., 1915, *The Pulleyns of Yorkshire*, Leeds.

Bibliography

Ramsay, J., 1892, *Lancaster and York*, 2 vols., Oxford.

Ramsey, N., 1985, 'Retained legal counsel, c.1275–c.1475', *TRHS*, fifth series 35, 95–112.

Rawcliffe, C., 1978, *The Staffords, Earls of Stafford and Dukes of Buckingham 1394–1521*, Cambridge.

Reddaway, T. F., 1975, *The Early History of the Goldsmiths' Company 1327–1509*, London.

Reid, R. R., 1921, *The King's Council in the North*, London.

Richmond, C. F., 1967, 'English naval power in the fifteenth century', *History*, 52, 1–15.

1970, 'Fauconberg's Kentish rising of May 1471', *EHR*, 85, 673–92.

1981a, *John Hopton: a fifteenth-century country gentleman*, Cambridge.

1981b, 'The expenses of Thomas Playter of Sotterley, 1459–60', *Proceedings of the Suffolk Institute of Archaeology and History*, 35 (1981–4), 41–52.

1986, '1485 and all that, or what was going on at the battle of Bosworth', in Hammond 1986, pp. 172–206.

Rogers, A., 1968, 'Parliamentary electors in Lincolnshire in the fifteenth century' (pt 1), *Lincolnshire History and Archaeology*, 3, 41–79.

Roskell, J. S., 1953, 'The office and dignity of protector of England, with special reference to its origins', *EHR*, 68, 193–233.

1959a, 'Sir John Wood of Molesey', *Surrey Archaeological Collections*, 56, 15–28.

1959b, 'William Catesby, counsellor to Richard III', *Bulletin of the John Rylands Library*, 42 (1959–60), 145–74.

1965, *The Commons and their Speakers in English Parliaments 1376–1523*, Manchester.

Ross, C. D., 1974, *Edward IV*, London.

1976, 'Some "servants and lovers" of Richard in his youth', *The Ricardian*, no. 55, 2–4.

1979, ed., *Patronage, Pedigree and Power in Later Medieval England*, Gloucester.

1981, *Richard III*, London.

Roth, C., 1920, 'Perkin Warbeck and his Jewish master', *Transactions of the Jewish Historical Society of England*, 9 (1918–20), 143–62.

Rowney, I., 1984a, 'Resources and retaining in Yorkist England: William lord Hastings and the honour of Tutbury', in Pollard 1984, chap. 7, pp. 139–55.

1984b, 'The Hastings affinity in Staffordshire and the honour of Tutbury', *BIHR*, 57, 35–45.

Scofield, C., 1923, *The Life and Reign of Edward the Fourth*, 2 vols., London.

Smith, J. Beverley, 1966, 'Crown and community in the principality of north Wales in the reign of Henry Tudor', *Welsh History Review*, 3 (1966–7), 145–71.

Somerville, R., 1953, *History of the Duchy of Lancaster* i, HMSO.

Starkey, D., 1981, 'The age of the household: politics, society and the arts c.1350–c.1550', in Medcalf, chap. 5, pp. 225–90.

1986, 'Which age of reform?', in Coleman and Starkey, chap. 1, pp. 13–27.

1987a, ed., *The English Court: from the Wars of the Roses to the Civil War*, London.

Bibliography

1987b, 'Introduction: court history in perspective', in Starkey 1987a, chap. 1, pp. 1–24.

1987c, 'Intimacy and innovation: the rise of the privy chamber, 1485–1547', in Starkey 1987a, chap. 3, pp. 71–118.

Steel, A., 1954, *The Receipt of the Exchequer, 1377–1485*, Cambridge.

Storey, R. L., 1958, 'English officers of state, 1399–1485', *BIHR*, 31, 84–92.

1966, *The End of the House of Lancaster*, London.

1972, 'The north of England', in Chrimes, Ross and Griffiths, chap. 6, pp. 129–44.

1982, 'Gentleman-bureaucrats', in Clough, chap. 4, pp. 90–129.

Surtees, R., 1816–40, *The History and Antiquities of the County Palatine of Durham*, 4 vols., London.

Sutton, A. F., 1976, 'The administration of justice whereunto we be professed', *The Ricardian*, no. 53, 4–15.

1981a, 'George Lovekyn, tailor to three kings of England, 1470–1504', *Costume*, 15, 1–12.

1981b, 'Richard III's secretary: the search continued', *The Ricardian*, no. 75, 438–47.

1982, 'The Hautes of Kent', *The Ricardian*, no. 77, 54–5.

1985, 'Richard III, the city of London and Southwark', in Petre, pp. 289–95.

1986a, ' "A curious searcher for our weal public": Richard III, piety, chivalry and the concept of the "good prince" ', in Hammond 1986, pp. 58–90.

1986b, 'William Shore, merchant of London and Derby', *Derbyshire Archaeological Journal*, 106, 127–39.

Sutton, A. F. and Hammond, P. W., 1978, 'The problems of dating and the dangers of redating: the acts of court of the mercers' company of London, 1453–1527', *Journal of the Society of Archivists*, 6, 87–91.

Thomson, J. A. F., 1972, 'The Courtenay family in the Yorkist period', *BIHR*, 45, 230–46.

1975, 'Richard III and lord Hastings – a problematical case reviewed', *BIHR*, 48, 22–30.

1986, 'Bishop Lionel Woodville and Richard III', *BIHR*, 59, 130–35.

Thorpe, J. D., 1928, 'History of the manor of Coates', *Transactions of the Bristol and Gloucestershire Archaeological Society*, 50, 135–274.

Tristram, E. W., 1950, *English Medieval Wall Painting: the thirteenth century*, 2 vols., Oxford.

Tuck, J. A., 1971, 'Richard II's system of patronage', in du Boulay and Barron, chap. 1, pp. 1–20.

Tudor-Craig, P., 1973, *Richard III*, National Portrait Gallery, London.

Victoria County Histories:

Buckinghamshire, 4 vols., London, 1905–27.

Hertfordshire, 4 vols., London, 1902–14.

Leicestershire, 5 vols., London, 1907–64.

Virgoe, R., 1981, 'The crown, magnates and local government in fifteenth-century East Anglia', in Highfield and Jeffs, chap. 4, pp. 72–87.

1982, 'Sir John Risley (1443–1512), courtier and councillor', *Norfolk Archae-*

ology, 38 (1981–3), 140–8.

Vivian, J. L., 1887, *The Visitations of Cornwall*, Exeter.

1895, *The Visitations of the County of Devon*, Exeter.

Waller, W. C., 1895a, 'An old church-chest, being notes of the contents of that at Theydon Garnon, Essex', *Transactions of the Essex Archaeological Society*, new series 5, 1–32.

1895b, 'Some Essex manuscripts', pt 1, *Transactions of the Essex Archaeological Society*, new series 5, 200–25.

1898, 'Some Essex manuscripts', pt 2, *Transactions of the Essex Archaeological Society*, new series 6, 101–21.

Warnicke, R. M., 1984, 'Sir Ralph Bigod: a loyal servant to king Richard III', *The Ricardian*, no. 84, 299–303.

Wedgwood, J., 1936, ed., *History of Parliament* I *Biographies of the Members of the Commons House, 1439–1509*, HMSO.

1938, ed., *History of Parliament* II *Register of the Ministers and of the Members of both Houses, 1439–1509*, HMSO.

Weever, J., 1631, *Ancient Funerall Monuments*, London.

Weiss, M., 1976, 'A power in the north? The Percies in the fifteenth century', *Historical Journal*, 19, 501–9.

Whitaker, T. D., 1818, *An History of the Original Parish of Whalley and Honor of Clitheroe in the Counties of Lancaster and York*, London, 3rd edn.

1878, *The History and Antiquities of Craven*, London, 3rd edn.

White, A. B., 1933, *Self Government at the King's Command*, Minnesota.

Wilkinson, B., 1964, *Constitutional History of England in the Fifteenth Century*, London.

Williams, B., 1983, 'The Portuguese connection and the significance of "the holy princess" ', *The Ricardian*, no. 80, 138–45.

Williams, C. H., 1928, 'The rebellion of Humphrey Stafford in 1486', *EHR*, 43, 181–9.

Williams, C. J., 1971, 'The Revell family of Carnfield', *Derbyshire Archaeological Journal*, 91, 141–63.

Williams, N., 1964, *Thomas Howard Fourth Duke of Norfolk*, London.

Wingfield, J. M., 1925, *Some Records of the Wingfield Family*, London.

Wolffe, B. P., 1971, *The Royal Demesne in English History*, London.

1974, 'When and why did Hastings lose his head?', *EHR*, 89, 835–44.

Wood, C. T., 1975, 'The deposition of Edward V', *Traditio*, 31, 247–86.

1986, 'Richard III, lord Hastings and Friday the thirteenth', in Griffiths and Sherborne, chap. 8, p. 155–68.

Wright, S. M., 1983, *The Derbyshire Gentry in the Fifteenth Century*, Derbyshire Record Society, 8.

Yeatman, J. P., 1882, *The Early Genealogical History of the House of Arundel*, London.

INDEX

Nobles are indexed under their surname (their maiden name in the case of women), as are ecclesiastics. Kings and their children are indexed under their Christian name. Welsh patronymics are indexed under Christian name.

Index

Index

358